Language Form and
Language Function

Language, Speech, and Communication

Language Form and Language Function

Frederick J. Newmeyer

A Bradford Book
The MIT Press
Cambridge, Massachusetts
London, England

This book was set in Times New Roman on the Monotype "Prism Plus" Post-Script Imagesetter by Asco Trade Typesetting Ltd., Hong Kong, and was printed and bound in the United States of America.

Library of Congress Cataloging-in-Publication Data

Newmeyer, Frederick J.
  Language form and language function / Frederick J. Newmeyer.
    p.   cm. — (Language, speech, and communication)
  "A Bradford book."
  Includes bibliographical references (p.   ) and index.
  ISBN 978-0-262-64044-2 (pb.: alk. paper)
  1. Linguistics—Methodology. 2. Linguistic analysis (Linguistics).
3. Formalization (Linguistics). 4. Functionalism (Linguistics).
I. Title. II. Series.
P126.N48   1998
410′.1—dc21   98-10471
                                                          CIP

The MIT Press is pleased to keep this title available in print by
manufacturing single copies, on demand, via digital printing technology.

For Marilyn, who makes me very happy

Contents

Preface

This work represents my attempt to pinpoint and evaluate the fundamental differences between the generativist program for linguistic theory and the functionalist program. While researching earlier books on the history and theoretical underpinnings of generative grammar, I had occasion to read a great deal of the functionalist literature, much of it critical of formal approaches to language. Even though I found in this literature little to sway me from my adherence to generative grammar, I was pleasantly surprised by the wealth of interesting generalizations that I found in the best functionalist writings. Several years ago, I resolved to devote a book to probing which of these generalizations are fully compatible with generative grammar and which appear to be major challenges to it. What you find between these covers is the final product of my investigations.

As Ray Jackendoff has reminded me, there is a phonological dimension to the issues that divide formalists and functionalists. Every major point of difference between the two camps with respect to the analysis of syntactic structure has a homologue in the analysis of phonological structure. I wish that I possessed the competency to pursue the latter as well as the former. With luck, it will not be long before some scholar submits the tension between formal and functional approaches to phonology to the same degree of analysis as I have done for the two approaches to syntax.

In this enterprise my greatest debt is to three individuals who provided me with detailed page-by-page comments on the entire prefinal manuscript: Anna Roussou, Neil Smith, and an anonymous referee for the MIT Press. I thank them wholeheartedly for making this book far better than it might have been otherwise. Other colleagues read one or more chapters and, with their comments, prevented me from burdening the reader with the myriad errors, misrepresentations, and faulty arguments that disfigured the draft that they read. They are Paul K. Andersen, Donna Andrews, Robert Borsley, Line Brandt, Lyle Campbell, Ronnie Cann, Lesley Carmichael, William Croft, Matthew Dryer, John Goldsmith, Myrna Gopnik, Jeanette Gundel, Alice Harris, Martin Haspelmath, Brian Joseph, Jurgen Klausenburger, Rob Malouf, Pascual Masullo, Edith Moravcsik, Muriel Norde, Sarah Thomason, Russell Tomlin, Gregory Ward, Gabriel Webster, David Wilkins, and Margaret Winters.

I could hardly hope to list every individual who set me on the right path when presented with some half-baked idea or who patiently told me that I should read such and such. The following stand out in my mind as especially worthy of acknowledgment: Leonard Babby, Alan Bell, Derek Bickerton, Heles Contreras, Wayne Cowart, Daniel Everett, Julia Herschensohn, Laurence Horn, Ray Jackendoff, Richard Janda, Soowon Kim, Simon Kirby, Shalom Lappin, Toshiyuki Ogihara, Ellen Prince, Elizabeth Riddle, Jerrold Sadock, Ivan Sag, Susan Steele, Karen Zagona, and Arnold Zwicky.

I presented some of this material in classes at the University of Washington and at the Universidad Nacional del Comahue in Argentina. Thanks to the students there for bearing with me and putting forward a number of suggestions that made their way into these pages.

Language Form and
Language Function

Chapter 1

The Form-Function Problem
in Linguistics

1 Setting the Stage with a (Not Totally) Imaginary Dialogue

Sandy Forman has just successfully defended an MIT dissertation entitled 'Gamma-Licensing Constraints on Dummy Agreement Phrases and the Theory of Q-Control: A Post-Minimalist Approach' and is at the Linguistic Society of America Annual Meeting hoping to find a job. Fortunately for Sandy, Minnesota State has advertised an entry-level syntax position, 'area of specialization open', and has asked for an interview. While waiting in the hallway, Sandy runs into an undergraduate classmate, Chris Funk, who is also killing time before a Minnesota State interview. Chris has just finished up at the University of California at Santa Barbara with a dissertation entitled 'Iconic Pathways and Image-Schematic Targets: Speaker-Empathy as a Motivating Force in the Grammaticalization of Landmark-Trajectory Metaphors'. After the two exchange pleasantries for a few minutes, Chris provokes Sandy with the following comment and the fur begins to fly:

Funk: It's just pure common sense that our starting point should be the idea that the structure of language is going to reflect what people *use* language for.

Forman: That hardly seems like common sense to me! To begin with, language is used for all sorts of things: to communicate, to think, to play, to deceive, to dream. What human activity *isn't* language a central part of?

Funk: Yes, language serves many functions. But any reasonable person would have to agree that communication—and in particular the communication of information—is paramount.

Forman: Well, I don't share those intuitions at all. It seems to me that a much more time-honored position, in fact, is that the primary function of language is to serve as a vehicle for rational thought. And you're not going to tell me that the 'perfect' vehicle for communication is going to look like the 'perfect' vehicle for rational thought!

Funk: I'm not going to tell you that language is the 'perfect' vehicle for anything. That's a caricature of the functionalist position. I am going to say, though, that the functions of language—including that of conveying meaning—have left their mark on language structure to a degree that it's hopeless to think that you can understand anything about this structure without working out how it's grounded functionally.

Forman: I'm skeptical about that for a whole lot of reasons. For one thing, all the people in the world have the same need to communicate. So if language structure were a response to meeting this need, we'd expect all languages to be virtually identical—right?

Funk: But that's assuming that there's only one way to respond to functional pressure. Why make that assumption? In the natural world, all organisms have the same need to ward off predators, but there are limitless ways to carry out this function. Humans who live in cold climates have to find ways to keep warm, but that doesn't mean that they're all going to do it the same way. It's the same thing with language. It's in everybody's communicative interest, say, to be able to modify a noun with a proposition that restricts the scope of that noun. If one language forms relative clauses one way and another a different way, that doesn't mean that there's been no response to communicative pressure.

Forman: Don't you see the trap that line of thinking gets you into? The more the different ways of carrying out the same function, the hazier the pairings of form and function turn out to be. That's why it makes sense to describe how the forms interrelate *independently* of their functions.

Funk: The fact that the coding by form of function is complex and, to a degree, indirect doesn't mean that the pairings are 'hazy'. In fact, the situation is just what we would expect. Since the functions of language place conflicting demands on form, we naturally expect to see those conflicts resolved in a variety of ways. And we also expect to see an arbitrary residue of formal patterns where there's *no* obvious direct link to function.

Forman: What you're calling an 'arbitrary residue' is part and parcel of a structural system right at the center of language. Surely, the fact that there are any number of structural generalizations that cut across functional lines shows that we generativists are on the right track when we characterize form without worrying about function.

Funk: Believe me, the discernible effects of function on form are more than robust enough to prevent me from giving up my commitment to *explaining* grammatical structure in favor of your mechanical "autonomist" approach that attempts to explain nothing.

Forman: I'll let that remark about 'explanation' pass for a moment. What makes me doubt your point about 'robustness' is the huge number of structural properties of language that seem to be not only useless but downright dysfunctional! Are you going to tell me that effective communication *needs* gender marking, agreement rules, irregular verbs, coindexing mechanisms that only Rube Goldberg could have dreamed up, and things like that? Yet they're all an integral part of the formal structural system in a particular language.

Funk: A lot of what might seem dysfunctional at first glance is probably anything but. I don't doubt for a minute that gender and agreement, for example, play an important role in tracking referents in discourse.

Forman: But you've got to agree that most of the profound generalizations about language structure that we've arrived at in decades of research in generative grammar have little, if anything, to do with the functions of language. What is communicatively necessary, or even useful, about rules being structure-dependent? About their applying cyclically? About abstract principles like the Empty Category Principle or Spec-Head Agreement?

Funk: A lot of your 'profound generalizations' are no more than artifacts of the narrow scope of the formalist enterprise. If all you're interested in doing is pushing symbols around, then you'll get generalizations about symbol pushing. Don't tell me, though, that they have anything to do with how language works.

Forman: That strikes me as a totally head-in-the-sand attitude, not to mention an unscientific one. Generalizations are generalizations. We wouldn't expect to find deep formal patterns in language if language weren't designed that way. What you're saying is that you won't accept any generalization that doesn't fit in with your preconceived ideas about how language is supposed to work.

Funk: I could say the same to you! *Your* head-in-the sand attitude has prevented you from even *asking* how much iconicity there is to syntax, to say nothing of discovering that there's an enormous amount. And that's only one example I could cite.

Forman: I've never been too impressed with what I've seen written about iconicity. But that would be a debate unto itself. In any event, I can't think of any functionalist principle that's stood the test of time. You guys can't even decide if old information is supposed to come before new information or if new information is supposed to come before old information!

Funk: You should talk! In one year and out the next is the rule for virtually every formal principle and constraint that I can think of.

Forman: But most of the time that's because the new principle has subsumed the old one and is more general. That's precisely how scientific progress is *supposed* to work.

Funk: What you don't seem to recognize is that, even on your own terms, a lot of generative principles have a pretty clear functional basis. To take the most obvious example of all, there's the Condition on Recoverability of Deletion. And do you think that it's just a coincidence that many, if not most, Subjacency and ECP violations are difficult to process? Isn't it obvious that structure-dependence and the cycle are simply grammar-particular instantiations of how human cognition represents complex structured information in general?

Forman: I've heard those points made many times, but I'm not impressed. Yes, at some fuzzily speculative level we can make up 'functions' for generative principles or analogize them to poorly understood properties that seem to govern other cognitive faculties. But when you look at them deeply, their 'motivations' disappear. GB and Minimalist principles are too grammar-specific, too abstract, and too removed from any function to be a response, even indirectly, to those functions.

Funk: Well, why *do* we have them in our heads, then?

Forman: Who knows? All we know is that they could never have been learned inductively by the child: they're much too abstract and kids have too little exposure to the relevant evidence. So we can safely conclude that they must be innate.

Funk: And I've heard *that* point made many times too! The fact is that you've never demonstrated that a theory of inductive learning can't acquire the principles of your theory, even if they are correct.

Forman: And you've never come up with a theory of inductive learning that *can* acquire them. This whole debate over innateness hasn't gone much beyond two kids screaming at each other over and over again: 'Can so!' 'Cannot!' 'Can so!' 'Cannot!'

Funk: So let me ask you again, Why on earth would these principles of yours ever have ended up being incorporated into the human genome?

Forman: And again, we just don't know. Maybe some day we will, but not knowing shouldn't keep us from trying to come up with the most adequate theory possible.

Funk: Now let me turn your question to me back to you. If the principles of grammar are innate, then why aren't all languages the same?

Forman: As you know, they have to be parameterized in specific ways. Different languages choose different parameter settings.

Funk: So what determines what the possible parameter settings are and why one language would choose one over another?

Forman: I assume that the possible settings are also innately provided. There might well be some principles that determine why some settings tend to cluster and why changes of settings don't take place randomly, though the fact is that those issues aren't very high on our research agenda.

Funk: Maybe they should be! Why would anybody be interested in a theory of language that doesn't place very high on its research agenda the question of how and why variation exists?

Forman: We're a lot more interested, frankly, in what all languages have *in common.* That's why language is a key to the nature of the human mind, and also why philosophers for thousands of years have thought that language is so important, by the way.

Funk: You can learn a lot more about the nature of the human mind by . . .

At this point a Minnesota State professor opens the door to the hallway and beckons Sandy to enter the interview room.

2   The Goals of This Book

The minidebate between Sandy and Chris, multiplied by several hundred pages, forms the subject matter of this book. By a not terribly subtle onomastic device, I have identified Sandy Forman as the archetypal formal linguist and Chris Funk as the archetypal functional linguist. I've tried to put in their mouths, as succinctly as possible, all of the major issues that I plan to take up in detail. Each statement that Sandy or Chris makes encapsulates a view characteristic of mainstream practitioners of formal linguistics and functional linguistics respectively. If there is anything unrealistic about their exchange, it is the fact that it could have taken place at all! Few functionalists and still fewer formalists are aware enough of the positions taken by the other side (caricatures of those positions aside) to make possible the back-and-forth to which we have just been exposed.

I will argue that, to a surprising extent, Sandy and Chris are both right. That is, formalists are absolutely correct in their commitment to characterizing form independently of meaning and function. But at the same time, functionalists are right that meaning and function can help to shape form. As we will see, there is no contradiction here, whatever Sandy and Chris might believe.

As many readers are no doubt aware, I have a reputation as an ardent defender of formal linguistics (see, for example, Newmeyer 1983, 1986b). In one sense, that ardor has not diminished one iota. My commitment to the 'generative enterprise' (Chomsky 1982b) is as firm as it ever has been. Indeed, these pages will add to my already substantial writings in defense of that enterprise (substantial in bulk if not in persuasiveness). But I have also in recent years become convinced that there is an ultimately self-destructive narrowness of outlook on the part of many generative grammarians. Put simply, they refuse to consider the possibility that anything of interest might have been uncovered in the course of functionalist-oriented research. I could not disagree with them more. On the contrary, I have found a wealth of interesting generalizations and suggestive avenues of research in the work carried out in that tradition. And significantly, I believe that what it will take to incorporate many of these generalizations into a comprehensive theory of language challenges important conceptions held by most mainstream formal linguists. While, crucially, this can be accomplished without abandoning the essential core of generativist theory, dealing with such generalizations involves, to say the least, broadening one's vision about what is going on in language and how best to deal with it.

I must stress that it is not the purpose of this book to unveil a new theory of language, or even to present a new synthesis that ties together previously adumbrated theories. Quite the contrary, in fact. I will be arguing, in chapter after chapter, that the Chomskyan approach to grammar, broadly defined, is fundamentally on the right track. I hope to accomplish this, however, not by demonstrating the superiority of one formal framework over its formalist or functionalist rivals. Rather, I will try to show that the basic principles of generative grammar, in interaction with principles from other domains at work in language, provide compelling accounts of phenomena that functionalists, in general, have taken to refute the generativist approach. These include phenomena such as prototype effects, grammaticalization, the grounding of formal structure in external pressure, and so on—phenomena that few generativists have, in the past, even thought worthy of consideration.

I've been using the terms 'formal linguistics' and 'functional linguistics' as if they have unique well-understood referents. Unfortunately, they do not. Before proceeding any further, it will be necessary to clarify the spectrum of positions identified with these terms.

3 The Two Orientations in Modern Linguistics

James McCawley (1982) once calculated that if one took 40 issues of interest to grammarians, each of which admits to two or more possible positions, and weeded out those combinations of positions that are inconsistent, incoherent, or blatantly false, one would still be left with at least thirty million theories of grammar. The fact that only a little over one millionth of that total have actually surfaced as named theories is troublesome enough for anyone who, like me, would wish to distill the fundamental controversies of the field to a couple of clearly counterposed positions.

There are, however, two broad *orientations* in the field. Leaving aside some (not insignificant) subtleties for the next chapter, they are as follows. One orientation sees as a central task for linguists characterizing the formal relationships among grammatical elements independently of any characterization of the semantic and pragmatic properties of those elements. The other orientation rejects that task on the grounds that the function of conveying meaning (in its broadest sense) has so affected grammatical form that it is senseless to compartmentalize it. It is the former orientation, of course, that I have been referring to as 'formalist' and the latter as 'functionalist'.

3.1 The formalist (structuralist, generativist) orientation
It should be obvious why the former orientation is called 'formalist': it focuses centrally on linguistic form. Despite their apparent mnemonicity, however, the terms 'formalist', 'formal linguistics', and 'formal linguist' are ill chosen and will not be used with reference to the first orientation in the subsequent pages of this work. The problem is the ambiguity of the

word 'formal' and its derivatives. The term is ambiguous between the sense of 'pertaining to (grammatical) form', as opposed to meanings and uses, and the sense of 'formal*ized*', i.e., stated in a mathematically precise vocabulary. This ambiguity has the danger of leading to confusion. When Pullum (1989), Chomsky (1990), and Ludlow (1992), for example, debate whether the 'principles and parameters' approach is a species of 'formal linguistics', they have the latter sense of the term in mind; functionalists' criticisms of 'formal linguistics' invariably refer to the former. And while functionalists have not produced formalized theories, many agree that in principle there is nothing about their orientation that should prevent them (someday) from doing so (see, for example, Li 1976: x; Croft 1995a: 503; Bybee 1998).

The question, then, is what to replace the term 'formalist' with. An obvious candidate is 'structuralist' and, indeed, some functionalists have used the term for that purpose (Noonan 1998). But 'structuralist' carries with it its own pernicious ambiguities. One problem is that many linguists in what (uncontroversially) is known as the 'structuralist tradition' in linguistics have taken what I have been calling a functionalist approach to syntax, even while focusing primarily on form at the phonological and morphological levels. This is the case, for example, for the linguists of the Prague School. As far as I am aware, however, they use the term 'structuralist' to refer to the entire body of their theorizing. Second, we find the nearly interchangeable use of the terms 'functionalist' and 'structuralist' by some European linguists, whose goal is to describe structural systems in terms of the 'functions' (in one sense of the term) of the elements of those systems.[1] Hence a Belgian historiographer of linguistics could write,

It is in any case undeniable that since the 1940s structuralism (or functionalism) has more than any other movement captured the attention of linguists and so, willy nilly, has become the driving force behind contemporary linguistics. (Leroy 1963/1967: 84)

And third, through a strange terminological twist, very few generative grammarians recognize themselves as being 'structuralists'. In the early

---

1. For representative recent work, see Dressler (1990) and the papers in Dressler et al. (1987). The basic idea of this approach to functionalism (called 'systemic functionalism' in Croft 1996b) is that grammars are shaped by forces driving them to become more efficient semiotic systems *internally*. I will have little to say about systemic functionalism in this book (but see the Croft paper and Labov 1994 for critiques).

1960s, Chomsky and his associates started using the word 'structuralist' to refer to those form-centered models that preceded generative grammar, in particular, to those in the American post-Bloomfieldian tradition. As a result, to many of us who were educated in generative-orientated departments in the first couple decades of that model's existence, the structuralists were the principal *opponents* of the generative grammarians. It hardly seems felicitous, then, to use the term 'structuralist' as a substitute for 'formalist'.

For better or worse, I have settled on the term 'generative' and its derivatives to refer to the first orientation. If what we mean by a generative grammar is a device that specifies the well-formed sentences of the language and their structures, then the first orientation, as I have characterized it, is for the most part a generative one. And surely, by definition, no practitioners of the second orientation have such a commitment. There are, unfortunately, terminological wrinkles here as well, primarily owing to the locution 'device that specifies'. Post-Bloomfieldian syntax was formalist, in the sense that it characterized the formal properties of sentences independently of their meanings and functions. However, in this tradition no generative device specified the set of sentences. Indeed, throughout most of the period in which post-Bloomfieldianism was ascendant in the United States, recursive function theory had not advanced to the point to which such a device was even imaginable. And current work in the principles-and-parameters tradition has progressively downplayed the construction of generative grammars in favor of the identification of universal principles governing grammatical form. Indeed, Chomsky has recently asserted:[2]

> The class [of well-formed (grammatical) expressions of *L*] has no significance. The concepts 'well-formed' and 'grammatical' remain without characterization or known empirical justification; they played virtually no role in early work on generative grammar except in informal exposition, or since. (Chomsky 1993: 44–45)

But notice that in the very passage in which Chomsky dismisses any interest in specifying the grammatical sentences of a language, he refers to his approach as 'generative grammar'. Hence I will follow him, and everyday usage in the field as well, by referring to the first orientation as a 'generative' one.

2. See Pullum (1996b) on how the last clause of the Chomsky quote could not possibly be true.

3.2 The functionalist orientation

The term 'functionalist' is no less problem-free than 'formalist'. In one
common usage, a 'functionalist' is simply a linguist who studies, 'among
other things perhaps, the discourse or processing functions of syntactic
forms' (Prince 1991: 79). As Prince notes, a functionalist in this sense need
not even reject generative grammar or the idea that syntax forms an
autonomous system. In the words of Susumu Kuno, whom Prince places
in this group,[3] 'In theory there is no conflict in principle between functional syntax and, say, the government and binding theory of generative
grammar' (Kuno 1987: 1).

   While I admit to extreme feelings of guilt at attempting to deprive
Prince and her cohort of the right to call themselves 'functionalists', in
this book I will not use that term to describe a linguist whose interests are
(simply) to study the interaction of form and meaning, discourse, and
processing. Rather, it will be reserved for those who believe that in some
profound way form is so beholden to meaning, discourse, and processing
that it is wrong-headed to specify the distribution of the formal elements
of language by means of an independent set of rules or principles. In other
words, to be considered a species of functionalism, a study will have to be
in line with the following statement by Johanna Nichols:

> [Functional grammar] analyzes grammatical structure, as do formal and structural
> grammar, but it also analyzes the entire communicative situation: the purpose of
> the speech event, its participants, its discourse context. Functionalists maintain
> that the communicative situation motivates, constrains, explains, or otherwise
> determines grammatical structure, and that a structural or formal approach is not
> merely limited to an artificially restricted data base, but is inadequate even as a
> structural account. (1984: 97)

   Functionalist work, then, is not addressed to formulating grammar-
internal principles characterizing the well- or ill-formedness of a set of
sentences. Instead, a generalization about grammatical patterning might
be attributed to the most orderly or efficient means of conveying information, the desirability of foregrounding or backgrounding events in the

---

3. In addition to herself and Kuno, Prince identifies the following linguists as
functionalists in her sense: Jacqueline Guéron, Jeanette Gundel, Georgia Green,
Tony Kroch, Gary Milsark, Tanya Reinhart, Michael Rochemont, Gregory
Ward, Yael Ziv, Anne Zribi-Hertz, Nomi Erteschik-Shir, and Laurence Horn. In
their overviews of various functionalist approaches, Nichols (1984) and Croft
(1995a) refer to this approach as 'conservative functionalism' and 'autonomist
functionalism' respectively.

discourse, the speaker's desire for economy, the hearer's demand for clarity, or cognitive propensities not specific to language, such as a general preference for iconic over arbitrary representations, and so on.

4 On the Variety of Generativist Approaches

Most, if not all, generativist approaches trace their ancestry to the work pioneered by Noam Chomsky in the 1950s (Chomsky 1955, 1957) and further developed by him in the next decade (Chomsky 1965). Broadly speaking, two trends in generative grammar have developed more or less in parallel since the mid 1970s (for more comprehensive discussion of this topic, see Newmeyer 1986a, 1996). The first trend is associated with the work of Chomsky and his associates and, for the greater part of the past couple decades, has predominated over the second in terms of number of practitioners and (more intangibly) influence. Since the early 1980s this trend has been known as the 'principles and parameters' (P&P) approach and has been embodied by two successive models of grammatical theory: the Government Binding theory (GB) (Chomsky 1981) and the Minimalist Program (MP) (Chomsky 1995).

The other trend consists of a dozen or more named theories, including Lexical-Functional Grammar (Bresnan 1982); Relational Grammar (Perlmutter 1983; Perlmutter and Rosen 1984; Postal and Joseph 1990); Generalized Phrase Structure Grammar (Gazdar et al. 1985); Head-Driven Phrase Structure Grammar (Pollard and Sag 1994); and Categorial Grammar (Steedman 1993).

Let me briefly outline the major differences between the P&P approach and its rivals. At the level of technical organization, the former postulates a multi-leveled theory, with transformational rules relating the levels. All of the latter models, in their various ways, generate surface structures directly.[4] Secondly, the former takes a 'deeply modular' approach to syntax in the sense that constructions are considered to be wholly epiphenomenal. Instead, parameterized principles of universal grammar (henceforth UG) interact to characterize the sentences of the language. The other approaches vary from being somewhat modular to reject-

---

4. Transformationless theories have been proposed both in GB (Koster 1986) and the MP (Brody 1995). However, their reliance on chains of coindexed elements leads to their having much more in common with P&P models than with non-P&P ones.

ing grammar-internal modularity outright. And thirdly, most non-P&P models posit a much closer linkage between form and meaning than does P&P. Most work in GB and MP has assumed that the only point of contact between form and meaning is at the abstract level of logical form, itself a product of transformational operations. But many non-P&P approaches assume that every syntactic rule (or statement) has an accompanying semantic rule (or statement), even while the basic mechanisms of these theories allow for an independent characterization of the formal elements of language.

Most of the approaches to meaning that fall under the rubric of 'formal semantics' presuppose, as might be expected, some version of generative syntax (for overviews, see Chierchia and McConnell-Ginet 1990; Cann 1993). Two important approaches to discourse phenomena do so as well. The first, already mentioned in §3.2, is that of Ellen Prince and her associates (Prince 1988; Green 1989; Ward, Sproat, and McKoon 1991). The other is known as 'Relevance Theory' (Sperber and Wilson 1986; Carston 1995).

For most of the issues that concern us in this book, the differences between P&P and its rivals are unimportant. Indeed, I have long taken the position that they tend to be exaggerated (see Newmeyer 1986a: 227; 1987). Nevertheless, it is worth pointing out that a leading functionalist (Croft 1998) has remarked that the non-P&P approaches are more congenial to the functionalist world view than P&P, given that they share with functionalism a 'surfacey' approach to characterizing grammatical form and that they posit very close linkages between form and meaning.

As I have stressed, it is not the purpose of this book to argue for new or improved principles of generative grammar. But still, I have to *present* the results of generative research by way of discussing the phenomena that divide generativists and functionalists. So the question I am faced with is: '*Which* generative research?' Or more concretely: 'The results of which framework?' With few exceptions, I have chosen the principles that have been arrived at within GB. Of all currently practiced frameworks, GB has, by far, the largest body of published research and, I think, the largest number of practitioners. I also happen to find the bulk of GB principles eminently plausible, at least in their general thrust. It is certainly possible that if I were to write this book several years from now, I would opt for the MP. However, at the present time, I find the concrete claims of the MP so vague and the total set of mechanisms that it requires (where I have been able to understand them) so *unminimalist*[5] that I see no reason to encumber the exposition with my interpretation of how the phenomenon in question might be dealt with within that approach. It is also worth pointing out that even leading developers of the MP typically appeal to strictly GB principles in presentations to general audiences of linguists (see, for example, Lasnik 1998).

5 On the Variety of Functionalist Approaches

Those who share the functionalist orientation differ in their basic assumptions far more than do those who are committed to the generativist approach. This is partly a consequence of there being a lot more possible ways that one can be against some theoretical conception (the compartmentalization of form) than one can be for it. Saying that the formal properties of language are not characterized as a system unto themselves leaves open a myriad of possibilities as to how they *should be* characterized. Another reason that there is so little consensus among functionalists is that the orientation is not dominated by one central figure to the extent that generative linguistics is. This can hardly be considered a bad thing, of course. For better or worse (and you will find partisans of both alternatives), Chomsky is looked upon as the pied piper by the majority of generative linguists. No functionalist has managed to play the pipes nearly as enticingly to the graduate students of Hamlin. To mix images, Elizabeth Bates has remarked that 'functionalism is like Protestantism: it is a group of warring sects which agree only on the rejection of the authority of the Pope' (cited in Van Valin 1990: 171).

The remainder of this section will briefly outline three current trends in functionalism: those that Croft (1995a) calls 'external functionalism' (including cognitive linguistics), 'integrative functionalism', and 'extreme functionalism'.

5.1 External functionalism (including cognitive linguistics)
External functionalism, like functionalism in general, rejects the project of characterizing the formal relationships among grammatical elements independently of any characterization of the semantic and pragmatic

---

5. My one sentence critique of the MP is that it gains elegance in the derivational component of the grammar only at the expense of a vast overcomplication of other components, in particular the lexicon and the morphology.

properties of those elements. That is, there are no purely syntactic rules
of any great generality. Nevertheless, external functionalism upholds
the idea of a synchronic *semiotic system*, in which formal elements are
linked to semantic and pragmatic ones. In most external functionalist
approaches, it is assumed that the links between form on the one hand
and meaning and use on the other are 'natural' ones, in that the properties
of the latter have helped to shape the former. Most of the named functionalist theories appear to represent external functionalism: some examples are Role and Reference Grammar (Foley and Van Valin 1984; Van
Valin 1993a, b), the Competition Model of Bates and MacWhinney
(1989); Functional Grammar (Dik 1981, 1989); and Systemic (Functional) Grammar (Halliday 1985).

The wing of external functionalism that seems to have the greatest
support world-wide consists of several related approaches that are generally referred to as 'cognitive linguistics'.[6] With the possible exception of
Role and Reference Grammar, no other functionalist school is as deeply
rooted historically in the generative tradition. Its two leading practitioners, George Lakoff and Ronald Langacker, were prominent generative semanticists in the 1970s, and, as such, were already committed to
a model of grammar that rejected 'boundaries' between syntax, semantics,
and pragmatics. Cognitive linguistics represents (as is acknowledged in
Lakoff 1987: 582) an 'updating' of generative semantics, purged of the
generative-derived formalism characteristic of that model and sensitive to
certain subsequent developments in cognitive psychology.

Indeed, not everybody thinks of cognitive linguistics as a species of
'functionalism' at all, though my impression is that the different sociological roots of cognitive linguistics from most other functionalist models
have become increasingly unimportant. In any event, Langacker (1987a:
4) refers to the 'natural affinity' of cognitive linguistics to the 'especially
significant' research in the functionalist tradition, while Lakoff (1991: 55),

6. The version of cognitive linguistics developed by Ronald Langacker and his
associates is called 'Cognitive Grammar'. A cluster of related approaches called
'Construction Grammar' contains models wholly within the cognitive linguistics
orbit (Barlow and Kemmer 1994), or mostly so (Goldberg 1996), and others (e.g.
Fillmore, Kay, and O'Connor 1988) with a strong resemblance to the generative
model of Head-Driven Phrase Structure Grammar. Word Grammar began as a
generative approach (Hudson 1984, 1990), but seems to be evolving in the direction of cognitive linguistics (see Hudson 1997).

reversing the more usual picture of the relationship, describes 'functional linguistics [as] a branch of cognitive linguistics'.

As the following quotes make clear, cognitive linguistics maintains that a grammar is a semiotic system, and therefore, by our terms, is a model of external functionalism:

Suppose we think of a language as a collection of form-meaning pairs, where the meanings are concepts in a given conceptual system. (Lakoff 1987: 539)

More specifically, the grammar of a language is defined as those aspects of cognitive organization in which resides a speaker's grasp of established linguistic convention. It can be characterized as a structured inventory of conventional linguistic units. (Langacker 1987a: 57)

Goldberg (1996: 3–4) has conveniently summarized the 'foundational assumptions' of cognitive linguistics. They could well be the foundational assumptions of external functionalism in general, though some models would attach greater or lesser stress to certain points than to others:

1. Semantics is based on speaker's construals of situations, not on objective truth conditions (Langacker 1985, 1987a, 1988; Fauconnier 1985; Lakoff 1987; Talmy 1978b, 1985).
2. Semantics and pragmatics form a continuum, and both play a role in linguistic meaning. Linguistic meaning is part of our overall conceptual system and not a separate modular component (Talmy 1978b, 1985; Haiman 1980a; Lakoff 1987; Langacker 1987a).
3. Categorization does not typically involve necessary and sufficient conditions, but rather central and extended senses (Rosch 1973; Rosch et al. 1976; Lakoff 1977, 1987; Haiman 1978a; Fillmore 1982; Hopper and Thompson 1984; Givón 1986; Brugman 1988; Taylor 1989; Corrigan, Eckman, and Noonan 1989).
4. The primary function of language is to convey meaning. Thus formal distinctions are useful to the extent that they convey semantic or pragmatic (including discourse) distinctions (Wierzbicka 1986a, 1988; Haiman 1985b; Lakoff 1987; Langacker 1987a; Croft 1991; Deane 1991).
5. Grammar does not involve any transformational component. Semantics is associated directly with surface form.
6. Grammatical constructions, like traditional lexical items, are pairings of form and meaning. They are taken to have a real cognitive status, and are not epiphenomena based on the operation of generative rules or universal principles (Lakoff 1987; Fillmore, Kay, and O'Connor 1988; Wierzbicka 1988; Goldberg 1995).

7. Grammar consists of a structured inventory of form-meaning pairings: phrasal grammatical constructions and lexical items (Fillmore and Kay 1993; Lakoff 1987; Langacker 1987a; Wierzbicka 1988; Goldberg 1995).

The stress laid by external functionalists on the systematic properties of language as a whole leave it with one foot in the structuralist door. Indeed, Van Valin (1993b: 1) has described Role and Reference Grammar as a 'structuralist-functionalist theory of grammar' and one functionalist has condemned this theory, along with Dik's Functional Grammar, for 'the practice of conferring functional-sounding labels on grammatical structures' (Givón 1995: 309).

5.2 Integrative functionalism

Integrative functionalists have a more 'immanent' view of grammatical structure than do external functionalists. As Croft (1995a: 516) characterizes integrative functionalism, 'Linguistic phenomena [are considered] systematic, and may be (partly) arbitrary, but they would involve such a close interaction of cognitive and external social factors that one could not reasonably describe the internal cognitive system as self-contained.' In other words, integrative functionalists do not deny the existence of systematicity in language, but they do deny the Saussurian dictum that it is meaningful to separate langue from parole and synchrony from diachrony.

Integrative functionalists are typically unwilling to distinguish between the functional role that a linguistic element might perform vis-à-vis other linguistic elements with which it is associated and the external functional motivation for that element. In this respect they differ dramatically from external functionalists. For example, Langacker (1987a: 413), speaking for the latter, notes that 'though functional considerations are undeniably critical in the shaping of linguistic structure, it does not follow that they should be incorporated directly into the grammar as descriptive statements' and has offered the view that only 'a *comprehensive* linguistic description will encompass both the grammar of a language *as well as* extensive accounts of the varied functional considerations that have shaped it' (Langacker 1991: 513; emphasis added).

The only named model of integrative functionalism of which I am aware is Paul Hopper's Emergent Grammar (Hopper 1987, 1988). Emergent Grammar rejects the idea that ' "grammar" [is] an object apart from the speaker and separated from the uses which the speaker might make of it' (Hopper 1987: 141). Instead, grammar is 'provisional and emergent, not isolatable in principle from general strategies for constructing discourses' (Hopper 1988: 132). That is, Hopper opts for a 'hermeneutic' approach in which temporality and context are key. In particular, Hopper denies the reality of linguistic representations: 'There is no room—no need—for mediation by mental structures' (1987: 145).

One characteristic of integrative functionalism—and much external functionalism as well—is the idea that the explanatory forces at work in shaping languages reveal themselves only when a large number of diverse languages are investigated. The belief has resulted in functionalists taking the lead in typological research. Indeed, one often makes reference to the 'functional-typological approach' to language.

The great majority of functionalists who do not adhere to one of the 'named' functionalist frameworks are not explicit as to how they stand on the issues that divide external and integrative functionalism. I do not think that it is unfair to say that it is common to find, combined within the same work, an integrative theoretical stance and an external analytical practice. No doubt this is to a large extent a consequence of the fact that the implications for grammatical analysis of integrative functionalism have barely begun to be explored. Along these lines, Croft (1995a: 520) points out that integrative functionalists have rarely addressed the question of how dynamic processes may be represented cognitively, and goes on to list three 'gaps and problems with the integrative model':

1. Integrative functionalism must provide a system of grammatical representation that can model a variable grammar and its acquisition and use.
2. Integrative functionalism must account for stable as well as dynamic characteristics of the grammatical system.
3. The role of functional (that is, cognitive and discourse) factors must be integrated with the role of social factors. (Croft 1995a: 520–521)

5.3 Extreme functionalism

Extreme functionalism is represented by work in the 'Columbia School' (García 1979; Diver 1995) and a proposal by Kalmár (1979) for predicate argument relations in Inukitut. Advocates of this approach believe that *all* of grammar can be derived from semantic and discourse factors—the only 'arbitrariness' in language exists in the lexicon. For reasons that will become clear as this work proceeds, very few linguists of any theoretical stripe consider such an approach to be tenable.[7]

5.4 On what to call 'the functionalist approach'

The even greater variety of functionalist approaches than generativist approaches gives me a correspondingly greater problem in deciding how to use the term 'functionalist' (without additional modification) in the remainder of this work. I have decided—I hope not too arbitrarily—to characterize as 'functionalism' any approach that embodies the following three positions, all of which are common to both external and integrative functionalism. First, the links between the formal properties of grammar and their semantic and pragmatic functions are tight enough to preclude any significant methodological or analytical 'parceling out' of form. Second, to a significant degree, the formal properties of grammar are motivated by the functions that language carries out, in particular its function of conveying meaning in communication. And third, by means of integrating functional explanation with typological investigation, one can explain why certain grammatical features in the languages of the world are more common than others and why, for particular languages, the appearance of one feature often implies the appearance of another.

6   A Look Ahead

Each chapter will focus on some aspect of the relationship between language form and language function, and hence on those issues that divide generativists and functionalists. Chapter 2, 'The Boundaries of Grammar', takes on the question of the 'compartmentalization of form', which is at the center of the debate. It lays out three different 'autonomy' theses, as follows:

1. *The autonomy of syntax* (AUTOSYN). Human cognition embodies a system whose primitive terms are nonsemantic and nondiscourse-derived syntactic elements and whose principles of combination make no reference to system-external factors.

7. Extreme functionalism does, however, provide a convenient caricature of functionalism in general for generative linguists, as it did, to an unfortunate extent, in Newmeyer (1983).

2. *The autonomy of knowledge of language with respect to use of language* (AUTOKNOW). Knowledge of language ('competence') can and should be characterized independently of language use ('performance') and the social, cognitive, and communicative factors contributing to use.

3. *The autonomy of grammar as a cognitive system* (AUTOGRAM). Human cognition embodies a system whose primitive terms are structural elements particular to language and whose principles of combination make no reference to system-external factors.

Current generative models adopt all three autonomy hypotheses, while integrative functionalists reject them. External functionalists reject AUTO-SYN, but (for the most part) seem to accept AUTOKNOW and AUTOGRAM. I will argue that all three hypotheses are motivated. Chapter 2 also takes on the question of innate grammatical principles, suggesting that conclusions of innateness based on classic 'arguments from the poverty of the stimulus' are problematic in a variety of ways. Nevertheless, recent findings that specific grammatical impairments can be transmitted genetically do point to an innate component to grammar, and hence to the correctness of AUTOGRAM.

Chapter 3, 'Internal and External Explanation in Linguistics', probes what it means to say that we have 'explained' some grammatical phenomenon. It stresses that the popular idea that explanation in generative grammar is entirely 'internal' and that functionalists opt for 'external' explanation is vastly oversimplified. Rather, both orientations make use of both modes of explanation. I argue that not only are the three autonomy hypotheses compatible with external (functional) explanation, but that central aspects of grammars *have* been motivated functionally. I identify parsing pressure and pressure for structure and meaning to be in iconic alignment as two central functional influences on grammars. I question, though, whether discourse has played much of a role in shaping grammatical form. Much of the chapter is devoted to the problem of 'competing motivations'—the fact that outside forces place conflicting demands on grammars. I argue that the since structure results from a number of external factors in competition with each other, grammars cannot be linkings of structures and their external motivations. I go on to show that competing motivations have equally profound implications for the functionalist program for language typology.

The fourth chapter is entitled 'On Syntactic Categories'. The classical view of syntactic categories, and one taken for granted by all generative models, is that they are discrete 'algebraic' entities, not admitting to a notional definition. The classical view has seen three challenges from the functionalist camp. In one, categories are embodied with a prototype structure, in which they have 'best case' members and members that systematically depart from the 'best case'. In this approach, the optimal grammatical description of morphosyntactic processes is held to involve reference to degree of categorial deviation from the 'best case'. The second challenge hypothesizes that the boundaries between categories are nondistinct, in the sense that one grades gradually into another. The third takes categories to be definable by necessary and sufficient semantic conditions.

Chapter 4 defends the classical view, arguing that many of the phenomena that seem to suggest its inadequacy are best analyzed in terms of the interaction of independently needed principles from syntax, semantics, and pragmatics. In an appendix to this chapter, I challenge the idea that grammatical constructions must be attributed a prototype structure. I try to show that when the facts are investigated in sufficiently thorough detail, no such conclusion is justified.

Chapter 5 is called 'Deconstructing Grammaticalization'. The phenomenon of 'grammaticalization'—roughly, the loss of independence of a grammatical structure or element—has been trumpeted by some functionalists as the key issue that shows the superiority of their approach over the generative. I agree that many of the mechanisms involved in grammaticalization—in particular certain types of natural semantic and phonetic changes—are not provided by generative theory. But neither are they incompatible with it. In fact, I conclude that grammaticalization is no more than a cover term for the intersection of certain common historical developments that any theory has to account for, and as such, has no special relevance to the generativist-functionalist dialogue.

Chapter 6 is called, and takes on, 'Language Typology and Its Difficulties'. How can we be sure that the typological generalizations that have always formed the explananda for functionalist theory, and increasingly for generativist theory as well, are real facts in need of explanation? After reviewing all of the difficulties inherent in the typological work, I conclude on a note 'somewhere between cautious optimism and reluctant skepticism'. *Some* typological generalizations do seem robust enough that we can regard them as explananda in theory construction.

I go on to argue that functionalists underestimate the need for formal analysis as a prerequisite to typological analysis, while generativists, by a rhetorical emphasis on innate parameter settings, are drawn away from investigating possible functional explanations for typological patterns. Both of these circumstances are unfortunate. There is nothing in the program of functional explanation of typological facts that is incompatible with the existence of an autonomous structural system. And there is nothing in the generative program that demands that all typological facts be attributed to the setting of innately specified parameters.

The final chapter, chapter 7, is a brief conclusion, stressing the main theme of the book: the three autonomy hypotheses are fully compatible with functional explanation of grammatical phenomena.

Chapter 2

The Boundaries of Grammar

1 Overview

This chapter addresses the question of where the boundaries of grammar lie. In particular, it is concerned with whether there exist autonomous systems dedicated to grammar or, alternatively, whether there is no principled separability between grammar and other faculties at work in language. Section 2 notes that there are three different ways that the autonomy hypothesis might be formulated: syntax is self-contained; grammatical knowledge is self-contained with respect to language use; and grammatical knowledge is self-contained with respect to other cognitive faculties. The sections that follow (§§3, 4, and 5 respectively) argue that each of the three autonomy hypotheses is correct.

2 The Three Autonomy Hypotheses

Perhaps the most hotly debated question in linguistic theory is whether language can and should be described as an autonomous 'self-contained system'. Glossing over a world of subtleties, generative linguistics posits such a system, while functional linguistics rejects it. But in fact there are (at least) three different autonomy hypotheses that have been debated among linguists, and which are to some degree independent of each other. Following the spirit, if not the letter, of the discussion in Croft (1995a), they are:

(1) a. *The autonomy of syntax* (AUTOSYN). Human cognition embodies a system whose primitive terms are nonsemantic and nondiscourse-derived syntactic elements and whose principles of combination make no reference to system-external factors.

b. *The autonomy of knowledge of language with respect to use of language* (AUTOKNOW). Knowledge of language ('competence') can and should be characterized independently of language use ('performance') and the social, cognitive, and communicative factors contributing to use.
c. *The autonomy of grammar as a cognitive system* (AUTOGRAM). Human cognition embodies a system whose primitive terms are structural elements particular to language and whose principles of combination make no reference to system-external factors.

The reader will have noted that there is a certain nonparallelism to these three hypotheses. AUTOSYN and AUTOGRAM are claims about the nature of linguistic knowledge vis-à-vis other cognitive systems, while AUTOKNOW is a claim about knowledge vis-à-vis use. AUTOGRAM can be thought of as a broader form of AUTOSYN, in which not just syntactic knowledge, but grammatical knowledge as a whole, forms a distinct cognitive system. In other words, AUTOGRAM is the classic 'Saussurean' position that language embodies a semiotic system, 'un ensemble où tout se tient', as Meillet put it. AUTOKNOW, however, differs from AUTOSYN and AUTOGRAM in that it is neutral with respect to whether the system of knowledge posited contains only grammatical primitives. It asserts that this knowledge (however it is to be characterized) must be clearly distinguished from the use to which it is put.

The relationship among these three hypotheses is therefore rather complex. AUTOSYN straightforwardly entails AUTOGRAM; if syntax is a distinct cognitive system, then ipso facto there must be a distinct *linguistic* system. In the event that syntax were the *only* grammatical component with a distinct cognitive reality, the domains of AUTOSYN and AUTOGRAM would be equivalent, though nobody has proposed a theory along such lines. AUTOSYN does not entail AUTOKNOW. To claim that syntax is autonomous is not to claim that the principles for characterizing the knowledge involved in syntax (whatever its nature may be) are necessarily distinct from the principles involved in putting that knowledge to use. For example, one could reasonably interpret the immediate-constituent approach to syntax of the post-Bloomfieldian linguists as a model of AUTOSYN. However, by virtue of their behaviorism, these linguists rejected AUTOKNOW.[1] One interpretation of Jerry Fodor's influential book *The*

1. Harris (1941: 345), for example, defined *langue* as 'merely the scientific arrangement of [*parole*]'.

Modularity of Mind (Fodor 1983) is that it assumes AUTOSYN, but rejects AUTOKNOW. Unlike Chomsky's view of modularity, which stresses that syntax embodies a distinct *system of knowledge*, Fodor does not clearly distinguish between knowledge of grammar and its implementation in language processing.[2]

Neither AUTOKNOW nor AUTOGRAM entail AUTOSYN. Two current schools of functionalist linguistics, Role and Reference Grammar and Functional Grammar, posit a semiotic system consistent with both AUTOKNOW and AUTOGRAM, but one in which there is no clear separation of semantic and syntactic primitives. Even given a basic framework of assumptions in the spirit of current principles-and-parameters work, one can imagine the possibility of a self-contained grammar module in which the task of accounting for syntactic patterning would be distributed among the various components, analogously to the way that in some approaches to morphology (e.g. Halle and Marantz 1993), there is no single component dedicated to expressing generalizations reasonably deemed 'morphological'.

Finally, we turn to the relationship between AUTOKNOW and AUTO-GRAM. AUTOGRAM does not entail AUTOKNOW for the same reason that AUTOSYN does not entail AUTOKNOW—to claim that a distinct linguistic system exists is not necessarily to claim that the principles for character-izing knowledge of that system are distinct from those characterizing its use. Perhaps 'connectionist' models of language can be interpreted as assuming AUTOGRAM, but not AUTOKNOW. Likewise, AUTOKNOW does not entail AUTOGRAM, since AUTOKNOW does not demand a set of specifically grammatical principles that are independent of those governing other aspects of cognition. In cognitive linguistics we sometimes find a rhetori-cal rejection of both AUTOKNOW and AUTOGRAM, which, as I will argue below (§5.1), is not carried out in practice.

This chapter will examine in turn the arguments for and against the three autonomy hypotheses. The conclusion will be that all are motivated.

3   The Autonomy of Syntax

The following sections take on issues pertinent to the hypothesis that syntax is autonomous. Section 3.1 discusses the historical roots of the hypothesis; §3.2 attempts to specify it precisely, while §3.3 deals with its

2. For illuminating discussion of Fodor's theory and its relationship to autonomy, see Higginbotham (1987) and Bock and Kroch (1989).

scope; §3.4 addresses methodological issues that arise in the course of discussions of the hypothesis; and §3.5 provides evidence that it is well motivated empirically.

3.1 The Historical Roots of AUTOSYN

By the mid 1940s, most American structural linguists (or, as they were commonly known, the 'post-Bloomfieldians') who took any interest in syntax at all believed that patterning of syntactic forms could and should be described independently of the meanings held by those forms. Matthews (1993) devotes a lengthy and, on the whole, compelling discussion on how they arrived at such a view. While Leonard Bloomfield, the teacher of and intellectual inspiration for most American linguists in this period, was agnostic on the question of AUTOSYN, his book *Language* (Bloomfield 1933) did provide an accessible terminology and implicit methodology for characterizing forms and their positions. This contrasted with the relative difficulty in analyzing meaning, for Bloomfield 'the weak point in language-study' (1933: 140). The post-Bloomfieldians were also mightily impressed by Sapir, who was able to provide numerous compelling examples of how 'the formal processes by which a language expresses concepts do not correspond in any simple fashion to the concepts themselves' (Matthews 1993: 115).

For the more empiricist of the post-Bloomfieldians, the need to provide a characterization of the purely formal relations among linguistic elements was a matter of theoretical necessity. As Trager and Smith (1951: 8) explained it:

The presentation of the structure of a language should begin, in theory, with a complete statement of the pertinent prelinguistic data.... This should be followed by an account of the observed phonetic behavior, and then should come the analysis of the phonetic behavior into the phonemic structure, completing the phonology. The next step is to present the recurring entities ... that constitute the morpheme list.... The analyses, *like any scientific analyses, are based on classifications of behavior events.* (Emphasis added.)

And for the others, it was a matter of methodological convenience—it is easier to exclude semantic considerations from grammar if progress seems to be forthcoming without appeal to them. The following passage from Matthews (1993: 122) acknowledges this point:

In a moment of reminiscence, Voegelin and his wife imply that Bloomfield himself was willing to push [exclusively distributional criteria] quite a long way. They recall his advice, 'repeated over and over again' at Linguistic Institutes, 'to postpone consideration of unsolved or unresolved semantic problems until the more formal problems of grammar (in phonology and syntax) were better stated'. 'Most Americanists', they say, 'heeded' it (Voegelin and Voegelin 1976: 18, 97 n. 7).

With the birth of transformational generative grammar in the mid 1950s, AUTOSYN took on a new dimension. The first nonintroductory chapter of Chomsky's *Syntactic Structures* (Chomsky 1957) is entitled 'The Independence of Grammar'. In that chapter, after several pages of discussion, he concluded 'that we are forced to conclude that grammar is autonomous and independent of meaning' (1957: 17). Chomsky stresses the independence of grammar and meaning so many times in that book that many commentators have assumed that he simply adopted without questioning the position of the post-Bloomfieldians, an assumption often going hand-in-hand with the implication that this demonstrates that he had not really broken completely from that tradition. But a careful reading of *Syntactic Structures* falsifies such a conclusion. First of all, the independence of grammar in no way followed from his approach to theory construction, as it did for many post-Bloomfieldians. Chomsky was clear that the question of the relation of grammar and meaning is an empirical one. He gave example after example in support of AUTOSYN: Speakers have intuitions that cannot be expressed in semantic terms; neither phonemic distinctness nor morpheme identity is wholly semantic; notions like 'subject' and 'object' defy strict semantic characterization; and so on. In fact, Chomsky used the apparent nonparaphrase relationship between the sentences *Everyone in the room knows at least two languages* and *At least two languages are known by everyone in the room* as evidence that Passive (and transformations in general) cannot be defined strictly in terms of meaning. In other words, he was arguing that the *assumption* that syntax is semantically based is false, and any theory built on this assumption must therefore be fundamentally deficient.

As AUTOSYN is formulated in (1a), there exist purely syntactic primitives, the mutual interrelationships of which are determined by system-internal principles of combination. But that formulation leaves open a wealth of interpretations as to what is required for a theory of syntax to meet the criterion of autonomy. These interpretations will be addressed in the next section.

3.2 The content of AUTOSYN

Exactly *how separate* does syntax have to be in order for it to be regarded as 'autonomous'? In an interesting discussion, Croft (1995a) notes that there are three positions pertinent to AUTOSYN, listed below in order of increasing strength:

(2) a. At least some elements of syntax are arbitrary (ARBITRARINESS).
    b. The arbitrary elements participate in a system (SYSTEMATICITY).
    c. That system is self-contained (SELF-CONTAINEDNESS).

A denial of arbitrariness would entail the claim that any syntactic construct in any language is replaceable in principle by a semantic or discourse-based construct. There are very few linguists in the world of any theoretical stripe who would accept such a claim—virtually all accept some degree of arbitrariness in the mapping between form and semiotic function. The following representative quotes from two leading function-alists (the second a major architect of the cognitive linguistics wing of functionalism) illustrate the consensus that any approach to syntax must allow for a certain number of arbitrary elements:

Linguistic forms represent generalizations, and ... generalizations are possible only if some features of a phenomenon are treated as more important than others. To the extent that all these features are real, generalizations must distort reality in some ways. To the extent that different generalizations are possible, some arbitrariness is possible. (Haiman 1983: 815)

It is commonly assumed that the full or partial arbitrariness of distributional classes demonstrates the autonomy of grammar [i.e. syntax].... [But] absolute predictability cannot in general be expected for natural language, and any assumption that a certain level of predictability is criterial for a particular type of structure is essentially gratuitous. (Langacker 1987a: 421)

It is easy to find examples of pure arbitrariness in syntax, that is, situations in which differences in form do not correlate with (relevant) differences in meaning. Hudson et al. (1996) catalogue a number of them from English, a few of which are illustrated below: *Likely* occurs in a 'raising' structure, while *probable* does not (3a–b); *allow* occurs with an infinitive marker, while *let* does not (4a–b); *enough*, unlike *sufficiently* and other degree modifiers, does not occur prenominally (5a–b):

(3) a. He is likely to be late.
    b. *He is probable to be late.

(4) a. He allowed the rope to go slack.
    b. *He let the rope to go slack.

(5) a. He isn't sufficiently tall.
    b. *He isn't enough tall. / He isn't tall enough.

If such cases of syntactic arbitrariness were in and of themselves sufficient to establish AUTOSYN, then close to all linguists would of necessity be
'autonomous syntacticians'. Clearly, in order for the concept to have any
utility, AUTOSYN should entail more than the existence of isolated examples of arbitrary syntactic patterning.

What about the other extreme? Can syntax be regarded as a self-
contained system? If self-containedness is interpreted so strongly that it
excludes any systematic points of contact between syntax and semantics,
then no one has advocated such an idea. In particular, Chomsky has
always assumed that points of contact exist between form and meaning
and that it is the linguist's task to flesh them out. Consider, for example,
the closing words of *Syntactic Structures*:

Nevertheless, we do find many important correlations, quite naturally, between
syntactic structure and meaning.... These correlations could form part of the
subject matter for a more general theory of language concerned with syntax and
semantics and their points of connection. (Chomsky 1957: 108)

Syntactic Structures itself reveals many such points of connection,
including the observation that 'there are striking correspondences between
structures and elements that are discovered in formal grammatical analysis and specific semantic functions' (1957: 101). Indeed, Chomsky's principal methodological (as opposed to empirical) argument for positing
AUTOSYN was that the nature and full extent of the correspondences would
be unascertainable if one simply *assumed* that form and meaning were in
lock step (for discussion see Newmeyer 1986a: ch. 2).

In fact, all current generative theories of syntax posit some variety of
rule linking syntactic and semantic structure, though they differ enormously in their specifics.

Perhaps then one could interpret 'self-containedness' in a somewhat
weaker sense, namely as allowing systematic links between form and
meaning, but disallowing any purely semantic construct from appearing
in the component dedicated to syntactic rules and principles. Self-
containedness, in this sense, has in fact been mooted over the years. It
is implicit in *Syntactic Structures* and is endorsed explicitly in *Aspects of
the Theory of Syntax*:

For the moment, I see no reason to modify the view, expressed in Chomsky (1957)
and elsewhere, that although, obviously, semantic considerations are relevant to
the construction of general linguistic theory ..., there is, at present, no way to
show that semantic considerations play a role in the choice of the syntactic or

phonological component of a grammar or that semantic features (in any significant sense of this term) play a role in the functioning of the syntactic or phonological rules. (Chomsky 1965: 226)

It was the view expressed in the above quote that provided the main target
for the generative semantic opposition to the *Aspects* model in the late
1960s and early 1970s.

The amount of allowable 'leakage' from the semantics into the syntax
has been a matter of some discussion since the 1970s. Chomsky (1975a)
contrasts an 'absolute autonomy thesis', in which semantic notions are
excluded entirely from the statement of grammatical patterning, with a
weaker 'parameterized' version, which allows such notions to appear in
restricted locations in the grammar, say, in the lexicon (see also Lightfoot
1976). He opts for the latter version, endorsing Putnam's view that lexical
entries of 'natural kind terms' (e.g. the entries for words such as *lemon* or
tiger) cannot ignore matters of fact and belief. Even this weaker version, however, makes a strong self-containedness claim, since the syntactic rules themselves (i.e. those distinguished from lexical rules) do not
incorporate semantic or pragmatic constructs. Certainly, no one has ever
argued that any syntactic rule or constraint is sensitive to the speaker's
beliefs about the definitional properties of lemons or tigers.

The last decade's work has resulted in many generative grammarians
proposing significant relaxations of the self-containedness condition. A
long tradition within generative grammar (see for example Fillmore 1968)
has posited that some syntactic processes are sensitive to the thematic role
('θ-role') borne by a particular element, where thematic roles are defined
as 'semantic properties assigned by heads' (Chomsky 1986b: 93). The idea
that θ-roles are relevant to syntax is incorporated into the Government-
Binding theory of Chomsky (1981) and subsequent work. For example,
the Theta-Criterion, a central construct of this theory, demands that the
syntax 'know' which syntactic elements bear θ-roles and which do not.
Along similar lines is the proposal of Chomsky (1986b) that 'c-selection'
(essentially, subcategorization) reduces to 's-selection' (essentially, the
thematic properties of the items involved).[3]

Not all generative grammarians agree that θ-roles have a place in syntactic theory. Culicover and Wilkins (1984), Culicover (1988), Jackendoff

---

3. For an alternative 'minimalist' approach to argument structure not involving
thematic roles, see Hale and Keyser (1993).

(1990), and Wilkins (1988) argue that all valid generalizations involving these roles are properly placed in the semantic component or the component linking syntactic and semantic structure, rather than syntactic component. Such a position leads ultimately to a semantic treatment of control, predication, and, perhaps, binding. Those who would admit them into syntactic and morphological theory disagree whether the grammar need only pay attention to whether an element bears *some* θ-role (see Rappaport and Levin 1988) or whether the actual θ-role *label* is relevant (as in the work of Stowell 1981). A popular view is that syntactic processes, but not morphological ones, ignore θ-role labels (for discussion of the relevance for autonomy of issues such as these, see Bouchard 1991).

So, we have seen that most functionalists accept arbitrariness (2a), and at least some generativists posit a model incompatible with a strict interpretation of self-containedness (2c). That leaves systematicity (2b). While few linguists would deny a significant degree of systematicity in syntax, the issue, as posed in (2b), is whether it is the *arbitrary* elements that partake of the system. That is, the question is whether the relationship between purely formally defined elements is so systematic that a grammar should accord a central place to formalizing the relationship among these elements without reference to their meanings or functions. *Here* we have the key difference between mainstream generative linguistics on the one hand and mainstream functional linguistics on the other. The former accept systematicity in this sense, the latter reject it.

Throughout this work, then, I will adopt the following litmus test for whether a particular model of language adopts or rejects AUTOSYN. If it posits rules and principles capable of generating the set of grammatically well-formed sentences of a language (and their associated structural descriptions) independently of their meanings and functions, then it is a model adopting AUTOSYN. If it posits no such rules and principles, then it is a model rejecting AUTOSYN.

One final word of caution is necessary, however. As Croft (1995a: 495) notes, just as no functionalist would deny that some elements of syntax are arbitrary, no generative grammarian would maintain that there is an airtight systematicity in the interrelationships of all formal elements. The unexpected post-adjectival occurrence of the degree modifier *enough* in (5b) illustrates such lack of total systematicity, since otherwise degree modifiers are pre-adjectival. Hence, while AUTOSYN entails that there exists a purely syntactic system, as described above, it does not entail total 'systematicity' (i.e. exceptionlessness) *within* that system.

I will attempt to demonstrate in the §3.5 that an adequate syntactic treatment of English involves, to a profound degree, the autonomous patterning of grammatical elements. Before undertaking this demonstration, however, we must deal with the issue of the scope of AUTOSYN (§3.3) and with some methodological questions that bear on its adequacy (§3.4).

3.3   The insufficiency of syntax and the scope of AUTOSYN

The question of whether the syntax is autonomous or not cannot be answered in a vacuum, but only with respect to the relative roles of theories of meaning and use. This point has been well understood since the earliest days of generative grammar. In *Syntactic Structures*, for example, Chomsky raised the issue of 'how ... the syntactic devices available in a given language [are] put to work in the actual use of this language' (Chomsky 1957: 93) and stressed that there is an intimate connection between the theories of grammar, meaning and language use:[4]

We can judge formal theories in terms of their ability to explain and clarify a variety of facts about the way in which sentences are used and understood.... we shall naturally rate more highly a theory of formal structure that leads to grammars that meet this requirement more fully. (Chomsky 1957: 102)

Over the years the scope of applicability of syntactic principles has varied, and as a consequence deviant sentences that at one time may have been ruled out by syntactic principles (and hence, in the technical sense of the term, deemed 'ungrammatical'), at another period may have been analyzed as violating principles of semantics or pragmatics. So, take sentences such as the following, in which pronominal elements are incorrectly bound to their antecedents:

(6) a. *Mary$_i$ likes her$_i$.
     b. *John$_i$ thinks that Mary likes himself$_i$.

---

4. A few years later Chomsky was to remark that 'the abilities that [a speaker of a language] develops constitute an implicit theory of the language that he has mastered, a theory that predicts the grammatical structure of each of an infinite class of physical events, *and the conditions for the appropriate use of each of these items*' (Chomsky 1962: 528; emphasis added). Chomsky has repeatedly stressed in recent work that the question 'How is knowledge of language put to use?' is one of the three basic questions of linguistics, standing alongside the questions 'What constitutes knowledge of language?' and 'How is knowledge of language acquired?' (see Chomsky 1986b: 3, 1988: 3, 1991: 6).

In the earliest work in transformational grammar, such sentences were considered ungrammatical, as they violated a condition on the transformational rule deriving pronouns and reflexives from their underlying full NPs (see Lees and Klima 1963). But in work in the late 1960s and early 1970s, their deviance was attributed to the semantic component, leaving them syntactically well-formed (Chomsky 1971; Jackendoff 1972). Since Chomsky (1973), most generativists have again attributed their deviance to the violation of syntactic principles (e.g. the subparts of the binding theory), though Jackendoff (1992) has revived the idea that the relevant principles might be semantic.

Nobody would deny that a full explication of (6a–b) has to involve, at some level, constructs such as 'coreference' and 'gender', and that these are semantic constructs par excellence. Yet from such a fact it does not follow that a syntactic treatment of these sentences violates strict self-containedness. That would be the case only if '(semantic) coreference' and '(semantic) gender' were mentioned in the syntactic rule or principle. But they are not. Most syntactic treatments of (6a–b) involve purely formal coindexing restrictions and grammatical gender. Neither of these constructs are semantic, though of course the rules interfacing form and meaning must capture the fact that the relationship between coindexing and coreference on the one hand and that between grammatical gender and semantic gender on the other are nonarbitrary.

Along the same lines, phenomena that are handled wholly within the grammar by some investigators might be given a partially extragrammatical treatment by others. For example, the grammar-internal Structure-Preserving Constraint of Emonds (1976) prohibits transformations with a particular formal property, namely 'root transformations', from applying in subordinate clauses. This constraint, for example, rules the following sentences ungrammatical, since the root transformations Topicalization and Preposing around *Be* have applied in the complement:

(7) a. *John regretted that liver he would never eat.
   b. *Mary feared that speaking at today's lunch would be our congressman.

Hooper and Thompson (1973), however, noted that the following sentences seem fully acceptable:

(8) a. John said that liver he would never eat.
   b. Mary repeated that speaking at today's lunch would be our congressman.

They proposed, in contradiction to Emonds' syntactic explanation of (7a–b), a partially discourse-based analysis, in which (oversimplifying somewhat) so-called 'root transformations' can apply only in clauses that make assertions. Such clauses are normally, but not always, the highest in the sentence.[5] Their analysis is as compatible with AUTOSYN as is Emonds's, though the balance of responsibility between syntax and pragmatics has changed.

To summarize, sentences do not come labeled 'Treat me in the syntax'. As generative grammatical theory has developed, new principles have been proposed in the domains of syntax, semantics, and use and existing ones have been modified. As the principles have changed, so has the nature of their interaction. Therefore, a sentence whose unacceptablility at one time was accorded a semantic or pragmatic explanation might well have later been explained by a syntactic principle, or vice-versa. The ever-changing scope of syntax has no bearing on whether or not it is autonomous.

3.4   Methodological preliminaries to an evaluation of AUTOSYN
The following subsections address some of the methodological issues surrounding the question of the autonomy of syntax. Section 3.4.1 takes on the question of whether AUTOSYN is an empirical hypothesis, and concludes that it is. Section 3.4.2 deals with whether the correctness of AUTOSYN should entail that speakers of a language have 'intuitions about form' distinct from intuitions about other aspects of language. It concludes that there is no such entailment. Section 3.4.3 makes the case that the use of introspective data does not bias matters in favor of AUTOSYN. Section 3.4.4 argues that many functionalists *do* prejudice the case against AUTOSYN by an unwarranted demand that a syntactic theory should attempt to account for why certain sentences are more likely to be uttered than others. And finally §3.4.5 argues that the demonstration that a particular structure has a consistent meaning or use is not in and of itself an argument that that structure should not be generated by autonomous syntactic rules or principles.

---

5. For other work anchoring 'root-transformation' phenomena in discourse, see Green (1976), Bolinger (1977a), and Lakoff (1984). Croft (1995a: 497–498) cites this work specifically to make the (correct) point that the provision of a discourse-based analysis of a particular phenomenon is compatible with the self-containedness of syntax.

3.4.1 Is AUTOSYN an empirical hypothesis?

A number of linguists have questioned whether there is any empirical content to the hypothesis that syntax is (to whatever degree) autonomous. George Lakoff is probably speaking for a sizable proportion of functional linguists when he writes that autonomy is built into the underlying *assumptions* driving work in generative grammar:

> Generative linguistics ... begins with the assumption that syntax is autonomous. It is not an empirical question *within* generative linguistics as to whether semantics, communicative function, etc. might play a necessary role in stating syntactic generalizations: that possibility is ruled out a priori. It is important to understand exactly why that possibility is ruled out. It follows from an a priori philosophical commitment.... This is the commitment to describe language in terms of the mathematics of symbol manipulation systems.... Thus, such things as meaning, communicative function, and general cognition *cannot by definition* enter into rules of formal grammar. (Lakoff 1991: 53–54; emphasis in original)

If Lakoff were correct, then it would be beside the point to adduce arguments for autonomy or even to debate the scope of the hypothesis. All one could do would be to examine whether the 'assumption' of autonomy is or is not a productive one. Presumably, following Lakoff, any illustration of 'such things as meaning, communicative function, and general cognition' entering into rules of formal grammar would suffice to show that it is not productive.

But Lakoff is not correct. In fact, questions such as whether syntactic rules refer to semantic constructs or to discourse notions such as 'topic' and 'focus' have been raised since the 1960s and have been given a broad spectrum of answers, each supported by empirical arguments. And the charge that autonomy is a consequence of a 'philosophical commitment ... to describe language in terms of the mathematics of symbol manipulation systems' is also false. There is nothing inherent to such systems that demands that syntactic and semantic constructs be segregated into different components. Indeed, the preliminary work in formalizing Lakoff's own theory of Generative Semantics (e.g. Dowty 1972; Keenan 1972) combined symbol manipulation and a rejection of autonomy. Around the same time, Bartsch and Vennemann (1972) presented a formalized theory of 'Natural Generative Grammar' whose central characteristic was an 'integrated' approach to form and meaning (for discussion of this theory and other attempts to combine formal symbol manipulation with non-autonomy, see the papers in Keenan 1975).

Lakoff goes on to criticize AUTOSYN by means of an appeal to the 'purposes' of language, which, it is said, are not well served by a system of 'uninterpreted symbols':

Intuitively the idea that a natural language is made up of uninterpreted symbols is rather strange. The primary purposes of language are to frame and express thoughts and to communicate, not to produce sequences of uninterpreted sounds. If thought is independent of language (as it seems, at least in part, to be), and if language is a way of expressing thought so that it can be communicated, then one would expect that many (not necessarily all) aspects of natural language syntax would be dependent in at least some way on the thoughts expressed. (Lakoff 1987: 228)

But AUTOSYN entails that a grammar is made up of 'uninterpreted symbols' only in the sense that it has a purely internal logic of combination. Clearly, that symbolic system is 'interpreted' (recognized, called into play, interfaced, etc.) by the other systems involved in thought and communication. Consider an analogy with our bodily organs. Each organ has a characteristic function or set of functions. Yet this fact does not challenge the profitability of describing the cellular, molecular, and submolecular processes implicated in the functioning of our organs in terms of their systematic formal properties abstracted away from their specific functions.

And no generative grammarian has ever denied 'that many (not necessarily all) aspects of natural language syntax [might] be dependent in at least some way on the thoughts expressed'. (I assume that what Lakoff means here is that syntactic structure is to some degree a reflection of conceptual structure.) While one might equally speculate that conceptualization is to some degree constrained by grammar, the idea that syntax has been shaped in part by conceptual constraints is fully compatible with AUTOSYN. Indeed, as we will see in the following chapter, this idea has a great deal of merit.

There is an 'assumption' underlying autonomy, however. That is that it is *possible* to describe the formal elements of language and their interrelationships independently of their semantic or pragmatic properties. But virtually everybody agrees that it is possible. The question of AUTOSYN revolves around whether it is *desirable* to do so. Most functionalists would argue that it is not desirable; most generativists would argue that it is. In §3.5 below, I will provide arguments that the latter are correct.

3.4.2 'Intuitions about form' and AUTOSYN   In his earliest writings in transformational generative grammar, Chomsky offered the opinion that

speakers have intuitions about form that can be distinguished from intuitions about meaning:

> Furthermore, the speaker has developed a large store of knowledge about his
> language and a mass of feelings and understandings that we might call 'intuitions
> about linguistic form'. For example, any speaker of English knows that
>
> (a) 'keep' and 'coop' begin with the same sound ...,
> (b) 'see' has a special relation to 'sight' that it does not have to 'seat' ...,
> (c) 'Are they coming?' is the question corresponding to 'They are coming' ...,
> (d) 'John read the book' and 'My friend plays tennis' are sentences of the same
> type (declaratives) ...,
> (e) many sentences can be understood in several different ways, e.g. 'They are
> flying planes' ...,
> (f) despite superficial similarities, the sentences 'The children laughed at the
> clown' and 'John worked at the office' are structurally quite distinct. (Chomsky
> 1955/1975: 62)

As is well known, in *Syntactic Structures* he suggested that the intuitions
of speakers of English distinguish the sentences *Colorless green ideas sleep
furiously* and *Furiously sleep ideas green colorless:* '[They] are equally
nonsensical, but any speaker of English will recognize that only the former is grammatical' (1957: 15).

But by a decade later, Chomsky and most other generative grammarians had come to the conclusion that, while speakers can judge sentences
as well-formed or deviant, it is not within their ability to judge the *nature*
of this deviance, i.e. whether it is syntactic or semantic:

> For example, we may make an intuitive judgment that some linguistic expression
> is odd or deviant. But we cannot in general know, pretheoretically, whether this
> deviance is a matter of syntax, semantics, pragmatics, belief, memory limitations,
> style, etc. (Chomsky 1977: 4; see also Chomsky 1965: 157, 1975b: 95)

If Chomsky's 'second opinion' is correct, what implications, if any,
does that fact have for AUTOSYN? To read certain commentators, the
implications would appear to be grave. For example, in the opinion of
Moore and Carling (1982), a speaker's inability to distinguish syntactic from
semantic deviance suffices to show that AUTOSYN is incorrect, while in the
opinion of Partee (1975), it suffices to show that it lacks empirical content.

Certainly, if a speaker could consistently distinguish syntactic from
semantic deviance and the division drawn by the speaker correlated with
the independently-motivated assignment of principles to the syntactic and
semantic components of the grammar respectively, that would count as
strong support for AUTOSYN. But from the speaker's *failure* to be able to

do that, nothing of interest follows as far as AUTOSYN is concerned. We simply do not know at this point what the connection is between the mental representation of language and a speaker's ability to make subtle judgments about the effects of the various modules that constitute that representation. Wayne Cowart has suggested a parallel with the modularization of faculties involved in vision:

I'm very skeptical that any reasonable training procedure for informants will yield 'raw' judgments that clearly reflect only form or only meaning. This is, however, of no particular import to the theoretical question. In the neuroscience of vision, the arguments for the independence of the color perception and form perception systems in the striate cortex do not depend on getting informants to do reports on their visual experience that clearly differentiate effects of color and form. Evidence of the autonomy of the two systems is, so far as I know, rather hard to come by in intact informants—and accessible only by way of the sort of indirect experimental manipulation I expect we'll need with sentence judgments. (personal communication, 18 August 1995)

3.4.3 Data sources and AUTOSYN The question of the correctness of AUTOSYN is sometimes linked to the question of the sources of the data upon which linguistic theory is constructed. Uncontroversially, this data has consisted in very large part on the intuitive judgments of the well-formedness of sentences by native speakers. A number of critics have complained that this fact disqualifies a generative grammar as being a model of *anything other than* those intuitions, i.e. that if one bases one's theory on introspective judgments, then AUTOSYN will follow as a logical consequence. For example:

Artificial-sounding sentences, in isolation of communicative function and communicative context, became the stock-in-trade of linguistic evidence [for generative grammarians], to be analyzed, dissected and 'explained'.... On the basis of such 'data', an independent level of grammatical organization—autonomous syntax—was postulated, with its so-called 'properties' studied in great depth, whose imputed existence bore little or no relation to natural language facts. (Givón 1979a: 25)

But Givón is surely wrong if what he means is that reliance on introspective data somehow leads irrevocably to AUTOSYN. For example, the bulk of the data appealed to by cognitive linguists is introspective, yet cognitive linguistics interprets the data in such a way as to conclude that AUTOSYN is ill-founded. Indeed, the data cited in typical functionalist work tends to be far more introspectively based than the Givón quote would imply.

The null hypothesis is that there is only one mentally represented model of grammar—not one that governs the introspective judgments that speakers make and another that is involved in, say, language processing or the act of communication. The attempts that have been made to show that a reliance on introspective data leads to a model of language incompatible with data from other spheres are all quite flawed in my opinion. For example, many make a giant leap from subjects' behavior in a laboratory experiment to a conclusion about the presence of some principle in those subjects' grammars (for discussion, see Newmeyer 1983: ch. 2).

A parallel criticism by Clark and Haviland (1974: 116) questions the use of introspective judgments as data because '[w]e do not speak in order to be grammatical; we speak in order to convey meaning'. But Wexler and Culicover (1980) replied that even if this is true:

No logical relation can be established between the purpose of our speech and the kind of data on which to base linguistic theories. Function can also be established in biology. For example, the function of certain molecules is associated with genetic transmission. But this function once again does not dictate choice of data. We do not say that the biologist's enterprise is odd because he uses X-ray photographs although it is not the purpose or function of the relevant molecules to provide photographs. (Wexler and Culicover 1980: 395)

3.4.4 AUTOSYN and the relevance of frequency of utterance type Many, if not most, functionalists regard the theoretical interest in some feature of grammar as being a function of the likelihood that such a feature would ever appear in a sentence occurring in actual discourse. For example, any number of functionalists have criticized generative grammarians for the (putatively undue) attention paid to sentence-types unlikely ever to be manifested in the speech of any speaker of the language. Sentence-types of low text count are simply dismissed as irrelevant to theory. Likewise, when studying a particular language, a functionalist, it is said, 'takes the position that cross-linguistic patterns should be taken into consideration at virtually every level of generalization' (Croft 1990: 6). This means that less importance is to be attached to patterns that are not manifested in many languages than those that are typologically widespread (Croft's specific examples involve English determiners; see also the discussion of English tag-sentences in Hagège 1976).

It is not difficult to see how such a position prejudices the case against AUTOSYN in advance of an empirical investigation of its correctness. There is no reason to believe that sentences that pattern similarly (i.e. that have the same formal properties) should be of equal text frequency. Some might very well never be used at all. The message that one wishes to convey at a particular time is, after all, a function of the communicative context, not of any particular feature of one's grammatical system. By ignoring little-used structural types, it is *guaranteed* that one will be led to overlook any number of profound formal patterns in the language. Yet presumably all available structural patterns bear equally on the nature of the *cognitive* system underlying language. Thus to determine whether AUTOSYN is correct or not demands treating all possible sentence types as equally relevant to grammatical theory.

In the remainder of this section, we will look at referential-indefinite subjects and then adjectives in definite NPs to illustrate the point that that there is as much to learn about language and mind from a look at rare sentence types as from common ones. Finally, I suggest that the fact that we have intuitions about sentences that we *never* hear points to a greater separation between form on the one hand and meaning and use on the other than many functionalists are comfortable with.

Givón (1979a) points out that referential-indefinite subjects are relatively rare among the languages of the world. Literal translations of English sentences like *A lawyer shot himself yesterday* are impossible in most languages. The question is whether the fact that English does allow such forms is a significant fact to be explained. Givón thinks not, since even in English the text count of such sentences is (reportedly) very low:

And a transformational-generative linguist will then be forced to count this fact as competence in Krio [a language disallowing such subjects] and performance in English. But what is the communicative difference between a rule of 90% fidelity [as in English] and one of 100% fidelity [as in Krio]? In psychological terms, next to nothing. (Givón 1979a: 28)

But Givón's remarks confuse explananda and explanans. Given that we wish to explain the cognitive state of the speaker vis-à-vis language, a goal that Givón shares (see especially Givón 1989), what a speaker of language has the possibility of saying in his or her language is crucial data. There is all the difference in the world between the mental state of the English speaker and that of the Krio speaker, as far as referential-indefinite subjects are concerned. By dismissing the fact that such subjects in English are possible, Givón necessarily precludes any explanation of *why* they are possible. If it were to turn out that their possibility is a function of independently necessary structural principles of English, that would be a significant and interesting finding.

In a commentary on Givón's treatment of this phenomenon, Van Valin (1981: 50–51) points out that to disparage any theoretical interest in the difference between what is possible in a language and what actually occurs is to return 'to the post-Bloomfieldian view that language equals text. This would be something of a step backward rather than forward and is especially puzzling in light of [Givón's] castigation of structuralist methodology'. Van Valin is correct; there is a very short step from demanding that statistical regularities in a corpus form the primary data base for theorizing to the rank empiricism that set the theoretical agenda for linguists in the United States in the 1940s and 1950s.

Now, of course, we would also like to know why referential indefinite subjects are so rare in actual English discourse, assuming such to actually be the case. Here, without question, one would seek a uniform (possibly external functional) principle unifying English and Krio. But to dismiss any psychological interest in what the grammars of different languages allow speakers of those languages to say or not to say is a curious move coming from someone who regards the study of language as part and parcel of the study of mind.

Turning now to the syntactic category 'adjective', Thompson (1988) is devoted to demonstrating that it is grounded in discourse. Of the 308 adjectives in her corpus of spoken English, Thompson found that 242 were used to predicate a property of an established discourse referent and 66 to introduce a new discourse referent. Of the 242 predicating adjectives, 209 (or 86%) occurred in predicate position, rather than prenominally. And only one adjective out of the total of 308 was found in a definite NP (*this Jewish guy*). Since the function of a definite NP is to re-identify or distinguish an already introduced referent, it is not surprising (she argues) that adjectives do not generally occur in them. Thompson goes on to blast standard generative work, in which one examines one's intuitions for 'context-free artificial examples' (1988: 178) for being incapable in principle of uncovering these generalizations.[6]

But such generalizations are not the sort that the program of generative syntax is designed to uncover. Rather, generative analyses characterize

---

6. The small number of prenominal attributive adjectives might, in fact, be a simple artifact of Thompson's corpus. Chafe (1982: 24) found that 'attributive adjectives were fairly common even in speaking', occurring 33.5 times per 1000 words. Not all such adjectives occurred in definite NPs, but some did: he gave the examples *the old house* and *now these are two distinct places*. Chafe also found 134.9 occurrences of attributive adjectives per 1000 words in writing.

the structural *possibilities* in a particular language, and explicate the degree to which they can be attributed to UG and the degree to which they are language specific. The extent to which a speaker might choose to *make use of* these possibilities is not a concern of the theory per se. *Can* speakers use adjectives within definite NPs? Of course. Could anybody deny that the following sentences, whether they occur in Thompson's corpus or not, are well-formed sentences of English?

(9) a. This is the best Chinese restaurant in Seattle.
     b. I'll take the lemon-filled doughnut in the back.
     c. Who's that fat guy over there?
     d. That crazy friend of yours made the outrageous statement that the American poor are responsible for their own poverty.

Indeed, superlatives, which are by nature predicating, do not occur in *indefinite* NPs (*a best Chinese restaurant*). However infrequently they might occur in a particular corpus, one would hardly want to be placed in the position of saying that such sentences are not English!

Furthermore, even if it is true that adjectives do not occur in definite NPs in the 'natural spontaneous conversational discourse' that formed Thompson's data base, they may clearly do so in other types of text. Lest one be skeptical of this claim, it must be pointed out that a single page of Thompson's paper (1988: 176) with 25 lines of text contains 14 instances of adjectives within definite noun phrases: *the successive discourse* (twice), *the new referent* (7 times), *the head noun* (once), *the sad thing* (once), *this new referent* (once), *the later discourse* (once), and *the other situation* (once).

In short, any adequate grammar of English must provide for the possibility of adjectives occurring in definite NPs. Since, apparently, such adjectives are scarce in (some) discourse corpora, then that only serves to demonstrate that discourse corpora are insufficient as data bases for the study of the mental representation of language. What we conclude from this case, and the previously discussed one, is that generalizations about language structure should not be confused with the explanation of why certain forms are more likely to occur than others in a particular assemblage of texts.

While Givón and Thompson attribute a low text count to referential-indefinite subjects and adjectives within definite NPs respectively, they do agree that such constructions occur. Remarkably, speakers have the ability to pass judgments on sentences that they have *never* encountered and those that have a text frequency approaching zero. Let me illustrate. An informal poll of students in my introductory syntax class for the past 15 years indicates that all accept sentence (10) as English, but none accept (11a) (where *reading* is transitive) or (11b):

(10) This is the paper that I filed before reading.

(11) a. *I filed the paper before reading.
     b. *This is the paper that I filed the notes before reading.

How on earth did they come to learn this? From direct instruction? That explanation is out of the question, since even most trained grammarians were unaware of the existence of such 'parasitic gap' sentences until the late 1970s (see Taraldsen 1981; Engdahl 1983). From memorization of past bits of language use? Such an explanation seems equally implausible. My guess is that sentences like (10) are anything but common in actual discourse, while (11a–b) are close enough to fully acceptable sentences to rule out analogy to sentences the speaker already knows to be unacceptable (from wherever such knowledge may have sprung) to be the explanation.

The only conclusion is that English speakers have some internal principle or principles that lead them to these judgments. Surely the study of such principles is logically prior to the study of how the structures *resulting from* the principles are actually put to work in discourse.

We find even more striking abilities to judge the acceptability of sentence-types that have never been encountered among child language learners. For example, an experiment with 33 three- to five-year-old (Gordon 1985) showed that they know that English allows irregular plurals inside compounds (e.g. *mice-eater*), but not regular plurals (e.g. **rats-eater*), as predicted by the level-ordered theory of lexical phonology of Kiparsky (1982). Gordon reviews the possible ways that a child could have acquired such knowledge; given the rarity of such compounds in children's input, he comes to the reasonable conclusion is that level-ordering is an innate structural property of the lexicon.

Again, if this conclusion is correct (and similar conclusions pertaining to other structures are reached in Bloom 1990; Crain and Fodor 1993; and Pinker 1989a), we have further evidence for the wisdom of studying grammatical structure independently of, and as a preliminary to, its implementation in discourse. That does not lead inevitably to the conclusion that AUTOSYN is correct—such a study might in principle lead to no autonomous structural principles at all being proposed. But it is clear that *not* to look at sentences independently of their frequency of use can never lead to the conclusion that at the heart of language is an autonomous structural system.

3.4.5 Autonomy and the 'fit' between form and meaning/function A great deal of the literature devoted to the correctness or not of AUTOSYN has centered around the question of the closeness of the fit between form on the one hand and meaning and function on the other. As Langacker (1987a: 421; 1988) points out, many of the arguments devoted to supporting the thesis (including my own—see Newmeyer 1983) have been based on the full or partial arbitrariness of many distributional classes with respect to meaning. On the other hand, works devoted to demolishing the thesis (see especially Lakoff 1972b) have primarily focused on showing the generally close fit between form and meaning, in particular, on showing that the occurrence of formal elements tends to be inextricably tied to particular semantic effects. Along the same lines, consider the following quote from a prominent functionalist:

Crucial evidence for choosing a functionalist over a traditional Chomskian formalist approach [embodying AUTOSYN] would minimally be any language in which a rule-governed relationship exists between discourse/cognitive functions and linear order. Such languages clearly exist. (Payne 1998: 155)

But the fact is that AUTOSYN entails no claim whatever about the closeness of the fit between form and meaning.[7] If it did, then every generative grammarian would qualify in Payne's terms as a 'functionalist', since absolutely *none* deny a 'rule-like' relationship between form and meaning/ function. Suppose that the form-meaning/function relation were utterly perfect, i.e. that every class of grammatical elements were associated with an invariable meaning or function. Would such a consequence render AUTOSYN incorrect? Not necessarily, since there still might be evidence supporting the existence of a grammatical system governed by non-semantic or nondiscourse-derived principles linked in a (necessarily) trivially simple fashion to the semantic system. Going to the other extreme, suppose that the relationship between form and meaning or function were utterly chaotic. Would that support AUTOSYN? Not necessarily; even given such a consequence, the optimal description of form-meaning/function relations might entail a vast number of individual schemas along the lines

---

7. This point is made forcefully in Moravcsik (1991).

that Langacker (1987a) proposes to represent irregular English past tense forms.

In short, it takes more than pointing to a fit, or lack of a fit, between form and meaning or function to impact AUTOSYN. To take a concrete example, consider Goldberg's (1989) analysis of the English ditransitive construction (now incorporated into Goldberg 1995), which Lakoff (1991: 62) cites as one of the 'hundreds of studies demonstrating the non-autonomy of syntax'. Goldberg argues that there is a central sense to the V NP NP construction, represented by such sentences as *Jo gave Bill an apple*, which involves transfer of a physical object to a recipient. Additionally, there are five major classes of extensions, based on different types of 'metaphorical transfer'.[8] So the metaphor that allows the construal of effects as objects licenses *The paint job gave the car a higher sales price*, the conduit metaphor depicting communication as traveling licenses *She wired Joe a message*, and so on.

There is no problem preserving Goldberg's basic generalizations within an AUTOSYN framework, should they turn out to be valid. Syntactic principles license structures with two noun phrases following the verb. *Give* and verbs of its class are specified as occurring in such structures along with a characterization of the semantic properties of the arguments. Principles of metaphorical extension at work in the semantics apply to derive the lexical entries of the verbs in nonbasic classes (along with their relevant semantic properties). While that might not be the correct analysis, it is by no means an a priori unreasonable one. In other words, simply showing that there is an intimate relation between form and meaning or even that metaphors have grammatical consequences is not sufficient to defeat AUTOSYN.

Along the same lines, consider the debate between Goldberg (1996) and Jackendoff (1996) on whether such grammatical constructs as syntactic features ($\pm$N, $\pm$V), bar levels, case, number, and gender support or refute AUTOSYN. This debate, I feel, largely misses the point. Goldberg stresses the degree to which they are 'conventionalized semantic categories' (1996: 13). Jackendoff stresses the conventionalization itself, while not denying that these constructs do have, to some extent, semantic correlates. But the only issue, as far as AUTOSYN is concerned, is the degree of integration of these constructs into a system containing other grammatical constructs. A

---

8. The idea that metaphors apply in the grammar will be criticized in the appendix to chapter 4.

tight degree of integration supports AUTOSYN, regardless of their degree of conventionalization.

3.5 Empirical support for AUTOSYN

Evidence for AUTOSYN, then, involves more than showing that the relationship between form and meaning is not one-to-one. Rather, it involves demonstrating the existence of *structural systems*, that is systems with formally defined elements entering into systematic interrelationship governed by an internal algebra. In the following three subsections, I will argue that this is indeed the case, pointing to evidence provided by English structures in which the subject follows the first element of the auxiliary verb (§3.5.1), by *wh*-constructions (§3.5.2), and by the principle of 'Lexical Government' (§3.5.3).

3.5.1 Inverted auxiliaries in English Lakoff and Brugman (1987) discovered, in their study of the preposed negative adverb construction in English, that auxiliary inversion is possible only when the nonoccurrence of the main clause event is entailed:[9]

(12) a. For no money would she sky-dive. (She wouldn't.)
       b. For no money, she would sky-dive. (She would.)

Lakoff (1991) concludes that this fact calls AUTOSYN into question:

But entailment is a semantic relation. The fact that it is part of the condition for the occurrence of the inversion construction shows that a purely autonomous syntax cannot be maintained while stating the correct generalization containing auxiliary inversion.... It is evidence against the claim that syntax is autonomous. (Lakoff 1991: 58)

Suppose that this were the extent of the relevant data. How would it bear on AUTOSYN? The answer is 'Not in the least'. The rules linking syntactic and semantic structures would simply specify the Lakoff-Brugman generalization. For facts such as these to challenge AUTOSYN one would minimally have to demonstrate that this particular syntax-meaning pairing is a nonarbitrary one, that is, to show that there is some reason rooted in grammar-external facts why inversion and lack of entailment should go hand-in-hand. But no such reason has ever been advanced.

Lakoff's conclusion is further undermined by the fact that his starting point was, as we have seen, the 'inversion construction'. What is a 'con-

9. Much of the material in this section was originally presented in Newmeyer (1991).

struction'? Within the cognitive linguistics branch of functionalism, constructions are *defined as* 'pairings of form and meaning' (Lakoff 1987: 378; see also Langacker 1987a: 82). Clearly, if constructions are defined in such a way, it will hardly be a surprising 'discovery' that the bond between form and meaning is tight. To avoid the danger of such circular reasoning, in investigating the nature of the fit between form and meaning, we need a neutral vocabulary, that is, one that does not presuppose any particular degree of relationship between the two. Let us examine the relevant data instead in terms of the more neutral 'structures', instead of 'constructions', where no presupposition is made, in advance of actual analysis, about how form and content are related. The first thing that we notice is that the inverted auxiliary structure is not restricted to preposed negative adverbs. The use of the inverted auxiliary is associated with many diverse semantic functions. For example, it can be used to signal a question, both of the 'yes-no' and the 'wh-' variety:

(13) a. Have you been working late?
      b. What have you been eating?

However, it is disallowed in embedded questions (14b) and (15b) and in main clause questions if the subject itself is a *wh*-phrase (16b):

(14) a. I wondered whether you had been working late.
      b. *I wondered whether had you been working late.

(15) a. I wondered what you had been eating.
      b. *I wondered what had you been eating.

(16) a. What has been bothering you?
      b. *Has what been bothering you?

Furthermore, the structure occurs after preposed negative adverbs (17a), but not after preposed positive adverbs (18a); with bare subjunctives, but not with those introduced by *if* (19a–b); and obligatorily after preposed *so*-clauses (20a–b):

(17) a. Under no circumstances will I take a day off.
      b. *Under no circumstances I will take a day off.

(18) a. *Given any possibility will I take a day off.
      b. Given any possibility I will take a day off.

(19) a. Had I known the dangers, I would have kept my distance.
      b. *If had I known the dangers, I would have kept my distance.

(20) a.   So tall is Mary, she can see into second story windows.
     b.   *So tall Mary is, she can see into second story windows.

Thus the environments in which the inverted auxiliary structure occurs defy a uniform semantic characterization. Furthermore, each of these environments *share formal idiosyncrasies*. For example, each allows only one auxiliary element to occur in inverted position:

(21) a.   *Have been you working late?
     b.   *What have been you eating?
     c.   *Under no circumstances, will be I taking a leave of absence.
     d.   *Had been I thinking about the dangers, I never would have
        done that.
     e.   *So competent has been Mary, she'll surely get the promotion.

Likewise, none may occur in embedded questions or subordinate clauses:[10]

(22) a.   *I asked had you been working late.
     b.   *I wondered what had you been eating.
     c.   *I think that had I known the dangers I would have kept my
        distance.
     d.   *I'm sure that so competent is Mary, she will get the promotion.

Anyone rejecting the necessity for a structural characterization of the process of auxiliary inversion in favor of a purely semantically or functionally based account would have to explain why *the same restrictions* occur on each separate use of the structure. And yet the key formal differences between the auxiliary-before-subject structure and the 'normal' auxiliary-after-subject structure is trivially easy to state (for a recent account, see Grimshaw 1993). Since the nonsemantic principles accounting for these formal differences are at work throughout the syntax of English (and many other languages), the facts surrounding the inverted auxiliaries support the idea of an autonomous structural system.

Children's acquisition of the auxiliary inversion structure also points to the correctness of AUTOSYN. Crain and Nakayama (1987) have shown that in acquiring this structure, children pay no attention to the semantic properties of the subject NP. In particular, there are no semantic proto-

---

10. Interestingly, (22a–d) appear to be grammatical in Belfast English, a fact that has been adduced in support of a parameter-setting model of grammar (Henry 1995).

type effects. All NPs are integrated into the system at once, whether referential, expletive, abstract, or whatever.

It seems clear that we learn that English has the option of fronting an auxiliary and we learn the contexts in which it is correct to do so. Presumably any linguist who wished to deny the reality of autonomous structures (or, more properly, the autonomous principles underlying them) would have to take the somewhat peculiar position that each time a new semantic function is learned for the inverted auxiliary, the construction itself would have be learned from scratch. For to say otherwise would be to make a fundamental concession to the principle of the autonomy of linguistic form.

Pursuing the matter further, a critic of AUTOSYN might speculate that what unites the various uses of the inverted auxiliary is the service of some broader discourse function. But this too is incorrect; its use has a diversity of discourse effects. For example, inverting the auxiliary can convey a question (23a), a request (23b), an offer (23c), an exclamation of desire (23d), and a statement of enthusiasm (23e):

(23) a. Can you take KLM from Seattle to Amsterdam?
     b. Could you pass the salt?
     c. Can I help you?
     d. Could I use a drink!
     e. Is linguistics easy!

Since all five types of speech acts represented in (23a–e) can also be carried out by means of other formal devices, we may conclude from a study of the inverted auxiliary that the principles involved in characterizing structures formally must be distinguished from those involved in determining their use in discourse. (For discussion of the pragmatic principles relevant to an understanding of the use of these sentences, see, for example, Searle 1975.)

The kind of grammar-internal evidence that bears on the validity of the autonomy thesis, then, is evidence that knowledge of a language consists in part of internalized generalizations about linguistic form. That is, that there are pervasive structural patterns that form part of our knowledge of language and that there are general form-based principles responsible for producing them. The inverted auxiliary is typical in that its properties point to the need for a theory that specifies these principles.[11]

___

11. For rather similar conclusions based on an examination of a different type of English inversion structure, as in *Outside stood a little angel*, see Green (1980).

3.5.2 English *wh*-constructions There are a number of constructions in English in which a *wh*-phrase occurs displaced from its subcategorized position and fronted. Among them are the following:[12]

(24) *Wh-constructions in English*
      Questions:
      a. Who did you see?
      Relative clauses:
      b. the woman who I saw
      Free relatives:
      c. I'll buy what(ever) you are selling.
      Wh (pseudo) clefts:
      d. What John lost was his keys.

The analysis of such constructions provides interesting evidence in support of AUTOSYN. Here again we have a profound mismatch between form and function. In each construction type, the displaced *wh*-phrase occupies the same structural position, namely, the left margin of the phrase immediately dominating the rest of the sentence (in GB terminology, the 'Specifier of CP'):

(25)

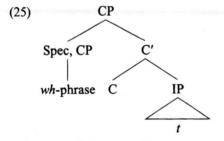

Despite their structural parallelism, the *wh*-phrases in the four constructions differ from each other *functionally*. A review of the functionalist literature reveals that a different sort of functional pressure was responsible for each. Givón (1990) gives a focus-based explanation for the fronting in simple *wh*-questions: sentence-initial position serves to focus the request for a piece of new information, where the entire clause is presupposed except for a single element. If Haiman (1985b) is right, however, the fronting in relative clauses has nothing to do with focusing. Rather, the iconic principle, 'Ideas that are closely connected tend to be placed together', is responsible for the fronting of the relative pronoun to place it

12. The full range of *wh*-constructions in English is presented in Zwicky (1986).

adjacent to the head noun. Free relatives, by definition, have no head noun, so why is the *wh*-phrase fronted? The explanation in Givón (1990) is an historical one: their diachronic origins are in full relatives that have lost their heads, and the fronted pronoun survives as a relic of their headed stage. Functionally, pseudo-clefts are different still. As Prince (1978) argues, the clause in which the *wh*-phrase is fronted represents information that the speaker can assume that the hearer is thinking about. But the function of the *wh*-phrase itself is not to elicit new information (as is the case with such phrases in questions), but rather to prepare the hearer for the focused (new) information in sentence-final position.

In short, we have a one-many relation between form and function. And crucially from the point of view of AUTOSYN, the formal principles involved in *wh*-fronting interact with *other* formal principles involved in other types of constructions. That is, not only do *wh*-constructions have an internal formal consistency, but they behave consistently within the broader structural system of English syntax. Let us look at two examples: Subjacency and Case Assignment.

As (26a–b) reveal, the relationship between the displaced *wh*-phrase and the gap with which it is associated is essentially the same in each of the four construction types. In each, for example, the gap may be indefinitely far from the *wh*-phrase:

(26) a. Who$_i$ did you ask Mary to tell John to see ____$_i$?
     b. the woman who$_i$ I asked Mary to tell John to see ____$_i$
     c. I'll buy what(ever)$_i$ you ask Mary to tell John to sell ____$_i$.
     d. What$_i$ John is afraid to tell Mary that he lost ____$_i$ is his keys.

Furthermore, as (27a–b) illustrate, the structural distance between the *wh*-phrase and the gap is constrained by the principle of Subjacency, formulated as in (28).

(27) a. *Who$_i$ did you believe the claim that John saw ____$_i$?
     b. *the woman who$_i$ I believed the claim that John saw ____$_i$
     c. *I'll buy what(ever)$_i$ Mary believes the claim that John is willing to sell ____$_i$.
     d. *What$_i$ John believes the claim that Mary lost ____$_i$ is his keys.

(28) *Subjacency*
     A movement operation cannot cross the boundary of one barrier, where a maximal projection other than VP is a barrier unless it is the complement of a verb or adjective. (Formulation adapted from Borsley 1991: 184)

But Subjacency, as it turns out, constrains movement operations that involve no (overt) *wh*-element at all. For example, Subjacency accounts for the ungrammaticality of the following two sentences:

(29) a. *Mary is taller than I believe the claim that Susan is.
     b. *Mary seems that it is likely that Susan likes.

In other words, the *wh*-constructions of (24) are integrated into the structural system of English, of which Subjacency forms an integral part.

Consider now the interplay of structures with *wh*-phrases with the process of Case Assignment. At first glance, there seems to be simple generalization about English: displaced NPs bear the case of their surface position; displaced *wh*-phrases bear the case of their subcategorized (underlying) position:[13]

(30) a. She / *Her was seen by Mary.
     b. She / *Her is easy to please.

(31) a. *Who / Whom did you see?
     b. Who / *Whom saw Mary?

In classical transformational grammar, the following rule ordering was posited to account for the facts (see Akmajian and Heny 1975):

(32) a. Passive
     b. Case assignment
     c. *Wh*-movement

Such an interaction between 'movement' processes and case assignment points immediately to the existence of the sort of structural system posited by AUTOSYN. That is, we find a systematic set of structural interactions stated in formal, not functional (or semantic) terms.[14]

As it turns out, the facts are more complicated and more interesting than those sketched above. The case marking of the *wh*-phrase is not in

---

13. This argument is constructable only for English dialects which distinguish between *who* and *whom*. Also, it is inapplicable to *wh*-clefts, as they do not allow personal pronouns in fronted position (**Who(m) John saw was Mary*).

14. More recently, these case marking effects have been derived from different properties of *wh*- and NP traces (Chomsky 1981) or from the postulation of a distinct level of 'NP-Structure' (Riemsdijk and Williams 1981). Since both of these approaches mimic the rule ordering analysis in crucial ways, for the purposes of this discussion the simplest expository course is to present the rule ordering analysis.

fact determined by its subcategorized position; rather, it is that of the last position that it occupies before *wh*-movement. Note the following sentence, in which it is the subject of a passive that has been *wh*-fronted. The case taken by the *wh*-phrase is nominative (the case of the subject of the passive), not objective (the case assigned by the verb that subcategorizes the *wh*-phrase):

(33) Who / *Whom do you think was seen by John?

To derive this effect nothing needs to be further assumed than the principle of cyclic application of transformational rules, one of the most long-standing and best motivated principles of formal grammar (for a summary, see Pullum 1979). In short, the principles involved in *wh*-constructions are part and parcel of a structural system, a system that interfaces with functional principles, but demands a statement in its own terms, that is the terms of an AUTOSYN.

3.5.3 Lexical Government Another means of providing support for AUTOSYN is to take some structural principle (i.e. one that does not lend itself to easy translation into a semantic or discourse-based vocabulary) and show that diverse grammatical phenomena are explained by it. Drawing on the discussion in Aoun et al. (1987) and Hornstein and Lightfoot (1991), I will argue that the subcase of the Empty Category Principle (ECP) called 'Lexical Government' has just these properties.

The ECP was first proposed in Chomsky (1981) to explain the distribution of empty elements in syntax. The version of the ECP outlined below is adapted from Aoun et al. (1987):

(34) *Empty Category Principle (ECP)*
$[_a e]$ (i.e. an empty category) must be properly governed.

(35) *Proper Government*
α properly governs β iff
1. α governs β and
2. (a) α is an overt (i.e. non-empty) Noun, Adjective, Verb, or Preposition) or
   (b) α is coindexed with β.

(36) *Government*
α governs β iff all maximal projections dominating α also dominate β *and* α is dominated either by all maximal projections dominating β or by all maximal projections dominating the maximal projection of β.

The ECP demands that an empty category be either governed by a lexical category (condition (2a) of (35)) or coindexed with a governor (condition (2b)). It is the former condition, namely 'Lexical Government', that we will be primarily concerned with. This condition is met when β is a sister to α, as in (37a) or is a 'niece' to α, as in (37b):

(37) a.   b.

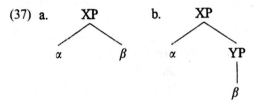

Phrase-structure diagram (37a) represents a classic head-complement relation, where we (arguably) have semantic parallelism across categories. But in (37b) the semantic relationship between α and β is quite different. For example, β could be an initial complementizer of YP. Nobody would argue that the semantic relationship of a head to a complementizer of a following subordinate clause is the same as that of a head to a direct object. Nevertheless, the structural conditions as stated above do not care; because the *that* complementizers in (38a–b) are in the correct structural position to be governed by the heads in the higher clause, they may be deleted:

(38) a. It was apparent (that) Kay left.
     b. The book (that) Kay wrote arrived.

If another projection intervenes, however, the government relationship is no longer met and ungrammaticality results:

(39) a. It was apparent yesterday *(that) Kay left.
     b. The book arrived yesterday *(that) Kay wrote.

Note that in (39) only the structural relationship among the relevant entities, not the semantic relationship, is different than in (38).

Now let us consider another, quite different, case. Subject to a set of fairly complex conditions, material in conjoined clauses in English and other languages can often be 'gapped' under identity to material in a preceding clause:

(40) Fay introduced Kay to Ray and Jay [ ] Don to Ron.

The principle of Lexical Government predicts that no material immediately to the right of the gap should be extractable: lexical governors cannot be empty. This prediction appears to be correct:

(41) *Which man$_i$ did Fay introduce e_i to Ray and which woman$_j$ (did) Jon [ ] e_j to Ron?

Finally, consider the well-known '*that*-trace phenomenon' in English. When a *wh*-phrase in object position is extracted, the complementizer *that* at the head of the embedded clauses may be deleted or not (42a–b). But when a *wh*-subject is extracted, then deletion of the complementizer is obligatory (42c–d):

(42) a.   I thought [(that) Ray saw Fay].
     b.   Who$_i$ did you think [e_i (that) Ray saw e_i].
     c.   Who$_i$ did you think [$e_i e_i$ saw Fay].
     d.   *Who$_i$ did you think [e_i that e_i saw Fay].

The condition on Lexical Government explains the ungrammaticality of (42d): the presence of the complementizer *that* blocks lexical government of the subject trace by the verb *think*.

In other words, we have seen three quite disparate phenomena explained by a single structural principle. It is evidence such as this that bears directly on the validity of AUTOSYN. The point is that we are not dealing here with some random 'arbitrariness', which linguists of all persuasions agree is to be found in grammar. Rather, we have what points to a structural *system* at work, that is, a system whose vocabulary contains structural primitives.

4   The Autonomy of Knowledge of Language with Respect to Use of Language

As was noted above in §2, the hypothesis that knowledge of language is autonomous with respect to language use has a somewhat different character from that of the autonomy of syntax, in that the former is not a hypothesis about how knowledge per se is to be characterized. Therefore, the arguments for AUTOKNOW will have a rather different character from those for AUTOSYN. I will begin in §4.1 by looking at the potential challenges posed for AUTOKNOW by certain ways that language knowledge and language use appear to interact. Section 4.2 contrasts two approaches that differ fundamentally in how they view these interactions. The first is the model of 'Emergent Grammar', the second approach has its roots in generative grammar. Section 4.3 takes a different tack in defending AUTOKNOW. It argues that the stability of adult grammars suggests that the traditional generative practice of sharply demarcating knowledge of language (competence) from use of language (performance) is correct.

4.1   On some interactions of knowledge and use

This section will explore the implications for AUTOKNOW of the existence of extragrammatical principles governing language use. Section 4.1.1 examines and rejects the claim that AUTOKNOW is refuted by the fact that the speakers' choices of available options in discourse are determined in part by such principles. Section 4.1.2 examines and rejects the claim that AUTOKNOW is refuted by the grammaticalization of such principles.[15]

4.1.1   Grammatical structure and speaker choice   The grammars of all languages provide the speaker with alternative means of expressing the same propositional content. The interpretations of *John hit the ball, the ball was hit by John, it was the ball that John hit, what John hit was the ball*, and so on all consist of predicate *hit*, actor *John*, and patient *the ball*. Likewise, the interpretations of *Mary bought some motor oil and went to the supermarket* and *Mary went to the supermarket and bought some motor oil*, whatever differences in meaning they may convey, consist of the same two propositions. All grammars also allow the speaker some choice in how to express arguments with the same understood reference. So, given the proper context, the direct objects in *I saw him, I saw Bill*, and *I saw my mother's second cousin* could be interpreted as having identical reference. Let us call 'stylistic variants' those sentences with differing word order but the same propositional content or with the same word order but a different expression of the same referent.

Principles from performance have been proposed to explain which of the available stylistic variants will be employed by the speaker in an actual discourse. Indeed, probably the most discussed topic in the functionalist literature is the principles of discourse that lead the speaker to choose one out of a set of stylistic variants. For example, there has long been interest in whatever principles govern word order choice in so-called 'free-word order' languages. The tradition of the Prague School (Mathesius 1929; Firbas 1964, 1966; Vachek 1966) maintains that this choice is governed by the principle of 'Communicative Dynamism', in which information moves from the more thematic to the less, where thematic information is that shared by speaker and hearer and connected in a specific way to the 'goal' of the discourse.[16] In Russian, for example, the

15. Much of the material in this section originally appeared in Newmeyer (1992).
16. This principle will be discussed in more detail in the following chapter (§4.6).

proposition 'Daddy has brought a Christmas tree' may be expressed in (at least) the following three ways:

(43) a. Pápa prinjós jólku. (SUBJ VERB OBJ)
  b. Jólku prinjós pápa. (OBJ VERB SUBJ)
  c. Jólku pápa prinjós. (OBJ SUBJ VERB)

In the Prague School view, these sentences differ in their information content in a precise way: In (43a), the subject is more thematic than the verb or the object. In (43b) and (43c), the object is the most thematic element, with the verb second-most thematic in (43b) and the subject second-most thematic in (43c).

Pressure from the parser is also said to constrain speaker choice. So, for example, both (44a) and (44b) are possible sentences of English:

(44) a. That Mary will be elected is certain.
  b. It is certain that Mary will be elected.

In the view of Hawkins (1994), pressure to identify the major constituents of the sentence rapidly is an important factor affecting language use. Since this is more easily accomplished by uttering (44b) than (44a), it follows (correctly) that the number of discourse tokens of sentences with extraposed sentential subjects will be greater than those with nonextraposed subjects.[17]

Is AUTOKNOW threatened by the fact that a speaker's choice of stylistic variants might be constrained by a performance principle? Not at all. Quite the contrary, in fact—speakers have to know what their options are before deciding (however unconsciously) which of them to use. And the choice of options is language particular and, to a large degree, idiosyncratic. Speakers of English do not have the same set of word order choices as do those of Russian, as far as the ordering of subject, verb, and object is concerned. And as for sentential subjects, they do not even appear to have been an option for English speakers until the last few hundred years.

The need for principles governing the distribution of possible sentences in a language is therefore unaffected by the fact that performance principles might affect a speaker's choice of which of those sentences to use in a particular situation. All that needs to be said with respect to cases in

17. The effects of the demand for rapid parsing on grammatical structure will be discussed in more detail in the following chapter (§4.4.2).

which the speaker has a choice of options, then, is that the grammar provides the options and the speaker makes the choice.

It is cases where the *choice of options* has been determined or constrained by an extragrammatical principle that appear to pose the greatest potential difficulty for AUTOKNOW. We turn now to an examination of such cases and their implications.

4.1.2 Grammaticalized performance principles Vachek (1966) claims that the principle of Communicative Dynamism has been grammaticalized in modern English so that subjects, which are in general considered to be 'more thematic' than verbs or objects, are literally *required* to occupy first position in the sentence. This grammaticalization was an historical development—the English of 1000 years ago allowed roughly the same set of options as does modern Russian. Along the same lines, Hawkins (1994) gives many examples of the grammaticalization of his parsing principle. Sentential subjects, disfavored in performance, are literally impossible in many languages, presumably as a result of the grammar responding directly to the parser.

The problem posed for AUTOKNOW by such examples is that it would appear at first sight that syntactic structure, rather than being determined by a set of internalized cognitive principles, is directly derivative of performance principles. If so, and if this is a typical situation, then might not the former be dispensed with in favor of some sort of direct mapping from discourse to grammatical structure?

The pertinent issue, then, is whether this mapping can bypass a characterization of whatever principles determine grammatical structure. And surely, in the two examples just cited, it cannot. One cannot replace the structurally defined notion 'subject' in English, for example, with, say, 'most thematic participant', since not all subjects are most thematic (e.g. expletive *there* and idiom chunks), while certain 'most thematic elements' are not subjects (e.g. topicalized objects). And as for sentential subjects, some languages have them and some do not. Grammars have to be written for both types of languages.

To conclude, if over time there has been functional pressure to push syntax and semantics into some particular type of alignment or if some discourse pattern has become grammaticalized, such facts in and of themselves do not bear on the correctness of AUTOKNOW. Rather, one would have to demonstrate that as a result of this (and other) pressure, the syntax had ceased to function as a system of knowledge whose categories and principles can be stated effectively without reference to language use.

4.2 Two approaches to the interaction of grammar and discourse

In §4.2.1 we will examine 'Emergent Grammar', a model of knowledge-use interaction that rejects AUTOKNOW. Section 4.2.2 looks at models of this interaction that accept AUTOKNOW.

4.2.1 Emergent Grammar A challenge to AUTOKNOW has been put forward in a series of publications by Paul Hopper and Sandra Thompson (Hopper and Thompson 1984, 1985; Hopper 1987, 1988; Thompson 1988). This view is embedded in an integrative functionalist model that has been dubbed 'Emergent Grammar' by Hopper.

The Hopper-Thompson theory rejects the idea of a grammar as a stored mental representation. Instead, grammar is 'provisional and emergent, not isolable in principle from general strategies for constructing discourses' (Hopper 1988: 132).

[Speaking is more a matter of] remembering procedures and things than ... following rules. It is a question of possessing a repertoire of strategies for building discourses and reaching into memory in order to improvise or assemble them. Grammar is now not to be seen as the only, or even the major, source of regularity, but instead grammar is what results when formulas are re-arranged, or dismantled and re-assembled, in different ways. (Hopper 1987: 145)

Emergent Grammar rejects 'the sort of decontextualization which characterizes intuitional data as a prerequisite to linguistic analysis' (1988: 120). In place of identifying the grammatical sentences of a language on the basis of context-isolated acceptability judgments, 'the major descriptive project of Emergent Grammar is to identify recurrent strategies for building discourses' (1987: 148) out of memorized bits of linguistic material, 'some of the most striking regularities [among which are] idioms, figures of speech, turns of phrase, proverbs, sayings, clichés, and so on' (1988: 120). In Hopper's view (1987: 144):

To a very considerable extent everyday language is built up out of combinations of such prefabricated parts. Language is, in other words, to be viewed as a kind of pastiche, pasted together in an improvised way out of ready-made elements.

In short, Emergent Grammar rejects AUTOKNOW.

Hopper and Thompson (1984, 1985) illustrate their ideas concretely by reference to the lexical categories 'noun' and 'verb'. Nouns and verbs, in their view, rather than being 'given' categories of a mental grammar encoded with a particular set of syntactic properties, manifest themselves in particular ways when required to do so by the discourse. They argue that what are commonly called nouns and verbs have prototypical discourse functions: nouns as 'discourse-manipulable participants' and verbs as 'reported events'. They observe that it is only when filling such functions that they manifest their full range of syntactic and morphological possibilities. Thus *bear* in (45a) fails to play its prototypical discourse role and it is as a consequence devoid of inflections; in (45b), where an individual bear is a full participant in the discourse, it can have all of the inflectional and modificational possibilities allowed to nouns:

(45) a. We went bear-trapping in the woods.
      b. We looked up and saw three old bears lumbering toward our
         picnic table.

Likewise, infinitives, lacking the ability to report events, are morphologically impoverished compared to 'full' verbs, which can report events (cf. 46a–b):

(46) a. To travel from Greece to Sweden takes a lot of time.
      b. We traveled from Sweden to Greece.

In other words, the more discourse-prototypical, the more 'nouny' or 'verby'. From this they conclude that 'linguistic forms are in principle to be considered as *lacking categoriality* completely unless nounhood or verbhood is forced on them by their discourse functions' (Hopper and Thompson 1984: 747; emphasis in original).

What would it take to get this idea to work? To answer this question, we must first ask what participants in a discourse have to know *prior* to the discourse. First, they would have to know the language-particular morphological details associated with nouns and verbs: that plurals are formed by suffixing -s, that *to* co-occurs with a bare stem, and so on. Second, they would have to know the structure of the phrases that these 'emergent' nouns and verbs can occur in: that *the old mill* is English, but not *mill the old*; that *she ran quickly down the street* is English, but not *ran she quickly down the street*. Finally they need to know that English is very permissive in allowing a bit of 'wordstuff' (to use a neutral term) to surface as either a noun or a verb (*to squirrel away*—Hopper and Thompson's example—and *I'm in the mood for a run*). This latter knowledge is highly language-specific, since such permissiveness is not universal.

Now it is worth asking how such a seemingly nonhomogeneous set of properties could ever be learned by the child. Becker, who takes a position similar to Hopper and Thompson's, explains: 'there's no such thing as language, only continual languaging', which children hear little bits of at a time. Having 'robust (if as yet unplanted) memories, they mimic and repeat the particular bits, and they gradually reshape these particular little texts into new contexts' (1991: 34).

While Becker goes on to clothe this view in phenomenological garb, one is struck by its resemblance to a classical associationist account of language acquisition, in which memory, repetition, and analogy play central roles. And all of the much-discussed problems of this type of account come immediately into play and beg for all of the following questions to be answered: In what form are the bits of language memorized? As indivisible wholes? Then how can 'little bits' be reshaped? As strings of words? Then why do some subparts tend to undergo reshaping more readily than others? Why do some analogies work and some fail? Since it is easy to construct an analogy that would lead to crashing ungrammaticality or even to constraint violations, why are these not more common than they are in actual speech?

It is clear that a vast amount of complex prior knowledge is entailed by the Hopper-Thompson view. The null hypothesis then is that the knowledge is stored in some systematic fashion. That is, it is stored in a grammar.

Hopper claims that such regularities as exist are 'provisional' and 'not homogeneous', and are 'only fragmentarily captured by the standard notion of "grammatical rules"' (1988: 120). It is more than a little ironic that he would use this fact as an argument *against* generative grammar. Chomsky has always appealed to the 'degenerate quality' of actual speech (Chomsky 1965: 58) to support the innateness of aspects of linguistic structure; given the complexity and heterogeneity of the input to the child, he reasons, it follows that an innately-specified system must underlie language, or it could never be learned. Labov was typical of an earlier-day opposition to such conclusions in replying:

[It is] the current belief of many linguists that most people do not speak in well-formed sentences, and their actual speech production, or performance, is ungrammatical. But those who have worked with any body of natural speech know that this is not the case. Our own studies (Labov 1966) of the grammaticality of everyday speech show that the great majority of utterances in all contexts are complete sentences, and most of the rest can be reduced to grammatical form by a small set of editing rules. (Labov 1972a: 221–222)

Given that the properties of spontaneous natural speech are at the crux of the differences between Chomsky and Labov, it would appear that in a fundamental respect Hopper has a more profound disagreement with the latter than with the former.

Thompson writes that she finds bizarre the idea 'that grammar somehow mysteriously "exists" for speakers to "deploy"' (1991: 96). But a mentally stored grammatical competence that is called upon in acts of speaking actually seems quite comparable to a mentally stored musical competence that underlies our ability to play an instrument or, for that matter a mentally stored recipe that is called up when we cook.

There still remains to discuss the fact noted by Hopper and Thompson that the more prototypical the discourse role a syntactic category plays, the more it manifests its full range of syntactic and morphological possibilities. I do not see how this fact challenges the basic tenets of generativist linguistic theory. Grammars provide speakers with a considerable array of options. As far as English grammar is concerned, it allows them the option of tensing verbs (i.e. in a fully inflected VP) or not tensing them (as in infinitives and gerunds). When the tense of the verb is relevant to the discourse, they will be more likely to tense the verb than when it is not. When tense is not important, they will be more likely to choose an infinitive or gerund. In short, the correlation between discourse functioning and categorial prototypicality boils down to no more than the observation that grammars of human languages allow speakers to express what they need to express.[18]

But a caveat is in order here. It may appear that I have given blanket endorsement to the (functionalist) dictum that 'grammars code best what speakers do most' (Du Bois 1985: 363). Clearly, grammar supports what speakers 'need to do' communicatively to a significant degree. After all, we do use language to communicate! But unless we have some independent means of measuring what these 'needs' are, there is a grave danger of circularity. Otherwise, it might just as well be the case that speakers do most what grammars code best.

Let me illustrate the divorce between 'need' and grammatical possibility with an example based on a discussion in Piattelli-Palmarini (1990) (which itself draws on unpublished work by David Dowty and Mürvet Enç). Suppose I have advance information that while John is away on

---

18. The issue of categorial prototypicality and discourse will be taken up in more detail in chapter 4.

vacation, his house will be broken into and his safe cracked. Can I accurately report what John will discover upon his return home as (47)?

(47) John will discover that his safe is empty.

No, I cannot, since (47) carries the direct (and incorrect) implication that his safe is empty at this very moment. Sentence (48) is also impossible since it implies that the safe will be cracked (leaving it empty) at some time after his discovery:

(48) John will discover that his safe will be empty.

All of the following are equally impossible:

(49) John will have discovered that his safe is / was / will be empty.

Piattelli-Palmarini concludes:

> Try it as you might, there just is no simple sentence forcing the hearer to lock onto this simultaneity of the two events at a time that lies in the future with respect to the time of utterance. The resources of tenses do not allow us to state this simple thought by syntactic means alone. We *have to* use some elaborate strained prolix periphrasis, supplemented with lexical pointers (1990: 753; emphasis in original)

So why *doesn't* grammar encode this nicety of tense? Presumably, a functionalist rejecting AUTOKNOW would attempt to build an explanation on the basis of the dictum that speakers don't need to make such a distinction. As Hopper puts it: 'The more useful a construction is, the more it will tend to become structuralized, in the sense of achieving cross-textual consistency' (1987: 150). But by what criterion would it not be 'useful' to make this tense distinction, which intuitively seems much more useful than a host of tense distinctions that grammars *do* facilitate (a passive perfect progressive such as *Mary has been being watched* comes immediately to mind). But the usefulness of a construction (which we have no noncircular means of measuring, in any event) is really beside the point. Even if we found that the real-life 'need' to describe situations such as outlined above is rare, how could we know that this lack of need might not have been shaped, in whole or in part, by the lack of a grammatical device to encode it? Only by adopting Hopper and Thompson's ideological (and manifestly incorrect) position that grammars have no existence independent of the discourse act itself can we avoid taking this possibility seriously.

   To adapt slightly an analogy from Jerrold Sadock (1984: 142), an emergent grammarian is like an anatomist who, realizing that birds can fly, loses all interest in the structure of their wings. Any attempt to derive the nature of grammatical structure from process of building discourses would be like an attempt to derive the structure of birds' wings from their capacity for flight. Clearly these structures enable their respective functions, while at the same time being vastly underdetermined by them.

4.2.2 Studies of grammar-discourse interactions in the generative tradition Almost two decades ago, Susumu Kuno outlined a methodology for the study of grammatical principles, discourse principles, and their interaction that is wholly consistent with AUTOKNOW:

Each theory of grammar must have a place or places where various functional constraints on the well-formedness of sentences or sequences of sentences can be stated, and each theory of grammar can benefit from utilizing a functional perspective in analysis of concrete syntactic phenomena. Therefore, in theory, there is no conflict between functional syntax and, say, the revised extended standard theory of generative grammar. Given a linguistic process that is governed purely by syntactic factors, this process will be described in the syntactic component of the grammar both by pure syntacticians and by functional syntacticians. On the other hand, given a linguistic process that is governed by both syntactic and, say, discourse factors, the syntactic aspect will be formulated in the syntactic component, while discourse factors that interact with this syntactic characterization will be described in, say, the discourse component of the grammar. Pure syntacticians would concentrate on the former characterization, and functional syntacticians, on the latter. There need not be any disagreement between the two. (Kuno 1980: 117–118)

Kuno's ideas can be exemplified by the robust tradition in which researchers committed to AUTOKNOW have explored how such discourse notions as 'topic' and 'focus' are best related to the syntactic structure that conveys them (see, for example, Prince 1981, 1985, 1988; Kamp 1981; Reinhart 1982; Gundel 1985; Rochemont 1986; Rochemont and Culicover 1990; Heim 1988; Primus 1991; Vallduví 1992; Erteschik-Shir 1995; Meinunger 1998). While it is not my intention to survey this literature here, I will give one example of a proposal put forward to capture a grammar-discourse interaction, followed by a brief discussion of two debates relevant to the handling of discourse phenomena within an AUTOKNOW-oriented model.

Rochemont and Culicover (1990) claim that the constituents in italics in the following sentences are all structurally-defined focuses, where— oversimplifying enormously—a 'focus' is the information conveyed in an utterance that is not construable from context (the traditional name of the rule the sentence exemplifies appears in parenthesis):

(50) a. John purchased for his wife *a brand new fur coat*. (Heavy NP shift)
      b. It was *a brand new fur coat* that John purchased for his wife. (*It* cleft)
      c. Mary was talking to a man at the party *who everybody knew*. (Relative clause extraposition)
      d. Into the room walked *John*. (Directional/locative adverbial preposing)
      e. There ran into the room *several overexcited fans*. (Presentational *there*-insertion)

Rochemont and Culicover note that in all these cases the focused elements appear in a position that is canonically governed by a lexical category which does not θ-govern or case-mark it. On this basis, they formulate 'The Focus Principle' as follows (1990: 156):

(51) *The Focus Principle*
      α is a *structural focus* if
      i.   there is a lexical head β that canonically governs α and α is neither Case-marked nor θ-marked by β
      ii. α is not a predicate that is θ-related to β

In other words, Rochemont and Culicover have provided a precise characterization of a form-discourse linkage in the grammar of English.

One important debate pertinent to the interface of grammar and discourse revolves around the relative 'burden' borne by the grammar itself and by pragmatic principles that interface with grammar (see above §3.3). There is a widespread belief among many of those who study grammar-discourse interactions that generative syntacticians are much too quick to ascribe to a *syntactic* principle the deviance of some sentence type, when a pragmatically-oriented one would be more adequate. Consider, for example, what is known as the 'definiteness effect' in English sentences with existential *there*. An old observation is that the definite article normally sounds very strange in such sentences, as in (52a):

(52) a. ?There's the dog running loose somewhere in the neighborhood.
      b. There were the same people at both conferences.

Syntacticians have generally opted for a purely syntactic explanation for the oddness of the definite article (Milsark 1977; Safir 1985; Reuland 1985). However, Ward and Birner (1995) have argued, convincingly in my opinion, that the correct explanation is a pragmatic one: NPs in such sentences are required to represent a hearer-new entity. Hence (52b) is impeccable. Ward, Prince, Kuno, and many others have taken syntacticians to task in like fashion with respect to a myriad of other phenomena (see, for example, Kuno 1987; Kuno and Takami 1993; and Prince 1991).

The second debate concerns whether discourse can profitably be regarded as a 'module' within linguistic theory, parallel to (or even subsumed within) the grammatical module. Kuno's reference to 'the discourse component of the grammar' indicates that he is a strong advocate of such a position. This idea has been defended most forcefully by Ellen Prince in many publications (see, for example, Prince 1988, 1995). Prince's argument that discourse analysis is 'part of the study of linguistic competence' (Prince 1988) is based on the high degree of arbitrariness of the relationship between syntactic structure and discourse function. As she points out in Prince (1995), quite commonly one syntactic structure can signal several different discourse functions, a single discourse function can be encoded syntactically in several different ways, and the links between the two are realized in different ways in different languages.

In the view of Sperber and Wilson (1986), on the other hand, pragmatic phenomena cannot be localized in a grammatical module. They stress that a full account of the ability of speakers and hearers to carry on successful discourses involves 'inferential comprehension'. But since the ability to draw inferences reflects the working of a 'central process' in the sense of Fodor (1983), rather than a modular one, discourse competence cannot be on a theoretical par with grammatical competence.

I suspect that at a certain level of abstraction, the Kuno-Prince approach and the Sperber-Wilson approach are integrable (for pertinent remarks, see Horn 1988). The focus of the latter is on the principles governing the structure of discourses per se; the former on the interaction between discourse and grammar. It seems likely that a competence module is the faculty responsible for governing this interaction, even while discourse itself may not be isolable and modularized (for detailed exposition of such a view, see Ariel 1998, forthcoming).

4.3   Some testing grounds for the autonomy of grammatical knowledge

This section will focus on specific phenomena that bear on the profitability of making a clear distinction between grammatical knowledge and use. First (§4.3.1), we will take on the question of whether the fact that many diachronic changes appear to be usage-driven challenges AUTO-

KNOW. I will argue that it does not. This question is often linked to the (independent) question of whether it is adults, children, or both who are responsible for initiating language change. My tentative conclusion is that while adults can clearly change their *speech*, it is not so obvious that they can change their *grammars*. This conclusion receives support from evidence that shows that adults lack the ability to transform pidgins into creoles (§4.3.2) and to acquire second languages by means of the same cognitive mechanisms available to children (§4.3.3). If such is correct, we have further support for AUTOKNOW.

4.3.1   AUTOKNOW, language change, and the stability of adult grammars   Croft (1995a: 517) poses the question of AUTOKNOW as follows:

Can the dynamic processes in language [i.e. processes involved in diachronic change] be conceived of as the interaction among self-contained grammars of individuals? Or is the interaction such that the grammars of individuals are more intimately interconnected with those dynamic functional forces—that is, can an individual adult speaker's grammar be influenced by those forces?

He notes that AUTOKNOW could be refuted by a demonstration that 'the cognitive processes that cause changes to the grammar are still (potentially) operative in the adult grammar.... If this is the case, then the simplest representation of grammatical knowledge will make reference to those forces' (1995a: 517).

Croft goes on to undertake such a refutation. He observes that 'sociolinguistic research has demonstrated overwhelmingly that language change occurs in variable patterns of use in the adult speech community' and that 'most speakers have most variants as part of their grammatical competence, and employ them differently depending on their social position in the speech community and the circumstances of the conversational interaction.... In this sense the grammar is not self-contained [i.e. AUTOKNOW is refuted]' (1995a: 518).

But the uncontroversial fact that speakers *use* different forms in different situations is irrelevant to whether their *grammars* are self-contained or not. The question is how those different forms entered the language to begin with—how the language change that introduced them was 'actuated', to use the terminology of Weinreich, Labov, and Herzog (1968). To challenge AUTOKNOW, one would minimally have to show that their actuation was so 'intimately interconnected with ... dynamic functional forces' that a speaker's knowledge state before and after the actuation could not profitably be separated *from* those functional forces. In a subsequent paper, Croft (1996a) does provide a number of examples designed to demonstrate this intimate interconnection. Many of the historical changes he discusses are familiar from the vast literature on grammaticalization (for comprehensive discussion, see chapter 5). So for example, he points to pleonastic negation, whereby language users come to insert an overt negative particle where a negative sense had previously been only covert. The (b) sentences of (53) to (55) are historical innovations based on the (a) sentences:

(53) a. That'll teach you to come early.
     b. That'll teach you not to come early.

(54) a. I really miss having a phonologist around the house.
     b. I really miss not having a phonologist around the house.

(55) a. I could care less.
     b. I couldn't care less.

What seems to have happened, then, is that some cognitive predisposition led language users to feel that an overt negative was 'needed' in such constructions. Examples such as these, however, are not sufficient to refute AUTOKNOW. The reason is that they do not demonstrate that 'the cognitive processes that cause changes to the grammar are still (potentially) operative *in* the adult grammar'. At most they demonstrate that such processes can lead to changes *to* the adult grammar. Implicit in Croft's discussion is the assumption that an autonomous system is, by definition, unable to interact with or be affected by external forces. But this is not true, as I will argue in detail in the next chapter.

Croft goes on to note that 'adoption of the usage-driven model ... would require abandonment of the child-driven model of actuation that is generally accepted by formal syntacticians' (1996a: ms. p. 42). Let us turn now to the question of adults versus children as 'actuators' of language change and whether the answer to this question bears on the adequacy of AUTOKNOW.

A tradition long antedating formal approaches to syntax holds that grammar-restructuring is primarily the work of children. Perhaps Hermann Paul was the first make this point (see Paul 1880/1920: 34f.); a similar position is endorsed by Jespersen (1921/1964: 161–190), Meillet (1931: 236), and Osgood and Sebeok (1954: 155), among others. Generativist theorists have largely taken it to be true (see, for example, Halle

1962; Lightfoot 1991; Clark and Roberts 1993; and Niyogi and Berwick 1995). Why might one believe this? Part of the answer is provided by Dan Slobin (1977), who points to the fact that the errors of children often parallel common historical changes, thereby giving credence to their key role in grammar-restructuring. Slobin concludes:

A fully developed human language must be pragmatically flexible, semantically expressive, rapid in tempo, readily decipherable, and semantically clear. *Children have the capacity to construct such languages*, and the human mind has the capacity to consistently maintain and adjust Language so that it remains in consonance with all of these goals. (Slobin 1977: 212; emphasis added)

The most detailed recent study of which I am aware that deals with language change in progress is Dorit Ravid's *Language Change in Child and Adult Hebrew* (1995). A quick glance at her conclusion might give the impression that she endorses the view that grammatical change takes place in adult grammars:

Thus it is not children's ontogenetic recapitulating of phylogenetic features that introduces language change, but rather cognitive structures in older children, adolescents, and adults that respond to certain areas of instability in Hebrew.... Thus young children do not cause language change: It is the population of older children and naive ... adult speakers who both provide the pool of possible variation necessary for change and induce change. (1995: 170)

But a careful reading of her book reveals that it is adults who *propagate* linguistic changes (lower socioeconomic status adults in the specific cases discussed). Every example she cites of functionally-motivated change was *initiated* in childhood and maintained by the initiators into adulthood.

Before proceeding further with the issue of the age of the actuators of language change, we must draw an important distinction. That is the distinction between change in *grammars*, i.e. change in grammatical competence, and mere additions to or deletions from the speaker's potential stock of *utterances*. Not every aspect of one's verbal habits, no matter how 'entrenched' it seems to be, necessarily points to a property of one's grammar. It may be difficult to determine in any particular case whether a form or construction in regular use is part of one's linguistic system, but it is often possible to do so. Consider, for example, the prestige usage of the nominative pronouns in *He and I left*, as opposed to nonstandard *Him and me left*. Emonds (1985: 238; 1986) and Sobin (1997) argue, quite plausibly, that such constructions are not part of our internalized competence at all and Emonds provides tests that bear out such an idea. Several factors point to their being a purely learned extra-grammatical phenomenon that English speakers 'tag onto' their grammars. First, college and business writing handbooks have to devote entire sections on subject pronouns. Second, widespread overcorrection of usage is attested (e.g. *Did you see he and I?*), suggesting that 'correct' usage has not been internalized. Third, the handbooks often resort to an 'avoid the construction' strategy for conjoined subject pronouns. And fourth, even middle class children go through a stage of producing *Him and me left.*

Clearly, adults have the ability to acquire forms and constructions that are new to them and to innovate entirely new forms and constructions. But it is not so easy to find clear-cut evidence that such forms and constructions have necessarily been assimilated into their grammatical competence. One measure of the stability of adult grammars is the fact that even when we *want* to change our grammars we find it extremely difficult, if not impossible, to do so. For example, Labov (1972a: 289–290) discusses how difficult it is for middle class blacks who did not grow up in vernacular culture to learn the vernacular as adults. As he notes, this fact cannot be due either to lack of motivation or to lack of exposure to the dialect. Labov's conclusion is that it is *too late* for them to master it—their system has already stabilized on the educated norm. Pointing out the well-known fact that one's childhood class dialect in England, Eliza Doolittle to the contrary, tends to betray one for life, he writes (1972a: 290): 'If it is true that Received Pronunciation cannot be mastered by someone who has been to the wrong school, this would stand as additional confirmation of the fact that the regular rules of the vernacular must be formed in the preadolescent years.'

In a classic paper, Andersen (1973) outlines the mechanisms by which adults can consciously change their *speech*, leading ultimately to children incorporating these changes into their *grammars*.[19] The bulk of his discussion involves the stigmatization of a certain consonant pronunciation in a dialect of Czech by speakers of neighboring dialects. The 'Peták speakers' (as Andersen calls them) initially formulated 'adaptive rules' ('A-rules') to imitate the norms of the 'Teták speakers'. However, he shows that these 'A-rules ... lack the intrinsic, structural motivation which characterizes the pronunciation rules that are part of phonological structure' (1973: 782). Instead, they 'form an additive system which can

19. See the interesting commentary on Andersen's paper in Pateman (1987).

be elaborated and revised throughout the speaker's life' (1973: 781). Thus, while not unsystematic, A-rules are not part of the basic system of linguistic competence that is acquired unconsciously by all speakers.

Examples of the effects of A-rules include the interpolation by many educated speakers of archaisms and even foreign expressions into their speech when the occasion seems to call for it:

> Many speakers of English are capable of producing anything from a pseudo-Gallic flavor to a real French pronunciation of lexemes which are marked 'French' in their lexical representation. Most educated speakers of English are able to derive an [x], probably from an underlying /k/, in lexemes or names of Scottish, German, or Slavic provenience. Some native speakers of General American English—among them some radio announcers—are able to simulate a more prestigious dialect by inserting an [i̯] in words like *duty* [di̯uti] and *new* [ni̯u], and sometimes in words like *noon* [ni̯un] and *noodle* [ni̯udl] as well. (Andersen 1973: 781)

The fact that I might say *Be that as it may* or drop a Latin phrase or two hardly counts as evidence that my grammar has retained the principles from 500 years ago for forming subjunctives or that I have a competence representation of even some small subpart of Latin.

Labov (1982) develops further the position that grammatical change is actuated primarily by children. The following passage summarizes his view of the relationship between children's grammars and adult grammars, as far as language change is concerned:

> If parents have acquired new forms in their later years, these will of course be transmitted to their children. *But research so far shows that such later acquisition is not likely to be highly systematic.* Research findings so far point to the following scenario:
>
> (1) Children learn their underlying forms from their parents.
> (2) Under the influence of pre-adolescent and adolescent peer groups, speakers may acquire low-level late rules of phonology and grammar in a systematic form.
> (3) The influence of peer groups on higher level rules and patterns of underlying forms is likely to be irregular.
> (4) *Changes in rules and underlying forms through the acquisition of superposed dialects later in life are normally irregular.* (1982: 69; emphasis added)

In other words, even if it happened to be an adult who first said, say, *I couldn't care less*, that would not be prima facie evidence that we have an example of a grammatical change actuated by an adult. That particular expression might well have been stored by that adult in some grammar-external stock of utterances, only to be integrated into grammatical competence by the next generation of language learners.

Is the question of whether grammatical change is actuated by children or by adults even relevant to the question of the correctness of AUTO- KNOW? Certainly if grammar-modification shuts off around puberty we would have support for AUTOKNOW—throughout most of life grammar would be a 'self-contained system' in the strongest sense possible. But suppose that our system of grammatical competence were able to develop during the entire course of one's life, rather than to shut off from further development after childhood. Would that challenge AUTOKNOW? In this regard, Chomsky has remarked:

Suppose contrary to apparent fact, that the system never hit a steady state but kept growing (like a carp) until termination of life. I don't see that anything much would change. (Cited in Pateman 1987: 91, n. 16)

I agree with Chomsky. What it would take to refute AUTOKNOW is the demonstration that adult grammars are in such flux that it is disadvanta- geous to describe them as *stored systems*. That is, one would have to show that grammatical structure is created 'on the fly', as it were, with whatever systematic properties grammars might possess emerging from the dynam- ics of the communicative interaction. This is the position of Emergent Grammar and, as noted above (§4.2.1), there appears to be little evidence to support it.

The following two sections bolster the idea that grammar construction is essentially completed in childhood by pointing to evidence that adults lack the ability to transform pidgins into creoles and to acquire full com- petence in a second language.

4.3.2 Adults and creole formation   Another obvious arena in which to investigate the stability and self-containedness of adult grammars is the process of creole formation. If one's internalized linguistic competence is (relatively) fixed by adulthood, then it follows that the 'sudden' (i.e. one- generation) transformation of pidgins into creoles by adults should not take place. Croft agrees; in fact, his belief that such a transformation *does* take place provides him with an argument against AUTOKNOW: 'Even creolization, considered a paradigm case of language in the making, can occur in an adult speech community, and is rarely solely due to child language acquisition (Mühlhäusler 1986: 51–95, esp. 85–86)' (Croft 1995a: 518). But the cited Mühlhäusler pages fail to document any one- generation creation of a creole by adults. Rather, the text gives examples of pidgins being gradually elaborated over several generations and does not contradict the idea that creolization itself is the work of children.

Unfortunately, well documented studies of the single generation formation of creoles are rare, since most took place hundreds of years before we had the luxury of written records and contemporary scholarly interest. There is one major exception, however: the formation of Hawaiian creole, which was accomplished at the end of the last century and the beginning of this one. Here, adults had every opportunity to create the creole, but they failed to do so. It took the next generation of children to accomplish the task.[20]

Sankoff and Laberge (1973) describe the dramatic contrast between the speech of adult pidgin speakers of Tok Pisin and that of their children, who have creolized it:

The children speak with much greater speed and fluency [than the adults], involving a number of morphophonemic reductions as well as reduction in the number of syllables characteristically receiving primary stress. Whereas an adult will say, for the sentence 'I am going home',

(1) Mi go long haus;

a child will often say

(2) Mi go l:aus;

three syllables rather than four, with one primary stress rather than two. (1973: 35–36)

Slobin's (1977) comments on this passage are quite interesting. He notes that 'the parents are also *fluent* speakers. Apparently there is something about child speech, or the nature of a *native* language, which plays a leading role in bringing Language to adhere to the third charge ["be quick and easy"]' (1977: 204; emphasis in original). He goes on to say: 'It seems, given the limited but suggestive evidence at hand, that it is adult speakers who invent new forms, *using them with some degree of variability in their speech*. Children, exposed to this variability, tend to make these new forms obligatory and regular' (1977: 205; emphasis added).

In short, while adults may modify pidgins into something more creole-like, it is only children who literally have the ability to *create* creoles, that is to create a new grammatical system. This contrast between the abilities of adults and children provides support for AUTOKNOW.

---

20. See Roberts (1996) for a debunking of the view (advocated by Goodman 1985; Holm 1986; and others) that Hawaiian creole developed gradually by means of diffusion of a structurally complex pidgin or creole from the Caribbean.

4.3.3 Adults and second-language acquisition One question that has been subject to vigorous debate in recent years among generative linguists is whether UG is active in second-language (L2) acquisition as well as in the first. The community is split down the middle on this question, with some taking the position that the adult second-language learner has full access to UG (Flynn 1987; White 1990; Epstein, Flynn, and Marto-hardjono 1996; Vainikka and Young-Scholten 1991); some positing par-tial access (Schachter 1989; Tsimpli and Roussou 1991; Strozer 1994); and some no access at all (Clahsen and Muysken 1986; Clahsen 1988; Bley-Vroman 1989).

Very few, if any, participants in the debate have commented on the implications of the question for AUTOKNOW. But clearly the strongest AUTOKNOW-compatible position is that adult learners have *no* access to UG. If UG has 'done its work' by puberty, then, by definition, adult grammars are fixed. Adult-acquired second languages, then, however flu-ent they might be, could not be systems of grammatical competence.

The null hypothesis, surely, is that adult-acquired second languages are *not* systems of grammatical competence. It is hardly news that adults are virtually never successful in mastering a foreign language perfectly. To this point, Bley-Vroman (1989: 43–49) lists nine fundamental ways that the process of second language acquisition differs from that of the first:

(56) a. *Lack of success.* Normal children inevitably achieve perfect
        mastery of language; adult foreign language learners do not.
     b. *General failure.* Complete success in adult foreign language
        learning is extremely rare, perhaps even nonexistent.
     c. *Variation in success, course, and strategy.* There is vastly more
        variation in the learning strategies followed by adults than by
        children, and, of course, more variation in degree of success.
     d. *Variation in goals.* The different degrees of importance attached
        by adults to different aspects of the process of second language
        acquisition is characteristic of general problem solving
        mechanisms, not the work of a dedicated mental faculty.
     e. *Fossilization.* Second language learners consciously or
        unconsciously decide to stop learning after a particular degree of
        attainment is reached; first language learners do not.
     f. *Indeterminate intuitions.* Even very advanced nonnative speakers
        lack the ability to make clear acceptability judgments, or they
        make them with a much greater degree of inconsistency than
        native speakers.

g. *Importance of instruction.* Children do not need formal
instruction; adults almost always do.

h. *Negative evidence.* Child language acquisition does not rely on the
availability of negative evidence; adult acquisition does.

i. *Role of affective factors.* Success in adult acquisition is highly
affected by personality, socialization, motivation, attitude, and
the like; children's success is unaffected by such factors.

These fundamental and, I would say, uncontroversial differences between L1 and L2 acquisition clearly put the burden of proof on advocates of the full-access hypothesis. I do not feel that the most recent
lengthy defense of this hypothesis, Epstein, Flynn, and Martohardjono
(1996), succeeds in explaining the differences pointed to by Bley-Vroman.
It puts forward two different sorts of arguments in support of the full-
access hypothesis. The first is the claim that we have to suppose that the
adult learner has full access to UG in order to explain how he or she
could even *begin* the task of learning a second language:

The hypothesis that L2 learning is not constrained by the language faculty is
empirically inadequate given what is known about the L2 learner's linguistic
knowledge as represented in a grammar. For example, the capacity to distinguish
between speech and other noises is provided by the language faculty. (1996: 681)

First, it is not clear that knowledge of phonemes, syntax, morphology, and so
on, ... can be attributed to the L2 by the learner without 'deep analysis' of the L2.
Second, for the learner to assume that the architecture of the L2 is 'not utterly
different' from the architecture of the L1 is tantamount to saying that the learner
is able to identify and presumably treat the L2 as an object that falls under the
domain of the language faculty. (1996: 683)

But, as Bickerton (1996) points out, these passages falsely equate any sort
of knowledge about language with UG and UG itself with the language
faculty as a whole. Surely we can discover things about language by
drawing on resources other than our UG. To take Epstein et al. literally,
no Martian, say, could ever discover that human language contains discrete segments, principles of combination, or any other basic property,
just as no human could ever learn the most elementary aspects of 'dolphin
language', should it turn out that they have one. That simply can't be
right.

Epstein et al. also present a considerable number of detailed empirical
arguments in support of the idea that UG is fully active in second language acquisition. Many of them are based on the idea that adult learners

have arrived at different 'parameter settings' from those of their native language—settings, they postulate, that could have only been provided by UG. The problem is that such arguments tend to assume in advance what they set out to prove. Suppose, say, that in the course of my studying Japanese, I come to learn that the language is verb-final. Is that evidence that UG reset the appropriate parameter for me? The answer can be 'yes' only if my adult-acquired Japanese is an internalized system of grammatical competence. If it isn't, then some other cognitive faculty steered me toward that knowledge. But the crucial (albeit difficult) task of showing that my knowledge representation of Japanese is identical in relevant respects to that of my knowledge representation of English remains to be demonstrated.

The most interesting sorts of arguments for UG driving L2 acquisition are modeled on the poverty of the stimulus arguments for an innate UG itself (see below, §5.3.1). For example, Finer and Broselow (1986) found that Korean learners of English postulated binding domains for English anaphors that were neither those of Korean, nor those of English. Rather, they appeared to be the domains that UG (as it was understood at the time) took to be the most unmarked. The problem is that experiments testing adult learners with respect to UG principles have led to mixed results. Johnson and Newport (1991) show that late learners of English accept Subjacency violations, something that should not happen if UG were shaping their acquisition of the language.

Epstein et al. appeal to 'grammar-external performance systems' that make learning a second language so difficult for most adults. For example, they propose a 'performance-based' explanation for why long-distance movement is difficult for Japanese learners of English: 'The assignment of a new parameter value can appear to "take time" in the course of acquisition, for example, if new parameter setting involves determining the features of certain lexical entries' (1996: 706). But the sketchy remarks on these putative performance systems make them look nothing like well-understood performance systems that affect language production. And, one might ask, how one might distinguish an explanation employing them from one which says simply that an L2 is 'parasitic' on an L1, so adult Japanese learners need to 'take time' as they assess the positive evidence and call into play whatever cognitive tricks they can muster to get English *Wh*-movement right. If UG were available to children and adults equally, we would expect adults to be even faster than children at 'time-taking' complex cognitive tasks, not slower. But apparently it takes adults longer than children to get their parameters reset. The conclusion then seems to be that adults aren't literally resetting parameters at all—they are simply doing their best with the parameters that they already have.

The necessity of having to resort to poorly understood performance factors to explain every difference between L1 and L2 acquisition undercuts Epstein et al.'s often repeated assertion that UG 'is fully available to the L2 learner', who has 'full access' to it in acquisition. Given the everyday English meanings of the words 'available' and 'access', this assertion is simply not true. UG may be there, but a host of mechanisms block available access to it for the normal adult. An analogy might help to illustrate my point. Imagine human vision being very different than it actually is. Suppose that in adulthood the neural wiring enabling vision remained essentially unchanged from childhood, but that most adults had the tendency to develop severely degenerated retinas, corneas, irises, and so on. As a result, few adults in this imaginary world would be able to see reliably enough to undertake any task in which good vision is required without, say, the accompaniment of a fully-sighted child. Would we be comfortable saying that in this world visual competence is 'fully available' to adults? How, I would ask Epstein et al., is such a world fundamentally different from the world that they posit, in which we have so little true access to our UG as adults that overwhelmingly our attempts to call it into play in learning a second language end in abject failure.

To summarize, then, I see no evidence that an adult-acquired second language is an internalized system of grammatical competence and therefore do not see that there is an argument against AUTOKNOW to be gleaned from the facts of second language acquisition.[21]

5   The Autonomy of Grammar as a Cognitive System

This section explores and defends the hypothesis that the human mind embodies a cognitive system dedicated to language. As noted above, any defense of AUTOSYN is ipso facto a defense of AUTOGRAM. Since I have already undertaken the former (§3), my remarks in this section will mostly

---

21. Interestingly, the brain activity of early and late bilinguals differ markedly. Kim et al. (1997) have provided MRI-based evidence that while second languages acquired in childhood have common frontal cortical areas, those acquired in adulthood are spatially separated from native languages. Such facts might bear on the question at hand, though at this point it would be mere speculation to suggest that they argue against the full-access hypothesis.

be devoted to more general remarks about the nature of the AUTOGRAM hypothesis. However, the last subsection (§5.3) will go into some detail on the question of the innateness of purely grammatical constructs and on how the phenomenon of genetic dysphasia might bear on this question.

5.1 Does *anybody* reject AUTOGRAM?

It is not easy to find many explicit rejections of AUTOGRAM in the published literature. Outside integrative functionalism, certain work in artificial intelligence comes closest. For example, according to Anderson (1983: 3), 'the language faculty is really the whole cognitive system'. Even Anderson acknowledges that there may be 'language-specific adaptions', though they are 'few in number'. But such work tends to be poorly informed linguistically, and not taken seriously by theoretical linguists of any stripe.

Talmy Givón, who is one of the world's leading functional linguists, is explicit in *defending* AUTOGRAM. For example, he has long deplored the 'perennial tendencies of cognitive psychologists to underestimate the unique organization of human language' (Givón 1984: 3). His recent book, *Functionalism and Grammar*, is in broad outline a series of arguments that 'formal structure assumes its own reality, communicatively, cognitively, and neurologically' (Givón 1995: 11). In other words, it is a series of arguments for AUTOGRAM.[22]

As mentioned above, there are passages in the cognitive linguistics literature that imply a rejection of AUTOGRAM, or at least agnosticism on the question. Langacker, for example, expresses his agnosticism as follows:

22. There are passages in Givón's (1995) book, such as that cited above, that have led commentators (on electronic bulletin boards) to conclude that he now accepts AUTOSYN. And other passages in the book suggest a *rejection* of AUTOGRAM: 'All functionalists [agree] that language (and grammar) can be neither described nor explained adequately as an autonomous system' (1995: xv). Without attempting a full review of the book, I feel that a close reading makes it clear that it accepts the latter, while rejecting the former. That is, consistent with AUTOGRAM, grammar as a whole functions as a semiotic system (but one with a certain amount of 'leakage' and with properties that cannot be explained without going outside the system). And, consistent with a rejection of AUTOSYN, there is no place for a purely syntactic component whose rules and principles specify all and only the grammatically well-formed sentences of the language. I take the following extract from the book to be a tersely colorful rejection of AUTOSYN: 'As the overripe Generative orthodoxy crumbles of its own weight of formal vacuity and methodological indifference ...' (1995: xvi).

What is controversial is whether these [linguistic] structures and abilities are unique to language, possibly constituting a separate modular package with special properties not reflective or derivative of other, more general cognitive functions. In my opinion, a convincing case has not yet been made for a unique linguistic faculty.... I hasten to add, though, that I take no position on the matter at present, nor does the question appear to have any overriding significance in assessing the viability of the proposed framework. I have some doubt that either linguistic or cognitive studies have advanced to the point where the issue can be addressed in truly substantive terms. (Langacker 1987a: 13)

In fact, however, AUTOGRAM is assumed throughout Langacker's work. Indeed, his very definition of what a grammar is presupposes AUTOGRAM:

More specifically, the grammar of a language is defined as those aspects of cognitive organization in which resides a speaker's grasp of established linguistic convention. It can be characterized as a *structured inventory of conventional linguistic units*. (Langacker 1987a: 57; emphasis in original)

Langacker's concrete analyses of specific grammatical phenomena, such as nominal constructions, auxiliaries, clause structure, and so on (see especially Langacker 1991) do in fact reject AUTOSYN, but at the same time are formulated in the context of an encapsulated grammar whose nature seems wholly compatible with AUTOGRAM.

Certain passages in George Lakoff's writings also appear to reject AUTOGRAM: 'Generative linguistics (in the Chomskyan tradition) takes for granted that there is an autonomous language faculty that makes no use at all of general cognitive capacities' (Lakoff 1987: 181). Lakoff goes on to remark that '[it] seems extremely unlikely that human beings do not make use of general cognitive capacities in language' (1987: 182). But a close reading of this book reveals that it does not reject AUTOGRAM at all—again, AUTOGRAM is assumed throughout. Rather, it merely posits that the structure of certain constructs internal to linguistic theory have parallels with (what Lakoff believes) to be the structure of certain constructs external to linguistic theory (in particular their formulation in terms of prototypes). That question is independent of AUTOGRAM. To illustrate this point, let us assume for purposes of argument that Chomsky is right that linguistic categories are discrete and also that other cognitive categories are discrete as well. Thus we would have a situation in which 'general cognitive capacities' (a propensity to favor discrete categories) were reflected in language. Would that refute AUTOGRAM? Of course not. Analogously, a discovery that both linguistic and other cognitive categories have a prototype structure would be equally irrelevant to AUTOGRAM.

Lakoff's concrete analyses are all compatible with AUTOGRAM. Consider, for example, his 'three assumptions' necessary for the adequate analysis of English *there*-constructions:

• Grammatical constructions are pairings of form and meaning.
• The structural aspect of meaning is describable using cognitive models.
• Grammatical constructions form radially structured categories. (Lakoff 1987: 378)

The first and third assumptions transparently assume the correctness of AUTOGRAM. Such assumptions, and the analyses based upon them, seem inconsistent with Lakoff's assertion that 'the simplest possible theory ..., the null theory, ... says there are no purely linguistic universals at all' (Lakoff 1977: 237). To the extent that these assumptions are valid cross-linguistically (and it is implied that they are), they embody 'purely linguistic' concepts (e.g. form-meaning pairings).

In any event, the kind of reductionist thinking that would a priori favor a theory with no purely linguistic universals has rarely proved productive in scientific inquiry. Rather, productive inquiry seeks the most elegant set of principles in the relevant domain, without respect to whether they are derivative of other principles. If they turn out to be so, well and good, but, as the experience with behaviorist thought in psychology teaches us, one is likely to be led astray by taking the absence of domain-specific principles as the null hypothesis.

Let us now turn to some general questions about the nature of AUTOGRAM and how linguistic theory might be situated within a broader cognitive framework.

5.2 The cognitive commitment

What I can only consider to be a pseudo-issue revolves around what Lakoff (1991: 54) has called the 'cognitive commitment', namely 'the commitment to make one's account of human language accord with what is generally known about the mind and brain from disciplines other than linguistics'. In Lakoff's opinion, the theory of cognitive linguistics is defined by the cognitive commitment, while generative grammar rejects it.[23]

23. Geeraerts (1991: 162) makes a similar point, arguing that generative grammarians 'reject or neglect a direct confrontation with the results of psycholinguistic language-acquisition research'. Nothing could be farther from the truth; scores of papers and books are published each year that present acquisitional evidence supporting the principal conceptions of generative grammar.

As we have seen, Lakoff maintains that the generative view is that 'human beings do not make use of general cognitive capacities in languages' (Lakoff 1987: 182). If what Lakoff means by this is that generativists reject the idea that linguistic theory must be situated in a neuropsychologically real overall theory of mind-brain, he is simply wrong. In Chomsky's words, 'a grammar is a cognitive structure interacting with other systems of knowledge and belief' (Chomsky 1975a: 86).

Lakoff appears to believe that the supposed rejection of the cognitive commitment by generative grammarians is a logical consequence of the idea that syntax is held to be a formal system (see above, §3.4.1). Since in formal (i.e. algorithmic) systems, generation takes place independently of semantic interpretation, Lakoff concludes that:

Generative grammar [has to be] *defined* so as to be independent of general cognitive capacities.... Any use of a general cognitive capacity would require a step outside of the formal system metaphor.... The paradigm in which generative linguistics is defined absolutely requires a strong assumption of the autonomy of syntax from semantics and of the language faculty from any cognitive influence. (Lakoff 1987: 181–182)

There are several errors here. First, no one has ever 'defined' generative grammar as independent of general cognitive capacities. The question of the relationship between generative grammar and other cognitive faculties (it is by no means clear what 'general cognitive capacities' are) is an entirely empirical question. Furthermore, Lakoff's wording implies that attributes characterizable by 'formal systems' are not part of general cognitive functioning, an idea for which he provides no support. Logically, one can imagine that there might exist a broader algorithmically-characterizable cognitive system which contains as one of its proper subparts a generative grammar, thereby realizing at one and the same time AUTOGRAM and the inseparability of grammar from 'general cognitive capacities'. And finally, as noted above, the idea that grammar is a formal system no more requires the separation of syntax from semantics than a formal phonological theory prohibits the phonetic grounding of phonological constructs. Nothing would prevent the existence of an algorithm generating intrinsically paired syntactic and semantic constructs or from generating semantic constructs, which are then mapped onto syntactic ones. Indeed, the program of early Generative Semantics was to do precisely the latter.

Lakoff's belief that for generativists the language faculty is divorced from cognitive influence leads him to conclude that generative grammar must adopt an 'objectivist' view of semantics, in which grammatical

structures must be interpreted model-theoretically. This is a curious conclusion. Many generativists, and in particular Chomsky, have rejected the
'objectivist semantics' that Lakoff also rejects (see, for example, Chomsky
1975a). Ray Jackendoff, another leading generativist, takes the same
position as Lakoff and Chomsky:

These treatments all make an assumption that we rejected, [namely] a fixed, pre-
established connection of truth between sentences and the real world. By contrast,
we are concerned with how the organism makes the judgment, or what is involved
in *grasping* an atomic sentence. We thus take the theory of categorization to concern not whether a particular categorization is true, but what information and
processing must be ascribed to an organism to account for its categorization
judgments. (Jackendoff 1983: 78)

In a series of books (Jackendoff 1983, 1987, 1990), one of which was
published before Lakoff (1987), but not cited in it, Jackendoff has developed a theory of conceptual semantics, with many features in common
with the semantic conceptions of cognitive linguistics. Most importantly,
Jackendoff sees the goal of a semantic theory to provide a mental representation of the world in relation to language. The fact that Jackendoff
adopts an autonomous generative syntax—and devotes considerable
space to explicating the correspondence rules linking them to conceptual
structure—would appear to present prima facie evidence that a non-
objectivist semantics and an autonomous syntax can go hand-in-hand.

The question of the parallelism between the structure of grammar and
that of other cognitive faculties has been most thoroughly addressed by
Jackendoff (see especially Jackendoff 1987), who explicitly defends both
AUTOSYN and AUTOGRAM, and by Leonard Talmy (see especially Talmy
1988), who (to my knowledge) takes no position on them. Talmy shares
with Jackendoff the view 'that there is a fundamental core to conceptual
structure that is common across cognitive domains' (1988: 200), and both
have pointed in particular to structural commonalities between the
grammatical and the visual system. Such commonalities pose no threat to
AUTOGRAM, though they may well, of course, threaten objectivist semantics. Talmy stresses that the grammatical system has *parallels* to other
faculties, not that it is derivative of them. That is, while grammar, vision,
and so on may share properties—a necessary consequence of the need for
humans to integrate a body of disparate conceptual material—grammar
is no more *dependent upon* vision or the other cognitive faculties taken as
a whole than any other faculty is dependent upon the others. Indeed,
Talmy even writes of grammar as 'the determinant of conceptual struc-

ture within one cognitive domain, language' (Talmy 1988: 166), a wording thoroughly in keeping with the spirit of AUTOGRAM.

It is clearly methodologically illicit to take some result (however well established) from cognitive psychology or neurobiology that has been shown to be applicable to some cognitive domain other than language and to assume that it must govern grammatical functioning as well. Lakoff is particularly prone to commit this error. On a number of occasions he has provided a list of 'empirical results from a number of disciplines' that 'the cognitive commitment forces one to be responsive to' (Lakoff 1990: 40), including:

• Categorization results from cognitive psychology, developmental psychology, and anthropology that demonstrate the existence of basic-level categorization and prototype effects.
• Psychophysical, neurophysiological, anthropological results about the nature of color perception and categorization.
• Results from cognitive psychology concerning human imaging capacities and the association of conventional imagery with language.
• Results from cognitive neuroscience and connectionism regarding the computational mechanisms of the brain. (Lakoff 1990: 40–41)

But 'results' are free for the taking in cognitive psychology and allied disciplines.[24] One could just as easily provide a completely different list to serve the purposes of generative grammar:

• Categorization results that demonstrate the existence of discrete well-defined categories in visual perception and representation.
• Psychophysical, neurophysiological, anthropological results about the nature of musical knowledge and abilities.
• Results from cognitive psychology indicating domain-specificity in the child's acquisition of cognitive faculties and their modularization in the adult.
• Results from work on cognitive development regarding the richness and complexity of the representations the mind has of the world.

The point is that even if basic-level categories and conceptual prototypes are well motivated for some aspects of cognition, nothing follows

---

24. Note that Paul Deane, a cognitive linguist, has remarked: 'In actual practice, however, cognitive linguists as a class may not seem particularly well versed in the other cognitive sciences. Cognitive linguists often seem to rely on a few key results from other disciplines' (1996: 82).

with regard to whether the boundaries of *grammatical* categories are discrete. The point is true all around, of course: from the fact that some conceptual categories are discrete, no conclusion can be drawn about whether or not grammatical categories are discrete.

It must be acknowledged that playing fast and loose with results from outside linguistics is as prevalent in the generative sphere as in the functionalist sphere. So, for example, Piattelli-Palmarini (1989) concludes that the parameter-setting model of generative grammar is supported on the basis of the fact that the concept of 'instructive learning' has been abandoned by many biologists in favor of mechanisms of internal selection and filtering, which affect a pre-programmed chain of multiple internal recombinations and internal 'switches'. He may well be right that the latter instantiates the former, but given the complexity and diversity of human knowledge acquisition, one can hardly point to such results as further confirmation of a particular approach to grammar.

In short, generative grammar and cognitive linguistics stand united in their devotion to the 'cognitive commitment'. I would be happy to substitute 'generative' for 'cognitive' in the following passage as an accurate statement of my own views:

> I view cognitive linguistics as defined by the commitment to characterize the full range of linguistic generalizations while being faithful to empirical discoveries about the nature of the mind/brain. (Lakoff 1990: 39)

What stands in the way of a reconciliation between the two approaches to language is not the principled question of whether a theory of language must be 'psychologically real', but the empirical one of how the results of linguistics are properly situated within a broader theory of mind.

5.3   AUTOGRAM and the question of innate grammatical constructs

Perhaps the most controversial hypothesis put forward in the course of generativist theorizing is the idea that central aspects of the autonomous linguistic system are provided by the human genome. In this section, we will examine the arguments that are put forward in support of an 'innate UG'.

5.3.1   From autonomy to innateness   How do we come to possess the autonomous cognitive system dedicated to the grammatical aspects of language? How do we 'know' that Lexical Government, Subjacency, and so on are principles of grammar? The conclusion arrived at by many

generative grammarians is that they could never have been learned inductively, and thus must be part of the innate cognitive make-up that every child brings to the task of language acquisition.

Typically, arguments for the innateness of a principle take one of three forms, all versions of what are called 'arguments from the poverty of the stimulus' (APS). The first is to emphasize that the *abstractness and/or complexity* of the principle is so great that no conceivable mechanism of inductive learning could have resulted in its acquisition. The second is to point out that the principle *appears at such an early age and so rapidly* that, again, no theory other than one that posits its innate origins can reasonably explain its possession by the child. And the third, more indirectly, points to some aspect of verbal behavior (normally judgments of sentential acceptability) that are at great remove from any aspect of verbal behavior likely to have been experienced. Therefore, it is concluded, an innate principle must underlie that behavior (even though we may not know the precise nature of the principle).

Let me give two examples of APS of the first type. One is Chomsky's well-known and often repeated argument for the innateness of the structure-dependent nature of grammatical rules (see, for example, Chomsky 1975b: 32–33; 1980c: 40). Chomsky reasons as follows: Suppose that a child learning English unerringly forms questions such as (57b) from declaratives such as (57a):

(57) a. The man is tall.
     b. Is the man tall?

In principle, the child could be working with one of two strategies for forming questions. The first is simply that they are formed by inverting the first occurrence of *is* (or an auxiliary). In the second, more complex, scenario, the child analyzes the sentence into abstract phrases and preposes the occurrence of *is* (or an auxiliary) that occurs after the first noun phrase. Questions formed from sentences such as (58a), in which the subject contains a relative clause with a copula, decide the matter—the child assumes the second hypothesis. Given the first hypothesis, the child would incorrectly produce (58b). However, following the second, the child correctly produces (58c):

(58) a. The man who is tall is in the room.
     b. *Is the man who tall is in the room?
     c. Is the man who is tall in the room?

How did the child come to possess the second hypothesis? Chomsky writes:

It is certainly absurd to argue that children are trained to use the structure-dependent rule, in this case.... A person may go through a considerable portion of his life without ever facing relevant evidence, but he will have no hesitation in using the structure-dependent rule, even if all of his experience is consistent with hypothesis 1.... The principle of structure-dependence is not learned, but forms part of the conditions for language learning. (Chomsky 1975b: 32–33)

Hoekstra and Kooij (1988) have constructed a similar argument in support of the innateness of the principle of Subjacency. Since this constraint prohibits the formation of *wh*-questions if a *wh*-phrase intervenes between the filler and the gap, it predicts correctly that (59a) is ambiguous as to the scope of *where*, while (59b) is not. Note that in (59a), *where* can refer both to the place of John's saying and the place of getting off the bus, while in (59b), *where* can refer only to the place of John's asking:

(59) a. Where$_i$ did John say ____$_i$ that we had to get off the bus ____$_i$?
     b. Where$_i$ did John ask ____$_i$ whether we had to get off the bus
        *____$_i$?

They argue that positive evidence alone could hardly suffice to enable the child language learner to come to the conclusion that (59b) does not manifest the same ambiguity as (59a)—the abstractness and complexity of the principle and the paucity of direct evidence bearing directly on it guarantee that the child could never figure Subjacency out 'for itself'. Thus knowledge of the permissible intervening structure between a *wh*-phrase and its co-indexed gap must be pre-wired into the language learner.

The second type of APS can be illustrated by the acquisition of anaphoric binding. Crain (1991) calls attention to the following sentences:

(60) a. The Ninja Turtle danced while he ate pizza.
     b. While he danced, the Ninja Turtle ate pizza.
     c. His archrival danced while the Ninja Turtle ate pizza.
     d. He danced while the Ninja Turtle ate pizza.

In (60a–b) *he* can be coreferential with *the Ninja Turtle*, as can *his* in (60c). However, in (60d) *he* and *Ninja Turtle* cannot corefer. The principles of grammar that explain this distribution of facts are quite complex and abstract. Furthermore, Crain and McKee (1986) have shown that even children as young as two years old accept (60a–b) and reject (60d).

The conclusion that Crain draws is that the principles of anaphoric binding must be innate.

We have already encountered the third type of APS in the above discussion of intuitions about sentences never heard (§3.4.4). Consider again
sentences (10–11), repeated below for convenience:

(10) This is the paper that I filed before reading.

(11) a. *I filed the paper before reading.
      b. *This is the paper that I filed the notes before reading.

While we may not know the precise principle or combination of principles
responsible for speakers' judgments on parasitic gap sentences, no inductive learning procedure seems plausible that might explain how they
arrived at these judgments. Hence, once again, an innate principle of UG
is implicated.[25]

5.3.2 Challenges to APS APS have been challenged on a variety of
grounds. To begin with, as John Hawkins has frequently reminded us
(Hawkins 1985: 583; 1988a; 1994), APS arguments for the innateness of
some principle will be convincing only to the extent that we are sure that
positive evidence would not suffice for its learning. The problem, as
Hawkins notes, is that we do not really have a theory of what *is* learnable
from positive evidence. Thus the claim that no child could come to
acquire some feature of his or her language without innate guidance is not
one based on the failure of some particular concrete and widely-accepted
theory of learning; rather, it is based more on the plausibility that no such
theory could possibly exist.

To give a concrete example of the depth of the problem, consider a
recent paper by Geoffrey Pullum (1996a). Pullum challenges the APS
argument for the innateness of structure-dependence on the grounds that,
contrary to what Chomsky's has written, a person may indeed 'face relevant evidence' for the principle. He reports that a corpus of articles from
the *Wall Street Journal* between 1987 and 1989 contains many dozens of
examples of sentences parallel to (58c) and none at all parallel to (58b).
Given the (arguable) assumption that such sentence types also form part
of the child's input experience, it is not so clear that the child might not

---

25. See Hyams (1998) for more arguments of this sort and references to the literature on the topic.

have been able, in this particular case, to induce the correct structure-dependent rule.

But at the same time it is not obvious that the child *would* be able to do so, and, even if he or she could do so, would be led to generalize structure-dependence to cases where the relevant evidence was *not* forthcoming. We simply do not know what the child's 'resources' are in this regard. Pullum cites recent work on data-driven learning algorithms (Brent 1993; Schütze 1997) capable of inducing many complex syntactic generalizations from raw text alone. But, of course, even if it were the case that such an algorithm could induce, say, Subjacency, that would not mean that the human brain *follows* that algorithm. Concluding the noninnateness of some hypothesized UG principle on the basis of an ingenious program drawing on the statistical distribution of grammatical elements (rather than on the basis of child development studies) carries with it its own dangers.

Another problem, as Matthew Dryer has pointed out (personal communication), is that while APS might lead irrevocably to innateness, it does not lead necessarily to innate principles of UG. That is, while the acquisition of the contrasts in (59a–b) might suggest that the child brings to the language learning process more than the ability to make simple generalizations from observed input, there is no logical necessity for the conclusion that a specifically linguistic faculty (i.e. an innate UG) is at work, rather than some sophisticated general cognitive faculty or some more specific faculty not restricted to language.

There have, in fact, been some proposals made to account for the effects of putative UG principles in terms of innate principles not specific to language. The most ambitious is William O'Grady's *Principles of Grammar and Learning* (O'Grady 1987).[26] In one sense, O'Grady proposes a theory that, up to a point, is consistent with AUTOSYN—a version of categorial grammar is responsible for constructing phrasal structure. However, he attempts to show that the bulk of the phenomena that have been handled by UG principles within standard versions of generative grammar can be explained in terms of notions such as 'adjacency', 'precedence', 'continuity', and 'dependency'—all of which have their roots outside the language faculty. Since the child exploits these notions in constructing his or her grammar, the need for innately endowed specifically linguistic principles appears to be vitiated.

26. For other important work along the lines of O'Grady's, see Deane (1992), Na and Huck (1993), Kuno and Takami (1993), and Van Valin (1994).

O'Grady's theory can be judged, first of all, simply on grounds of descriptive adequacy. If the principles that he puts forward lack sufficient generality then it hardly matters if they are innate or not. The problem is that his analysis of (mostly) English syntactic phenomena is far too sketchy to do an adequate evaluation in this regard. As he himself points out, 'it would be unrealistic to think that the [233 page] work of any one person could equal in descriptive coverage the combined effort of hundreds of people over a twenty-five year period' (1987: xi). But too many phenomena are omitted from analysis that form crucial evidence for or against the UG principles that he wishes to replace. One hopes for further expansion of his theory in terms of its descriptive coverage before an adequate evaluation can be undertaken.

More serious is the question of whether his claimed replacement of purely syntactic principles by ones derived from general principles of cognition is any more than terminological. For example, one proposed principle leads the child to disfavor discontinuous constituents, thereby predicting subjacency effects. Displaced *wh*-phrases and other displaced constituents are licensed by other learning strategies that override the aforementioned one. These principles are so language-specific (or incorporate so many language-specific elements) and are at such a remove from what are generally accepted principles of learning that it seems to me that UG, in a somewhat different form, enters through the back door.[27]

5.3.3 Does innateness even matter?   To read the critical literature, one would think that there is some logical connection between the generativist research program and the need to posit a set of purely syntactic innate universals—a distasteful conclusion for so many. But innateness is a conclusion, not an assumption, and plays no role in the *formulation* of the principles. In other words, the question of the adequacy of such principles is independent of the question of where they 'come from'. If somebody were able to show that they could be learned inductively, then well and good. The generative research program would not have to budge one centimeter.

---

27. Similar criticisms apply to work in the cognitive linguistics tradition that claims that there is no innate UG, while at the same time postulating that the image-schematic structure underlying grammatical knowledge is innate (Deane 1992, 1996; Langacker 1993).

Keeping that point in mind, there *are* recent findings which I feel provide incontrovertible evidence that AUTOGRAM is correct and that, furthermore, there are innate, purely grammatical, principles. These are the findings by Myrna Gopnik and her colleagues that certain purely grammatical deficits can be transmitted genetically (see especially Gopnik 1990; Gopnik and Crago 1991; Gopnik et al. 1996). Such cases of 'genetic dysphasia', to be discussed in the following section, lend themselves to no reasonable interpretation that excludes a distinct cognitive model of grammatical competence.

5.3.4 Genetic dysphasia   The idea that grammatical impairments might be transmitted genetically ('genetic dysphasia') raises a number of extremely interesting issues, which we will address in this section.[28] Genetic dysphasia is, by definition, a specific language impairment (SLI) transmitted genetically. And SLI is, by definition, a language disorder unaccompanied by nonlinguistic deficits, such as an abnormally low IQ, a hearing deficit, a brain injury, a significant medical history, environmental deprivation, or an obvious emotional or behavioral disturbance. One's first thought, therefore, might be that any case of SLI (genetically transmitted or not) would ipso facto support both AUTOKNOW and AUTOGRAM.[29]

Things are not so simple, however. SLI is defined broadly enough to encompass language disorders that are not necessarily deficits in linguistic competence per se, and therefore may have no bearing whatever on AUTOKNOW. For example, deficits to the peripheral mechanisms involved in language production and comprehension are (or can be) SLI's. But unless in some specific case one is able to successfully demonstrate that the deficit leaves the competence system intact (no easy task!), that case would neither provide evidence for or against AUTOKNOW.

In other words, not every case of SLI provides evidence for AUTOKNOW. But it is equally the case that a language impairment that is accompanied by cognitive or other nonspecifically linguistic deficits (and is therefore, by definition, not a case of SLI) can be fully compatible with both AUTO-

28. This section has been published in Newmeyer (1997). The reader should consult that work for discussion of whether and how evidence from dysphasic speech might bear on questions internal to grammatical theory.

29. The first work to suggest that SLI might result from a disorder of the autonomous grammatical system was Cromer (1978).

KNOW and AUTOGRAM. For example, a dysphasia that always happened to be accompanied by, say, problems with articulation or cognition would weigh against the correctness of these hypotheses only if the problems in grammar followed as a consequence of those external to grammar. If the same underlying factors (genetic or otherwise) were at the root of all the impairments, then the facts would present no challenge to the notion of an autonomous grammatical system.

Indeed, it is within the realm of plausibility that a prior degree of grammatical knowledge is a prerequisite to the development of the full set of normal cognitive abilities. Thus, if we find a case in which grammatical and cognitive deficits cooccur, it might well be the former (i.e. an impairment to the autonomous grammatical system) that is the root cause of the latter.

In the past few decades, hundreds, if not thousands, of individuals have been diagnosed with SLI, providing an immense potential pool to test the hypothesis that a grammatical system can be impaired in the absence of deficits in other capacities, whether linguistic or nonlinguistic. Unfortunately, it is all but impossible to extract relevant evidence for this hypothesis from the great majority of such cases. Not only are diagnoses arrived at on the bases of wildly different criteria, but only rarely are enough grammar-probing tests applied to allow firm conclusions to be drawn.[30]

In the best studied case of SLI of all, however, the evidence for a differential loss of grammatical competence seems incontrovertible. This is the working-class British family described in Gopnik (1990) and elsewhere, and referred to in the literature as 'the KE family' (or simply as 'the K family'). With the exception of some problems with articulation (see below), the only deficit shared by all affected members of this family is a partial and consistent loss of grammatical function. All attempts have proved fruitless to circumvent the conclusion that the locus of their deficit is the autonomous grammatical system. To begin with, environmental causes can be ruled out. There is no difference in the broader communicative context that might account for why one family member is afflicted and another not:

---

30. Fletcher and Ingham (1995: 620) point to 'the absence of a clear etiology, and the consequent lack of clear identificatory criteria, plus the confounding influences of development and remediation in older subject groups, [which] virtually guarantee extensive variation in any sample selected for research purposes'.

The fact that these close interactions occur between the impaired and the unimpaired members of the family means that the impaired subjects are receiving constant linguistic input from the speakers who do not have any linguistic impairment and yet ... they are never able to construct a normal grammar. The fact that they were all raised in the same neighborhood insures that they all have the same dialect of English, therefore differences in their linguistic performance cannot be attributed to a difference in dialect. (Gopnik 1994b: 1).

Furthermore, the dysphasia affects the formal features of language only, leaving those manifesting the syndrome with no loss of ability in the conveying or understanding of meaning or in the pragmatics of language use. For example, loss of the ability to produce tense markers implies no decreased ability to mentally represent 'presentness' or 'pastness' (Gopnik 1994c); the loss of ability to produce number markers implies no decreased ability to differentiate semantic singularity and plurality (Gopnik and Crago 1991; Gopnik 1992); and so on.

As might be expected, there have been attempts to attribute the deficit manifested by affected KE family members to systems at work in the *use* of language, and thereby undercut the theory that it is the grammatical system per se that is affected. For example, Leonard (1989, 1992, 1994) and Leonard et al. (1992) have hypothesized that an auditory processing deficit is responsible for the dysphasia—subjects have difficulty processing morphological inflections because they are not acoustically salient. However, as Goad and Gopnik (1994) and Gopnik (1994d) have shown, such an explanation cannot be correct. Affected members of the KE family perform excellently on phoneme-recognition tasks, and, moreover, have no difficulty perceiving unstressed word-final segments that mimic the form of inflectional suffixes (e.g. the final alveolar in words like *wand*).

Fletcher (1990, 1996), on the other hand, posits an articulatory deficit—affected individuals, for example, lack the ability to produce the final alveolar consonant in past tense forms. But Gopnik (1994a) reports that clinical assessments by a neurologist and a speech-language pathologist indicate no reduction in range or movement or tone of the mouth or tongue musculature, thereby ruling out a diagnosis of dysarthia, as defined in Bishop (1988). It is true that the affected members of the KE family manifest problems in articulation. But these problems could not be the root cause of their grammatical impairment—no deficit in articulation could explain why they make errors with suppletive past tenses (*was, went*) and with irregular pasts, regardless of the sound that happens to occur in final position (*took, drove, got, swam,* etc.).[31] And, as observed by Goad and Gopnik, 'it is very hard to see how articulatory problems could prevent them from making correct grammaticality judgments or ratings which require them to just nod yes or no or to circle a number' (1997: 9).

It is absolutely true, as pointed out in Vargha-Khadem et al. (1995) and elsewhere, that virtually all of the affected members of the KE family have other problems, ranging from dyslexia to spatial rotation to depression to schizophrenia to apraxia.[32] But the point is that none of these problems reliably occur with the language disorder and therefore cannot be the root cause of it. And, of course, any number of individuals manifest one or more of these disorders without an accompanying grammatical deficit. In short, there seems to be no avoiding the conclusion that the dysphasia affecting the KE family is a condition affecting the grammatical system per se, and, by virtue of that fact, there seems to be no avoiding the conclusion that such a system must exist.

It has been known for some time that SLI tends to run in families (Bishop 1987; Tallal, Ross, and Curtiss 1989). Researchers have now had the opportunity to study the linguistic deficits of familial SLI manifested by speakers of four different languages: English (16 impaired individuals in three generations of the KE family); Japanese (several children who have a positive familial history of SLI [Fukuda and Fukuda 1994]); Inuktitut (a single speaker from a family in which SLI has been reported in three generations [Crago and Allen 1996]); and Greek (18 children, 9 of whom have a positive family history of SLI [Dalalakis 1994]). Now, as observed in Pinker (1994b: 48–49), the fact that a behavioral pattern runs in families does not prove that it is genetic: 'Recipes, accents, and lullabies run in families, but they have nothing to do with DNA'. Nevertheless, no

31. Piggott and Kessler Robb (1994) suggest that the seeming articulatory deficit is in reality a deficit in the prosodic rules of English that govern the formation of multisyllabic words.

32. Vargha-Khadem et al. (1995) is perhaps the most accessible publication that attempts to attribute the KE family members' dysphasia to nongrammatical factors. A telling criticism of this publication is that it ignores all work done by Myrna Gopnik and her associates that appeared after 1991. As a consequence, it ignores the bulk of the facts upon which the hypotheses of the Gopnik group have been based and distorts many others. For discussion of the Vargha-Khadem et al. paper, see Gopnik and Goad (1997).

Table 2.1
Percent of concordance in twin pairs with SLI

Monozygotic	Dizygotic	Source
80	38	Tomblin and Buckwalter 1994
86	48	Lewis and Thompson 1992
89	48	Bishop, North, and Donlan 1995

environmental explanation seems forthcoming for why approximately half the members of the KE family are affected, including one fraternal twin. Indeed, the heritability of (some types of) SLI is suggested by its increased occurrence in monozygotic, as compared to dizygotic twins. Table 2.1 (reprinted from Gopnik et al. 1996: 229) illustrates.

In addition, there is a ready genetic explanation for the distribution of the language-impaired and the nonimpaired in the KE family. As a geneticist has noted:

The relatively clear-cut difference between affected and unaffected members [of the family] and the occurrence of 15 definitely affected members out of 29 over three generations affecting both sexes equally, is highly indicative of autosomal dominant inheritance ... such a concentration of a rare distinct disorder in 15 members of one family makes polygenetic and multifactoral inheritance very unlikely. (Pembrey 1992: 54–55)

In other words, we have strong evidence for the genetic transmission of specific strictly grammatical traits.

6   Conclusion

In this chapter, we have examined three distinct autonomy hypotheses that are at the center of debate among theoretical linguists: the autonomy of syntax, which holds that there exists a cognitive system of nonsemantic and nondiscourse-derived syntactic elements whose principles of combination make no reference to system-external factors; the autonomy of linguistic knowledge from use, which postulates a system embodying knowledge of language that is characterizable independently of language use; and the autonomy of grammar as a cognitive system, namely the idea that there is a cognitive system exclusively dedicated to language. In each case, I have argued that the hypothesis is correct.

Chapter 3

Internal and External
Explanation in Linguistics

1 Overview

This chapter takes on the difficult question of what it means to 'explain' why grammatical structure has the properties that it does and why some sorts of proffered explanations are better than others. Section 2 is a short survey of the problem, calling attention to the useful distinction between 'internal' and 'external' explanation. In §3 I focus on the former, a mode of explanation that is generally identified with the generative program. I argue that not only is the common functionalist criticism of internal explanation per se ill-founded, but functionalists themselves make recourse to that mode of explanation. Section 4 introduces the plethora of types of external explanatory factors that have been advanced in the course of linguistic theorizing, from parsing to iconicity to innateness. Indeed, it seems that an open-ended number of external factors have been claimed to shape grammatical structure. But not all are equally convincing; in §5, I make some suggestions about how convincing ones can be identified and go on to identify two of them—one parsing-based and one semantically-based. I argue that appeals to information flow, frequency, and economy can be dispensed with in syntax. Section 6 addresses the problem of 'competing motivations', namely external influences on syntactic structure that pull on it in different directions. I suggest that their existence renders problematic two aspects of the functionalist program. The first is the idea that grammars per se should link external motivations and structure. The second is the practice of attempting to explain why some grammatical feature has the typological breakdown that it does. Section 7 argues that external explanation is fully compatible with the autonomy of syntax and §8 is a short conclusion.

2   On Explanation in Linguistics, Internal and External

Hardly a publication appears in the field that is not committed to 'explaining' some aspect of language or to demonstrating that some existing explanatory device can or cannot be extended to some new domain of data. Only the most theoretically nihilistic linguists—and they are few in number—would deny that some proposed explanations are 'better' or 'worse' than others. But the situation in linguistics is complicated—as it is in other cognitive sciences—in two ways. First of all, what the very facts are that need to be explained (the 'explananda') is a controversial topic. As we saw in the previous chapter, for example, certain linguists dismiss any interest in explaining judgments by native speakers about sentences that would rarely, if ever, be used in an actual discourse. For others, however, explaining the source of such judgments is a central goal, since the possession of such knowledge in the absence of direct experience points to a complex, and possibly innate, cognitive faculty dedicated to language.

And one also debates what counts as an acceptable explanation. That is, one debates the 'explanans' as well as the explananda. Broadly speaking, one can divide explanans into two types—internal and external. An internal explanation in linguistics is one in which a set of facts fall out as a consequence of the deductive structure of a particular theory of grammar. An external explanation is one in which a set of facts is derived as a consequence of principles outside the domain of grammar.

There is a rough correspondence between internal explanations and what are called 'formal' explanations and between external explanations and what are called 'functional' explanations. However, following Hyman (1983: 68), I will generally avoid the terms 'formal explanation' and 'functional explanation', as they are inherently misleading. The term 'formal', as noted in chapter 1, is ambiguous between the sense of 'pertaining to (grammatical) form', and that of 'stated in a mathematically precise vocabulary'. We would not wish to say that internal explanation *requires* formalization, as useful as that may be. Also, the extensions of 'functional explanation' and 'external explanation' are not identical. An explanation of some grammatical property on the basis of, say, a cognitive disposition toward iconic representations is certainly external, though there is nothing self-evidently 'functional' about it.

Explanatory devices that for one linguist are primary motivating factors of grammatical structure are rejected by another as inherently deficient or, at best, uninteresting. A popular view is that generativists embrace internal explanation, but dismiss external; that functionalists embrace the latter, but dismiss the former. As we will see, this popular view—though it embodies a kernel of truth—is grossly oversimplified. Both approaches adopt both types of explanation.

3   Internal Explanation

This section begins with an overview of the explanatory devices of generative grammar, which exemplify internal explanation par excellence (§3.1). Section 3.2 discusses and evaluates criticisms that have been leveled against internal explanation, and §3.3 illustrates that functionalists as well as generativists have had recourse to this mode of explanation.

3.1   The explanans of generative grammar

The central explanans of generative grammar is internal, in the sense that a set of principles formulated in a vocabulary of grammar-internal primitives interact to yield the set of grammatical sentences in a particular language and their structures. Generativists say that the latter are 'explained' by the former. So, for example, the ungrammaticality of sentence (1a) is explained by the fact that the principles of the grammar fail to generate it. Likewise, the dual structural description of (1b) is explained by the fact that the principles of the grammar are organized in such a way that two structures for this sentence follow as a consequence of their formulation:

(1) a. *Mary is been liked by Sue.
     b. Alice likes Mary more than Sue.

But the notions 'ungrammaticality' and 'dual structural description' are themselves wholly theory-internal. By what criteria, then, can we claim to have explained anything about *English* (or about human language in general)? After all, an internally-consistent deductive system could be designed to rule (1a) grammatical and give (1b) only a single structure. The answer is that one assumes a consistent—though not mechanical— correspondence between the predictions of the grammar and observations of language performance. Since the ungrammaticality of (1a) is matched by its unacceptability to native speakers of English and the dual structure attributed to (1b) is matched by the fact that speakers find it ambiguous, one concludes that the principles in question are correct. Indeed, one goes on to say that the judgments of the native speaker are explained by their internalization of these principles.

Many explanations provided within generative grammar thus fit a weak form of the deductive-nomological model (Hempel 1965). That is, a general principle is formulated and paired with a set of initial conditions. A phenomenon is said to be 'explained' if it can be deduced from this pairing. Consider, for example, the 'Case Filter', a UG principle proposed in Rouveret and Vergnaud (1980) and Chomsky (1980a) and which played a central role in the Government-Binding theory of the 1980s. The Case Filter requires overt noun phrases to be Case-marked; (2) is one statement of the filter from Chomsky (1981: 49):

(2) *The Case Filter*
    *NP if NP has phonetic content and has no Case

Independently arrived at assumptions about phrase structure lead to the conclusion that any NP in the position indicated 'NP' in the following configuration cannot receive Case:

(3) It is unclear [[who] [NP to see t]]

Hence it is deduced that the following sentence will be ungrammatical:

(4) *It is unclear who John to see.

Since (4) is indeed unacceptable to native speakers, we have evidence in favor of the Case Filter, from which the deduction follows.

The problems with exclusive reliance on the deductive-nomological mode of explanation are well known (for a review, see Salmon 1984, 1989). In a nutshell, for any complex phenomenon, the initial conditions and the data to be explained are themselves typically fluid enough that giving them a slight reinterpretation allows one to explain away any failed deduction without abandoning the proposed principle. Suppose, for example, that contrary to fact, we *did* find sentences of the form of (4) of unquestioned acceptability. Would the failure of the deduction then falsify the Case Filter? Not necessarily. The problem might lie with the initial conditions—themselves hypotheses about the nature of grammar. Or as another possibility, it might be the case that the proposed structure is incorrect, or correct at one level of grammar, but incorrect at the level at which the Case Filter is thought to apply. Or as yet another possibility, one might argue that in this particular case, speakers have some particular reason to accept sentences that their grammar does not generate.

Furthermore, we have no theory-independent way of knowing which facts are consequences of which principles. Suppose we encountered a set of ungrammatical sentences bearing a resemblance to those that are recognized as Case Filter violations, but which the Case Filter (as currently formulated) could not exclude. Would that be sufficient to falsify the (current formulation of) the Case Filter? Not necessarily—perhaps some other, possibly yet unformulated, principle is responsible for excluding them. An analogous issue came up in the early 1980s. In the context of a critique of a trace-theoretic explanation of the contraction of *want to* to *wanna*, Postal and Pullum (1982) pointed out that the proposals in Jaeggli (1980) and Chomsky (1980b) failed to explain (among other things) the impossibility of contraction in (5a–b):

(5) a.   I want to dance and to sing.
     b. *I wanna dance and to sing.

With some irony, they faulted Jaeggli and Chomsky for claiming 'explanatory success' when their proposals failed to even *describe* the set of facts that simple reflection might lead one to believe that they should describe. But in a reply to Postal and Pullum, Aoun and Lightfoot (1984) argued that the set of facts under the purview of a particular theoretical proposal is not given in advance:

> [Postal and Pullum] find it theoretically suspicious that trace theory advocates can claim to have achieved explanatory success when in fact their descriptions fail. We would argue that one can explain some facts even if others are left undescribed; it is unreasonable to say that one has no explanation until all facts are described. In order to have an explanation (of greater or lesser depth) one needs to describe the *relevant* facts. It is important to note that there is no theory-independent way of establishing which facts are relevant. (Aoun and Lightfoot 1984: 472)

Given the difficulties inherent in the deductive-nomological mode of explanation, how does one then determine if a proposal (or, for that matter, an entire theory) is an explanatory one? There is no simple answer to this question. Most philosophers of science today would appeal, not to the successful deduction of a set of facts from a set of premises, but to more intangible matters, such as a theory's internal consistency, to its meeting standards of simplicity and elegance, and above all its ability to contribute to an *understanding* of the matter at hand.

To illustrate, consider two competing internal treatments of the English auxiliary: a item-and-arrangement phrase structure analysis of the type current in the 1950s and the analysis proposed by Chomsky in *Syntactic*

Structures. The former, by any criterion, is cumbersome and uninsightful. The latter analysis, however, treated the superficially discontinuous auxiliary morphemes *have -en* and *be -ing* as unit constituents generated by (a simplified set of) phrase structure rules, and posited a simple transformational rule to permute the affixal and verbal elements into their surface positions, thus predicting the basic distribution of auxiliaries in simple declarative sentences. Moreover, Chomsky was able to show that the permutation rule, 'the Auxiliary Transformation' (later called 'Affix Hopping' by other linguists), interacts with rules forming simple negatives and simple *yes-no* questions to specify neatly the exact locations where 'supportive' *do* appears.

Most grammarians agreed at the time that the *Syntactic Structures* account was more 'explanatory' than the alternative. But why? Certainly not because of its empirical coverage, which was no better than that of any purely phrase structural account. The analysis was considered more explanatory because it was elegant, simple, and, by virtue of being able to bring new facts into its domain with only a minimum of additional assumptions, seemed to lead to a deeper understanding of English grammar as a whole.

3.2 Criticisms of internal explanation

Criticisms of internal explanation cannot, in general, be disassociated from criticisms of the various autonomy hypotheses. A common line of reasoning in the functionalist literature concludes from the nonautonomy of, say, syntax that it is irrational to attempt to explain some syntactic phenomenon on the basis of a syntactic principle. Indeed, the assumption is made that any explanation of a syntactic phenomenon demands 'linking' it to something external to syntax.

Even if syntax were nonautonomous, that conclusion would not necessarily follow. Unless one were to dismiss the possibility of *any* syntax-internal generalization, it would still be legitimate to attempt to derive lower level generalizations from higher level ones. But nobody can reasonably reject the idea that *some* generalizations are stateable in purely grammar-internal terms. For example, the reason for (i.e. the explanation of) the fact that subjects of tensed passive verbs in English occur in the nominative case is the fact that *all* subjects of tensed verbs occur in the nominative case. In other words, we have provided an internal explanation, and one which surely no functionalist could dispute. One could go on to ask why subjects have a particular case marking, but that, of course, is a different question.

The correctness of the autonomy theses invites the search for *deep* internal explanations. Given the autonomy of syntax, which posits a rich set of syntax-internal principles, one is naturally led to attempt to formulate the most general, comprehensive, and insightful set of principles possible. In other words, one is led to construct a formal model from which the syntactic properties of the language under consideration follow as an automatic consequence.

One does, to be sure, frequently encounter claims that any model employing theory-internal constructs is *in principle* nonexplanatory:

> In essence, a formal model is *nothing but* a restatement of the facts at a tighter level of generalization.... There is one thing, however, that a formal model can never do: It cannot *explain* a single thing.... The history of transformational-generative linguistics boils down to nothing but a blatant attempt to represent the formalism as 'theory', to assert that it 'predicts a range of facts', that it 'makes empirical claims', and that it somehow 'explains'. (Givón 1979a: 5–6; emphasis in original)

Givón's remarks are addressed in some detail in Newmeyer (1983: 123f.), so I will provide only a brief response to them here. Essentially, Givón confuses two types of models: descriptive (iconic) and theoretical (explanatory). The former indeed *are* 'nothing but a restatement of the facts' and that is all they are intended to be. Zellig Harris, for example, who endeavored to provide a 'compact one-one representation of the stock of utterances in the corpus' (Harris 1951: 366), was committed to a descriptive model. But 'the function of a [theoretical] model is to form the basis of a theory, and a theory is intended to explain some phenomenon' (Harré 1970: 52).

A generative model is a theoretical model and therefore one in which the relationship between data and theory can be extremely indirect. For that reason it is extremely odd to claim that a generative model is 'nothing but a restatement of the facts'. Among other things, such a statement contradicts another frequent criticism of generative work, made by Givón and others, that generative methodology is such as to lead one to *ignore* classes of pertinent facts. A standard functionalist complaint about generative grammar is that its principles, by virtue of their abstractness and great remove from language as it is actually used, *fail* to be, in any ordinary sense of the terms, 'descriptive' or to be responsible to the 'facts'.

I conclude, then, that an internal explanation is, by any criterion, a 'real' explanation. The only question is whether internal explanation is *sufficient*. After a brief look at internal explanation in functional linguistics, we will turn to the question of external explanation.

3.3 Internal explanation in functional linguistics

At a rhetorical level many functionalists have rejected internal explanation in toto. And certainly they put their rhetoric into practice when it comes to dealing with systematic regularities of grammar—there is an absence of any attempt to derive these regularities from deep principles that are themselves grammar-internal. Some functionalists, e.g. Givón, go so far as to claim that there is an ultimate external explanation for every state of grammatical affairs, no matter how seemingly complex: 'In each instance a crazy synchronic state of the grammar has arisen via diachronic changes that are highly natural and presumably motivated independently by various communicative factors' (1979a: 235). Others, e.g. Tomlin (1990), are happy to admit an amount of 'ultimate arbitrariness' to language, that is, to acknowledge that not all structure is a product of function.[1] But it is a defining characteristic of functionalism in linguistics that any 'real' explanation of a grammatical regularity must be external to grammar itself.

Internal explanations are not unknown in functional linguistics, however. They may be found in the large body of literature on the phenomenon of grammaticalization (for overviews, see especially Heine, Claudi, and Hünnemeyer 1991b; Hopper and Traugott 1993). Grammaticalization will be dealt with in detail in chapter 5; for our purposes here it suffices to follow Heine, Claudi, and Hünnemeyer (1991b: 2) in describing it as a case of 'a lexical unit or structure assum[ing] a grammatical function, or ... a grammatical unit assum[ing] a more grammatical function.' Hence, grammaticalization can be exemplified by a verb in the course of time developing auxiliary properties or by an auxiliary reducing to a clitic or tense inflection.

A central hypothesis of most functionalist research is that grammaticalization is unidirectional. That is, it is claimed that we never find an affix upgrading to an auxiliary or an auxiliary upgrading to a true verb. On the

---

1. Tomlin refers approvingly to Robert Merton's rejection of the 'postulate of indispensability' in sociology, which assumes that there is a functional explanation for any existing social structure (see Merton 1949: 32–37).

basis of this assumption, it is common to make deductions about changes in grammars for which we have no direct attestation, as in Heine's work, where complex sequences of historical development are posited for many African languages.

Since unidirectionality is a grammar-internal hypothesis governing the evolution of grammatical forms, appeals to it are as much internal explanations as are appeals to the Case Filter to explain the ungrammaticality of a previously uninvestigated set of sentences. One might object that unidirectionality is 'observed' in language change (and is therefore directly verified), while the Case Filter has never been 'observed'. Even if that were true, it would not bear on whether unidirectionality-based explanations were internal or not. Observability can hardly be a requirement for external explanation, since many such explanations, as we will see below, appeal to human dispositions that are anything but observable. But, in any event, a unidirectionality-based proposal that a particular form in, say, Ibo has the properties that it does is no more directly verifiable on the basis of observable evidence than are claims that the Case Filter is responsible for the ungrammaticality of sentence (4). All that is observed are individual unidirectional changes, not the principle of unidirectionality itself. In fact, the Case Filter has a principled 'observability' that unidirectionality lacks. One can imagine the possibility that the uttering of every sentence claimed to be a Case Filter violation might be accompanied by a characteristic electrical response in the brain. That would constitute direct (external) evidence bearing on the correctness of the filter. Compelling external evidence for unidirectionality would necessarily be more indirect, given that, to the extent that it is correct, it is a consequence of the interaction over historical time of several independent processes, each of whose presumptive unidirectionality has to be defended and explained independently (again, see chapter 5).

4   External Explanation

External explanations for grammatical phenomena are those that appeal to forces outside of grammar proper. In the following sections, we will examine the nature of and justification for the principal forms of external explanations that have been proffered in the literature. Section 4.1 points out that, despite what many might think, to attribute a grammatical principle to innateness is to provide an external explanation for it. Sections 4.2 through 4.7 introduce and discuss external explanations based on processing, iconicity, other aspects of cognition, information flow, text frequency, and economy respectively.

4.1   Innateness as an external explanation

As generative grammar has evolved, the focus of much work has shifted from writing more or less detailed grammars of individual languages to proposing and exploring candidate principles of universal grammar (UG) (for discussion, see Newmeyer 1986a). As noted in the previous chapter (§5.3), the abstractness of these principles and their seeming presence at the earliest stages of language acquisition has suggested that they could never be literally 'learned' by the child—they had to be, in effect, pre-wired into the human brain. Thus the explanans of the theory became in large part a set of innate principles of grammar.

Now, of course, languages differ in their structural properties; we come to know a considerable amount about our grammars that are not shared by the grammars of other languages. In Chomsky (1981), it was suggested that such principles must be 'parameterized' to a certain degree from language to language. That is, each principle admits to a certain degree of possible variation (specified by UG). The child's acquisition process then consists in part of 'fixing the parameters' of his or her language. The full set of possible interactions among parameters yields the set of possible grammars of human languages. In one view expressed by Chomsky, the set of possible parameter settings are innate as well:

What we 'know innately' are the principles of the various subsystems of S_0 [the initial state of the language faculty] and the manner of their interaction, and the parameters associated with these principles. What we learn are the values of these parameters and the elements of the periphery (along with the lexicon, to which similar considerations apply). The language that we then know is a system of principles with parameters fixed, along with a periphery of marked exceptions. (Chomsky 1986b: 150–151)

We are presented with a picture of generative grammar, then, in which via internal explanation one arrives at a set of principles and their possible parameter settings. One explains the existence of these principles and parameters, in turn, by attributing them to the human genome.

To attempt to explain why grammars are organized the way that they are by hypothesizing that certain of their properties are innate is to provide an external explanation for them. For example, to theorize that the Case Filter is innate is to provide an external explanation for why the Case Filter exists in the grammars of human languages. True, we could go on to ask *why* the Case Filter is innate, but then we could ask why *any* proposed external explanation should hold. After all, any explanans is itself an explanandum. Suppose, for example, that we had concluded that a cognitive propensity to favor iconic representations was the explanation for why causative constructions have the properties that they do (see §4.3.2). It naturally then would be fair to go on to ask why we have this cognitive propensity.

Despite these truisms, it is astonishing to see appeals to innateness being dismissed as *inherently* nonexplanatory, as in the following quote (see also Givón 1984: 7; Comrie 1989: 25):

> To 'explain' these facts [about the form of grammars of natural language] by saying that the specification is innate is to my mind to give a non-explanation. We are saying in effect: human languages are the way they are because they are the way they are. (Bach 1974: 169)

Not so at all. We are saying, rather, that they 'are the way they are because evolution did what it did'. Why it did it is another question.

Furthermore, if innate syntactic principles are inherently nonexplanatory, then presumably *any* appeal to a putatively innate human attribute should be inherently nonexplanatory as well. But explanations appealing to innate cognitive dispositions are frequently encountered in the functionalist literature, particularly in work dealing with grammaticalization (again, see chapter 5). For example, Haspelmath (1992: 196) speculates that 'it is very plausible that the fact that human languages change in particular ways but not in others (constrained by theories of language change like Grammaticalization Theory) is ultimately due to innate properties of the human mind (Claudi and Heine 1986)'. The innate predispositions to metaphorical extension that Claudi and Heine have in mind might well exist, and an innate Case Filter might not, but there is no sense in which an appeal to the former has the property of being potentially explanatory, while an appeal to the latter does not.

So the question is not whether 'innateness' qualifies as an external explanation or does not qualify as one; the only question is whether in any particular case it qualifies as a *good* one. And that, in general, is not an easy question to answer (for discussion, see ch. 2, §5).

4.2 Parsing explanations

While there do exist openly 'Platonistic' approaches to formal grammar (e.g. Katz 1981), I think that it is fair to say that most generative grammarians believe that the mental grammars posited by the linguist are actually *used* in the course of speech production and comprehension. For example, in comprehension (which is far easier to theorize about than production), there is evidence that we construct an on-line grammatical representation of the utterance we are hearing and use that representation to access the meaning of the sentence. In standard terminology, we 'parse' the sentence.

It has long seemed reasonable to many generative grammarians that certain features of the grammar arise to allow parsing to take place rapidly and efficiently. That is, the demands of real-time language processing may have 'left their mark' on grammars, in the sense that some grammatical features can be attributed to an accommodation of the grammar to the parser. The following two sections will discuss some proposals along these lines: §4.2.1 reviews some of the earliest parsing explanations for grammatical structure, while §4.2.2 focuses on John A. Hawkins' theory of 'Early Immediate Constituents'.

4.2.1 Some parsing explanations from the 1970s and the 1980s Bever and Langendoen (1971) observed that relative pronouns are freely deletable in Standard English when they originate in object position, but not if they originate in subject position. Note that corresponding to (6a), we have grammatical (6b), while (7b), corresponding to (7a), is ungrammatical:

(6) a. I saw the man who Mary was talking about.
     b. I saw the man Mary was talking about.

(7) a. The man who wants to see the boss is waiting downstairs.
     b. *The man wants to see the boss is waiting downstairs.

Bever and Langendoen attributed the ungrammaticality of (7b) to a parsing strategy (they used the term 'perceptual strategy') that leads the hearer to take an incoming NP-V sequence as the main clause of the sentence. The effects of this strategy were incorporated into the grammar, prohibiting the rule of Relative Pronoun Deletion from applying to produce (7b).

To take another example, Janet Fodor (1978, 1984) has proposed what she calls the 'Nested Dependency Constraint' to explain why sentence (8) has interpretation (9a), but not interpretation (9b). This constraint forbids referential links between gaps and fillers from crossing each other (as in 9b), but does allow them to be nested (as in (9a)). She argues that this

constraint arose as a result of pressure from the parser, which finds interpretations such as (9b) difficult to process:

(8) What are boxes easy to store in?

(9) a. What$_i$ are boxes$_j$ easy to store ____$_j$ in ____$_i$

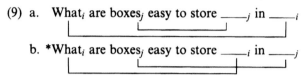

    b. *What$_i$ are boxes$_j$ easy to store ____$_i$ in ____$_j$

Berwick and Weinberg (1984) have argued that the principle of Subjacency also is motivated by parsing pressure. As will be recalled from
Chapter 2, §3.5.2, this principle blocks the extraction of elements from
clauses with certain structures, in particular those headed by complex NPs
(contrast 10a–b) and those with *wh*-phrases in their embedded COMP
position (contrast (11a–b)):

(10) a. You believed the claim that Harry would eat what?
    b. *What did you believe the claim that Harry would eat?

(11) a. You wondered where Jane put what?
    b. *What did you wonder where Jane put?

Berwick and Weinberg take as a starting point the fact that part of the
parser's job is to identify an element's antecedent. But the material
between an antecedent and its coindexed gap can be arbitrarily long. How
then can the parser store all the context to the left of the element that it is
currently analyzing? This is possible, Berwick and Weinberg argue, only if
the left context required for parsing decisions is finitely representable. In
other words, a solution to this parsing problem has resulted in the Subjacency constraint, which helps the parser in precisely the required way,
being built directly into the grammar.

Finally, there have long been attempts to provide parsing explanations
for typological (that is, cross-linguistic) generalizations about grammars.
Kuno (1974), for example, put forward an explanation for some of the
universal tendencies first noted in Greenberg (1963) by appealing to the
perceptual difficulties engendered by center-embedded structures. Greenberg noted that SOV languages invariably have prenominal relative
clauses, while VSO languages invariably have postnominal relatives.
Kuno showed that these correlations are a consequence of the parser's
desire to avoid center-embedded structures. The opposite correlations
would increase the amount of center-embedding in the language. Kuno

also constructed analogous arguments to explain the fact that complementizers and prepositions tend to occur on the left periphery of S' and PP respectively in SVO and VSO languages, and the right periphery in SOV languages.

4.2.2 Early Immediate Constituents By far the most comprehensive of all accounts of the grammaticalization of parsing principles is presented in John A. Hawkins impressive work *A Performance Theory of Order and Constituency* (Hawkins 1994). The central insight guiding this book is that it is in the interest of the parsing mechanism to recognize the syntactic groupings and immediate constituents of a sentence as rapidly as possible. The parser's preference is realized both in performance and in the grammar itself. As far as the former is concerned, when speakers have a choice of word order options, they will, in general, choose that option that the parser prefers. As for the latter, languages will be more likely to grammaticalize preferred orders than nonpreferred ones.

The central parsing principle that Hawkins proposes is called 'Early Immediate Constituents' (EIC) and is stated as follows (1994: 77):

(12) *Early Immediate Constituents (EIC)*
      The human parser prefers linear orders that maximize the
      IC-to-non-IC ratios of constituent recognition domains (CRD).

A 'constituent recognition domain' for a particular phrasal mother node M consists of the set of nodes that have to be parsed in order to recognize M and all of the ICs of M.

EIC explains (among other things) why in Verb-Object languages there is a tendency for heavy constituents to occur at the right margins of their verb phrases; why, for example, (13b) and (14b) are preferred to (13a) and (14a) respectively:

(13) a. ?I consider everybody who agrees with me and my disciples
            about the nature of the cosmos (to be) smart.
      b. I consider (to be) smart everybody who agrees with me and my
            disciples about the nature of the cosmos.

(14) a. ?I met the 23 people who I had taken Astronomy 201 with last
            semester in the park.
      b. I met in the park the 23 people who I had taken Astronomy 201
            with last semester.

Consider (14a–b), whose structures are depicted in (15a–b) respectively. The CRD for the VP in (15a) comprises the distance between the element that constructs the first constituent of VP, namely *met* (which constructs V) and the element that constructs the last constituent of VP, namely *in* (which constructs PP). Expressed as the ratio of the number of constituents of VP (3) over the number of words in the CRD (15),[2] we get a ratio of 3/15 or 20%. The CRD for VP in (15b), however is expressed as a ratio of 3/5 or 60%. The NP is constructed on its left periphery by D, so the remainder of the material in the 'heavy' NP does not count. Since speakers can improve the ratio from 20% to 60% by shifting the NP, EIC predicts (correctly) that they will do just that.

(15) a.

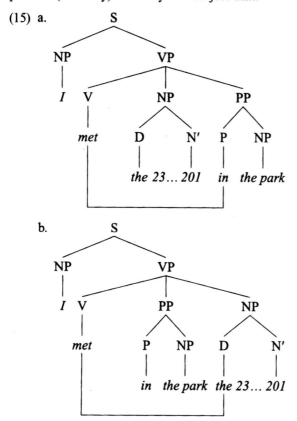

2. Technically, the denominator of the ratio is the number of non-IC constituents, not the number of words. Hawkins often simplifies the calculation by appeal to words, however, and so shall I.

Consider now some typological predictions. As is well known, VO languages, like English, tend to extrapose S′ subjects, while OV languages, like Japanese, tend to prepose S′ objects. Hence in English discourse, the subject of (16a) will almost always be extraposed to (16b), while in Japanese discourse, the object of (17a) will frequently be preposed to (17b):

(16) a. That John will leave is likely.
      b. It is likely that John will leave.

(17) a. Mary-ga [kinoo   John-ga kekkonsi-ta to]   it-ta
          Mary   yesterday John   married   that said
          'Mary said that John got married yesterday'
      b. [kinoo John-ga kekkonsi-ta to] Mary-ga it-ta

EIC provides an explanation. By extraposing the sentential subject in English, the CRD for the main clause is dramatically shortened, as illustrated in (18a–b).[3] By preposing the sentential object in Japanese, we find an analogous CRD shortening, as in (19a–b):

(18) a. $_S[_{S'}$[that $_S$[John will leave]] $_{VP}$[is likely]]

      b. $_S[_{NP}$[it] $_{VP}$[is likely $_{S'}$[that $_S$[John will leave]]]]

(19) a. $_{S_1}$[Mary-ga $_{VP}[_{S'}[_{S_2}$[kinoo John-ga kekkonsi-ta] to] it-ta]]

      b. $_{S_2}[_{S'}[_{S_1}$[kinoo John-ga kekkonsi-ta] to] Mary-ga $_{VP}$[it-ta]]

The above English and Japanese cases illustrate the grammar giving a choice of options to the speaker, who tends to follow the option favored by EIC. Hawkins also applies EIC to explaining the distribution of *grammaticalized* orders, that is, cases where the speaker has no choice about the positioning of phrases. Consider, for example, the explanation of the tendency, observed by Greenberg (1963), for VO languages to be

---

3. Phrase structure (18b) assumes that the extraposed subject is adjoined as a daughter of the topmost S. If, following Reinhart (1983), it is adjoined to VP, things are a little more complicated. The CRD for S is shortened even further. However, the CRD for VP increases, since that node now has three constituents. Hawkins calculates the ratios for an entire sentence by aggregating (i.e. averaging) the ratios for each phrasal domain in the sentence (i.e. the ratios for S and VP will be averaged together). By this method, the aggregate ratio for the sentence with Extraposition will still be higher than for the one without.

prepositional and OV languages to be postpositional. There are four logical possibilities, illustrated in (20a–d): VO and prepositional (20a); OV and postpositional (20b); VO and postpositional (20c); and OV and prepositional (20d):

(20)

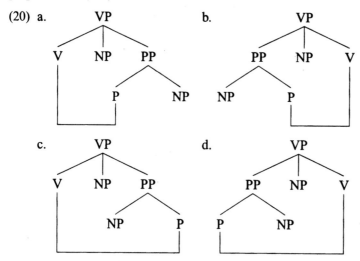

Assuming that both NPs are two words long, the ratio for VP in (20a) and (20b), the two typologically preferred structures, are 3/4, or 75%. But in (20c) and (20d), they are only 3/6, or 50%. Furthermore, the longer the object of the prepositional phrase gets, the worse the ratios will be for (20c) and (20d), while those for (20a) and (20b) will remain the same.

EIC is supplemented with a method for calculating the relative processing ease of constituents with nonoptimal ratios. The essential idea is that linear orderings will be preferred that place the shorter ICs in a leftward position within CRDs.

> [The left-to-right IC-to-non-IC ratios are calculated by] counting the ICs in the domain from left to right (starting from 1), and then counting the non-ICs (or words alone) in the domain (again starting from 1). The first IC is then divided by the total number of non-ICs that it dominates (e.g. 1/2); the second IC is divided by the highest total for the non-ICs that it dominates . . . ; and so on for all subsequent ICs. The ratio for each IC is expressed as a percentage, and these percentages are then aggregated to achieve a score for the whole CRD. (Hawkins 1994: 82–83)

This procedure can be illustrated by considering the 12 logically possible combinations of a noun, an adjective, and a complementizer—sentence sequence within a noun phrase:

(21) a. [N Adj [C S]]   g. [N [C S] Adj]
     b. [Adj N [C S]]   h. [Adj [C S] N]
     c. [[S C] N Adj]   i. [N [S C] Adj]
     d. [[S C] Adj N]   j. [Adj [S C] N]
     e. [N Adj [S C]]   k. [[C S] N Adj]
     f. [Adj N [S C]]   l. [[C S] Adj N]]

These combinations break down into 4 groups as far as EIC is concerned. In (21a–d) the ICs of the NP are recognized in rapid succession—the adjective, the noun, and the complementizer (which constructs the dominating S′) are contiguous. In (21e–l) the constituents of NP are recognized more slowly, since the full sentence intervenes between either the adjective and the complementizer or the noun and the complementizer. By the left-to-right measure, (21e–f) come out fairly well, since the heavy complementizer-final S′ comes late. In (21g–j), recognition is slower, since S′ intervenes between N and Adj; and in (21k–l) slowest of all, since the heavy S′ is the initial constituent of NP and the complementizer is to its left. (22a′), (22e′), (22g′), and (22k′) below illustrate this for (21a), (21e), (21g), and (21k), indicating for each NP first the IC-to-word ratio and then the left-to-right IC-to-word ratio (we assume that S′ dominates 4 words):

(22) a′.   NP   e′.   NP

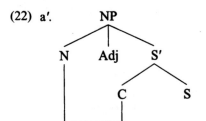

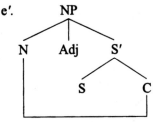

- IC-to-word ratio = 3/3 = 100%
- Left-to-right IC-to-word ratios are 1/1 (100%); 2/2 (100%); 3/3 (100%)
- Aggregate = 100%

- IC-to-word ratio = 3/6 = 50%
- Left-to-right IC-to-word ratios are 1/1 (100%); 2/2 (100%); 3/6 (50%)
- Aggregate = 83.3%

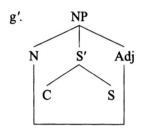

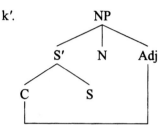

- IC-to-word ratio = 3/6 = 50%
- Left-to-right IC-to-word ratios are 1/1 (100%); 2/5 (40%); 3/6 (50%)
- Aggregate = 63.3%

- IC-to-word ratio = 3/6 = 50%
- Left-to-right IC-to-word ratios are 1/4 (25%); 2/5 (40%); 3/6 (50%)
- Aggregate = 38.3%

EIC makes precisely the right typological predictions: Languages with orders (21a–d) are widely attested; those with (21e–f) are attested, but are not common; of (21g–j), only (21j) has been attested as a marked variant; and no languages at all with orders (21k–l) are known to exist.

EIC also serves to explain the relative cross-linguistic rarity of center-embeddings (for earlier processing accounts, see Kuno 1973, 1974; Dryer 1980) and even greater rarity of self-embeddings (Frazier 1985) and subsumes a number of the individual parsing principles proposed in that latter work.

Hawkins is absolutely clear that the explanation for typological universals that he proposes 'would have been impossible without the structural insights of generative grammar' and, in fact, 'provide strong support ... for many abstract syntactic analyses of the kind generative grammarians have proposed' (1994: 411). But what about specific *models* of generative syntax, in particular the principles-and-parameters approach? Here things are a bit more complicated. In particular, there is nothing in his approach that rules out the idea that learning a language centrally involves setting a series of parameters from which the central structural properties of the language may be derived. However, Hawkins argues that EIC provides a better *explanation* for the ranking and entailment relations among parameter settings than does simply attributing such relations to an innate UG. We will return to contrast the UG with the

EIC-performance approaches to predicting typological generalizations in chapter 6, §7.3.[4]

4.3 Iconicity

A theme pervading much work in the functionalist tradition is that language structure to a considerable degree has an 'iconic' motivation.[5] Roughly, this embodies the idea that the form, length, complexity, or interrelationship of elements in a linguistic representation reflects the form, length, complexity, or interrelationship of elements in the concept, experience, or communicative strategy that that representation encodes.

In this section, I will review some of the evidence for the iconicity of linguistic representations. Section 4.3.1 attempts to define the notion 'iconicity' and §4.3.2 illustrates it with respect to match-ups between syntactic structure and meaning.

4.3.1 Defining 'iconicity'   The notion of 'iconicity' was first introduced into discussions of the relation between form and content, I believe, in work by Charles Sanders Peirce (see especially Peirce 1867/1931, 1885/ 1933, c. 1902/1932). While the following statement hardly does justice to the subtlety and richness of his theory of signs, Peirce identified three different ways that a sign can stand for its referent. In an *iconic* relation, there is some sort of similarity between sign and referent (a map is an obvious example); in an *indexical* relation, the sign points to the referent (as a man's 'rolling gait' points to his being a sailor (Peirce c. 1902/1932: 160)); in a *symbolic* relationship the sign-referent link is an arbitrary one (e.g. the use of the word *bird* in English to refer to a feathered vertebrate).

Peirce identified a type of iconic relation which has been claimed to be manifested widely in language. He wrote: 'Those [icons] which represent the relations ... of the parts of one thing by analogous relations in their own parts, are *diagrams*' (Peirce c. 1902/1932: 157). Much of the linguistic literature on iconicity has pointed to cases of such 'diagrammatic iconicity', in which relations among linguistic structures are paralleled by

---

4. Rohdenburg (1996) takes up from Hawkins's work, demonstrating that the choice of a particular construction in discourse (e.g. a subordinate clauses which is introduced by *that* versus one which is not) is also a function of processing complexity.

5. The material in this section first appeared (in more detailed form) in Newmeyer (1992).

relations among concepts or elements of discourse. In what follows, I will characterize a property of language as 'iconic' only where it bears physical or diagrammatic resemblance to its conceptual or discourse referents.

Unfortunately, the waters are muddied somewhat by the fact that linguistic properties are often referred to as 'iconic' when neither Peirce's characterization nor the ordinary English sense of the term suggest that they should be. Indeed, there is a tendency to label virtually any functional motivation for a linguistic structure as an 'iconic' one, a practice which carried to its logical conclusion results in the terms 'functionally motivated' and 'iconic' becoming all but interchangeable. The most extreme examples of the extended use of the term 'iconicity' that I have discovered are in Givón (1985), where it would appear that any non-arbitrary relation in language qualifies as an iconic one. For example, he takes as an exemplification of iconicity the fact that the position of a main verb on a particular semantic scale correlates with the likelihood of the complement verb being marked for aspect (1985: 200). The reader must therefore take care to interpret the remarks of this section as following as strictly as possible the Peircean sense of the term, rather than its extension by some functionalists.

The major works dealing with iconicity in language (Haiman 1980b, 1983, 1985a, 1985b; Bolinger 1982; Verhaar 1985; Dik 1989: ch. 16–17; Givón 1990: ch. 21, 1991; Croft 1990: ch. 7; Simone 1995) are devoted primarily to defending three distinct claims, though their distinctness is rarely acknowledged. They are:

(23) a. Grammatical structure is an iconic reflection of conceptual structure.
   b. Iconic principles govern speakers' choices of structurally available options in discourse.
   c. Structural options that reflect discourse-iconic principles become grammaticalized.

In this section, I will be concerned only with (23a), structure-concept iconicity. The question of whether grammatical structure iconically reflects discourse structure will be addressed in §4.5 and §5.3.1.

4.3.2 Structure-concept iconicity A number of ways have been suggested in which linguistic structure can iconically reflect conceptual structure. In Newmeyer (1992) I refer to them as iconicity of 'distance',

'independence', 'order', 'complexity', and 'categorization'. Let us briefly
survey each in turn.

Iconicity of distance goes back at least to a principle articulated by
Otto Behagel in 1932: 'This is the most important principle: that which is
closely correlated mentally will also be closely associated physically'
(Behagel 1932: 4; my translation). To illustrate, as is well known, lexical
causatives (e.g. *kill*) tend to convey a more direct causation than periphrastic causatives (e.g. *cause to die*). Hence, we see that where cause and
result are formally separated, conceptual distance is greater than when
they are not. Along the same lines, Haiman (1983, 1985b) suggests that
in no language will the linguistic distance between X and Y be greater in
signaling inalienable possession, in expressions like 'X's Y' than it is in
signaling alienable possession.

Iconicity of distance is illustrated by the fact that the modifiers of a
head tend to form a constituent with that head, a fact first observed in
Bazell (1953: 33–37), if not earlier (see also Rijkhoff 1990). Along the
same lines, Bybee (1985a, 1985b) provides evidence to show that the more
'relevant' an inflection is to a head, the closer it is likely to be to that head
and the more likely it is to be bound to that head (as opposed to occurring
as an independent word), where the 'relevance' of an inflection is measured in terms of the degree to which it directly modifies the head. Thus,
as Greenberg (1963) noted, where number and case morphemes are not
fused, the former are almost always closer to the head than the latter and
less likely to be expressed as independent words. Similarly, the order of
suffixes in West Greenlandic Eskimo correlates with their semantic scope
(Fortescue 1980), the more distant from the head the wider the scope, a
generalization which Foley and Van Valin (1984: 208f.) and Hengeveld
(1989) illustrate for aspect morphemes for a wide variety of languages.

Iconicity of independence is defended in Haiman (1983), where it is
posited that 'the linguistic separateness of an expression corresponds to
the conceptual independence of the object or event which it represents'
(1983: 783). For example, Givón (1980, 1985) argues that the more conceptual control a main verb exerts over a complement verb, the more
likely the latter is to be incorporated with the former and the less likely a
complementizer is to occur in the embedded clause. In both cases, the
number of constituent boundaries between the two verbs correlates with
their conceptual independence. A final example along these lines, provided by Haiman (1983) and Mithun (1984), relates to noun incorpo-

ration. When nouns are incorporated morphologically as subparts of larger words, they tend to have less conceptual independence, as measured by their ability to have independent reference or to be focused or stressed, than do nonincorporated nouns.

Iconicity of order is illustrated by the fact that the order of morphemes or words tends to reflect logical relations among their referents. This is particularly true for scope phenomena in a number of languages. So in English, if one quantifier or negative element precedes another, it is generally interpreted with wider scope (Jackendoff 1972). Greenberg (1963: 103) has claimed that it is often the case that 'the order of elements in language parallels that in physical experience or the order of knowledge'. He points to his 'Universal 14' to illustrate this point: 'In conditional statements, the conditional clause precedes the conclusion as the normal order in all languages' (1963: 111) (for more discussion of the iconic structure of conditional clauses, see Traugott 1974 and Haiman 1978b). Finally, Tai (1985) has observed that in Chinese, the temporal order of constituents is often a grammaticalization of the temporal order of the notions that they encode, and Croft (1991) notes that in Yao, the order of verbs that make up compound verbs is the same as the causal order of the concepts that they denote.

Consider now iconicity of complexity. The idea that linguistic complexity reflects conceptual complexity has long been an important aspect of markedness theory. Marked forms and structures are typically both structurally more complex (or at least longer) than unmarked ones and semantically more complex as well (for discussion within the context of generative grammar, see Lapointe 1986). Reduplicative plurals illustrate iconicity of complexity in an obvious way. And in the realm of syntax, conceptual and structural complexity tend to go hand in hand. Any modification or elaboration of one meaning-bearing grammatical element by another (as in processes of relativization, subordination, or whatever), leads to the increase of both types of complexity.

As far as iconicity of categorization is concerned, concepts that fall into the same grammatical category tend to be cognitively similar. Thus grammatical subjects tend to correlate with agents and grammatical objects with patients. In general, differences in case correlate with semantic differences. For example, in Spanish sentences with accusative-dative minimal pairs, accusative case tends to suggest a more direct link between verb and object than dative. As Haiman (1983) notes: '*Contestar la pregunta* 'answer the question' means to succeed in answering the question. The

intransitive counterpart *contestar a la pregunta* means to contribute a
response to the question (but not a satisfactory one)' (1983: 790).

A great number of studies have shown that lexical categories tend to
have semantic (or, in some cases, discourse) correlates (see Bolinger 1966;
Dixon 1977; Givón 1979a, 1984: ch. 3; Hopper and Thompson 1984,
1985; Wierzbicka 1986b; Langacker 1987b; Thompson 1988; Croft 1991).
Conventions for naming types of living things also illustrate iconicity of
categorization. Rosch (1978) demonstrated that there is a level of 'basic'
perceptual categories that have special psychological salience. For example, life forms at the specific level are generally regarded as conceptually
more complex than those at the generic level; the former are perceived
as being subcases of the latter. Linguistic categorization reflects this. In
many languages, names for species are compounds consisting of the
names for genera and a distinguishing feature (Berlin 1978).

4.4 Some other cognitively-based explanations
The functionalist literature points to a great variety of other cognitively-
based explanans for grammatical structure, a few of which will be mentioned in this section. One is a propensity to classify the objects of our
experience in terms of prototypes and degrees of divergence from the
prototype. It is claimed that this propensity has left its mark on grammar:
virtually every grammatical construct, from semantic and syntactic categories, to intonation contours to grammatical constructions, has been
argued to be endowed with a prototype structure (for an overview, see
Taylor 1989). We will return to discuss the putative grammatical reflection of prototype-categorization in some detail in chapter 4.

Another cognitively-based factor said to play a role in explaining why
grammatical structure has the properties that it does is metaphor. Bybee
and Pagliuca (1985: 75) write of a cognitively based 'natural propensity
for making metaphorical extensions'. The notion of metaphor playing a
prominent place in the grammar has been a consistent theme in the work
of George Lakoff and others in cognitive linguistics. The basic idea is that
grammatical categories have a radial structure, where elements are related
by means of metaphoric principles. Consider, for example, the Japanese
classifier *hon* (Lakoff 1987; Lee 1988). *Hon* has a central sense of classifying long, thin, rigid objects, such as sticks, canes, pencils, candles, and
trees. However, metaphors, *still said to be operative in the grammar of
Japanese*, motivate extended senses of *hon*: it classifies martial arts contests (since they are fought with long thin rigid staffs and swords), judo

matches (by analogy to martial arts contests), letters (since they were originally written on long stick-like scrolls), and telephone calls (by metaphorical extension from letters). I will discuss further the question of metaphor and grammar in the appendix to chapter 4.

Finally, Ferguson and Barlow (1988) have even suggested that grammatical structure might be in part a response to a human propensity to 'playfulness', speculating that grammatical agreement might persist and even spread 'in response to the same kind of factors at work in the conventionalization and persistence of rhymed word-pairs, prose rhythms, patterned repetitions, and the like' (1988: 17–18).

4.5   Explanations based on information flow in discourse

A commonly appealed to form of external explanation is based on the self-evident facts that language is used to communicate, and that communication involves the conveying of information. Consequently, it is argued, the nature of information flow should leave, and has left, its mark on grammatical structure. This has been the guiding assumption in probably the great majority of functionalist publications. For example, the Introduction to a major anthology on word order variation begins by offering the opinion that:

> Explanatory factors behind word order variation are to be found in studies of how the mind grammaticizes forms, processes information, and speech act theory considerations of speakers' attempts to get their hearers to build one, rather than another, mental representation of incoming information. (Payne 1992: 2)

Consider, by way of example, a suggested explanation of why ergative clause patterns are so common cross-linguistically (that is, cases in which the subject of an intransitive verb and the object of a transitive verb receive the same (absolutive) morphological marking). Du Bois (1985, 1987) studied narratives in Sacapultec, an ergative language, and found that clauses with two full noun phrases are quite rare. Typically only one occurs in actual discourse: either the intransitive subject or the transitive object. Furthermore, it is just these argument types that are used to introduce new participants in the discourse. Du Bois suggests that the combination of a verb and absolutive NP is a 'preferred argument structure' and concludes: 'We may thus hypothesize that the grammaticization of morphological ergativity in Sacapultec is ultimately a crystallization of certain patterns in discourse' (1985: 353). In other words, ergativity is motivated by principles of information flow.

Information-flow-based explanations have commonly been given to explain the ordering of clausal and phrasal elements. In English, for example, (24a) and (24b) are both possible sentences:

(24) a. Mary bought some motor oil and went to the supermarket.
     b. Mary went to the supermarket and bought some motor oil.

These sentences both convey the same propositions, namely 'Mary bought some motor oil' and 'Mary went to the supermarket'. However, they differ in that (24a) normally conveys the idea that Mary bought the oil before going to the supermarket and (24b) that Mary did so at the supermarket or after going there. Schmerling (1975) has suggested that speakers follow Grice's maxim governing successful conversation: 'Be orderly' (Grice 1975). This principle leads them to produce and interpret temporally sequenced constituents in temporal order. The evidence that an extragrammatical discourse principle shapes the spoken order of conjuncts (rather than, say, a rule of semantic interpretation) is the fact that the interpretation in which grammatical ordering parallels real-time ordering can be canceled by the speaker: *Mary bought some motor oil and went to the supermarket—but not in that order.* In Gricean terms, then, (24a) conversationally implicates, but does not entail, that Mary bought the oil before going to the supermarket.[6]

Tai (1985) points to the Chinese serial VP construction as a case of where the above-mentioned Gricean maxim has been grammaticalized, so that speakers have no choice but to interpret sequences of constituents which can be assigned a temporal order in that temporal order:

(25) a. Zhāngsān [dào túshūguǎn] [ná shū]
        Zhangsan reach library   take book
        'John went to the library to get the book'

---

6. 'Be orderly' is a submaxim of the Maxim of Manner, which encompasses principles such as 'Avoid obscurity of expression'. A pragmatic account of sentences like (24a–b) is defended in Wilson (1975: ch. 5), Gazdar (1979: ch. 3), Levinson (1983: ch. 3), Horn (1989: §6.2), and Carston (1993), but rejected in favor of a semantic account in Bar-Lev and Palacas (1980), McCawley (1981: ch. 3), and Kempson (1986). For a more sophisticated approach to temporal interpretation, one which integrates Gricean-style maxims with a formal theory of default-reasoning (and thereby accounts for discourses like *Caesar died. Brutus stabbed him*), see Lascarides and Asher (1991).

   b. Zhāngsān [ná shū]   [dào túshūguǎn]
      Zhangsan take book reach library
      'John took the book to the library'

An interpretation of (25a) in which John had the book before going to the library is impossible, as is one of (25b) in which John did not handle the book until after reaching the library.[7]

Information-flow-based principles have also been appealed to in order to explain the ordering of the major elements within a clause. To repeat an example from the previous chapter, in Russian, the proposition 'Daddy has brought a Christmas tree' may be expressed in (at least) the following three ways (Vachek 1966: 90):

(43) a. Pápa prinjós jólku. (SUBJ VERB OBJ)
      b. Jólku prinjós pápa. (OBJ VERB SUBJ)
      c. Jólku pápa prinjós. (OBJ SUBJ VERB)

It has been suggested that speakers of Russian exploit different word order possibilities depending on the relative information content contributed by the subject, verb, and object. As we noted in chapter 2, an early consensus view was that information generally moves from the more thematic to the less, where thematic information is that shared by speaker and hearer and connected in a specific way to the 'goal' of the discourse.[8] This idea has been expressed by Firbas (1964, 1966, 1987) in terms of the notion 'Communicative Dynamism' (CD):[9]

---

7. Tai does not analyze (25a–b) as a grammaticalization of a Gricean implicature. Rather, he appeals to an independent 'Principle of temporal sequencing' under which he subsumes Chinese cases parallel to (24a–b) as well. So if in Chinese two sentences are separated by the simple conjunction *bingqie* 'and', as in English, temporal sequence is conversationally implicated, but not entailed. For reasons that I do not understand, functionalists virtually never appeal to Gricean maxims, but tend to propose instead discourse-based principles of lesser generality.

8. Alongside the opposition thematic vs. non-thematic (or rhematic), we also have old information vs. new information, ground vs. figure, topic vs. comment, and a number of others. These terminological distinctions are used differently by different investigators, and in some approaches coexist (in different senses) in one particular analysis.

9. Jakobson (1963) deemed this principle an iconic one, since the flow of information from old to new matches the flow in time of the speech act.

By a degree of CD I understand the relative extent to which a linguistic element contributes towards the further development of communication.... [The analyst] can arrange the elements [of a sentence] interpretively in accordance with a gradual rise of CD. (Firbas 1987: 291–292)

It has been claimed that the effects of this principle are also found in languages in which the speaker has little choice in the ordering of elements. Consider English, where the subject must rigidly appear before the verb—a 'grammatical word order language', in the terms of Thompson (1978). Thompson claims that it is just such languages that have a number of what are described in the generative literature as 'movement transformations' i.e. processes that promote material from post-verbal position to signal its functioning as a discourse theme and demoting subjects to signal their playing the discourse role of focus. Among the former are Passive, *Tough*-movement, and Raising; among the latter are *It*-cleft and *wh*-cleft:

(27) a. Tom's latest theory has just been proven wrong.
     b. Linda is fun to speak French with.
     c. George is likely to need a ride.

(28) a. It's Vicki who made the announcement.
     b. What Robbie needs is someone to sign with.

In other words, we have a discourse-based explanation for the existence of such 'transformational' processes in languages like English.

Along the same lines, a thematic-first explanation has been applied to an explanation of why, in the overwhelming majority of the world's languages, subjects precede objects. The ordering follows automatically, given the assumption (defended in Lyons 1977: 510–511) that subjects are more likely to be thematic than objects.[10]

However, beginning with the publication of Tomlin and Rhodes (1979)'s work on Ojibwa, evidence began to accumulate that in some languages thematic information (old information, the topic, etc.) tends to

---

10. For attempts to explain the general tendency for subjects to precede objects, see also Mathesius (1929), Behagel (1932), Jakobson (1963), Chafe (1970, 1976), Pullum (1977), Emonds (1980), Mallinson and Blake (1981), Hawkins (1983), Du Bois (1985, 1987), Tomlin (1986), Lambrecht (1987), Manning and Parker (1989), and Croft (1990: ch. 3). Not all of these explanations take 'communicative dynamism' as a basic explanans. Tomlin (1986), for example, attempts to derive the theme-before-rheme principle from the more fundamental process of attention in human cognition.

come *late* in the sentence, rather than early. In a sweeping reanalysis of previously accepted wisdom, Givón (1988) presents a pragmatic principle incompatible with Communicative Dynamism to explain constituent ordering, namely the principle of 'Communicative Task Urgency'. A communicative task is said to be more urgent when the information to be communicated is either less predictable or more important. Predictability and importance are claimed to control word order in the following way:

Given the preceding discourse context, less predictable information is fronted. . . . Given the thematic organization of the discourse, more important information is fronted. (1988: 275)

Givón illustrates the principle of Communicative Task Urgency by citing studies of Ute (Givón 1983), Papago (Payne 1987), and Cayuga (Mithun 1987), as well as Ojibwa.

4.6   Text frequency as an explanatory factor

Language users possess what William Labov (1994: 598) has aptly described as an 'extraordinary sensitivity . . . to frequency'. In particular, language changes at every level of grammar appear to be related in some way to the relative frequency of use of a particular word or grammatical element. For example, it is well known that certain sound changes are diffused through the lexicon earliest in frequently-occurring items (see Labov 1994 and the references cited there). My own Philadelphia dialect of English illustrates this fact. Reflexes of Middle English short /o/ have advanced to diphthong status in common words, but retain the more 'standard' American /a/ in those that are less common. Hence I have the contrasts illustrated in table 3.1.[11] These facts seem to show that speakers are in some sense 'aware' of the relative frequency of use of certain words, and this awareness must form some component of a full explanation of sound change.

As far as morphology is concerned, one of the tests for whether a member of a grammatical opposition is marked or unmarked is its relative text frequency (see Greenberg 1966; Croft 1990, 1991; Hawkins 1996). Unmarked singulars are more frequent in discourse than more marked plurals, which in turn are more frequent than still more marked duals. The text frequencies of nominatives are higher than that of accusatives, which are higher than that of datives. Here again, as frequency

---

11. Labov's own dialect is apparently similar (see Labov 1994: 530).

Table 3.1
Some vowel contrasts in the author's dialect of English

/ɔw/	/a/
on, off	honor, offal, don, doff, Goth
dog	frog, log, bog
loss	floss
strong, song, wrong	gong, tong, King Kong
cost, frost	Pentecost

decreases, markedness increases. As is well known, morphological change tends in the direction of reduced markedness. Hence, a language will lose a dual inflection before a plural inflection and languages which at one time had a nominative-accusative-dative (NAD) case system may syncretize AD or all of NAD, but rarely, if ever, syncretize NA, preserving D, or syncretize ND, preserving A. Quite plausibly, then, frequency plays a role in explaining why morphological systems have the properties that they do.

At the level of syntax, changing text frequency has been argued by Lightfoot (1991) to be a central component of the loss of OV order in the history of English. In Old English, speakers had the choice of both OV and VO order, but (for reasons we can ignore here) OV was basic. However:

As matrix instances of object-verb diminished [in frequency] to a certain point, underlying object-verb order became unlearnable and the verb-order parameter came to be set differently.... Changes in the primary linguistic data, if they show a slight cumulative effect, might have the consequence of setting a grammatical parameter differently. That is what seems to have happened with English verb order. (Lightfoot 1991: 67–68)

All linguists would agree that text frequency is a response to a variety of factors, from cognitive complexity to pragmatic usefulness. The question is to what extent frequency itself can legitimately be called upon as an 'explanation' for whatever phenomena seem to be sensitive to it. Hawkins (1996), in fact, has argued that frequency provides a 'direct explanation' for the performance-grammar correlations that we observe in the morphological hierarchies described above. He represents two alternatives schematically as in figures 3.1 and 3.2. In the first, there is a chain of explanation, in which frequency is an intermediate link in the chain

Figure 3.1
Morphological hierarchies as a direct consequence of frequencies.

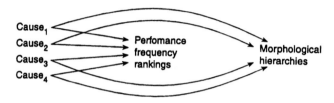

Figure 3.2
Morphological hierarchies as an indirect consequence of frequencies.

between ultimate cause and ultimate effect. In the second, the hierarchies and the frequency effects are both direct effects of the ultimate causes.

Hawkins opts for the situation depicted in figure 3.1, in which the properties of morphological systems can be attributed to a *direct* effect of frequency and provides three reasons for his decision. First, he argues that the plausible causes for frequency rankings are not necessarily plausible as direct explanations for morphologization. Let's say that a clause containing a dative is cognitively more complex than a clause containing a nominative. That may provide a reason, he suggests, for using datives less frequently than nominatives, but not for removing a distinct dative morpheme from one's morphological inventory. Second, it is likely that speakers are unconsciously more aware of frequency rankings than of the causes of those rankings. And third, Hawkins argues that considerations of generality favor the model depicted in figure 3.1 over that depicted in figure 3.2.

While Lightfoot does not claim that the changes in word order frequency 'explain' the change in underlying order, typically functional linguists do refer to (changes in) frequency as 'explaining' syntactic change. Consider, for example, the discussion in Dryer (1995) of developments in O'oodham (Papago). That language has apparently been undergoing a change from GenN order to NGen order and a change from postpositions to prepositions. At the same time, Dryer notes, VS and VO order have become more frequent than SV and OV (which in turn is a consequence of

O'oodham word order being driven by definiteness). In Dryer's view, it is
these S-V-O frequency changes that are most directly responsible for
speakers shifting to postposed genitives and prepositions. He writes that
'it is necessary to appeal to the frequency facts in order to explain word
order changes that have been occurring in the language' (1995: 132).[12]

4.7 Economy
A frequently appealed to external motivation is 'economy'. The basic idea
of economy is that, all other things being equal, the desire of speakers and
hearers to perform the 'least (amount of) effort' or to do things in the
'simplest' way will leave their mark on grammatical structure. Haiman
(1983) gives a number of examples. Most illustrate the reduced expression of predictable information. For example, in a number of languages
reflexivity can be expressed both by a full form and by a reduced form,
say an affix. The desire for economy has led to the reduced form being
most common with verbs whose reflexivity is the norm (e.g. *shave*).

4.8 Summary
As we have seen, a multitude of factors have been put forward as possible
(partial) explanations for why grammatical structure has the properties
that it has. In the next section, we will take on the question of identifying
which of them can be regarded as *convincing* explanations.

5   Convincing and Unconvincing External Explanations

Given the seemingly open-ended number of potential motivators of
grammatical structure, only a subset of which were outlined in the previous section, one might wonder if there is any reliable means of identifying which are convincing and which can be dispensed with. I will
suggest that there is and, in §5.1, will put forward three criteria by which
a convincing external explanation might be identified. In §5.2 I will suggest that two proposed external principles, the parsing principle of Early
Immediate Constituents and pressure for structure-concept iconicity,
come close to fulfilling these criteria. Section 5.3 explains why I regard
appeals to information flow, frequency, and economy to be unsatisfactory
potential explanans for the nature of syntactic structure.

12. For other functionalist work crucially appealing to frequency, see Fox (1987),
Dryer (1989a), and Fox and Thompson (1990).

5.1 Three criteria for identifying an external motivation

Suppose that we have been presented with some factor that has been claimed to be an external motivation for linguistic structure. How can we test such a claim? I would suggest that in order to be confirmed in this regard, the candidate motivation must meet three criteria. First, it must lend itself to precise formulation. We would be loath to identify cigarette smoking as a cause of lung cancer if we had no precise way of gauging whether and how much people smoked. Consider, by way of contrast, the popular idea that one's 'state of mind', 'attitude toward life', 'personality type', and so on are factors in the incidence of cancer. While there may ultimately be something to such ideas, we can hardly rank them with smoking as a cause of the disease—they simply are not precise enough. Along the same lines, the first criterion automatically excludes appeal to such notions as 'predispositions toward metaphor', 'speaker empathy', 'playfulness', and many others from being convincing external explanations for the nature of grammatical structure. That does not mean, of course, that they are *not* motivating factors. It is simply that, given their fuzziness, we have at the present time no way of testing whether they are or not.

Second, we have to be able to identify a *linkage* between cause and effect. For cigarette smoking and cancer, the linkage—that is, the effect of the components of smoke upon cells—is well understood. The linkage problem is much greater, unfortunately, when we are dealing with cognitive structures rather than with overt biological ones. Any argument appealing to cause and effect will necessarily be more indirect, particularly given the poorly understood relationship between neurological structures and cognitive structures. Nevertheless, as I will suggest in the next section, the linkage problem can to a certain degree be overcome in evaluating potential external causative factors for grammatical structure.

And third, any proposed external motivation must have measurable typological consequences. Just as we know that the more people smoke, the more likely they are to contract lung cancer, we have to demonstrate that the more the proposed grammar-affecting factor is manifest, the more languages will reflect its operation.

5.2 Two prime candidates for external explanans

I am convinced of the existence of only two external motivating factors for grammatical structure. The first, Early Immediate Constituents (EIC), already meets the three criteria that I feel are necessary for confirmation in this regard. The second, external pressure for structure-concept iconicity has the *potential* to be confirmed, though the necessary testing remains to be carried out.

The question of innateness as an external motivation for grammatical structure raises special problems, some of which have been addressed in the previous chapter (§5.3) and above (§4.1). As far as 'linkage' is concerned, for any innate grammatical principle such must have taken place at the level of the evolution of the species. Much of Newmeyer (in preparation) will be devoted to the question of the plausibility of such a development.

5.2.1 Early Immediate Constituents EIC meets all three criteria for a compelling explanans. First, it can be and has been formulated precisely (see §4.2.2). The notions 'IC-to-non-IC ratios' and 'constituent recognition domain' are sufficiently rigorous to allow the predictions of EIC to be tested. More problematic, however, is the fact that for most sentences there is little accord among grammarians as to their correct constituent structure. Hawkins is able to show that in many cases EIC makes the same predictions for each alternative proposed structure for a given sentence or sentence type. But often the predictions are different, admittedly weakening any claim as to EIC's success.

Second, there is a highly plausible linkage between EIC and grammatical structure. The advantage of parsing sentences rapidly can hardly be cast into doubt. Grammars are models of *knowledge*. Speaking and understanding involve drawing on that knowledge and 'packaging' and 'unpackaging' it in real time. Hence, procedures for doing this (un)packaging have to exist. It stands to reason, then, that grammatical structure might have been shaped in part as a response this need. And we know that parsing is fast and efficient. In language production, every word has to be identified from an ensemble of more than 50,000 stored forms in less than a third of a second and assembled into a structure that correctly represents the meaning intended by the speaker. The hearer has to perform the same process in reverse and rarely makes mistakes in assigning the correct grammatical structure to the incoming flow of speech. In other words, we have a link between parsing efficiency and grammatical structure that seems as compelling as that between the carcinogens of a cigarette and the cancerous mutations of cells.

And third, the typological predictions of EIC have been confirmed. There is a direct correlation between strength of the EIC effect and the typological frequency of the structural type in question—one that Hawkins and his collaborators have been able to demonstrate for literally dozens of grammatical features.

In short, we have every reason to accept EIC as a factor that has contributed to the shaping of grammatical structure.

5.2.2 Pressure for structure-concept iconicity According to structure-concept iconicity, grammatical structure reflects, to a significant degree, conceptual structure. Let us suggest that external pressure for this reflection (henceforth PSCI) is an important external motivating factor for grammatical structure. Why should this pressure exist? What might be pushing form and meaning into a high degree of alignment? I suggest that this pressure has its roots in parsing as much as does the fact that grammatical structure is organized to facilitate the rapid recognition of constituents. In other words, I think that Givón is on the right track when he suggests that 'all other things being equal, a coded experience is easier to store, retrieve, and communicate if the code is maximally isomorphic to the experience' (Givón 1985: 189). Experimental evidence bears out the idea that semantic interpretation of a sentence proceeds on line as the syntactic constituents are recognized (Marslen-Wilson 1975; Potter and Faulconer 1979; Frazier 1985). For purely functional reasons, then, one would expect grammatical and semantic constituents to exhibit a certain degree of alignment.

PSCI seems quite capable of precise formulation. So, for example, one might consider integrating Jackendoff's principle of Argument Fusion into a processing model that prefers 'simple' fusions (however they may be defined) to complex ones, thereby yielding iconicity of distance:

(29) *Argument Fusion*
    To form the conceptual structure of a syntactic phrase that has been
    linked with an LCS (lexical conceptual structure), fuse the
    conceptual structure of each indexed syntactic position into the
    coindexed conceptual constituent in the LCS. (Jackendoff 1990: 264)

As far as iconicity of order is concerned, Hawkins (1997: 761) has already suggested that it can be derived from a processing preference that he calls 'Dependent Nodes Later':

(30) *Dependent Nodes Later*
    If a node Y is semantically and/or syntactically dependent on a node
    X, then the human parser prefers to receive and parse X before Y.

PSCI remains to be tested as rigorously as EIC has been tested. My guess is that as the structurally definable distance increases between two nodes, the less likely it is that those nodes will form a semantic unit, whether within the grammar of a single language or cross-linguistically. Likewise, I suspect that one would find analogous effects with semantic dependence and linear order. If so, then I would not hesitate to point to PSCI as an important factor in giving shape to grammatical structure.

In summary, EIC and PSCI strike me as the two best candidates for external forces shaping grammatical structure.

5.3 Appeals to information flow, frequency, and economy—three problematic explanans of syntactic patterning

There are undoubtedly external motivations for grammatical structure beyond those discussed in the previous section. However, I will argue in this section that three that have been suggested—information flow, frequency, and economy—are highly problematic. The first appears to be empirically unmotivated, while the latter two, it seems, can generally be reduced to processing effects.

5.3.1 Is information flow irrelevant to syntax?
In this section, I will address claims that syntactic structure is to a significant degree a response to discourse pressure to optimize information flow (see §4.5). I will conclude that there is little reason to believe that this is actually the case.

In one crucial instance where parsing-based and information flow-based principles make different predictions about grammatical structure, it is the former that are borne out. Recall that two conflicting pragmatic principles have been put forward to explain the order of the major constituents of a sentence: 'Communicative Dynamism' and 'Communicative Task Urgency'. The former leads, in general, to the prediction that given information should precede new information (GN) and the latter to the prediction that new information should precede given information (NG).[13] Both make predictions that are at odds with EIC. Hawkins

---

13. Hawkins notes, correctly in my opinion, that 'The Prague School theory of given-before-new ordering seems to be particularly *non*functional: why should each sentence begin with what has already been presented, delaying the newest information till the very end? There are plausible cognitive explanations for the positioning of a topic before a comment (cf. Sasse 1987), but the theory of communicative dynamism is more general than this, claiming that given before new holds for all adjacent items throughout a sentence' (1994: 116–117).

(1994: §4.4) argues, on the basis of the relative orderings of NPs and PPs in English, Hungarian, German, and Japanese, that it is the predictions made by EIC that are correct. Using several different methods of measurement, Hawkins found that the correlations between order and syntactic weight are considerably more robust than those between order and information status. Interestingly, where EIC predicts short before long ICs (as in English, Hungarian, and German), we tend to find given before new; where EIC predicts long before short ICs (as in Japanese), we tend to find new before given. Hawkins asks:

> Is this to be expected? Most certainly it is. It follows logically because new information for the hearer will generally require more linguistic material for referent identification, and hence longer NPs and PPs, whereas predictable items can regularly be referred to by single-word pronouns or proper names, or by short(er) definite full NPs. So if EIC predicts short before long, there should be a correlation with given before new, and conversely for long before short. (1994: 238)

In other words, the discourse-based explanans of longest standing, that of given information preceding new information, *and* its converse, are both incorrect.

It is important to stress that Hawkins is not denying that there might exist *conventionalized associations* between syntactic position and discourse function. Clearly there are such associations. Subjects in English do tend to be the most 'topical arguments'. As noted in chapter 2, §4.2.2, there are structural focus positions in English. Many languages go even further, and grammaticalize particular discourse-configurational nodes, as is exemplified by the topic and focus constituents in Hungarian. However, he argues that the ultimate explanation for the *positioning* of constituents conveying particular discourse-relevant information is primarily processing-based, rather than discourse based. Subjects in English are associated with givenness, not because given information naturally comes early, but because given information tends to be short and the processing of English, a head-initial language, is more efficient if short constituents precede long constituents.

Other purported effects of discourse on syntax are equally dubious. Recall, for example, Du Bois' attempt to ground ergativity patterns in information flow (see §4.5). While his remarks are certainly thought-provoking, problems remain that vitiate his account. First, and perhaps least seriously, it provides no explanation of why most languages as far as NPs are concerned are either wholly ergative or wholly nominative, rather than split along person. Second, there is the question of morphological vs.

syntactic ergativity. A minority of languages are ergative morphologically; a tiny minority syntactically (Sacapultec Maya, Du Bois' language, is hardly ergative syntactically at all—see Du Bois 1987: 809). Why should this be, if discourse pressure is such a major 'motivator' of grammar? Third, Du Bois' account is challenged by the many other explanations that already exist for the origins of ergative systems, including those with split ergativity (Anderson 1977, 1988; Chung 1978; Garrett 1990b; Harris and Campbell 1995: §9.2.8). It is clear that many of these point to pressure from within the linguistic system itself for the rise of ergative case marking. For example, Garrett (1990b) has proposed an alternative, and (in my view) more compelling account of the origins of NP-split ergativity than that put forward by Du Bois, namely that ergatively marked NPs develop from instrumentals in null-subject languages. From the fact that instrumental NPs are overwhelmingly third person, it follows that their descendant ergatives will be far more likely to be third person than first or second. Fourth, Herring (1989) shows that verb-absolutive pairings seem to form a 'preferred argument structure' for the presentation of new information only because Du Bois excluded from consideration nonarguments of the verb. And finally, O'Dowd (1990) has argued that Du Bois' results are an artifact of the structure of narratives per se. When other types of discourses such as lectures or dialogues are examined, we do not find subjects of intransitives and objects of transitives lining up together.

By way of a general critique of information flow explanations for grammatical phenomena, consider the question of whether the passive construction is in some sense 'discourse-iconic', that is, whether its structure reflects to some significant degree its use. The classical functionalist answer, based on Communicative Dynamism, is 'yes': logical patients are promoted to subject position to downplay the agent of the action if it is unknown or unimportant and at the same time to express the topichood of the nonagent. This in itself is normally related to maximizing the efficiency of the exchange of information in discourse.

But an information flow explanation of the properties of passives—indeed for the properties of *any* construction—fails for several (rather different) reasons. First, to the extent that topics do occur before nontopics (in English), we do not need to appeal to the flow of discourse at all. As discussed above, EIC predicts this ordering. Second, it is often the case that when the use of a passive is determined by some property of the discourse, that property is not a pragmatic one based in information flow. Weiner and Labov (1983) have found that the use of a passive is to a significant degree a function of the use of a passive in the preceding utterance or of a propensity to maintain coreferential subjects in the same syntactic position (see also Estival 1985). In other words, the desire of speakers to maintain structural parallelism is an important motivating force in actual speech. Other studies have found analogous parallelism effects in the use of questions (Levelt and Kelter 1982) and indirect object constructions (Bock 1986).

Third, there is little reason to believe that the conveying of information is a central function of language to begin with. As Van Valin (1981: 59) has noted:[14]

Language is used to establish, reinforce, maintain, and express social relationships rather than convey information. In the literature of the ethnography of communication there are numerous case studies of verbal interactions in which the exchange of information is minimal but the social aspect is maximal (see Bird and Shopen 1979; Keenan and Ochs 1979; Haviland 1980).

Fourth, information flow-based explanations of grammatical structure attribute to speakers and hearers more knowledge, whether overt or covert, than they actually are likely to have. At any given point in a conversational exchange, do we really have a clue as to what our information state is, or what that of our addressee might be? I doubt it. Labov (1994: 549–550) is surely correct in pointing out that 'there is no reason to think that our notions of what we intend or the intentions we attribute to others are very accurate, or that we have any way of knowing whether they are accurate.... If functional theories of language change and variation are theories of intentions, they will be leading us down a very slippery path indeed'.

And finally, the temporal precedence that a grammatical analysis of a string takes over a pragmatic analysis increases the plausibility that the former factor would exert its influence on grammatical structure more readily than the latter. Hawkins (1994: 116) remarks that:

The recognition of linguistic form, i.e. sound units, word units, and larger syntactic units, logically precedes the assignment of meaning to these units, because

---

14. Van Valin rejects the position of Givón (1979a: 52) that 'narrative [is] the most basic discourse type' (see also Hinds 1979 and Longacre 1979 for a similar idea). He writes (1981: 58) that underlying this approach 'is an essentially Aristotelian view of the nature of language and its function, a view which treats the social function of language as secondary or derivative'.

one cannot begin to assign a meaning to a given form, activating in the process one's grammatical knowledge of form-meaning pairings, unless one knows what form it is that is to be interpreted. Hence, form processing must, in general, have priority over content, given that both semantic and pragmatic processing require prior access to form.

The spectacular failure of Communicative Dynamism and Communicative Task Urgency has led Hawkins to 'a radical and controversial conclusion: pragmatics appears to play no [explanatory] role whatsoever' in linear ordering (1994: 240–241). Indeed, a convincing example of a thoroughgoing iconic reflection of a discourse function by a syntactic structure is such a rarity that Prince has remarked that 'the felt iconicity of some syntactic constructions with respect to some discourse function is no doubt simply a metalinguistic illusion: if a syntactic construction "feels" iconic to the speakers of its language . . . , then it must be the case that such feelings of iconicity are acquired with the language' (1988: 171).

5.3.2 Text frequency and syntactic patterning There can be no doubt that language learners and users are, in some sense, sensitive to the frequency of occurrence of (certain) grammatical elements. From this observation, nevertheless, I am loath to go on to conclude that frequency is a legitimate explanatory factor insofar as the nature of grammar is concerned. Consider, for example, the well-known markedness hierarchy for grammatical number: singular > plural > dual. This hierarchy is manifested in a number of ways, of which I will call attention to two. First, morpheme length increases in the direction of increased markedness. Second, the existence of a morpheme lower on the hierarchy implies the existence of one higher. The existence of a dual morpheme, for example, implies the existence of a plural.

To what extent is it necessary to appeal to the increased text frequency of singulars over plurals and of plurals over duals to explain these facts? None at all, I would say. It is not frequency per se that makes singular morphemes shorter than plural morphemes. Rather it is some principle involving ease of production that makes frequent items shorter than infrequent ones. Likewise, it is not infrequent use that encourages speakers to jettison duals before they jettison plurals. Rather, it is lack of usefulness that makes infrequent items dispensable.

To be more concrete, let's say that at one stage in its history, Language L had three morphologically distinct numbers: singular, plural, and dual. At a later stage it had only a singular and a plural. A language learner at the first stage would presumably have registered the fact that he or she heard duals used less often than singulars and plurals and plurals less often than singulars. Now, how does that fact in any way explain why that particular learner, let us say, stopped using the dual form? In a nutshell, it doesn't. Rather, we have to appeal to an economy principle that says something like: 'The less frequent an item is, the more dispensable it is'. (Lack of) frequency in other words is not the explanation for the loss of the dual form; rather it is part of the background conditions that make the explanation possible.

As the reader will recall, in §4.6 I presented Hawkins (1996)'s alternative models of the relationship between morphological hierarchies and frequency. In the first, represented schematically by figure 3.1, the hierarchies are a direct consequence of frequencies. In the second, represented by figure 3.2, they are an indirect consequence. As the above discussion should have made clear, contrary to Hawkins, I opt for the second model.

In closing this section, I would like to raise (but, unfortunately, not resolve) an issue pertaining to the sensitivity of language users to frequency. It seems transparently obvious that we have this sensitivity when it comes to phonological, morphological, and lexical units. But in the realm of syntax, it is not clear to me what units users might be sensitive to. The basic elements of phonology, morphology, and even lexicon are finite, simple, and relatively few in number. The idea that language users have the ability to keep them all 'in their heads' and to track their frequency seems totally reasonable. But it is far from clear what the syntactic analogues are to phonemes, morphemes, and words, or if there even exist such analogues. Many would say that these analogues are 'constructions'. But constructions are many orders of magnitude more complex than their lower-level counterparts. Is it plausible to suppose that speakers have the ability to assign frequency rankings to each and every one? The existence of such an ability seems especially suspect when one recalls that any particular sentence may be an instantiation of an indefinite number of constructions. The sentence *What had been given to Mary by Paul?* at one and the same time reflects the ditransitive construction, the passive construction, the initial *wh*-construction, the perfect auxiliary construction, and no doubt many more. Each time that sentence is uttered, do the speaker and hearer really tick off in their mental note pads one more use of each? To further complicate the issue, in principles-and-parameters approaches, there are no analogues to phonemes and morphemes in the syntax at all. Constructions are regarded as purely epiphenomenal by-products of the interaction of parameterized principles. It is therefore difficult to imagine what language users would even 'tally', and even more difficult to imagine how and why they would be driven to use the results of that tally to change their grammars.

Nevertheless, formalists and functionalists alike have assumed that language users are sensitive to the frequency of syntactic units. What precisely these units are is a matter for further research.

5.3.3 Economy and least effort as external explanations As we have seen, many external explanations for properties of grammatical structure have been put forward that appeal to notions such as 'economy' and 'least effort'. The question naturally arises as to whether such notions are merely cover terms for *any* type of external explanation. Surely appeals to EIC and PSCI are, in some relevant sense, appeals to economy. As for the former, it is more 'economical' for the hearer (as measured in terms of amount of effort expended) to recognize the constituents of the sentence rapidly rather than slowly. An analogous point can be made for the latter. One can easily imagine the greater processing effort that would be required if there were a near random alignment of formal elements and semantic elements, rather than a very close one.

Some investigators have, in fact, attempted to equate iconicity with economy, or to derive one from the other. Givón (1985), for example, takes economy to be a major motivation for iconicity, so any iconic motivation is ipso facto an economic one, while DeLancey (1985) and Givón (1991a), on the other hand, view economy as a form of iconicity. Haiman (1983, 1985a) however, attempts to distinguish economic motivation from other types, in particular iconic. His examples of the latter for the most part involve reductions of structure—gaps, deletions, phrasal conjunctions, and so on. These are all cases, of course, where the meaning is recoverable elsewhere in the structure, either from the position of the coreferential antecedent or from the preservation of the relevant phrasal structure (that is, the structure from which the meaning is determined). One can easily imagine that such cases are based ultimately on parsing ease. Surely it is more efficient to process only those syntactic nodes that are necessary for meaning recovery than to have to process an essentially duplicate set as well. While I would not suggest (and neither has Hawkins, to my knowledge) that EIC is able to predict preferences for reductions of structure, there seems to be little call for a distinct species of 'economic motivation' governing such cases.

In the remainder on this book I will phrase explanations in terms of 'economy' and 'least effort' only when referring to phonetic reductions, where these terms have a long-established use and a reasonably concrete interpretation (they were just appealed to above in §5.3.2 and will play a fairly central role in my discussion of grammaticalization in chapter 5). However, I will avoid these terms in any discussions of the nature of grammatical structure.[15]

6   The Problem of Competing Motivations

In this section I will explore the consequences of the fact that external motivations for grammatical structure can be 'in competition' with each other. I will argue that this fact poses a severe challenge to the full functionalist program for external explanation. Section 6.1 gives a number of examples of competing motivations. In §6.2 I argue that the fact that structure results from a number of external factors in competition with each other leads to the conclusion that grammars cannot link structures and their external motivations.[16] In §6.3 I show that competing motivations have equally profound implications for the functionalist program for language typology.

6.1   Competing motivations
Jack Du Bois has pointed out,

Volumes of so-called functionalism are filled with ingenious appeals to perception, cognition or other system-external functional domains, which are used to 'explain' why the language in question simply has to have the grammatical particularity that it does—when a moment's further reflection would show that another well-known language, or even the next dialect down the road, has a grammatical structure diametrically opposed in the relevant parameter. (Du Bois 1985: 353)

But *why don't* particular languages 'simply have to have' the grammatical peculiarities that they do? Indeed, if grammatical structure is a response

---

15. In this chapter I deliberately fail to discuss the sorts of 'least-effort' considerations that have been claimed to be at work in the Minimalist Program of Chomsky (1995). It is not obvious to me that the term 'effort' is employed there in any sense but a metaphorical one. However, in chapter 5, §7.2, I do discuss the claim that formal grammars might be shaped by a 'least-effort strategy' (Roberts 1993), since this claim is relevant to the question of grammaticalization.

16. Much of the material in sections 6.1 and 6.2 has appeared (in somewhat different form) in Newmeyer (1994a).

to externally motivating factors, then it is reasonable to ask why all languages are not the same. The answer, at least in part, is that the number of factors that might plausibly exert a functional influence on language is so great that it is highly implausible that any one of them would dominate as the sole influencing factor in any given case. So most functionalists have come to recognize that a convincing account of a particular grammatical phenomenon must specify the combination and interaction of contributing factors at work.

Further complicating a satisfactory function-based account of any particular phenomenon, however, is the fact that functions can be *in conflict* with each other, thereby opening up the possibility that a linguistic structure might exhibit influences from both. Many examples have been adduced of such 'competing motivations' in the realm of syntax. In the major study along these lines, Haiman (1983) argues that the desire for economy (such as might result in the simplification or omission of redundant material) can come into conflict with pressure to make grammatical structures iconic. In the view of Dik (1989), iconicity can conflict with the prominence of participants. Thus, in indirect object constructions, the V-DO-IDO order is an iconic one, in that it reflects the movement of the object in question from the donor to the recipient. The V-IDO-DO order, on the other hand, is also functionally motivated in that it places the more 'prominent' indirect object before the less prominent direct object.[17] A conflict between an iconic principle and a different cognitive principle is discussed in Tai (1985), based in part on work by Osgood (1980). Tai claims Chinese manifests 'natural word order'. In Chinese, word order is said to be highly iconic, in that the order of words in a sentence corresponds to a high degree to the order that the elements involved are perceived. However, many other languages manifest what he calls 'salient word order', that is, an ordering based on 'a speaker's interests, involvements, focus, etc.' (1985: 64). So we have two motivations in conflict, whose resolution is different in different languages.

Functionalists also point to external factors in competition with internal structural ones. Comrie (1984a: 89–90) suggests that 'Universal 15' from Greenberg (1963) represents just such a case:

17. See also Thompson and Koide (1987) for a somewhat different competing motivations approach to the indirect object construction.

(31) *Universal 15*

In expressions of volition and purpose, a subordinate verbal form always follows the main verb as the normal order except in those languages in which the nominal object always precedes the verb.

Comrie provides a competing motivations explanation for the universal. The subordinate form following the head is attributed to iconicity: when wishes and statements of purpose precede their realizations, 'the form of an expression is brought into direct correspondence with some aspect of its meaning' (1984a: 89). However, in rigidly verb final languages, form wins out over function: 'It is simpler to have a rule that the verb of the main clause follows all constituents, irrespective of their semantics' (1984a: 89).

As a result of competing motivations, it will virtually never be the case that a grammatical structure is a simple mirror of an external functional motivation. In functionalist parlance, the various external pressures on language structure are a cause of 'arbitrariness' in language: 'Where [competing principles] conflict, apparent arbitrariness results.... To the extent that different generalizations are possible, some arbitrariness is possible' (Haiman 1983: 814–815).

Motivations in conflict are said to have three different outcomes: one motivation might win out over the other; each motivation might have its own grammatical consequence (i.e. multiple structural possibilities); and there might be a compromise, in which the resultant structure or structural subsystem fails to reflect any one motivation.

Haiman (1983) illustrates the first case. Considerations of economy would dictate that Hua subordinate clauses should have a reduced structure, since they are typically used to express given or familiar information. But considerations of iconicity should result in their *not* undergoing reduction, since failure to undergo reduction 'is an icon of the conceptual independence of these clauses' (1983: 814). As it turns out, there is no reduction: 'economy conflicts with a kind of iconicity, and economy loses' (1983: 814).

Another case of one motivation being said to win out over another is illustrated by the grammaticalization of the Gricean maxim 'Be Orderly' in Chinese (see the discussion in §4.5 above). However, there are sentences in which the reverse temporal order reading is the normal one. This is the case, for example, if the first conjunct contains the particle *qian* 'before':

(32) Wǒ chū mén qián,   yídìng guān hǎo mén chuāng
     I   out door before must   shut well door window
     'I must close the door and window before I go out.'

Croft (1995a: 508) has a competing motivations account of this fact, arguing that in adverbial subordinate clauses tense-iconicity competes with and loses out to another external motivation. Citing Reinhart (1984) and Talmy (1978a), he suggests that 'the relationship between clauses in adverbial subordination signifies a Gestalt figure-ground pattern, a conventionalized semantic relation that can override an implicature of tense iconicity'.

The second case is illustrated by Dik's analysis of the indirect object construction mentioned above. English allows both orders (i.e. *Mary gave the book to John* and *Mary gave John the book* are both possible), so iconicity and prominence each has its attendant ordering. Another way that the second case might be instantiated is by both principles yielding their consequences in the same construction. This is the situation in double case marking patterns of the sort where a possessor constituent is marked both for its own possessor case and also for the case of the entire noun phrase it is part of, as in Old Georgian and many Australian languages.

The third outcome of motivations in conflict has been exemplified by the 'crazy rules' that it has been suggested that every grammar has (Givón 1979). Givón recognizes that the grammars of many languages appear to be arbitrary and 'unnatural', in the sense of 'communicatively disruptive' (1979a: 236). For example, Swahili 'represents a certain bewildering complexity in the morphology and syntax of relativization' (1979: 252). Givón suggests that such a situation might be expected to cause processing difficulties relative to one where a language has only one device to express relativization. But he offers the opinion that this seeming arbitrariness is simply a reflection of the interaction of a number of thoroughly natural functional pressures, not all pulling in the same direction, which, in their in mutual interaction, have produced what, on the face of it, is an arbitrary state of affairs.

6.2 Competing motivations and synchronic analysis
We turn now to the question of whether external functional forces are incorporable into synchronic grammatical analysis per se. That is, I will examine the implicit assumption in much functionalist work that an

optimal grammatical description specifies direct linkages between the formal properties of language and the external forces that are responsible for them.[18] I will argue on the basis of the fact that these forces are in competition with each other that it is hopeless to think of grammatical descriptions in such terms.

6.2.1   On stating functional forces in the grammar itself   Let us begin with Simon Dik's account of indirect object constructions that we alluded to above. In his view, English grammar shows the effects of both iconicity and prominence; when the direct object precedes the indirect object, we see the effects of iconic motivation, when the indirect object precedes the direct object, we see relative prominence of participants as the primary motivating factor. How might a functionalist deal with this aspect of English in a grammatical description? Presumably, by positing a direct relationship from the external functions of iconic motivation and prominence to their attendant grammatical orderings.

But not all languages allow the indirect object both to precede and follow the direct object.[19] Let us consider Bini, which allows only the DO-IDO order. A functionalist might therefore say that Bini's exclusive use of this order is motivated by and hence (in some manner) linked to the principle of iconicity. Or consider Hausa, which allows only the IDO-DO order. An functionalist might therefore say that this aspect of the grammar of Hausa is motivated by and hence linked to prominence.

There is a fundamental problem with such an approach. It might very well be the case that over time prominence and iconicity have helped to shape the respective orders of direct and indirect objects of the three languages in their different ways. But from that fact it does not necessarily follow that in the synchronic grammars of the languages the same motivating factors are at work. This point can be driven home by noting that it is frequently the case that the original motivating factors have *ceased to exist*. The example of Swahili relativization referred to above is typical.

18. One must be careful to distinguish external forces (or motivations) from functions themselves. Nobody denies that it is part of the task of a linguistic theory to specify the functions (discourse or otherwise) carried out by grammatical form. The question is whether the forces *responsible* for form are to be stated as part of a grammatical description.

19. Sedlak (1975) lists 19 languages with both orders, 15 with only the IDO-DO order, and 11 with only the DO-IDO order.

Givón posits an original SOV order for Swahili. Given this order, a processing strategy motivated a particular relativization pattern. Swahili word order changed to SVO, so the processing strategy no longer favored the pattern. But nevertheless the pattern survived as conventionalized structure. Since speakers of Swahili can hardly know what happened in the past, the synchronic grammar of Swahili clearly cannot relate this pattern to its (original) functional motivation.

One might attempt to save a strictly synchronic appeal to competing motivations by calling convention itself a 'motivation'. Such a move would solve one problem—virtually all synchronic structure is now motivated!—but create a far graver one. The attraction of any functionalist account lies in its reductionist potential. That is, by showing that independently motivated principles of cognition, discourse, physiology, and so on conspire to shape language structure, one is spared the need to proliferate causal factors or to postulate effects that have no cause. But appeal to convention is fundamentally different from appeal to parsing efficiency, discourse facilitation, and so on in the following way: the more one can demonstrate the effects of the latter, the stronger one's functionalist theory; the more one can demonstrate the effects of convention, the weaker one's functionalist theory. This is because convention by definition plays no role in shaping grammatical structure, only in preserving structure that itself was shaped by (presumably) functional factors.

6.2.2 Competing motivations and natural classes I am aware of one attempt to provide substance to a synchronic appeal to competing motivations. Haiman (1983) likens them to the motivations for natural classes in phonology, with construction types such as (33a–c) playing the role of phonemes (X, A, and Y represent morphemes):

(33) a. $X \# A \# Y$
      b. $X \# Y$
      c. $X + Y$

Haiman writes:

It seems to me that competing motivations for any of the constructions schematized in [(33a–c)] are exactly analogous to competing motivations for indeterminate sounds like /T/ in phonemic analysis. With respect to one feature, voicing, /T/ patterns with /t/, and its identification with the phoneme /t/ is motivated; with respect to another feature, tenseness, /T/ patterns with /d/, and its identification with /d/ is also motivated. (Haiman 1983: 815)

Just as phonemes are phonetically motivated, 'linguistic categories may be derived from, and ultimately may be similar to, conceptual categories' (Haiman 1983: 816). Haiman discusses two principles grounded in iconicity that relate syntactic constructions to their conceptual underpinnings, which I will call the 'Distance Principle' and the 'Separateness Principle':

(34) *The Distance Principle*
     The linguistic distance between expressions corresponds to the conceptual distance between them.

(35) *The Separateness Principle*
     The linguistic separateness of an expression corresponds to the conceptual independence of the object or event which it represents.

The linguistic distance between two expressions is measured by the nature and number of the boundaries between them. Hence in (33a–c) above, the linguistic distance between X and Y decreases from (33a) to (33c). The Distance Principle can be illustrated by the examples given in §4.3.2 illustrating iconicity of distance.

The linguistic separateness of an expression is a function of the grammatical fusion of its component parts. A construction composed of two words is more linguistically separate than one containing a word and a bound morpheme; one composed of two full clauses is more separate than one containing a full clause and a reduced clause. The Separateness Principle can be illustrated by the fact that incorporated object nouns separated by a morpheme boundary from the verb are invariably nonreferential, as opposed to object NPs separated by a word boundary, which can refer.

These principles make predictions about the conceptual status of verb-incorporated object constructions (i.e. constructions with the structure of (33c) above). The Distance Principle predicts that the conceptual distance between the verb and the incorporated object should be very low (syntactic proximity goes along with low conceptual distance). The Separateness Principle predicts that conceptual separateness of the verb and the incorporated object should also be very low (as noted above, grammatical fusion goes along with a low degree of individuation for the object).

Haiman tests these predictions, drawing on work on Greenlandic Eskimo presented in Sadock (1980). As it turns out, Greenlandic violates the Distance Principle. Unfortunately for that principle, the conceptual distance between verbs and incorporated objects is very high. However,

Haiman notes, the Separateness Principle does appear to be followed: the conceptual separateness of incorporated objects is very low.

Haiman concludes that what we have here is a clash between the Distance Principle and the Separateness Principle, and the latter wins out. But this is unproblematic, according to Haiman, since we find the same sort of situation in phonology: just as it is arbitrary for a particular rule whether /T/ might pattern with voiceless segments or with nontense segments, it is arbitrary which *conceptual* generalization a grammatical structure will reflect. And just as each class involved in a phonological rule tends to be a natural (i.e. phonetically motivated) one, any particular grammatical structure will also generally be a natural one, in that it is likely to reflect *some* conceptual generalization, even though, because of competing motivations, it cannot reflect all of them.

Upon close examination, however, Haiman's analogy to phonology breaks down and we are left with a situation analogous to the object order case described above, in which a convenient motivating factor is said to 'explain' the distribution of data and an inconvenient one is simply ignored.

The passage from Haiman quoted above leaves two interpretations open as to the nature of /T/. In one interpretation, it is simply a nontense voiceless stop. If so, then /T/, /t/ and /T/, /d/ form natural classes with respect to the features of voicing and tenseness respectively. This is the case, of course, regardless of whether /T/ happens to be participating in a phonological rule in which voicing or tenseness are relevant. That is, /T/ does not become [+VOICED] if it participates in a phonological rule where its [−TENSE] feature is relevant. But incorporated objects in Greenlandic unexpectedly shift from [+LOW CONCEPTUAL DISTANCE] to [+HIGH CONCEPTUAL DISTANCE] when their [+LOW CONCEPTUAL SEPARATENESS] feature is relevant. Nothing of the sort is known in phonology: what we have in phonology is a case of *different* generalizations; what we have in Haiman's syntactic example is a case of *conflicting* generalizations.

In another interpretation (suggested by Haiman's use of the term 'indeterminate sound'), /T/ is an archiphoneme (or possibly a morphophoneme), unspecified for voicing and tenseness, and whose value is supplied by regular rules. A classic example is provided by German, in which /T/ is realized as voiceless and tense word-finally. In this interpretation, Haiman's phonological analogy is even more remote. Voicing and tenseness do not 'compete' with each other in German and other languages with parallel phenomena, with one 'winning out', thereby violating some principle grounding phonology in phonetics. But, as we have seen, in Haiman's treatment of verb-incorporated constructions, a principle grounding syntax conceptually is indeed violated.

In short, the analogy to phonology cannot be sustained; we have no reason to reevaluate the conclusion that competing motivations make the idea that a synchronic grammar consists of direct mappings between form and functional motivation extremely problematic.

6.2.3 Summary I have attempted to make the case in this section that there is no coherent way that external motivations can enter into the formulation of a synchronic grammar. The fact that forces motivating grammatical structure can be in competition with each other renders such a possibility inherently unfeasible. Thus competing motivations provide us with one further argument for the autonomy of knowledge of language with respect to use of language (see ch. 2, §4).

6.3 Competing motivations and typology
One could reject the idea that motivations be literally incorporated into grammatical statements, but still appeal to competing motivations to attempt to explain of the distribution of typological features of the world's languages. Consider some typological generalizations: A certain percentage of languages are verb-initial, a certain percentage are verb-final; a certain percentage allow null subjects, a certain percentage do not; if a language is verb-second, it will usually (but not always) have prepositions, rather than postpositions; and so on. As mentioned above, most functionalists would say that this typological variation is a consequence of different, and competing, external forces. Perhaps, then, one might think that we can *explain* the typological breakdown of whatever feature of grammar by appealing to the relative strength of the external forces.

I will argue in this section that *in principle* such an approach makes perfect sense. However, given the open-ended multiplicity of motivating factors that have been put forward in the literature and our inability to provide any independent measure of their relative weight, we have no hope of explaining typological generalizations by means of appeal to them. In brief, any conceivable state of affairs, existing or nonexisting, could be attributed to some reasonable functional force or combination of forces, thereby explaining nothing.

6.3.1 Vacuous appeals to competing motivations Let us begin with a look at Tomlin (1986), which is one of the best known works dedicated to explaining the typological distribution of some grammatical feature. Tomlin proposes three principles which interact to explain what he takes to be the relative frequency of the basic orderings of subjects, objects, and verbs in the world's languages:[20]

(36) a. SOV = SVO (most common)
     b. VSO
     c. VOS = OVS
     d. OSV(least common)

The three principles are as follows:

(37) a. *The Theme-First Principle*
       More thematic information tends to precede less thematic
       information.
     b. *Verb-Object Bonding*
       In a transitive clause, the object is more tightly 'bound' to the
       verb than it is to the subject.
     c. *The Animated-First Principle*
       Animated NPs tend to precede other NPs.

The frequency ranking in (36) is claimed to follow from the interaction of the three principles. SOV and SVO languages are consistent with all three, VSO languages with two of them, VOS and OVS languages with only one, while the OSV languages violate each principle. But, one might ask why the lower ranked orderings exist at all. Tomlin suggests that VOS languages like Ojibwa obey a 'Theme-Last' principle. In other words, Theme-First and Theme-Last compete, and the latter is, at times, powerful enough to eclipse the former.

The problem with explanations such as Tomlin's, as is noted in Croft (1988b), is that they are essentially vacuous. To provide an explanation of why feature A is more common than feature B, one must do more than simply declare that the motivation for A is stronger than the motivation for B. Rather, one is obliged to provide independent motivation to explain *why* this should be the case. Otherwise, one has accomplished nothing more than to find a different way of saying that A is more com-

---

20. For comments on Tomlin's ordering breakdown, see ch. 6, §3.1.3.

mon than B.[21] Tomlin does, to be sure, provide evidence, based on cognitive principles of information flow, for the Theme-First Principle (which is, of course, a variant of Communicative Dynamism). But no explanation is given why a significant set of languages should violate it, i.e. what principle, cognitive or otherwise, should lead some languages to place themes last and why this principle is so much weaker than those leading to the initial positioning of themes. In the absence of an explication of the relative strength of competing principles, one has, as best, explained why both types of languages exist, without moving even slightly to advance the typologists' goal of explaining their relative frequency.

The same point has been made by Hammond, Moravcsik, and Wirth (1988) with respect to Comrie's attempted explanation of Greenberg's Universal 15 discussed above. Comrie posits a functional and a formal principle in conflict. But Hammond et al. ask:

> Why doesn't the explanation work? Briefly, because the facts to be explained—that one subset of languages has one word order in these constructions, and that another subset (rigid nominal OV languages) has a different order—do not follow from the explanatory principles suggested. Although this failure is partly due to the vagueness of the explanatory principles referred to, it is primarily because no basis is given for the assumption that the interaction works the way it is asserted to work. If the form of grammar (i.e. rules or principles of grammatical form) is to be explained by functional principles, then what licenses the 'pre-emption' of the functional principle by principles of form? The explanation has an air of circularity about it. Without further explication and justification, this sketch cannot count as an explanation. (1988: 16–17)

To summarize the problem pointed to in this section, we have seen situations in which some languages manifest feature A and some languages manifest feature B, where A and B are incompatible. Furthermore, it seems reasonable to appeal to motivation M_1 to explain A and to motivation M_2 to explain B. But since our only means of gauging the relative strengths of M_1 and M_2 is the typological distribution itself, our appeal to M_1 and M_2 to account for this distribution is vacuous—nothing, in fact, has been explained.

Can one find a way out of this dilemma? In the next section we will examine a suggestion by William Croft that attempts to do so.

---

21. Lass (1980) regards *all* functional explanation as vacuous in this way, a conclusion that I feel is overly nihilistic. For interesting comments on Lass, see Nettle (1998).

6.3.2 An attempt to save competing motivations explanations from vacuity Croft (1990: §7.4) puts forward a strategy designed to rescue external explanation of typological distribution in the context of competing motivations. He does not question the conclusion that one needs independent evidence as to the strength of each motivation in order to explain why a certain percentage of languages have one feature and another percentage another feature. Nor does he deny that such evidence is, in general, impossible to come by. However, he argues that one can still explain why certain features do *not* exist. The logic of his argument is as follows. Suppose that we have two proposed motivations that are in conflict, i.e. that cannot be fulfilled simultaneously. We may therefore expect to find patterns in language where one motivation, but not the other, is fulfilled. However, we predict that there can be no language which manifests patterns that satisfy *neither* motivation. Hence, appeals to competing motivations can, after all, be nonvacuous. He illustrates with two examples from the realm of syntax, which I will now present, followed by general discussion and then specific criticism.

Croft's first example is taken from Haiman (1985b). Haiman (1985b: 237–238) proposes three motivations, all of which we have already discussed, which interact to yield the set of word order possibilities. The first, (38a), is Communicative Dynamism; the second, (38b), we have called 'structure-concept iconicity'; and the third, (38c), is Communicative Task Urgency:

(38) a. What is old information comes first, what is new information
          comes later, in an utterance.
      b. Ideas that are closely connected tend to be placed together.
      c. What is at the moment uppermost in the speaker's mind tends to
          be first expressed.

These three principles compete with each other. Principles (38a) and (38c) can conflict—what is uppermost in the speaker's mind could obviously be new information. (38b) and (38c) can conflict—two ideas might be 'closely connected' (in some sense), while only one might be uppermost in the speaker's mind. And (38a) and (38b) can conflict—of the two closely connected ideas, only one might be old information. Do these conflicts render vacuous any appeal to these competing motivations? Neither Haiman nor Croft think so, and they discuss some typological facts involving the 'fronting' of relative and interrogative pronouns to support their position.

Interrogative pronouns, they argue, are subject to two competing motivations, namely (38b) and (38c). Since they are 'closely connected' to their predicates and clausal coarguments, one might expect, by (38b), for them to remain close to them. But semantically they are in focus—i.e. uppermost in the speaker's mind. Therefore, by (38c) we would expect them to front. Relative pronouns, on the other hand, are not in focus, so (38c) does not apply. Principle (38b) alone determines that they will appear closest to the element to which they are most closely connected— their head noun.

Since interrogative pronouns are subject to forces pressuring them to front and not to front, it would seem to be predicted (correctly) that they will front in some languages, but not in others. But relative pronouns are subject *only* to the pressure that attracts them to their head nouns. Therefore no language should exist, Haiman and Croft conclude, in which relative pronouns do not front—even if that language does not front interrogative pronouns.

Croft's other example in defense of the idea that there can be non-vacuous appeal to competing motivations is taken from the analysis of ergativity in Du Bois (1985, 1987) (see above, §4.5 and §5.3.1). Given that the alignment of subjects of intransitives with objects of transitives is motivated by preferred information flow, one might first think that all languages should be ergative. Du Bois appeals, however, to a principle that competes with preferred information flow. This is the predisposition to mark cognitively similar entities (in this instance, human agentive topics) the same way (i.e. with nominative case) over long stretches of discourse. Du Bois claims to have avoided vacuity (and Croft agrees) on the basis of the behavior of split-ergative languages: when there is a person split, first and second are nominative, and third ergative. Since first and second person are never new participants in a discourse, but are always 'given' (Chafe 1976), his theory predicts that when ergativity is split, they will be marked nominatively, not ergatively. Thus the theory satisfies the goal of limiting language types: a split ergative system with ergative first person and nominative third person will never occur.

There are two *general* problems with the structure of Croft's attempt to defend the existence of nonvacuous appeals to competing motivations. The first is in confirming any hypothesis that begins 'no language exists in which'. As I will argue in some detail in chapter 6, we have no reason to believe that the accidental sample of languages in the world today stands in any close relationship to the class of *possible* human languages. The nonoccurrence of a particular feature in a sample, however large, may simply not be that conclusive with respect to the question of its possibility.

Second, and even more problematically, we have no way of placing limits on what the relevant set of possible motivating factors are for any particular phenomenon. When it comes to the position of relative pronouns, why should we assume that it is only the three motivations discussed by Haiman that have to be taken into consideration? Or with respect to ergativity and nonergativity, why just the two mooted by Du Bois? No constraints have ever been proposed—nor is it even clear that such constraints exist—on what might conceivably act as an external motivation for grammatical structure.

Croft (I would have to say unwittingly) illustrates just this problem in his discussion of the 'predictions' of markedness theory. He suggests that the motivations of economy and iconicity are at work in the determination of the relationship between markedness and the number of morphemes used to express a category. By the motivation of economy, the more frequent value should be expressed by fewer morphemes than the less frequent; by the principle of iconicity, there should be only one morpheme per value, whether marked or unmarked. Crucially, 'The excluded type is the one in which uneconomically, the more frequent value is assigned an 'extra' morpheme, while uniconically the other value, the marked one, is expressed by no morpheme' (Croft 1990: 193).

But later in the same book, Croft gives an actually occurring example of just this 'excluded' type. In some modern Slavic languages, many nouns have nonzero nominative singular affixes and zero genitive plural forms. Croft writes:

The origin of this exception to the markedness of number and case is due to competing motivation from a completely independent source: the loss of the short high vowels ('jers') of Common Slavic, including the short vowel that formerly marked the genitive plural in some declensions. In fact, since the phonological system of a language is quite independent of the syntactic-semantic system, conflicts in externally motivated processes between the two systems are rather common in languages, and hence lead to synchronic 'exceptions'. (1990: 216)

In other words, we have found another motivating factor to come to the rescue. Again, since the number of potential motivations is, as far as we know, open-ended, any attempt to explain the typological distribution of a feature on the basis of an appeal to them is extremely problematic.

This point can be driven home by means of a closer look at Haiman's discussion of interrogative and relative pronouns. He assumes that only one motivating factor is relevant to the positioning of relative pronouns—principle (38c), which, on the basis of the conceptual closeness between them and their heads attracts the former to the latter. But surely, in Haiman's terms, another potential motivation is in competition with pressure for conceptual closeness. The principle of economy (which he accepts as a distinct motivating factor in other circumstances) should work to reduce the number of possible structural patterns in a language. This principle, then, should *discourage* the attraction of the relative pronoun to the head, since the resultant structure involves a departure from the canonical ordering of subject, object, and verb.[22]

Furthermore, the nonfronting of the relative pronoun would allow principle (38b) to be fulfilled in a different way, since by not fronting an object relative pronoun, the verb and its object would remain contiguous. In other words, the principle of conceptual closeness competes with itself! What we must conclude, then, is that Haiman's account is vacuous after all—no possible language type is excluded by it. And, indeed, Haiman himself cites two languages in which the relative pronoun is not attracted to its head—Luganda and Haya.

As far as Du Bois' information flow-based explanation of ergativity is concerned, since it is seriously flawed to begin with (see §5.3.1), there is little hope in salvaging an argument from it in support of a nonvacuous appeal to competing motivations.

The problem of weighting motivations is increased astronomically by the fact that there is no simple correspondence between experimentally ascertained preferences of language users and properties of grammars (and, therefore, by extension, typology).[23] This problem is discussed at length in Kirby (1998a, 1998b). Experimental results show that relative clauses are easier to process if the head of the relative clauses and the gap within the relative clause have the same grammatical function (Sheldon 1974; MacWhinney and Pléh 1988). Hence, subject-subject and object-object relatives are easier to process than subject-object and object-subject

---

22. Haiman (1985b: 240–241) notes that when relatives are formed by means of anaphoric pronouns rather than by relative pronouns, the former do tend to remain in their 'underlying' position, but that with the latter, 'there is ... no analogical pressure to maintain the relative pronoun in its grammatical slot' (1985b: 241). But there is, nevertheless, economic pressure.

23. This point is acknowledged by at least some functionalists (e.g. Bybee and Newman 1995: 653).

relatives. One might predict, then, that parallel function relatives would predominate over nonparallel function relatives or that there would be an implicational relationship demanding that if a language has the latter it would necessarily have the former. But neither appears to be true. Kirby suggests that the reason for this is rooted in the properties of UG: structural principles governing predication and *Wh*-Movement essentially demand that a language user acquire object-subject relatives when subject-subject relatives are acquired and subject-object relatives when object-object relatives are acquired.[24]

Along the same lines, Fodor (1984) has pointed out that, however much grammar might have *some* basis in parsing, it is hopeless to think that one can derive grammatical principles directly from parsing principles. The relationship between what the principles of UG allow and exclude and what the parser might be expected to find easy or hard respectively is far from being one-to-one. We find sentences that are constraint violations that pose no parsing difficulty (39a–b) and pairs of sentences of roughly equal ease to the parser, where one is grammatical and the other is a violation (40a–b) and (41a–b):

(39) a. *Who were you hoping for ____ to win the game?
     b. *What did the baby play with ____ and the rattle?

(40) a. *John tried for Mary to get along well with ____.
     b. John is too snobbish for Mary to get along well with ____.

(41) a. *The second question, that he couldn't answer ____ satisfactorily
        was obvious.
     b. The second question, it was obvious that he couldn't answer
        ____ satisfactorily.

In other words, the parser 'competes' with factors that, given our present state of knowledge, are simply unquantifiable. In short, given the

---

24. Kirby (1998a) is a highly original work whose methodology involves computational simulations of the effects of processing pressure on grammatical form. Kirby's main explanans is the parsing theory of Hawkins (1994) (see above), which he shows to compete with both pressure for morphological simplicity and with pressure from UG itself. While not free from some of the problems that I have called attention to with respect to appeal to competing motivations, I consider Kirby's work the most promising step taken to date in the attempt to provide substance to how a variety of factors compete to yield the typological breakdown of grammatical features.

wealth of possible motivations and our inability to provide an independent evaluation of their relative weight, no conceivable state of affairs is excluded from occurring.

One sometimes hears it said that appeals to competing motivations in linguistics are no different from such appeals in other domains, where they are never challenged. For example, we are not loath to pinpoint cigarette smoking as a 'cause' of lung cancer, even though the great majority of people who smoke will not get lung cancer and many who do not smoke *will* contract it. Is it not the case, it might be asked, that we are appealing to 'competing motivations' in order to explain this state of affairs? That is, don't we have a 'competition' of genetic make up, smoking habits, personal health history, environmental factors, as well as factors that are not currently known, all of which might affect the percentage of the population that will be afflicted?

But there is a huge difference between identifying *one cause* for *one disease* and attempting to 'explain' the full set of grammatical properties of the world's languages in terms of the full set of competing motivations. We can pinpoint cigarette smoking as a cause of lung cancer because we know that the more people smoke, the more likely they are to develop cancer and, furthermore, we have a pretty good understanding of the causal relationship between the components of cigarette smoke and the modifications that cells undergo when they become cancerous. Importantly, we can hold other, potentially competing, factors (more or less) constant, and study the direct correlation between smoking and cancer.

I suggest, then, that we lower our sights, as far as external explanation is concerned. It seems utterly hopeless, given the potentially open-ended number of factors that might plausibly be in competition with each other, to attempt to explain the typological breakdown of some grammatical feature. But, as we have seen, all is not lost. We may not be able to assess the relative weights of external motivations, but that does not mean that we cannot *identify* certain of them. Just as we can identify cigarette smoking as a cause of lung cancer, we have been able, in parallel fashion, to identify two convincing external motivations for grammatical structure: parsing motivations (as embodied in EIC) and structure-concept iconicity.

7   External Explanation and the Autonomy of Syntax

One important task remains in this chapter, namely, to demonstrate that its results are compatible with those of the previous one. A central theme of chapter 2 is that syntax is autonomous; of the present chapter 3 that syntax is, to a considerable degree, motivated externally. Many might wonder if and how the two conclusions can be compatible. Surely, one might reasonably believe, the 'self-contained' nature of syntactic systems should cut them off from being a response to any kind of external pressure.

I will argue here that syntax can be both autonomous and externally influenced. I begin in §7.1 by showing that Chomsky holds just such a position. Section 7.2 demonstrates that an iconic relationship between form and meaning is literally built into generative grammar. And finally, in §7.3, I take on the theoretical issues involved in reconciling autonomy and external motivation.

7.1 Chomsky on external explanation

It has become commonplace in the functionalist literature to portray generative grammarians as *denying* that external function might exert any direct influence on grammatical form. This section will show that such a portrayal is incorrect, by making reference to Chomsky's published remarks on the topic.[25]

Bates and MacWhinney (1989) express lucidly the view that generativists believe that grammar is immune to external influence. They point in particular to Chomsky (1975b) as arguing 'for a kind of autonomy of syntax that would cut it off from the pressures of communicative functions. In the Chomskian vision, language is pure and autonomous, unconstrained and unshaped by purpose or function' (1989: 5). Or consider the following similar remarks by Givón (1979b: xiii):

The dogma of autonomous syntax ... precludes asking the most interesting questions about the grammar of human language, namely, why it is the way it is; how it got to be that way; what function it serves, and how it relates to the use of human language as an instrument of information processing, storage, retrieval, and—above all—communication.

Chomsky (1975b), however, says nothing remotely resembling what Bates and McWhinney attribute to him; indeed, he says the precise opposite. In a reply to Searle (1972/1974), which presages the objections of Bates and MacWhinney, Chomsky writes that 'there are significant connections between structure and function' (1975b: 56) and to Searle's

25. This section has been previously published as Newmeyer (1994b).

contention that 'it is quite reasonable to suppose that the needs of communication influenced [language] structure', he responds: 'I agree' (1975b: 58). While he goes on to express skepticism that that any comprehensive external explanation of the formal properties of language is likely to be forthcoming and points to a fundamental linguistic principle (the structure-dependency of rules) that would appear to have no grounding in communicative function, he is absolutely clear that there is no *principled* reason that aspects of the language faculty might not have been shaped to meet some external need.

A similar somewhat prejudicial reading of Chomsky's views on the possibility of external motivation for linguistic principles is found in Traugott (1985). Implying that Chomsky sees this possibility as incompatible with the foundations of his theory, she argues: 'Yet it is clear that not all of language is arbitrary, and that the linguistic faculty, however conceived, must include the capacity to construct and understand sentences in nonarbitrary, iconic ways' (1985: 289). Traugott cites the following passage from Chomsky in support of her interpretation of his views:

It seems to me that one must deplore the common tendency to insist that the mechanisms of language must be special cases of 'generalized learning strategies' or general cognitive mechanisms of some sort. . . . There seems to be little reason to suppose, for the moment, that there are general principles of cognitive structure, or even of human cognition, expressible at some higher level, from which the particular properties of particular 'mental organs', such as the language faculty, can be deduced, or even that there are illuminating analogies among these various systems. (Chomsky 1980b: 214–215)

But nowhere in this passage does Chomsky imply that 'all of language is arbitrary'. Rather, he simply 'deplore[s] the common tendency' (which he has spent the previous dozen pages illustrating) to assume that the major principles of language *'must be'* nonarbitrary. While, 'for the moment' he remains unconvinced that general principles of cognitive structure would lead to much of linguistic structure being 'deduced', he hardly rejects out of hand the possibility that *certain* aspects of linguistic structure might be externally motivated.

In any event, not many pages later he characterizes the suggestion that 'functional considerations determine the character of linguistic rules' as a 'productive' one (1980b: 230–231) and notes that it makes the most sense to speak of functional explanation as applying at the evolutionary level, whether biological evolution or the evolution of a particular language (for similar remarks, see Chomsky 1979: 85–87).

The most egregious misrepresentation of Chomsky's views is found in Haiman (1985b: 6). Haiman cites the following passage from Chomsky (1972) to bolster his claim that Chomsky rejects the possibility that grammatical structure might be in part a response to pressure for an iconic match up between form and content:

Animal languages ... make use of a fixed number of linguistic dimensions, each of which is associated with a particular non-linguistic dimension in such a way that selection of a point along the linguistic dimension determines and signals a certain point along the non-linguistic dimension.... The mechanism and principle, however, are entirely different from those employed by human language ... (Chomsky 1972: 69)

Completion of the ellipsis by which Haiman interrupted Chomsky's last sentence perhaps puts the latter's view into better perspective:[26]

... to express indefinitely many new thoughts, intentions, feelings, and so on.

Surely Haiman does not believe that the expression of particular human 'thoughts, intentions, feelings, and so on' is representable as a point along a single dimension. I therefore fail to see how he could reasonably interpret Chomsky's passage as having any bearing on the *general* question of the influence of content upon form.

In short, there is no evidence from Chomsky's writings that he would regard the discovery that aspects of linguistic structure are externally motivated as a threat to his approach to language. Indeed, he has even suggested a couple of functional motivations. In his seminal 'Conditions on transformations' paper, Chomsky (1973) speculated that the roots of the Specified Subject Condition and the A-over-A Principle might lie in ambiguity-reduction, that is, in increasing the reliability of a perceptual strategy that matches appropriate predicates and arguments. Translated into today's theory, that would entail that aspects of Binding Theory and Bounding Theory have a functional motivation. And Chomsky and Lasnik (1977) point out that the filters they argue for might have a perceptual motivation as well. Since, most of these filters were subsumed by Case theory, one might conclude that this module of UG has a partly functional motivation.

---

26. Givón (1991a: 86) also elides crucial material from the same Chomsky passage to make a similar point.

In recent work, Chomsky (1995) suggests that two central aspects of the language faculty may have been imposed as a result of external pressure. One is the existence of a phonological component; another that of movement operations that displace elements from the position at which they appear at LF (and thereby violate the strictest minimalist scenario). These may well exist by virtue of the fact that 'the information provided by L[anguage] has to be accommodated to the human sensory and motor apparatus' (1995: 221); that is, they involve 'considerations of language use' (1995: 317).[27]

7.2 Iconicity and generative grammar

I have argued above that pressure in the direction of structure-concept iconicity is a plausible external motivation for grammatical structure. In this section I will illustrate that, indeed, a high degree of such iconicity is built into current models of generative grammar.[28]

While the terms 'iconicity' or 'iconic' rarely appear in generativist writing,[29] generative theorizing has always posited a considerable degree of structure-concept iconicity. In the 'standard theory' of Chomsky (1965), for example, all semantic rules applied at deep structure, the level defined by the application of the phrase structure rules and rules of lexical insertion. But by the early 1970s most syntacticians had concluded that that level provided suitable input for only certain aspects of semantic interpretation. In particular, deep structure was seen as the syntactic level best reflecting the main propositional content of the clause: the semantic

27. Chomsky remarks, 'if humans could communicate by telepathy, there would be no need for a phonological component, at least for purposes of communication; and the same extends to the use of language generally' (1995: 221). Here, as elsewhere in his writings, he implies that 'language would be perfect if only we didn't have to talk' (Jackendoff 1997: 19).

28. This section is a condensation of §4 of Newmeyer (1992) and omits and oversimplifies much material that is given extensive treatment there. The reader should consult that work for a more detailed picture of the historical treatment of iconic relationships within generative grammar.

29. But see Chomsky (1965: 11), where Chomsky suggests that certain 'unacceptable grammatical sentences often cannot be used, for reasons having to do, not with grammar, but rather with memory limitations, intonational and stylistic factors, "iconic" elements of discourse,... and so on.' Later in the book (1965: 224–225) he called attention to Jakobson's idea that an iconic relation exists between surface structure order and order of importance.

relations between the predicates and the major participants, such as
arguments and adjuncts (see Chomsky 1971; Jackendoff 1972). Following
the introduction in Chomsky (1973) of the idea that traces are left at sites
of movement, it was soon realized that traces could be exploited to allow
all aspects of meaning to be interpreted at the surface, since at a surface
level they would encode the underlying position of the moved element.
Nevertheless, since traces simply allow access to the structural relations
holding at the deeper level, main propositional content was still, in effect,
interpreted at deep structure (see Chomsky 1975b, 1976).

The relationship between D-structure (as deep structure was rechris-
tened in the late 1970s) and meaning has been explored in greatest detail
within generative grammar in Jackendoff (1983, 1987, 1990). In his
model, each major constituent in a sentence maps into a conceptual constituent (see Jackendoff 1983: 67). Interpretation is carried out by the
principle of Argument Fusion (see §5.2.2 above). In 'linking' (i.e. associating particular semantic roles with particular syntactic positions), a one-
to-one relation does not exist between thematic roles and grammatical
relations. Each can be characterized by a hierarchy, however. The linking
rules (oversimplifying somewhat) link in turn the highest available
thematic role on that hierarchy with the unlinked grammatical relation
that is highest on its own hierarchy.

Let us consider how some of the iconic relations between form and
meaning outlined in §4.3.2 can be handled within the Jackendovian
model. As far as iconicity of distance is concerned, the matter is straightforwardly captured by Argument Fusion. Elements that are structurally
distant from each other (i.e. non-co-constituents) are interpreted as conceptually distant. Iconicity of independence is handled straightforwardly
as well. An incorporated element, by definition, forms a constituent with
the element with which it is incorporated. Therefore the two elements are
predicted to have a 'close' semantic relationship, while elements separated
by major constituent boundaries are predicted not to. Along the same lines,
if a complementizer intrudes between two elements, they will not form a
constituent and therefore will be interpreted as semantically distant.

Furthermore, the linking rules are highly iconic, thereby capturing
(some aspects of) iconicity of categorization. Many instances of iconicity
of complexity fall out as well, though for largely uninteresting reasons.
The greater the syntactic (or morphological) complexity, the more elements capable of bearing meaning. The more elements of meaning, the

more complex the meaning. It is not obvious to me that anything more needs to be said.

Returning to iconicity of distance, Croft (1990: 179) makes the interesting suggestion that this hypothesis, if correct, 'could account for almost all of constituent structure (that is, constituency and contiguity, not word order) in one stroke'. But as he realizes, there are a number of problematic cases. For example, it is quite common for a constituent to be displaced from the position in which it is contiguous to the elements with which it forms a conceptual unit. Sentences containing 'raised subjects' are obvious examples. Compare the following two sentences:

(42) a. It seems that John won the race.
       b. John seems to have won the race.

I take it as uncontroversial that in the above sentences the argument conveyed by *John* and the predicate conveyed by *won the race* together form a conceptual unit. Quite simply, the predicate *won* has two arguments: the actor argument *John* and the theme argument *the race*. In (42a), the conceptual closeness of *John* and *won the race* is represented iconically: they form a syntactic clause. In (42b), the conceptual relation between argument and predicate is the same as in (42a). But this relation is not represented iconically on the surface. Iconicity of distance holds only at the level of D-structure, where *won the race* and its conceptual subject do form a constituent. In other words, the level of D-structure allows the full iconicity of the raised subject construction to be captured.

One might have the uneasy feeling that some circularity is inherent in the demonstration that the level of D-structure allows iconic relations in language to be captured to their fullest. Is it not the case, one might wonder, that the level of D-structure was *set up* to exhibit structurally canonical relations between verbs and arguments, and so it is therefore hardly a great 'discovery' that this level represents these relations iconically.

However, the primary motivation for this abstract level is *not* semantic. Rather, it is syntactic: by positing such a level (along with the subsequent movement processes that such a level requires) one is able to capture syntactic parallels between structures with displaced constituents and those with anaphoric expressions. Thus, by placing the traces of NP movement and anaphors (such as reflexives) in the same syntactic class, a single principle, Principle A of the Binding Theory (see Chomsky 1981),

explains a wide class of grammaticality distributions, including the ungrammaticality of the following two sentences:

(43) a. *John seems (that) won the race.
     b. *John thinks that himself won the race.

There is no compelling semantic motivation for identifying these two
types of elements; indeed, the semantic properties of traces of moved NPs
are wholly obscure. However, *syntactically* they behave in like fashion, a
generalization that would go uncaptured without a level of D-structure
and trace-leaving movement rules applying to that level.

By the early 1970s it had become clear that D-structure is not the sole
syntactic level relevant to semantic representation (again, see Chomsky
1971 and Jackendoff 1972). The different interpretations of the following
two sentences seemed to indicate the scope of quantifiers and negatives
are interpreted at a more superficial level:

(44) a. Many men read few books.
     b. Few books are read by many men.

In the preferred interpretation of (44a), *many men* c-commands *few books*
and has wider scope over it; precisely the opposite is true in (44b).[30] Thus
the asymmetry of the scope relationship is iconically reflected by the
asymmetry of the structural c-command relationship.

Reinhart (1983) exploited the asymmetry inherent in c-command to
handle aspects of coreference iconically. For example, the antecedent of an
anaphor must c-command it and a definite pronoun cannot c-command
its antecedent:

(45) a. *Himself saw John. (*Himself* c-commands *John*.)
     b. John saw himself. (*John* c-commands *himself*.)

(46) a. Because she$_i$ is clever, Mary$_i$ will succeed. (*She* does not
         c-command *Mary*.)
     b. *She$_i$ thinks that Mary$_i$ is clever. (*She* c-commands *Mary*.)

Functionalists frequently point out that cognitive asymmetry often
corresponds to structural asymmetry (see especially Haiman 1985c).

---

30. A node α c-commands a node β if neither α nor β dominate the other and if the
first branching node dominating α also dominates β. For discussion of the relationship between c-command and quantifier scope, see Langacker (1969), Ross
(1969), Lasnik (1976), and, especially, Reinhart (1976, 1981, 1983).

The structural vocabulary of generative grammar is laden with terms manifesting an inherent asymmetry of participants: 'precede', 'dominate', 'command', 'govern', 'bind', 'control' and so on. It is instructive to observe how well suited these concepts are to capturing cognitive asymmetry.

In sum, generative grammar posits a highly iconic relationship between structure and meaning. However, few generativists have gone so far as to posit a *causal link* between the two. That is, few have suggested that the reason that form and meaning are 'in line' to the extent that they are is because of pressure from the latter on the former. Nevertheless, as we have seen, such an idea seems eminently plausible.

7.3   External explanation and autonomous syntax

Let us now address the question of *how* syntax can be both autonomous and externally motivated. As so often has been the case in our discipline, the point can be illustrated by means of a chess analogy. The principles of chess, like those of a generative syntax, form an autonomous system. That is, the layout of the board, pieces, and possible moves make no reference to principles from outside the game itself. Through a mechanical application of these principles, every 'grammatical' game of chess can be 'generated'. But the 'autonomy of chess' does not exclude the possibility that aspects of the system were motivated functionally. Perhaps its original developers worked out the most optimal set of moves to make chess as satisfying a pastime as possible or over time players themselves have exerted an influence on the rules (say, by tacitly agreeing on changes in them). Furthermore, in any actual *game* of chess, the players have free choice as to which pieces they choose to move and where to move them, subject to the rules of the game. Such factors are, of course, irrelevant to the autonomy of chess. By the same reasoning, the autonomy of syntax is not challenged by the fact that external factors may have affected the grammar of some language or by the fact that a speaker of a language can choose what to say at a particular time. The only issue, as far as the autonomy of syntax is concerned, is whether one's syntactic competence incorporates such external motivating factors. As we have seen, it does not do so. In short, the autonomy of syntax maintains that as a synchronic system, grammatical principles have an internal algebra. This fact, however, does not exclude the possibility that pressure from outside the system might lead to a changed internal algebra.

Let me illustrate further by means of another analogy, this one involving our bodily organs. They are self-contained systems in the same sense
that grammars are. That is, they have their own systematic structural
properties: one can describe, for example, the cellular, biochemical,
molecular, etc. make up of livers in general and the structure of any individual liver. But livers can surely 'be affected by external changes'.
A bout of heavy drinking might raise my SGOT levels to the danger
point. My liver's structure has thereby changed, though it has hardly
ceased to be a self-contained system in the relevant respects. Surely
the 'simplest representation' of the structure of my liver would not refer
to the forces that caused the structural changes (though, obviously,
they would be relevant to an explanation of why those changes came
about).

And now to give a linguistic example, suppose that at age 40 I had
succumbed to the functional pressure that has been claimed to disfavor
indefinites in subject position (ch. 2, §3.4.4.) and stopped saying things
like *A man wearing a green hat came to see you today.* How would that
bear on the autonomy of syntax? First of all, one would have to ask what
the evidence would be that my grammar had changed *at all.* Clearly, I
would still have the competence to say, and understand, sentences of that
type. But suppose, contrary to all that is plausible, my grammar did all of
a sudden fail to allow for such sentences. What would that demonstrate?
Only that my internal representation was affected by something external,
not that I lacked such a representation altogether.

It may prove useful to schematize the classic functionalist view of the
relationship between structure and motivation with the one that I am
advocating here. They are illustrated in figures 3.3 and 3.4 respectively.[31]

In the functionalist view, represented by figure 3.3, the relationship
between structure and motivation, while indirect and many-many, is not
mediated by an 'intermediate' autonomous structural system. In my view
(figure 3.4), such a system does intermediate between the two. Again, the
fact that this system is in part a response to external pressure does not
prevent it from being characterized in terms of its own system-internal
principles.

31. Both figures allow for motivations for structure to be both internal and external. Many functionalists, of course, believe that all motivation is (ultimately)
external.

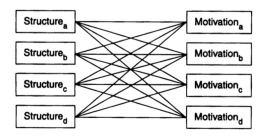

Figure 3.3
A classical functionalist view of the structure-motivation interrelationship.

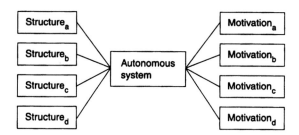

Figure 3.4
A view of the structure-motivation interrelationship compatible with *both* autonomy and external explanation

Let me close with some speculative remarks on *why* syntax should be autonomous.[32] Language serves many functions, which pull on it in many different directions. For this reason, virtually all linguists agree that there can be no *simple* relationship between form and function. However, two external forces do seem powerful enough to have 'left their mark' on grammar—the desirability for form and meaning to be in alignment (pressure for iconicity) and the desirability of being able to identify the structure of the sentence as rapidly as possible (parsing pressure). But even these two pressures can conflict with each other, however—in some cases dramatically. The evolutionary 'problem', then was to provide grammar with the degree of stability rendering it immune from the constant push-pull of conflicting forces. A natural solution to the problem

32. These remarks are developed in greater detail in Newmeyer (1991, in preparation). For a similar view, see Hawkins (1994: 439).

was to provide language with a relatively stable core *immune* to the immanent pressure coming from all sides. That is, a natural solution is to embody language with a *structural system* at its core. Put another way, an autonomous syntax as an intermediate system between form and function is a clever design solution to the problem of how to make language both learnable and usable. Such a system allows language to be nonarbitrary enough to facilitate acquisition and use and yet stable enough not be pushed this way and that by the functional force of the moment.

8   Conclusion

This chapter has taken on the question of explanation in linguistics. We have seen that the useful distinction between 'internal' and 'external' explanation does not match up one-to-one with the program of generative and functional linguistics respectively. Functionalists are wrong in dismissing internal explanations as inherently inadequate or uninteresting. But at the same time, many generativists fail to appreciate that some external explanations (besides innateness) are well motivated. In particular, it seems incontestable that the pressure for parsing efficiency and an (often countervailing) pressure for syntactic and semantic structure to be in alignment have left their mark on grammatical structure. The problem, then, is that if more than one force can affect grammatical structure, how to assess their relative weights. I have argued that because of such 'competing motivations', we cannot set our sights as high as many functionalists might wish. Competing motivations render it impossible, for example, at least at the present time, to explain the typological distribution of particular grammatical features on the basis of the external forces helping to shape that distribution. The chapter ended with a discussion of the compatibility of external explanation with the autonomy of syntax and came to the conclusion that they are fully compatible.

Chapter 4

On Syntactic Categories

1 Prototypes, Fuzzy Categories, and Grammatical Theory

This chapter explores in depth one central issue dividing generativists and functionalists—the nature of syntactic categories. In particular, the latter have argued that categories have a prototype structure and that the boundaries separating one category from another are fuzzy. I will argue that the (very real) facts offered in support of such an approach are consistent with the generativist view that categories are discrete entities. However, these facts do point to the necessity of a 'modular' approach to language, in which complex phenomena are explained by the interaction of principles from different domains.

1.1 Introduction

There are many diverse approaches to generative grammar, but what all current models share is an *algebraic* approach to the explanation of grammatical phenomena. That is, a derivation consists of the manipulation of discrete formal objects drawn from a universal vocabulary. Foremost among these objects are the syntactic categories: NP, V, S, and so on. The inventory of categories has changed over the years and differs from model to model. Likewise, their distribution has been constrained by proposals such as X-bar theory, feature subcategorization schemes, and the current (albeit controversial) distinction between lexical and functional categories. Nevertheless, what has remained constant, for the past two decades at least, is the idea that among the primitives of grammatical theory are discrete categories whose members have equal status as far as grammatical processes are concerned. That is, the theory does not regard

one lexical item as being 'more of a noun' than another, or restrict some
process to apply only to the 'best sorts' of NP.[1]

This classical notion of categories has been challenged in recent years
by many functional linguistics (see especially Dixon 1977; Hopper and
Thompson 1984, 1985; Langacker 1987b, 1991; Thompson 1988; Comrie
1989; Taylor 1989; Croft 1991; Cruse 1992; Heine 1993). In one alternative view, categories have a *prototype* structure, which entails the following two claims for linguistic theory:

(1) *Categorial Prototypicality*
    a. Grammatical categories have 'best case' members and members
       that systematically depart from the 'best case'.
    b. The optimal grammatical description of morphosyntactic
       processes involves reference to degree of categorial deviation from
       the 'best case'.

Representatives of both the 'functional linguistics' and 'cognitive linguistics' wings of functionalism have taken categorial prototypicality as fundamental to grammatical analysis, as the following quotes from Hopper
and Thompson (leading advocates of the former) and Langacker (a
developer of the latter) attest (I have added emphasis in both passages):

It is clear that *the concept of prototypicality* (the centrality vs. peripherality of
instances which are assigned to the same category) *has an important role to play in
the study of grammar.* Theories of language which work with underlying, idealized
structures necessarily ignore very real differences, both cross-linguistic and intralinguistic, among the various degrees of centrality with which one and the same
grammatical category may be instantiated. (Hopper and Thompson 1985: 155)

How then will the theory achieve restrictiveness? Not by means of explicit pro-
hibitions or categorical statements about what every language must have, but

---

1. In most generative approaches, categories have an internal feature structure,
which allows some pairs of categories to share more features than others and
allows individual categories to be unspecified for particular features. Head-Driven
Phrase Structure Grammar (HPSG) goes further, employing default-inheritance
mechanisms in the lexicon. These lead, in a sense, to some members of a category
being 'better' members of that category than others (see, for example, the HPSG
treatment of auxiliaries in Warner 1993a, 1993b). A similar point can be made for
the 'preference rules' of Jackendoff and Lerdahl (1981) and Jackendoff (1983).
Nevertheless, in these (still algebraic) accounts, the distance of an element from
the default setting is not itself directly encoded in the statement of grammatical
processes.

rather *through a positive characterization of prototypicality and the factors that determine it....* The theory will thus incorporate substantive descriptions of the various kinds of linguistic structures with the status of prototypes. (Langacker 1991: 513–514)

These approaches attribute prototype structure to (virtually) all of the constructs of grammar, not just the syntactic categories (see, for example, the treatment of the notion 'subject' along these lines in Silverstein 1976; Bates and MacWhinney 1982; Langendonck 1986; and Van Oosten 1986). However, the main part of this chapter will focus solely on the syntactic categories; the appendix will argue that there is no motivation for attributing a prototype structure to syntactic constructions.

Another functionalist position that challenges the classical approach to grammatical categories is that they have nondistinct boundaries:

(2) *Fuzzy Categories*
    The boundaries between categories are nondistinct.

My impression is that the great majority of functionalists accept categorial prototypicality and a sizeable percentage accept fuzzy categories. Comrie (1989) and Taylor (1989), for example, are typical in that respect. However, Langacker (1991), while accepting an internal prototype structure for categories, rejects the idea that the boundaries between them are nondistinct, arguing that syntactic categories can be defined by necessary and sufficient semantic conditions. Wierzbicka (1990) accepts this latter conception, but rejects prototypes. She writes:[2]

In too many cases, these new ideas [about semantic prototypes] have been treated as an excuse for intellectual laziness and sloppiness. In my view, the notion of prototype has to prove its usefulness through semantic description, not through semantic theorizing. (1990: 365)

And Heine (1993), on the basis of studies of grammaticalization, was led to accept fuzzy categories, but to reject categorial prototypicality. In his view, the internal structure of categories is based on the concept of 'degree of family resemblance' rather than 'degree of prototypicality'.

The specific goal of this chapter is to defend the classical theory of categories. First, it will provide evidence against categorial prototypicality by rebutting (1b), namely the idea that descriptively adequate grammars need to make reference to the degree of prototypicality of the categories

2. While the quote refers explicitly to semantic prototypes, the surrounding discussion makes it clear that Wierzbicka is equally skeptical of prototypes in syntax.

taking part in grammatical processes. To the extent that it is successful, it will thereby provide evidence against (1a) as well. Since grammatical behavior gives us the best clue as to the nature of grammatical structure, any refutation of (1b) ipso facto presents a strong challenge to (1a).

To be sure, it is possible to hold (1a), but to reject (1b). Such a view would entail the existence of judgments that categories have 'best-case' and 'less-than-best-case' members, without the degree of 'best-casedness' actually entering into grammatical description. Does anybody hold such a position? It is not clear. George Lakoff seems to leave such a possibility open. He writes that 'prototype effects ... are superficial phenomena which may have many sources' (1987: 56) and stresses at length that the existence of such effects for a particular phenomenon should not be taken as prima facie evidence that the mind represents that phenomenon in a prototype structure (see in particular his discussion of prototype effects for even and odd numbers in chapter 9). On the other hand, his discussion of strictly grammatical phenomena suggests that he does attribute to grammatical categories a graded structure with inherent degrees of membership and the degree of membership is relevant to syntactic description (see his discussion of 'nouniness' on pages 63–64, discussed in §4.3.3 below).

In any event, in this chapter I will be concerned only with theories advocating the conjunction of claims (1a) and (1b). That is, I will attend only to approaches in which descriptively adequate grammars are said to make reference (in whatever way) to graded categorial structure.

Limitations of space force me to ignore a number of topics that are relevant to a full evaluation of all facets of prototype theory. In particular, I will not address the question of whether nonlinguistic cognitive categories have a prototype structure. Much has appeared in the psychological literature on this topic, and a wide variety of opinions exist (see, for example, Rosch and Lloyd 1978; Mervis and Rosch 1981; Armstrong, Gleitman, and Gleitman 1983; Lakoff 1987; Smith and Osherson 1988; Keil 1989; Kamp and Partee 1995; Fodor and Lepore 1996; and Dryer 1997). However, the evidence for or against a prototype structure for grammatical categories can, I feel, be evaluated without having to take into account what has been written about the structure of semantic, perceptual, and other cognitive categories.

Second, I will argue against fuzzy categories. Nothing is to be gained, either in terms of descriptive or explanatory success, in positing categorial continua. And third, I will challenge the most comprehensive defense of the idea that categories are characterizable in notional terms, and will conclude that the possibility of providing a semantic definition of the categories 'noun', 'verb', and 'adjective' seems remote.

The remainder of §1 provides historical background to a prototype-based approach to syntactic categories. Section 2 discusses how prototype theory has been applied in this regard and discusses the major consequences that have been claimed to follow from categories having a prototype structure. Following earlier work, I call these consequences 'syntagmatic simplicity' and 'paradigmatic complexity'. Section 3 argues that the former consequence is explicable without reference to prototypes, while §4 does the same for the latter. In §5, I contrast the claims of markedness theory with those of prototype theory. I argue that under one interpretation of prototype theory, it is indistinguishable from markedness theory; under another interpretation it is less adequate empirically. Section 6 argues against fuzzy categories, and §7 against the notional definition of syntactic categories. Section 8 is a short conclusion.

1.2 Squishes and their legacy

Prototype theory was first proposed in Rosch (1971/1973) to account for the cognitive representation of concepts and was immediately applied to that purpose in linguistic semantics (see Lakoff 1972a, 1973).[3] This work was accompanied by proposals for treating *syntactic* categories in non-discrete terms, particularly in the work of J. R. Ross (see especially Ross 1973a, 1973b, 1975). Ross attempted to motivate a number of 'squishes', that is, continua both within and between categories, among which were the 'Fake NP Squish', illustrated in (3), and the 'Nouniness Squish', illustrated in (5). Consider first the Fake NP Squish:

(3) *The Fake NP Squish* (Ross 1973a)
   a. Animates
   b. Events
   c. Abstracts
   d. Expletive *it*
   e. Expletive *there*
   f. Opaque idiom chunks

---

3. For more recent work on prototype theory and meaning representation, see Coleman and Kay (1981); Lakoff (1987); Geeraerts (1993); and many of the papers in Rudzka-Ostyn (1988) and Tsohatzidis (1990). For a general discussion of prototypes, specifically within the framework of cognitive linguistics, see Winters (1990).

Progressing downward from (3a) to (3f) in the squish, each type of noun phrase was claimed to manifest a lower degree of noun phrase status than the type above it. Ross's measure of categorial goodness was the number of processes generally characteristic of the category that the NP type was able to undergo. Consider the possibility of reapplication of the rule of Raising. The 'best' sort of NPs, animates, easily allow it (4a), 'lesser' NPs, events, allow it only with difficulty (4b), while 'poor' NPs, idiom chunks, do not allow it at all (4c):

(4) a. John is likely to be shown to have cheated.
     b. ?The performance is likely to be shown to have begun late.
     c. *No headway is likely to have been shown to have been made.

With respect to the Fake NP Squish, Ross did not employ the vocabulary of the then nascent prototype theory. However, as observed in Taylor (1989: 189), his reference to 'copperclad, brass-bottomed Noun Phrases' (p. 98) to refer to those at the top of the squish leaves no doubt that he regarded them as the most 'prototypical' in some fundamental sense.

Ross proposed the 'Nouniness Squish' to illustrate a continuum *between* categories. Progressing from the left end to the right end, the degree of sententiality seems to decrease and that of noun phrase-like behavior to increase:

(5) *The 'Nouniness Squish'* (Ross 1973b: 141)
     that clauses > *for to* clauses > embedded questions > Acc *ing*
     complements > Poss *ing* complements > action nominals > derived
     nominals > underived nominals

Ross put forward the strong claim that syntactic processes apply to discrete segments of the squish. For example, preposition deletion must apply before *that* and *for-to* complements (6a), may optionally apply before embedded questions (6b), and may not apply before more nouny elements (6c):

(6) a. I was surprised (*at) that you had measles.
     b. I was surprised (at) how far you could throw the ball.
     c. I was surprised *(at) Jim's victory.

Given the apparent fact that different processes apply to *different* (albeit contiguous) segments of the squish, Ross was led to reject the idea of rigid boundaries separating syntactic categories.

In other words, Ross's approach involved hypothesizing both categorial prototypicality and fuzzy categories. By the end of the 1970s, however, very few syntactic analyses were still being proposed that involved squishes. Ross's particular approach to categorial continua was problematic in a number of ways. For one thing, it did not seek to provide a more general explanation for why categories should have the structure that he attributed to them. Second, his formalization of the position occupied by an element in the squish, the assignment of a rating between 0 and 1, struck many linguists as arbitrary and unmotivated. No reasonable set of criteria, for example, was ever proposed to determine if an abstract NP merited a rating of, say, .5 or .6 on the noun phrase scale. Third, Ross dealt with sentences in isolation, abstracted away from their extra-linguistic context. Since at that time those linguists who were the most disillusioned with generative grammar were the most likely to take a more 'sociolinguistic' approach to grammar, Ross's silence on the discourse properties of the sentences he dealt with seemed to them to be only a slight departure from business as usual. And finally, some doubts were raised about the robustness of the data upon which the squishes were based. Gazdar and Klein (1978) demonstrated that one of them (the 'Clausematiness Squish' of Ross 1975) did not exhibit statistically significant scalar properties that would not show up in an arbitrary matrix.

But while Ross's particular approach was abandoned, the central core of his ideas about grammatical categories has lived on. In particular, many linguists continued to accept the idea that they have a prototype structure and/or have fuzzy boundaries. The 1980s saw the development of functionalist alternatives to generative grammar that have attempted to incorporate such ideas about categorial structure into grammatical theory. It is to these approaches that we now turn, beginning with an examination of prototypes within functional linguistics.

2   Prototype Theory and Syntactic Categories

In this section, we will overview claims about the prototypical correlations of syntactic categories (§2.1) and see that these correlations have been implicated in both their syntagmatic and paradigmatic behavior (§2.2 and §2.3 respectively).

2.1   The claims of prototype theory for syntactic categories

Among linguists who take a prototype approach to syntactic categories there is considerable disagreement as to how to define the prototypical semantic and pragmatic correlates of each category. Just to take the category 'adjective', for example, we find proposals to characterize its prototypical members in terms of a set of concepts such as 'dimension', 'physical property', 'color', and so on (Dixon 1977); their 'time-stability' (Givón 1984); their role in description, as opposed to classification (Wierzbicka 1986b); and their discourse functions (which overlap with those of verbs and nouns respectively) of predicating a property of an existing discourse referent and introducing a new discourse referent (Thompson 1988).

This lack of consensus presents a bit of a dilemma for anyone who, like this author, would wish to evaluate the success of prototype theory for syntax without undertaking an exhaustive critique of all positions that have been put forward as claiming success in this matter. My solution will be to adopt for purposes of discussion what I feel is the best motivated, most elaborate, and most clearly explicated proposal for categorial prototypicality, namely that presented in Croft (1991). His proposals for the prototypical semantic and pragmatic properties of noun, adjective, and verb are summarized in table 4.1.

In other words, the prototypical noun has the pragmatic function of reference, it refers to an object with a valency of 0 (i.e. it is nonrelational), and it is stative, persistent, and nongradable. The prototypical verb has the pragmatic function of predication, it refers to an action, it has a valency of 1 or greater, and is a transitory, nongradable process. The links between semantic class and pragmatic function are, of course, non-accidental (see Croft 1991: 123), though I will not explore that matter here.

Table 4.1
Prototypical correlations of syntactic categories

	Syntactic category		
	Noun	Adjective	Verb
Semantic class	object	property	action
Valency	0	1	≥ 1
Stativity	state	state	process
Persistence	persistent	persistent	transitory
Gradability	nongradable	gradable	nongradable
Pragmatic function	reference	modification	predication

From Croft 1991: 55, 65.

Table 4.1 characterizes the most prototypical members of each category, but not their internal relative degrees of prototypicality. Most prototype theorists agree that definite human nouns are the most prototypical, with nonhuman animates less prototypical, followed by inanimates, abstract nouns, and dummy nouns such as *it* and *there*.

As far as adjectives are concerned, Dixon (1977) finds that words for age, dimension, value, and color are likely to belong to the adjective class, however small it is, suggesting that adjectives with these properties make up the prototypical core of that category. Words for human propensities and physical properties are often encoded as nouns and verbs respectively, suggesting that their status as prototypical adjectives is lower than members of the first group.

Finally, Croft notes that it is difficult to set up an elaborated prototypicality scale for verbs. However, there seems to be no disagreement on the point that causative agentive active verbs carrying out the pragmatic function of predication are the most prototypical, while nonactive verbs, including 'pure' statives and psychological predicates are less so.

It is important to stress that the approach of Croft (and of most other contemporary functional and cognitive linguists) differs in fundamental ways from that developed by Ross in the 1970s.[4] Most importantly, it adds the typological dimension that was missing in Ross's squishes. Prototypes are not determined, as for Ross, by the behavior of particular categories with respect to one or more grammatical rules in a particular language. Rather, the prototypes for the syntactic categories are privileged points in cognitive space, their privileged position being determined by typological grammatical patterns. Hence, no direct conclusion can be drawn from the hypothesized universal (cognitive) properties of some prototypical syntactic category about how that category will behave with respect to some particular grammatical process in some particular language. Indeed, it is consistent with Croft's approach that there may be languages in which the category Noun, say, shows no prototype effects at all. Another difference has to do with the structure of categories themselves. Ross assumes that all nonprototypical members of a category can be arranged on a one-dimensional scale leading away from the prototype, that is hierarchically. Croft, on the other hand, assumes a radial categorial structure (Lakoff 1987). In such an approach, two nonprototypical

---

4. I am indebted to William Croft (personal communication) for clarifying the differences between his approach and Ross's.

members of a category need not be ranked with respect to each other in terms of degree of prototypicality.

Croft's theory thus makes weaker claims than Ross's. One might even wonder how the notion 'prototypicality' surfaces at all in grammatical description. Croft explains:

These [markedness, hierarchy, and prototype] patterns are universal, and are therefore part of the grammatical description of any language. Language-specific facts involve the degree to which typological universals are conventionalized in a particular language; e.g. what cut-off point in the animacy hierarchy is used to structurally and behaviorally mark direct objects. (Croft 1990: 154)

In other words, grammatical processes in individual languages are sensitive to the degree of deviation of the elements participating in them from the typologically-established prototype.

2.2 Prototypicality and syntagmatic simplicity

An important manifestation of categorial prototypicality is what Moravcsik and Wirth (1986) call 'syntagmatic simplicity'.[5] All other things being equal, less structure is required (as measured by the number of necessary morphemes) to express the prototypical correlation of semantic and pragmatic properties than the nonprototypical. Croft (1990: 142) has provided convenient tables to illustrate how a category's bearing prototypical correlations goes hand-in-hand with a more concise use of morphemes. Table 4.2 provides a general look at the sorts of morphemic elaboration that we find as we move away from the basic correlations, while table 4.3 illustrates how the predictions are borne out with respect to English derivational morphology.

Prototypical correlations of semantic and pragmatic properties yield simple monomorphemic nouns, adjectives, and verbs. Where the correlations are not prototypical, extra morphemes are necessary. As tables 4.2 and 4.3 illustrate, adjectives and nouns used for (nonprototypical) predication are often marked with a copula or other special coding device. Ns with a valency of 1 (i.e. possessives) often register this nonprototypicality by means of a special marker. And Ns used (nonprototypically) as properties often register this fact by means of a special affix (7a), as do V's used (nonprototypically) as modifiers (7b):

---

5. To be accurate, Moravcsik and Wirth (1986) used this term with respect to the predictions of markedness theory, not prototype theory. I will discuss the relationship between the two in §5.

Table 4.2
A general illustration of syntagmatic simplicity

	Reference	Modification	Predication
Objects	*unmarked nouns*	genitive, compounds	predicate nominals
Properties	deadjectival nouns	*unmarked adjectives*	predicate adjectives
Actions	nominalizations, complements, infinitives, gerunds	participles, relative clauses	*unmarked verbs*

From Croft 1990: 142.

Table 4.3
Syntagmatic simplicity, illustrated with respect to English derivational morphology

	Reference	Modification	Predication
Objects	dog	dog*'s*	*be* a dog
Properties	happi-*ness*	happy	*be* happy
Actions	fly-*ing*, *to* fly, *that* ... fly, fli-*ght*	fly-*ing*, fl-*own*, *which* ... fly	fly

From Croft 1990: 142.

(7) a. happi+*ness*
    b. the fly+*ing* object

Furthermore, there is some evidence that the greater the distance from the prototypical correlation, the more likely it is that an extra morpheme will be needed. For example, prototypical Ns are less suitable for predication than prototypical As, since the former, prototypically, have a valency of zero. An apparent consequence of this is the following hierarchy of predication (Croft 1995a):[6]

(8) *Predication Hierarchy*
    Action word (V) < Property word (A) < Object word (N)

---

6. See chapter 6, §6 for broader discussion of the theoretical implications of such hierarchies. Croft informs me (personal communication) that this particular hierarchy is counterexemplified in Mangarayi.

That is, no language will require a special morpheme for verbal predication if it does not require one for adjectival and nominal predication; no language will require a special morpheme for adjectival predication if it does not require one for nominal.

2.3 Prototypicality and paradigmatic complexity

Another purported manifestation of categorial prototypicality is what one could call, again following Moravcsik and Wirth (1986), 'paradigmatic complexity'. The prototypical member of a category is claimed to manifest more distinct forms in an inflectional paradigm than the nonprototypical and to occur in a broader range of construction types. The inflectional consequences of prototypicality are discussed and defended in Croft (1991: 79–87). As he notes, each major syntactic category is associated with a range of inflectional categories, though of course languages differ as to which they instantiate:

Nouns: number (countability), case, gender, size (augmentative, diminutive), shape (classifiers), definiteness (determination), alienability;
Adjectives: comparative, superlative, equative, intensive ('very Adj'), approximative ('more or less Adj' or 'Adj-ish'), agreement with head;
Verbs: tense, aspect, mood, and modality, agreement with subject and object(s), transitivity. (Croft 1991: 79)

Croft argues that there is systematicity to the possibility of a particular category's bearing a particular inflection. Specifically, if a nonprototypical member of that category in a particular language allows that inflection, then a prototypical member will as well. Crosslinguistically, participles and infinitives, two nonpredicating types of verbal elements, are severely restricted in their tense, aspect, and modality possibilities. (Nonprototypical) stative verbs have fewer inflectional possibilities than (prototypical) active verbs, e.g. they often cannot occur in the progressive. Predicate Ns and (to a lesser extent) predicate As are often restricted morphosyntactically. Predicate Ns in many languages do not take determiners; predicate As do not take the full range of adjectival suffixes, etc. The same can be said for mass nouns, incorporated nouns, and so on— that is, nouns that do not attribute reference to an object.

Furthermore, nonprototypical members of a syntactic category seem to have a more restricted syntactic distribution than prototypical members. As Ross (1987: 309) remarks: 'One way of recognizing prototypical elements is by the fact that they combine more freely and productively than do elements which are far removed from the prototypes'. This point is amply illustrated by the Fake NP Squish (3). Animate nouns are more prototypical than event nouns, which are more prototypical than abstract nouns, which are more prototypical than idiom chunks. As degree of prototypicality declines, so does freedom of syntactic distribution. The same appears to hold true of verbs. In some languages, for example, only action verbs may occur in the passive construction.

3   Syntagmatic Simplicity and Prototypes: An Evaluation

I find no reason to question that lexicalizations of the purportedly proto-typical semantic-pragmatic correlations are less complex morphemically (i.e. simpler syntagmatically) than those of nonprototypical correlations. However, that generalization does not entail the conclusion that gram-matical statements should refer to degree of prototypicality per se (§3.1). Indeed, generative-oriented acquisition research has led to the derivation of essentially the same generalization (§3.2).

3.1   Syntagmatic simplicity does not lead to a prototype approach to categories

Where the prototypical correlations of semantics and pragmatics hold, it is claimed, less structural complexity (in terms of number of morphemes) will be involved than when the prototypical correlations do not hold. But why one should find this surprising, or, for that matter, as bearing on the adequacy of one grammatical theory over another? If it really is the case that predicating actions, referring to objects, and modifying by means of attributing properties are the three most important types of things that speakers find it useful to do, then we should not be surprised that the grammar-lexicon interface is organized to facilitate their doing so. And speakers do appear to find such things useful, at least for the conjunction of properties that yield prototypical nouns and verbs. Croft (1991: 87–93) performed text counts on texts in Quiché, Nguna, Soddo, and Ute and found that in all four languages, the correlations referring expression-object and predication-action were significantly more frequently employed than other pragmatic-semantic correlations.[7]

The question is what there is to be gained by calling the conjunction of semantic and pragmatic properties a 'prototype' (except in the most

---

7. The correlation of properties suggested to characterize prototypical adjectives (modification-property word), however, was not particularly evident in the texts.

informal sense of the term) and according it some special theoretical status. To make an analogy, it is well known that in casual speech fewer phonological segments are used to express any given proposition than would be used in formal speech (Kaisse 1985). But we hardly need to postulate a 'prototype' of a casual speech rule to explain that. Rather, economy considerations suffice to do the trick. There is no reason to make the additional—and superfluous!—assumption that we mentally represent the most unmarked conjunction of the semantic and pragmatic properties that make up the prototype.

It should also be stressed that relating morphemic complexity to the degree of deviation from a particular correlation of meaning and use in and of itself has no implication that categories are nondiscrete. True, deviations from the prototypical correlation do not occur in discrete quanta. But that point is irrelevant to the question of whether their *effects* can be captured by (the interaction of) discrete principles. In fact, the evidence (to be presented below) is that they can be. The sorts of pressures under discussion might lead the noun whose meaning is 'dog' to be monomorphemic and the noun whose meaning is 'whiteness' to be bimorphemic (see table 4.3). But for all that it does not follow that the latter is less of a noun than the former.

3.2   The notion of Canonical Structural Realization
Interestingly, there is a position internal to generative grammar that could provide an explanation for syntagmatic simplicity. In models of grammar whose roots lie in the Extended Standard Theory of the 1970s, including the Government-Binding Theory (Chomsky 1981) and the Minimalist Program (Chomsky 1995), it is assumed that there are two 'interface levels', Phonetic Form (PF) and Logical Form (LF). The former provides grammatical information to the performance system involved in articulation and perception; the latter to the conceptual-intentional system.

There is a vast literature on the phonetic interpretation of phonological features (see, for example, Beckman 1988; Keating 1988). While there is a correspondingly vast literature on certain aspects of the semantic interpretation of syntactic structure, in particular properties related to quantification and reference, there is next to nothing in the literature of grammatical theory on the semantic interpretation of syntactic categories and features. It is generally assumed that the categories N, A, P, and V are decomposed into features, as in table 4.4, but there is almost nothing

Table 4.4
Categories and features

	+N	−N
+V	A	V
−V	N	P

From Chomsky 1970: 208. ('P' was added to the system in later work.)

on what semantic values, if any, to attribute to those features (though see Chomsky and Lasnik 1977: 430 and Muysken and van Riemsdijk 1986).[8]

In fact, there is little reason to believe that this or any pair of binary feature specifications for the four major categories could be well motivated. To begin with, *any* such breakdown necessarily makes the very weak claim that 4 of the 6 combinations involving 2 categories are 'natural'; in the system illustrated in table 4.4, only the pairs A-P and V-N are unnatural. And yet, it is difficult to see what might be unnatural about either of them. In the course of the history of English, for example, we have seen adjectives become prepositions (e.g. the word *like*), and nouns become verbs (e.g. gerunds). And even more problematically, there are numerous attested generalizations involving 3 out of the 4 categories—P, A, and V are case assigners in some languages, and, in English, N, A, and P, but not V, allow QP specifiers (for more examples, see Reuland 1986 and Muysken and van Riemsdijk 1986).

I conclude, then, that the standard feature system for categories is not a promising place to start one's investigation of the semantic interpretation of syntactic categories. There is, however, a view of the semantic basis of syntactic categories that comes out of generative-inspired language acquisition research. According to the 'semantic bootstrapping hypothesis' (Pinker 1984: 41), UG provides default interpretations of syntactic categories, also known as their 'canonical structural realizations' (CSRs), as follows:

(9) *Default Canonical Structural Realizations (CSRs)*
 a. N   name of person or thing
 b. V   action or change of state
 c. A   attribute
 d. P   spatial relation path or direction

---

8. For alternative ways of decomposing categories into features, see Jackendoff (1977), Hale and Platero (1986), and Reuland (1986).

Put simply, children have a head start in the acquisition process; they are born expecting that the concepts enumerated above will be encoded in categorially different ways. This idea is also taken up and developed, along somewhat different lines in Grimshaw (1981), MacNamara (1982), Pinker (1987, 1989b, 1994a), and Bloom (1994).

I will leave it to acquisition specialists to debate whether UG provides CSRs for names of persons or things, actions or changes of state, and so on.[9] But the consequences of this idea and the idea that discourse pressure leads categories to prototypically manifest a certain correlation of semantics and pragmatics are striking in the parallel nature of their conclusions.[10] Indeed, they lead to a parallel explanation for syntagmatic simplicity. Given CSRs, reasons of economy *tout court* will dictate against creating special morphemes for what is provided innately.[11]

4 Paradigmatic Complexity and Prototypes: An Evaluation

Let us now examine paradigmatic complexity, again, the idea that prototypical elements have a greater number of distinct forms in an inflectional paradigm than less prototypical elements or occur in a larger range of construction types than less prototypical elements. In this section, I will challenge the idea that any correlation other than the most rough sort holds between paradigmatic complexity and presumed degree of prototypicality. My conclusion will serve to undermine the grammatical evidence for the idea that grammatical processes are sensitive to degree of prototypicality.

9. I have found surprisingly little discussion in the recent acquisition literature on the idea that children have innate canonical meanings for each category. Gleitman and Landau (1994) is the single work that one might most *expect* to take on this question, but most of the contributions to that volume either skirt around it or ignore it completely. The best evidence seems to be provided by the correlation of noun and physical object; infants appear to have cognitive representations of physical objects at a very early age and to treat them in a uniform way in their nascent grammars.

10. Though CSRs are defined in purely semantic terms, not in a conjunction of semantic and pragmatic. Presumably an advocate of the CSR hypothesis could explain why actions would be most likely to be predicated, objects to be referred to, and so on.

11. Prototype models have also been applied to language acquisition (for a general overview and literature references, see Bates and MacWhinney 1982).

Section 4.1 outlines the various positions that could be—and have been—taken to instantiate this correlation in a grammatical description. Section 4.2 shows that for three well-studied phenomena, the postulated correlation is not robust. Section 4.3 presents alternative explanations for phenomena that have been claimed to support the idea that syntactic behavior is sensitive to degree of prototypicality.

4.1 Paradigmatic complexity and claims about grammar-prototype interactions

The idea that inflectional and structural elaboration declines with decreasing categorial prototypicality has been interpreted in several different ways. Four positions can be identified that express this idea. In order of decreasing strength, they are 'Direct Mapping Prototypicality', 'Strong Cut-Off Point Prototypicality', 'Weak Cut-Off Point Prototypicality', and 'Correlation-Only Prototypicality'. I will now discuss them in turn.

According to Direct Mapping Prototypicality, morphosyntactic processes make direct reference to the degree of prototypicality of the elements partaking of those processes. In other words, part of our knowledge of our language is a Prototypicality Hierarchy and a grammar-internal mapping from that hierarchy to morphosyntax. Ross's squishes are examples of Direct Mapping Prototypicality. As I interpret his approach, the correlation in English between the position of a noun on the Prototypicality Hierarchy and its ability to allow the reapplication of Raising (see (4a–c)) is to be expressed directly in the grammar of English.

In Strong Cut-Off Point Prototypicality, the effects of prototype structure are encoded in the grammar of each language, but there is no language-particular linking between gradations in prototypicality and gradations in morphosyntactic behavior. To repeat Croft's characterization of this position:[12]

These [markedness, hierarchy, and prototype] patterns are universal, and are therefore part of the grammatical description of any language. Language-specific facts involve the degree to which typological universals are conventionalized in a particular language; e.g. what cut-off point in the animacy hierarchy is used to structurally and behaviorally mark direct objects. (Croft 1990: 154)

12. Such a view will be scrutinized further in chapter 6, §6.

One can think of Strong Cut-Off Point Prototypicality as a constraint on possible grammars. For example, it would prohibit (i.e. predict impossible) a language in other respects like English, but in which the reapplication of Raising would be *more* possible with nonprototypical NPs than with prototypical ones.

Weak Cut-Off Point Prototypicality allows a certain number of arbitrary exceptions to prototype-governed grammatical behavior. Thus it would admit the possibility that the reapplication of Raising could apply to a less prototypical NP than to a more prototypical one, though such cases would be rather exceptional. I interpret the analyses of Hungarian definite objects in Moravcsik (1983) and English *there*-constructions in Lakoff (1987) as manifesting Weak Cut-Off Point Prototypicality.[13] The central, prototypical, cases manifest the phenomenon in question, and there is a nonrandom, yet at the same time unpredictable, linking between the central cases and the noncentral ones.

Correlation-Only Prototypicality is the weakest position of all. It simply states that there is some nonrandom relationship between morphosyntactic behavior and degree of prototypicality.

4.2   On the robustness of the data supporting cut-off point prototypicality
In this section, I will demonstrate that for three well-studied phenomena, cut-off point prototypicality, in both its strong and weak versions, is disconfirmed. At best, the data support Correlation-Only Prototypicality.

4.2.1   The English progressive   English is quite poor in 'choosy' inflections, but it does permit one test of the correlation between prototypicality and paradigmatic complexity. This is the marker of progressive aspect, *-ing*. Certainly it is true, as (10a–b) illustrates, that there is a *general* correlation of categorial prototypicality and the ability to allow progressive aspect (note that both verbs are predicating):

(10) a.   Mary was throwing the ball.
     b. *Mary was containing 10 billion DNA molecules.

However, we find the progressive with surely nonprototypical temporary state and psychological predicate verbs (11a–b), but disallowed with presumably more prototypical achievement verbs (12):

---

13. For discussion of the latter, see the appendix to this chapter.

(11) a. The portrait is hanging on the wall of the bedroom.
     b. I'm enjoying my sabbatical year.

(12) *I'm noticing a diesel fuel truck passing by my window.

Furthermore, we have 'planned event progressives', where the possibility of progressive morphology is clearly unrelated to the prototypicality of the verb (cf. grammatical (13a) and ungrammatical (13b)):

(13) a. Tomorrow, the Mariners are playing the Yankees.
     b. *Tomorrow, the Mariners are playing well.

In short, the English progressive falsifies directly the idea that there is a cut-off point on the scale of prototypicality for verbs and that verbs on one side of the cut-off point allow that inflection, while those on the other side forbid it. Furthermore, the exceptions, i.e. the verbs of lesser prototypicality that allow the progressive, do not appear to be simple arbitrary exceptions. Therefore, the facts do not support Weak Cut-Off Point Prototypicality either.

One could, of course, attempt to by-pass this conclusion simply by exempting English progressive inflection from exhibiting prototype effects in any profound way. One might, for example, appeal to semantic or pragmatic principles that account for when one finds or does not find progressive morphology. Indeed, I have no doubt that such is the correct way to proceed (for discussion, see Goldsmith and Woisetschlaeger 1982; Kearns 1991; Smith 1991; Žegarac 1993; and Swart, forthcoming). But the point is that degree of verbal prototypicality fails utterly to account for when one finds progressive morphology in English. Therefore the facts lend no support to Croft's claim that the prototypical member of a category manifests more distinct forms in an inflectional paradigm than the nonprototypical member.[14]

---

14. Along the same lines, Robert Borsley informs me (personal communication) that Welsh and Polish copulas provide evidence against the idea that prototypical members of a category necessarily have more inflected forms than nonprototypical members. One assumes that the copula is a nonprototypical verb, but in Welsh it has 5 (or 6) tenses compared with 3 (or 4) for a standard verb, and in Polish it has 3 tenses, compared with 2 for a standard verb. On the other hand, one might take the position expressed in Croft (1991) that copulas are categorially auxiliaries, rather than verbs.

4.2.2 Adjectives Dixon (1977: 22–23) cites two languages which distinguish a certain subset of adjectives morphologically. Rotuman (Churchward 1940) has an open-ended adjective class, but only the (translations of) the following 12 have distinct singular and plural forms: *big; long; broad; whole, complete; black; small; short; narrow, thin; old; white; red; female.* Acooli (Crazzolara 1955) has a closed class of about 40 adjectives, 7 of which have distinct singular and plural forms: *great, big, old (of persons); big, large (of volume); long, high, distant (of place and time); good, kind, nice, beautiful; small, little; short; bad, bad tasting, ugly.* The remaining adjectives translate as *new; old; black; white; red; deep; shallow; broad; narrow; hard; soft; heavy; light; wet; unripe; coarse; warm; cold; sour; wise.*

These two languages, then, refute Strong Cut-off Point Prototypicality. While 11 of the 12 Rotuman adjectives fall into the prototypical adjective classes of 'age', 'dimension', value', and 'color' (*female* would appear to be the exception), any number of adjectives in these classes do not have distinct singular and plural forms. Since there is an open-ended number of adjectives in the language, and there is no reason to think that *old* is more prototypical than *new* or *young,* or *female* more prototypical than *male,* there is no cut-off point separating the prototypical from the non-prototypical. And in Acooli there are even *more* putatively prototypical adjectives in the class with only one form for number than in the class with two forms.

Weak Cut-Off Point Prototypicality does not fare much better. It is true that no nonprototypical adjectives (except for the word for 'female' in Rotuman) have two number possibilities. But in this language the 'exceptions' turn out to be the norm: 12 forms out of an open-ended number and 7 out of 40 do not provide very convincing support for what is put forward as a universal statement about prototypicality.

Weak Cut-Off Point Prototypicality is in even more serious trouble for Turkish. Croft (1991: 128), citing work by Lewis (1967), mentions that only a subset of Turkish adjectives allow reduplication for intensification. These include 'basic color terms, "quick," "new," and "long," as well as less prototypical adjectives'.[15]

---

15. And it should be pointed out that Dixon says that words in the semantic field of 'speed', e.g. *quick*, tend to lag behind the 4 most prototypical classes in their lexicalization as adjectives.

4.2.3 English verbal alternations As we have noted, Strong Cut-Off Point Prototypicality predicts that there should be no grammatical processes applying *only* to nonprototypical forms. Levin (1993) has provided us with the means to test this hypothesis with respect to English verbal alternations. Depending on how one counts, she describes from several dozen to almost one hundred such alternations. Significantly, many of these are restricted to nonprototypical stative and psychological predicates. The following are some of the alternations that illustrate this point.

Various subject alternations
(14) a. The world saw the beginning of a new era in 1492.
     b. 1492 saw the beginning of a new era.

(15) a. We sleep five people in each room.
     b. Each room sleeps five people.

(16) a. The middle class will benefit from the new tax laws.
     b. The new tax laws will benefit the middle class.

There-insertion
(17) a. A ship appeared on the horizon.
     b. There appeared a ship on the horizon.

Locative inversion
(18) a. A flowering plant is on the window sill.
     b. On the window sill is a flowering plant.

4.3 Some explanations for prototypicality effects
We have seen several examples that seem to falsify cut-off point prototypicality. And yet, there are undeniable *correlations* between prototypicality and the possibility of morphosyntactic elaboration. In general, actives do progressivize more easily than statives; it would seem that in general certain adjective classes allow more structural elaboration than others; and undeniably there are more verbal alternations in English involving active verbs (or an active and its corresponding stative) than statives alone.

Any theory of language should be able to explain why this correlation exists. This section will examine a number of English syntactic processes that manifest such correlations and have thereby been invoked to suggest that categories are nondiscrete. For each case, I will argue that the facts fall out from a theory with discrete categories and independently needed principles.

4.3.1 Measure verbs and passive An old problem is the fact that English measure verbs (*cost, weigh, measure,* etc.) do not passivize:

(19) a. The book cost a lot of money.
    b. John weighed 180 pounds.

(20) a. *A lot of money was cost by the book.
    b. *180 pounds was weighed by John.

The earliest work in generative grammar attempted to handle this fact by means of arbitrarily marking the verbs of this class not to undergo the rule (Lakoff 1970). But there has always been the feeling that it is not an accident that such verbs are exceptional—there is something seemingly less 'verb-like' about them than, say, an active transitive verb like *hit* or *squeeze.* Translated into prototype theory, one might suggest that measure verbs (or, possibly, their objects) are 'on the other side of the cut-off point' for passivization in English. And, in fact, such an analysis has been proposed recently in Ross (1995) (though Ross refers to 'defectiveness' rather than to 'lack of prototypicality').

I will now argue that these facts can be explained without recourse to prototypes.[16] I believe that Bresnan (1978) first called attention to the distinction between the following two sentences (see also Bach 1980):

(21) a. The boys make good cakes.
    b. The boys make good cooks.

Notice that the NP following the verb in (21a) passivizes, while that following the verb in (21b) does not:

(22) a. Good cakes are made by the boys.
    b. *Good cooks are made by the boys.

Bresnan noted that the argument structures of the two sentences differ. *Good cakes* in (21a) is a direct object patient, while *good cooks* in (21b) is a predicate nominative. Given her theory that only direct objects can be 'promoted' to subject position in passivization, the ungrammaticality of (22b) follows automatically.

Turning to (19a–b), we find that, in crucial respects, the semantic relationship between subject, verb, and post-verbal NP parallels that of (21b).

16. I would like to thank Pascual Masullo and Ray Jackendoff (personal communication) for discussing with me the alternatives to the prototype-based analysis.

'A lot of money' and '180 pounds' are predicate attributes of 'the book' and 'John' respectively. In a relationally-based framework such as Bresnan's, the deviance of (20a–b) has the same explanation as that of (22b). In a principles-and-parameters approach, a parallel treatment is available. Since 'a lot of money' and '180 pounds' are predicates rather than arguments, there is no motivation for the NP to move, thereby accounting for the deviance of the passives.[17] Crucially, there is no need for the grammar of English to refer to the degree of prototypicality either of the verb or of the NP that follows it.

4.3.2 *There* as a nonprototypical NP   Recall Ross's Fake NP Squish, repeated below as (23):

(23) The Fake NP Squish
    a. Animates
    b. Events
    c. Abstracts
    d. Expletive *it*
    e. Expletive *there*
    f. Opaque idiom chunks

Expletive *there* occupies a position very low on the squish. In other words, it seems to manifest low NP-like behavior. First, let us review why one would want to call it a NP at all. The reason is that it meets several central tests for NP status. It raises over the verb *seem* and others of its class (24a); it occurs as a passive subject (24b); it inverts over auxiliaries (24c); and it can be coindexed with tags (24d):

(24) a. There seems to be a problem.
    b. There was believed to be a problem.
    c. Is there a problem?
    d. There is a problem, isn't there?

---

17. Adger (1992, 1994) offers a treatment of measure verbs roughly along these lines. In his analysis, measure phrases, being 'quasi-arguments' (i.e. not full arguments), do not raise to the specifier of Agreement, thereby explaining the impossibility of passivization. Indeed, thematic role-based analyses, going back at least to Jackendoff (1972), are quite parallel. For Jackendoff, measure phrases are 'locations'. They are unable to displace the underlying 'theme' subjects of verbs such as *cost* or *weigh*, since 'location' is higher on the thematic hierarchy than 'theme'. Calling them 'locations', it seems to me, is simply another way of saying that they are not true arguments.

The null hypothesis, then, is that *there* is an NP, with nothing more needing to be said.

Now let us review the data that led Ross to conclude that rules applying to NPs have to be sensitive to their categorial prototypicality. He gives the following ways that *there* seems to behave like less than a full NP (the asterisks and question marks preceding each sentence are Ross's assignments): it doesn't undergo the rule of 'promotion' (25a–b); it doesn't allow raising to reapply (26a–b); it doesn't occur in the '*think of . . . as X*' construction (27a–b) or the '*what's . . . doing X*' construction (28a–b); it doesn't allow '*being*-deletion' (29a–b); it doesn't occur in dislocation constructions (30a–b); it doesn't undergo *tough*-movement (31a–b), topicalization (32a–b), 'swooping' (33a–b), 'equi' (34a–b), or conjunction reduction (35a–b). In each case an example of a more prototypical NP is illustrated that manifests the process:

(25) *Promotion*
a. Harpo's being willing to return surprised me. / Harpo surprised me by being willing to return.
b. There being heat in the furnace surprised me. / *There surprised me by being heat in the furnace.

(26) *Double raising*
a.   John is likely ____ to be shown ____ to have cheated.
b. ?*There is likely ____ to be shown ____ to be no way out of this shoe.

(27) *Think of . . . as NP*
a.   I thought of Freud as being wiggy.
b. *I thought of there as being too much homework.

(28) *What's . . . doing X?*
a.   What's he doing in jail?
b. *What's there doing being no mistrial?

(29) *Being deletion*
a. Hinswood (being) in the tub is a funny thought.
b. There *(being) no more Schlitz is a funny thought.

(30) *Left dislocation*
a.   Those guys, they're smuggling my armadillo to Helen.
b. *There, there are three armadillos in the road.

(31) *Tough movement*
   a. John will be difficult to prove to be likely to win.
   b. *There will be difficult to prove likely to be enough to eat.

(32) *Topicalization*
   a. John, I don't consider very intelligent.
   b. *There, I don't consider to be enough booze in the eggnog.

(33) *Swooping*
   a. I gave Sandra my zwieback, and she didn't want any. / I gave Sandra, and she didn't want any, my zwieback.
   b. I find there to be no grounds for contempt proceedings, and there may have been previously. / *I find there, which may have been previously, to be no grounds for contempt proceedings.

(34) *Equi*
   a. After he laughed politely, Oliver wiped his mustache. / After laughing politely, Oliver wiped his mustache.
   b. After there is a confrontation, there's always some good old-time head busting. / *After being a confrontation, there's always some good old-time head-busting.

(35) *Conjunction reduction*
   a. Manny wept and Sheila wept. / Manny and Sheila wept.
   b. There were diplodocuses, there are platypuses, and there may well also be diplatocodypuses. / *There were diplodocuses, are platypuses, and may well also be diplatocodypuses.

I wish to argue that all of these distinctions follow from the lexical semantics of *there* and the pragmatics of its use.[18] What does expletive *there* mean? The tradition in generative grammar has been to call *there* a meaningless element, or else to identify it as an existential quantifier with no intrinsic sense. Cognitive linguists, on the other hand, following earlier work by Dwight Bolinger (1977c), have posited lexical meaning for it. To Lakoff (1987), for example, expletive *there* designates conceptual space itself, rather than a location in it. To Langacker (1991: 352), *there* designates an abstract setting construed as hosting some relationship. In fact,

---

18. Lakoff (1987) attempts to provide an independent explanation of many of the properties of expletive *there* by basing it on the deictic use of *there*. Rather than evaluate his treatment here, I will present a general critique of his treatment of *there*-constructions in the appendix to this chapter.

we achieve the same results no matter which option we choose. Meaningless elements / abstract settings / conceptual spaces are not able to intrude into one's consciousness, thus explaining (25b) and (27b). Example (28b) is bad because abstract settings, etc., cannot themselves 'act'; rather they are the setting for action. Furthermore, such elements are not modifiable (33) to (34) nor able to occur as discourse topics (30) to (32). Example (29b) is ungenerable, given the uncontroversial requirement that *there* occur with a verb of existence. In my opinion and that of my consultants, (26b) and (35b) are fully acceptable.

In short, the apparent lack of prototypical NP behavior of expletive *there* is a direct consequence of its meaning and the pragmatics of its use. Nothing is gained by requiring that the rules that affect it pay attention to its degree of prototypicality. Syntax need no more be sensitive to prototypicality to explain examples (25) to (35) than we need a special syntactic principle to rule out (36):

(36) The square circle elapsed the dragon.

As a general point, the possibility of syntactic elaboration correlates with the diversity of pragmatic possibilities. Concrete nouns make, in general, better topics, focuses, new referents, established referents, and so on than do abstract nouns. We can talk about actions in a wider variety of discourse contexts and for a greater variety of reasons than states. The syntactic accommodation to this fact is a greater variety of sentence types in which objects and actions occur than abstract nouns and states. There is no reason to appeal to the prototypicality of the noun or the verb.

4.3.3 English idiom chunks Notice that in the Fake NP Squish, idiom chunks occupy an even lower position than expletive *there*. Lakoff (1987: 63–64), in his presentation of cognitive linguistics, endorsed the idea that their behavior is a direct consequence of their low prototypicality and even went so far as to claim that idiom chunk NPs can be ranked in prototypicality *with respect to each other*. Drawing on unpublished work by Ross (1981), he ranked 4 of them as follows, with *one's toe* the highest in prototypicality, and *one's time* the lowest:

(37) a. to stub one's toe
       b. to hold one's breath
       c. to lose one's way
       d. to take one's time

Lakoff (for the most part citing Ross's examples), argued that each idiom was more restricted in its syntactic behavior than the next higher in the hierarchy. For example, only *to stub one's toe* can be converted into a sequence of past participle, noun.

(38) a.   A *stubbed toe* can be very painful.
      b.   **Held breath* is usually fetid when released.
      c.   **A lost way* has been the cause of many a missed appointment.
      d.   **Taken time* might tend to irritate your boss.

To stub one's toe and *to hold one's breath* allow gapping in their conjuncts:

(39) a.   I stubbed my toe, and she hers.
      b.   I held my breath, and she hers.
      c.   *I lost my way, and she hers.
      d.   *I took my time, and she hers.

Pluralization possibilities distinguish *to stub one's toe* from *to hold one's breath* and both of these from *to lose one's way* and *to take one's time*. When *to stub one's toe* has a conjoined subject, pluralization is obligatory; for *to hold one's breath* it is optional; and for the latter two it is impossible:

(40) a.   Betty and Sue stubbed their toes.
      b.   *Betty and Sue stubbed their toe.
      c.   Betty and Sue held their breaths.
      d.   Betty and Sue held their breath.
      e.   *Betty and Sue lost their ways.
      f.   Betty and Sue lost their way.
      g.   *Betty and Sue took their times.
      h.   Betty and Sue took their time.

Finally, Lakoff judges all but *to take one's time* to allow pronominalization:

(41) a.   I stubbed my toe, but didn't hurt *it*.
      b.   Sam held his breath for a few seconds, and then released *it*.
      c.   Harry lost his way, but found *it* again.
      d.   *Harry took his time, but wasted *it*.

Lakoff concludes:

In each of these cases, the nounier nouns follow the general rule ..., while the less nouny nouns do not follow the rule. As the sentences indicate, there is a hierarchy of nouniness among the examples given. Rules differ as to how nouny a noun they require. (Lakoff 1987: 64).

In all cases but one, however, I have found an independent explanation for the range of judgments on these sentences. Beginning with the passive participle test, we find that (for whatever reason) *held* and *taken* never occur as participle modifiers, even in their literal senses:

(42) a. *Held cats often try to jump out of your arms.
     b. *The taken jewels were never returned.

I confess to not being able to explain (38c), since *lost* does occur in this position in a literal sense:

(43) A lost child is a pathetic sight.

Turning to Gapping, sentences (44a–d) show that the facts cited by Lakoff have nothing to do with the idioms themselves:[19]

(44) a. I lost my way, and she her way.
     b. I took my time, and she her time.
     c. ?I ate my ice cream and she hers.
     d. In the race to get to the airport, Mary and John lost their way, but we didn't lose ours (and so we won).

Examples (44a–b) illustrate that the idioms *lose one's way* and *take one's time* do indeed allow gapping in their conjuncts. The correct generalization appears to lie in discourse factors. Gapping apparently requires a contrastive focus reading of the gapped constituent. Hence (44c) seems as bad as (39c–d), while (44d) is fine.

In the examples involving plurals, what seems to be involved is the ability to individuate. We can do that easily with toes and less easily, but still possibly, with breaths. But we cannot individuate ways and times. So, nonplural (45a) is impossible—legs demand individuation—while plural (45b) is impossible as well, for the opposite reason. Rice in its collective sense is not individuated:

(45) a. *Betty and Sue broke their leg.
     b. *My bowl is full of rices.

Finally, (46a) and (46b) illustrate that *time* in *take one's time* is not resistant to pronominalization. (46a) is much improved over (41d) and (46b) is impeccable:

19. I am indebted to Ronnie Cann for pointing this out to me.

(46) a. Harry took his time, and wasted it.

     b. Harry took his time, which doesn't mean that he didn't find a way to waste it.

Again, there is no reason whatever to stipulate that grammatical processes have to be sensitive to the degree of prototypicality of the NP. Independently needed principles—none of which themselves crucially incorporate prototypicality—explain the range of acceptability.

4.3.4   English possessives   Taylor suggests that in NP's N constructions, the prototypicality of the possessor NP is relevant to acceptability:

> Consider the kinds of noun which can serve as the head of the 'possessor' NP. A noun like *teacher* is readily available: *the teacher's house, the teacher's work, the teacher's arrival,* and so on. Nouns which are semantically more distant from the prototype are less satisfactory; *the table's surface* and *the building's age* are still (perhaps) OK, but *the sky's color* and *the doorway's height* are more dubious. . . . And the ease with which nouns can designate a 'possessor' appears to correlate with closeness to the *semantically* defined prototype. (1989: 192–193; emphasis in original)

The situation, however, is vastly more complex than that. *Tuesday's lecture* (*the lecture on Tuesday*) is possible, but not *Van Gogh's lecture* (*the lecture about Van Gogh*); possessives of some nouns are impossible regardless of the degree of prototypicality (*Mary's familiarity with botany/ Susan* alongside **botany's/Susan's familiarity*); *the wind's destruction* is fine with *wind* understood as the cause of the destruction, but *John's destruction* is best interpreted with John as causee (but compare *John's destruction of the papers*); nonprototypical expletive *it* possessivizes (*its being 12 o'clock*), but not equally nonprototypical expletive *there* (**there's being not enough beer*); and so on. While nobody would claim to have a full understanding of the conditions licensing the possessor NP, what is at work appears to be a complex interaction of argument and event structure, along with some purely idiosyncratic factors (for discussion of the problem, see Anderson 1983; Randall 1984; Lebeaux 1986; and Grimshaw 1990).

4.3.5   Event structure and inflectional possibilities   Let us further explore why there is in general a correlation between degree of prototypicality and inflectional possibilities. Since Vendler (1967) it has been customary to divide the aspectual properties of verbs (and the propositions of which they are predicates) into four event types, generally referred to as 'states', 'processes', 'achievements', and 'accomplishments'. States (*know, resemble*) are not inherently bounded, have no natural goal or outcome, are not evaluated with respect to any other event, and are homogeneous. Processes (*walk, run*) are durative events with no inherent bound. Achievements (*die, find, arrive*) are momentary events of transition, while Accomplishments (*build, destroy*) are durative events with a natural goal or outcome. There have been a number of proposals for the representation of event structure (Dowty 1979; Grimshaw 1990; Pustejovsky 1995). The following are the proposals of Pustejovsky (1991):

(47) a. *States*

b. *Processes*

c. *Achievements* and *accomplishments* have the same schematic structure (both are called 'transitions'), though the former are non-agentive and the latter agentive:

Two observations are in order. The first is that there is a general increase in the complexity of event structure from states to accomplishments. The second is that this increase in complexity corresponds roughly to the the degree of prototypicality for verbs. From these observations, we may derive the reason for the correlation between prototypicality and inflectional possibilities to hold for verbs as a general tendency. There is clearly a mapping between the event structure of a proposition and those aspects of morphosyntactic structure in which tense, aspect, modality, and so on are encoded. In standard varieties of principles-and-parameters syntax, this is the 'functional structure' representation of the sentence. Now, the more complex the event structure of a proposition, the more aspectual possibilities that it allows. Hence, the more complex (in terms of number of projections) the functional structure can be. And, of course, it follows that the possibilities for inflection will be greater. In other words, we have derived a general correlation between degree of prototypicality and potential richness of verbal inflection without any reference to prototypicality per se.

It should be pointed out that this approach demands that functional projections exist only where they are motivated, i.e. that there can be no empty projections. Otherwise, there would be no difference in functional structure between states and accomplishments. In other words, it presupposes the principle of Minimal Projection, proposed and defended in Grimshaw (1993). According to this principle, a projection must be functionally interpreted, that is, it must make a contribution to the functional representation of the extended projection of which it is part.[20]

The correlation between semantic complexity and inflectional possibilities holds for nouns as well. Objects, e.g. people, books, automobiles, etc. can be individuated and specified in a way that abstract nouns such as *liberty* and dummy nouns like *there* cannot. So it follows that the semantic structure of concrete nouns will have the general potential to map onto more layers of nominal functional structure than that of abstract nouns.

The situation with adjectives is instructive in this regard. Virtually any adjective lends itself to being compared, intensified, equated, and so on. Not surprisingly, then, adjectives of different degrees of semantic prototypicality, but performing the same discourse function, do not differ in their inflectional possibilities.

One predicts, then, that languages in which categories are not distinguished by inflection will, all other things being equal, have more 'fluid' categories than those languages with rich inflection. That is, in inflection-poor languages the same root will often be assigned to more than one category and there will be considerable migrating of categorial assignments over time. This appears to be true. Consider Chinese, for example. For these very reasons there has been a long-standing debate over whether Chinese even *has* distinguishable syntactic categories (see Simon 1937; Chao 1968). While nobody would take the negative side of this debate today, it seems clear that categorial instability is, to a large degree, a product of the amount of available inflection. That might vary from language to language, but the overarching controlling factor is derivable

20. Grimshaw (1997) derives Minimal Projection from the principles of Economy of Movement and Oblig Heads.

from the semantics of the item in question and the pragmatics of its use, not its degree of prototypicality.

I will close this section by pointing to two problems that are faced by an exclusively semantic account of restrictions on inflection. The first is that some languages have inflections that are restricted to some forms but not others, even though there appears to be no semantic explanation for the restriction. For example, Croft notes that process verbs in Quiché take tense-aspect inflectional prefixes, while stative verbs do not, and writes,

> There is no apparent reason for this, since there is no semantic incompatibility between the inflectional prefixes ..., and in fact in a language like English stative predicates do inflect for tense. It is simply a grammatical fact regarding the expression of stative predicates in Quiché. As such, it provides very strong evidence for the markedness of stative predicates compared to process predicates. (1990: 82)

While I do not pretend to have a full explanation for cases such as these, I would venture to guess that what we have here are pragmatic factors overriding semantic ones. Both process verbs and stative verbs can logically manifest tense, aspect, and modality, though in many discourse contexts such distinctions are irrelevant for the latter. Thus pragmatic factors have kept the grammars of Quiché and languages manifesting similar phenomena from grammaticalizing tense, aspect, and modality for stative verbs. No appeal to prototypicality is necessary.

A second problem with a semantic approach to inflection is that inflections that appear to be semantically *empty* also manifest prototype effects. Take agreement inflections, for example. As is noted in Croft (1988a), where languages have a 'choice' as to object agreement, it is always the more definite and/or animate (i.e. more prototypical) direct object that has the agreement marker. Does this fact support prototype theory? Not necessarily: In the same paper Croft argues that agreement has a *pragmatic function*, namely to index important or salient arguments. So, if agreement markers are not 'pragmatically empty', then their presence can be related to their discourse function and need not be attributed to the inherently 'prototypical' properties of the arguments to which they are affixed.

5 Prototypes and Markedness

This section will overview the relationship between prototype theory and markedness theory (§5.1) and conclude that given the latter, there is no need for the former (§5.2).

5.1 Distinguishing 'prototype theory' from 'markedness theory'

The Prague School linguists of the 1930s developed the conception that, given two grammatical elements in paradigmatic opposition, one member of the opposition can generally be identified as 'marked' and the other as 'unmarked'. Markedness theory was developed first in Trubetzkoy (1931) for phonology and soon thereafter in Jakobson (1932/1971) for morphosyntax and semantics. The criteria applied by the Prague School to identify the marked and unmarked members of oppositions were based (again, to use the terminology of Moravcsik and Wirth 1980) on syntagmatic complexity, paradigmatic complexity, and distribution. The unmarked value requires no more morphemes than the marked (i.e. it is simpler syntagmatically), it has more distinct forms in an inflectional paradigm than the marked or occurs in a larger range of construction types (i.e. it is more complex paradigmatically), and it occurs more frequently in actual spoken or written text. So, for Russian, masculine gender is held to be unmarked with respect to feminine, singular number with respect to plural, the present tense as opposed to the preterite, indicative mood as opposed to subjunctive, and so on.

Modern work in linguistic typology, initiated by Greenberg (1963), has added a new dimension of complexity to the idea of markedness, first by intensive investigation of the cross-linguistic applicability of marking conventions and second by expanding the domain of markedness from simple marked-unmarked oppositions to hierarchies of *relative* markedness. As to the first point, as more and more languages have been investigated, it has turned out that oppositions tend to have the same markedness values in each language in which they can be identified.[21] We would be surprised, for example, to find a language in which the preterit was unmarked and the present marked. As to the second, it was found that nonbinary oppositions tend to have the same systematic manifestation of marking properties as binary ones. So, for example, the grammatical category of 'number' manifests itself in different ways in different languages. Some, like English, have only a singular and a plural, with the

---

21. Though the matter is complicated by the fact that the structure of the overall system in which the particular opposition exists affects markedness values. So, in English, objective case is unmarked with respect to nominative; in Russian nominative is unmarked with respect to objective. However, since Russian overall has a greater number of cases than English, we can cannot treat the English nominative-objective opposition as 'the same thing' as the nominative-objective opposition in Russian. For discussion of this problem, see Battistella (1990).

plural meeting the criteria for markedness. However, other languages have dual number, and still others a trial or a paucal. As it turns out, a hierarchy of markedness can by formulated as in (48) (Greenberg 1963: 94; Croft 1990: 97):

(48) singular < plural < dual < trial/paucal

The same sorts of criteria that lead to the conclusion that the plural is marked with respect to the singular lead to the conclusion that the dual is marked with respect to the plural and the trial and paucal with respect to the dual.

Now, where do prototypes fit in? Occasionally, the term is used informally as the virtual synonym of 'unmarked': the prototypical number is singular, the prototypical gender is masculine, and so on. But more often prototypes are regarded as properties of *categories*, including syntactic categories.[22] Where unmarked values of various traits cluster, we have the prototype of that category. In phonology, for example, we might say that the prototypical vowel is voiced, sonorant, syllabic, nonnasalized, nonglottalized, and so on, since vowels tend to be unmarked for each of those properties.

---

22. The ontological status of both markedness and prototypicality is murky, as is the relationship between them. Perhaps the most common view is that markedness is a structural relationship within a grammar, while prototypicality is a fact about cognitive representations (see Battistella 1990: 43 for exposition of such a view). Thus, 'markedness is a term used by linguists to describe a kind of prototype effect' (Lakoff 1987: 60). However, at least some hierarchies of markedness might possibly be attributed psychological reality, e.g. the Animacy Hierarchy, and certainly not every manifestation of markedness can be described as a prototype effect.

Prototypes are sometimes attributed a cognitive reality that the mere fact of unmarkedness is not. Consider for example, the idea that the prototypical transitive clause manifests the unmarked values of a set of semantic and pragmatic properties such as telicity, agentiveness, activity, and so on (Hopper and Thompson 1980). Such seems to imply that speakers have a 'gestalt' of a transitive clause, i.e. that it has a distinct cognitive reality.

To complicate matters still further, the notion of 'markedness' (but not that of 'prototypicality') is accorded an important role in certain models of generative grammar, where its interpretation is explicitly psychological. That is, markedness is either a property of parameter settings *within* core grammar (Manzini and Wexler 1987) or a property of the distance of a rule or principle *from* core grammar (Hyams 1986).

Analogously in syntax, categorial hierarchies of prototypicality reflect the convergence of whatever markedness hierarchies. So for example, the degree of prototypicality for nouns is derivable to a considerable degree from two markedness hierarchies: the Animacy Hierarchy and the Definiteness Hierarchy (see Croft 1991: 126–129). The former, first formulated in Silverstein (1976), is as follows, where nouns with the highest degree of animacy are on the left, the lowest on the right:

(49) *Animacy Hierarchy*
1st, 2nd person pronouns < 3rd person pronouns < proper names < human common nouns < nonhuman animate common nouns < inanimate common nouns (Dixon 1979: 85)

The Definiteness Hierarchy is as follows:

(50) *Definiteness Hierarchy*
definite < referential indefinite < nonreferential indefinite (Croft 1990: 115)

Note that the two hierarchies converge to a certain degree, e.g. first and second person pronouns are always definite, while many abstract (and therefore inanimate) common nouns are always nonreferential. Furthermore, the semantic end points of these two hierarchies jibe well with the pragmatic criteria for prototypicality, since definite personal pronouns are the most 'referential' of all NPs.

In other words, a common view—and one that will be adopted here— is that markedness is a relative concept, while prototypicality is an absolute concept. The unmarked subject NP may be animate and the unmarked instrumental NP may be inanimate, but the prototypical NP *in general*, i.e. the NP which is unmarked for the largest number of features, is animate.

5.2 Markedness overrides prototypicality
In this section I will provide one more reason to abandon the notion of 'prototypicality' in grammatical analysis. When the (absolute) degree of prototypicality conflicts with some (relative) hierarchy of markedness, it is always the latter that determines grammatical behavior.

Consider the phenomenon of 'markedness reversals' (or 'local markedness'). In such a case, we have the normally unmarked value of an opposition taking on the value of the marked member, and vice-versa. Croft (1990: 134–147) provides several examples. Normally, deictic terms and common nouns referring to places are marked with respect to animate nouns. However, when they occur as locatives, markedness is reversed. So, for example, Malay locatives denoting a person are syntagmatically more complex than those denoting a place:

(51) a. kĕ-φ 'to' / dari-φ 'from' + noun phrase denoting a place
     b. kĕ-*pada* 'to' / dari-*pada* 'from' + noun phrase denoting a person

Hence we find the effects of prototypicality being overriden by those of markedness. The same point can be made with respect to noun number. Singulars are more prototypical in an absolute sense than plurals. However, for nouns denoting objects that tend to occur in a group, plural is unmarked with respect to singular. Hence many languages have a collective-singulative contrast, where the (semantically plural) collective form is syntagmatically simpler than the (semantically singular) 'singulative' form. Croft (1990: 149) goes on to note that as far as pronominal systems are concerned, different markedness hierarchies rank the different persons differently:

We may summarize the typological patterns as follows (using '? <' again for a less-certain ranking of values):

G[rammatical] R[elations] hierarchy: 1, 2 < 3
Non-imperatives: 3 < 1 < 2
Imperatives: 2 < 1, 3
Number: 1 < 2? < 3
Gender: 3? < 2 < 1
Politeness: 2 < 3 < 1

Again, we see markedness overriding prototypicality.

   To conclude, if 'prototypical' is simply another word for 'unmarked', then it is redundant to make any appeal to the former term in grammatical analysis. On the other hand, if the two are distinguishable along the lines that we have been assuming, then the former can be dispensed with on the grounds of empirical adequacy.

6   The Nonexistence of Fuzzy Categories

We turn now to the question of whether categories have distinct *boundaries*, or, alternatively, whether they grade one into the other in fuzzy squish-like fashion. I examine three phenomena that have been appealed to in support of fuzzy categories—English *near* (§6.1), the Nouniness

Squish (§6.2), and Russian number names (§6.3)—and conclude that no argument for fuzzy categories can be derived from them.

6.1 English *near*

Ross (1972) analyzes the English word *near* as something between an adjective and a preposition. Like an adjective, it takes a preposition before its object (52a) and like a preposition, it takes a bare object (52b):

(52) a. The shed is near to the barn.
 b. The shed is near the barn.

So it would appear, as Ross concluded, that there is a continuum between the categories Adjective and Preposition, and *near* is to be analyzed as occupying a position at the center of the continuum. A prototype theorist would undoubtedly conclude that the intermediate position of *near* is a consequence of its having neither prototypical adjectival nor prototypical prepositional properties.

In fact, *near* can be used either as an adjective or a preposition. Maling (1983) provides evidence for the former categorization. Like any transitive adjective, it takes a following preposition (53a); when that preposition is present (i.e. when *near* is adjectival), the degree modifier must follow it (53b); it takes a comparative suffix (53c); and we find it (somewhat archaically) in prenominal position (53d):

(53) a. The gas station is near to the supermarket.
 b. Near enough to the supermarket
 c. Nearer to the supermarket
 d. The near shore

Near passes tests for Preposition as well. It takes a bare object (54a); when it has a bare object it may not be followed by *enough* (54b), but may take the prepositional modifier *right* (54c):

(54) a. The gas station is near the supermarket.
 b. *The gas station is near enough the supermarket.[23]
 c. The gas station is right near (*to) the supermarket.

It is true that, as a Preposition, it uncharacteristically takes an inflected comparative:

23. Maling judges sentences of this type acceptable, and on that basis rejects the idea that *near* is a P. I must say that I find (54b) impossible.

(55) The gas station is nearer the supermarket than the bank.

But, as (56) shows, other prepositions occur in the comparative construction; it is only in its being inflected, then, that *near* distinguishes itself:[24]

(56) The seaplane right now is more over the lake than over the
      mountain.

Thus I conclude that *near* provides no evidence for categorial continua.

6.2 The Nouniness Squish

Recall Ross's Nouniness Squish (5), repeated below:

(5) *The Nouniness Squish*
     that clauses > *for to* clauses > embedded questions > Acc *ing*
     complements > Poss *ing* complements > action nominals > derived
     nominals > underived nominals

This squish grades nouns (or, more properly, the phrases that contain them) along a single dimension—their degree of nominality. Subordinate and relative clauses introduced by the complementizer *that* are held to be the least nominal; underived nominals (i.e. simple nouns) are held to be the most nominal. But, according to Ross, there is no fixed point at which the dominating phrase node ceases to be S and starts to be NP; each successive element on the squish is held to be somewhat more nominal than the element to its left.

As Ross is aware, demonstrating a fuzzy boundary between S and NP entails (minimally) showing that syntactic behavior gradually changes as one progresses along the squish, that is, that there is no place where S 'stops' and NP 'starts'. We will now examine two purported instances of this graduality. As we will see, the facts are perfectly handlable in an approach that assumes membership in either S or NP.

First, Ross claims that 'the nounier a complement is, the less accessible are the nodes it dominates to the nodes which command the complement' (Ross 1973b: 174). That is, it should be harder to extract from a phrase headed by an underived N than from a *that* clause. He illustrates the workings of this principle with the data in (57) and concludes that 'the

---

24. Presumably the inflectional possibilities of *near* are properties of its neutralized lexical entry, rather than of the ADJ or P branch of the entry.

dwindling Englishness of [these] sentences supports [this principle]'
(1973b: 175):

(57) a. I wonder who he resented (it) that I went steady with.
     b. I wonder who he would resent (it) for me to go steady with.
     c. *I wonder who he resented how long I went steady with.
     d. ?I wonder who he resented me going out with.
     e. ??I wonder who he resented my going out with.
     f. ?*I wonder who he resented my careless examining of.
     g. ?*I wonder who he resented my careless examination of.
     h. ?*I wonder who he resented the daughter of.

But one notes immediately that, even on Ross' terms, we do not find
consistently 'dwindling Englishness': (57c) is crashingly bad. Furthermore, he admits (in a footnote) that many speakers find (57h) fine. In fact,
the data seem quite clear to me: (57a–b, d–e, h) are acceptable, and (57c,
f–g) are not. The latter three sentences are straightforward barriers violations, given the approach of Chomsky (1986a), while the others violate
no principles of UG. The degree of 'nouniness' plays no role in the explanation of these sentences.

   Second, Ross suggests that the phenomenon of pied piping—that
is, Wh-Movement carrying along material dominating the fronted wh-
phrase, is sensitive to degree of nouniness. He cites (58a–f) in support of
this idea. It would appear, he claims, that the more nouny the dominating
phrase, the more pied piping is possible:

(58) a. *Eloise, [for us to love [whom]] they liked, is an accomplished
         washboardist.
     b. *Eloise, [us loving [whom]] they liked, is an accomplished
         washboardist.
     c. *Eloise, [our loving [whom]] they liked, is an accomplished
         washboardist.
     d. ?*Eloise, [our loving of [whom]] they liked, is an accomplished
         washboardist.
     e. ?Eloise, [our love for [whom]] they liked, is an accomplished
         washboardist.
     f. Eloise, [a part of [whom]] they liked, is an accomplished
         washboardist.

Again, there is no support for a categorial continuum in these data. *For
to* clauses, Acc *ing* complements, and Poss *ing* complements are all

Table 4.5
The apparent adjective-to-noun squish of Russian numeral names

Property	odin '1'	dva '2'	tri '3'	pjat' '5'	sto '100'	tysjača '1000'	million '1,000,000'
(a)	A	N	N	N	N	N	N
(b)	A	N	N	N	N	N	N
(c)	A	(A)	N	N	N	N	N
(d)	A	A/(N)	A/(N)	N	N	N	N
(e)	A	A	A	A	(N)	N	N
(f)	A	A	A	A	A	N	N
(g)	A	A	A	A	A	A/N	N

Properties (a) through (g) represent morphosyntactic properties that test for N or A.

dominated by the node S, which can *never* pied pipe. Hence (58a–c) are ungrammatical. On the other hand, (58d–e) are all fully grammatical, though this is masked by the stylistic awkwardness of the *loving ... liked* sequence. By substituting *was a joy to our parents* for *they liked* some of the awkwardness is eliminated and both sentences increase in acceptability.

6.3   Russian number names
A particularly interesting categorial continuum was first proposed by Corbett (1978) and brought to the attention of the broader community of linguists in Comrie (1989: 107–109). It would appear that adjectival behavior decreases and nominal behavior increases as Russian numerals increase in value. In table 4.5 (a) through (g) are tests for adjectives and nouns in that language. The first four, (a) through (d), are tests for adjective status: (a) is number agreement with the head noun, on a singular/plural opposition; (b) is case agreement with the head noun; (c) is gender agreement with the head noun; (d) is animacy agreement with the head noun. The last three, (e) through (g), are tests for noun status: (e) is the ability of the head noun to take number independently of the dependent noun; (f) is the ability of the head noun in the quantitative construction to take an attributive agreeing with it; (g) is the invariable appearance of the noun dependent on the head noun in the genitive, and, if countable, in the genitive plural.

Table 4.5 suggests that adjectivalness decreases and nouniness increases as the numerals increase in value. That is, the word for '1' passes all the adjective tests and fails all the noun tests. The word for '1,000,000' fails all the adjective tests and passes all the noun tests. The words for '2', '3', '5', '100', and '1000' seem to display increasing nouniness as their value increases.

Comrie provides a prototype-squish explanation for the facts:

> In Russian, in general, the distinction between nouns and adjectives is clear cut, so that we can establish criteria that correlate with the focal values (prototypes) of noun and adjective. Numerals, however, fall in between these two prototypes, in a way that makes impossible any establishment of non-arbitrary cut-off points ... The situation is rather that we have clear prototypes, and a continuum separating those prototypes from one another, much as with color terms, even though here we are clearly dealing with grammatical categories. (1989: 107–109)

Babby (1987, forthcoming) has provided an analysis of these facts that does not appeal to categorial continua. In his analysis, the apparent mixed adjectival and nominal properties of 2–10 derive from the fact that they were historically either adjectives (2–4) or nouns (5–10), which were reanalyzed as a new category when the dual was lost. In Modern Russian, *odin* '1' is an adjective and *million* '1,000,000' is a noun. The numbers in between are neither; they are a new category 'Q' (i.e. Quantifier) headed by QP. Importantly, QP occupies a new position that was created in the NP (see Babby 1987 for details). Thus many of the unique properties of NPs containing numbers can be explained in terms of X-bar structure. For example, *tysjača* '1000' can behave like a noun and be head of NP or it can behave like a number (i.e. a Q) and be head of the QP, which is itself contained in the NP. *Pjat'* '5' can only be the head of QP, and *million* can only be head of NP. So, much of the squish-like behavior of numbers falls out from discrete categories and their projections in X-bar structure.

It still remains to be explained why 2–4 have adjectival properties. In Babby's view, the categorial reanalysis introduced a new feature [Q] to the categorial features making up nouns and adjectives, and [Q] was projected to the phrase's maximal projection along with the other categorial features. The apparent varying degree of adjectivalness of the lower numbers follows from independently needed constraints on the distribution of this feature.

6.4 Summary

We have looked at three phenomena that appear to suggest the need for fuzzy boundaries between categories. Analyzed carefully, however, none lead to that conclusion.

7 Against Langacker's Notional Definitions of 'Noun' and 'Verb'

Langacker (1987b) attempts to provide necessary and sufficient conditions for membership in the categories 'noun' and 'verb' in English.[25] In particular, 'a noun designates a region in some domain' (1987b: 58), where a 'region' is a 'set of interconnected entities' (1987b: 62) and a 'domain' is any cognitive structure, such as 'a novel conceptualization, an established concept, a perceptual experience, or an entire knowledge system' (1987b: 56). For example, the noun *bicycle* consists of a set of interconnected entities (the parts that compose it) in the domain of vehicles. A noun like *beep*, on the other hand, is internally homogeneous, so 'the major burden of delimitation necessarily falls on contrast with surroundings' (in this case, silence).

Such a definition would appear to admit the words *yell* and *red* into the class of nouns—couldn't one construe yells as regions in the domain of shouting and specific colors as regions in the general domain of color? Langacker's solution to this problem is to distinguish between nominal and relational predications, which differ as to how content is construed and profiled. A nominal predication presupposes interconnections among a set of conceived entities and profiles the region, while a relational predication presupposes a set of entities and profiles the interconnections among them.

Relational predications are further divided into those that involve summary scanning and those that involve sequential scanning. With respect to the former, namely, complex atemporal relations, 'all facets of [a complex conceptualization] are simultaneously available, and cohere as a single gestalt' (Langacker 1987b: 72). With respect to the latter, namely processes, 'the various phases of an evolving situation are examined serially, in non-cumulative fashion; hence the conceptualization is dynamic, in the sense that its contents change from one instant to the next' (Lan-

---

25. While all of Langacker's examples are from English, he does say that his characterizations 'are no doubt universal rather than language-specific' (1987b: 54).

gacker 1987b: 72). Nominal predications are, of course, nouns. Relational predications that denote processes are verbs; those that denote complex atemporal relations are prepositions, adjectives, adverbs, infinitives, or participles.[26] Consider, for example, the distinctions between the words *group* and *together* or between the nominal sense of *square* and the adjectival sense. The nominals *group* and *square* presuppose the interconnections that define them, while highlighting the entire gestalt. The use of the relational predicates *together* and *square*, on the other hand, presupposes the entities which they predicate and profile their relations to each other.

While Langacker's attempt to characterize notionally the distinction between nouns and verbs is certainly of interest, his presentation of the relevant parameters leaves so many questions open that he cannot be said to have come close to establishing his case. To begin with, as noted by Croft (1991: 285), it is not clear how he would handle inherently relational nouns. Kinship terms and words like *friend, translator,* and so on do more than profile interconnections internal to a domain. Crucially, they relate entities of one domain to those of another. Notice how difficult it is to conceive of 'daughters', 'friends', and so on in the abstract—one is almost compelled to conceptualize pairs of entities to which they refer. But that should lead them to be categorized as verbs (or at least as some type of relational predication), not as nouns, given Langacker's definitions.

Conversely, there are *non*-relational verbs and adjectives. Words for referring to the weather provide perhaps the best example. In sentences such as *It rained yesterday* and *It is sunny*, what are the entities among which interconnections are profiled for the verb *rain* and the adjective *sunny*? Along the same lines, I doubt very strongly that no 'sequential scanning' is involved in the interpretation of the noun *rain* in the sentence *The rain lasted for 8 hours,* or even for the noun *rain* removed from a normal sentential context.

Even more troublesome are those verbs which do not appear to be sequentially scanned. Croft (1991: 106–107) notes, correctly in my opinion, that such verbs as *be (at), have,* and *see* are implausibly analyzed as processes; certainly there is no essential 'sequential' aspect of their interpretation.

---

26. And hence the latter two categories are not considered to be verbs or a subclass of verbs.

An unfortunate consequence of Langacker's definitions is that infinitives and participles must be entirely divorced from the category 'verb'. Thus he loses the advantage of both the generative analysis, which sees them as (subclasses of) verbs, and the prototype approach, which sees a categorial continuum between them and 'true' verbs. There is another peculiarity of his analysis. The participle *running*, being atemporal, cannot be a verb. However, the stem *run-* is analyzed as a process, and hence is called a verb (Langacker 1987b: 75). But surely the stem itself is atemporal as well; it takes a tense inflection to make the sentence a temporal predication—in this case an inflection on the preceding copula. I suspect that Langacker was led to this analysis by the (totally reasonable) desire to capture the traditional statement that the word *run* is a verb. But the stem of the participle cannot be one, given how he defines that syntactic category.

In summary, Langacker's attempt to define notionally the syntactic categories noun and verb is not successful.

8 Conclusion

The classical view of syntactic categories assumed in most models of generative grammar has seen three major challenges. In one, categories have a prototype structure, in which they have 'best case' members and members that systematically depart from the 'best case'. In this approach, the optimal grammatical description of morphosyntactic processes is held to involve reference to degree of categorial deviation from the 'best case'. The second challenge hypothesizes that the boundaries between categories are nondistinct, in the sense that one grades gradually into another. The third takes categories to be definable by necessary and sufficient semantic conditions.

This chapter has defended the classical view, arguing that categories have discrete boundaries, are not organized around central 'best cases', and are not definable notionally. It has argued that many of the phenomena that seem to suggest the inadequacy of the classical view are best analyzed in terms of the interaction of independently needed principles from syntax, semantics, and pragmatics.

Appendix: On Prototypes Constructions

In this appendix, we will take a quick look at another notion that has been attributed a prototype structure, the grammatical construction, and conclude that here too there is no reason to appeal to prototypes to explain their properties.

A.1 George Lakoff on deictic constructions

Undoubtedly the most extensive argument that syntactic constructions are endowed with a prototype structure is George Lakoff's 123-page discussion of English deictic *there* and *here* constructions (Lakoff 1987: 462–585). These all have the role of 'pointing out', that is, focusing the hearer's attention upon an entity in the speaker's consciousness. These constructions are named and illustrated in (59a–k):

(59) *Deictic here and there constructions*
    a. *Central*: There's Harry with the red jacket on.
    b. *Perceptual*: There goes the bell now!
    c. *Discourse*: There's a nice point to bring up in class.
    d. *Existence*: There goes our last hope.
    e. *Activity Start*: There goes Harry, meditating again.
    f. *Delivery*: Here's your pizza, piping hot!
    g. *Paragon*: Now there was a real ballplayer!
    h. *Exasperation*: There goes Harry again, making a fool of himself.
    i. *Narrative Focus*: There I was, in the middle of the jungle ...
    j. *New Enterprise*: Here I go, off to Africa.
    k. *Presentational*: There on that hill will be built a new university.

In Lakoff's analysis, not all of these constructions have equal status as far as the grammar of English is concerned. Rather, the Central Deictic, in which initial deictic *there* designates a location in physical space, is the prototype deictic construction and the others are based on it, not by a 'derivation', in the generative sense, but by a network of relationships radiating out from it. In broad outline, the grammar specifies the properties of the prototypical central construction, along with the properties that minimally distinguish each of the subconstructions from it. Lakoff observes:

The result is a cognitive structure that is very much like the category structures that occur elsewhere in the conceptual system. The point is that structures like this are to be expected, given the way people normally construct categories. Prototype theory *explains* why such a grouping of constructions should exist in a language. According to traditional generative theories, such a clustering of categories is simply an anomaly. (Lakoff 1987: 482; emphasis in original)

Thus we have a relationship between the Central Deictic and the other deictic constructions as is schematically illustrated in (60):

(60)

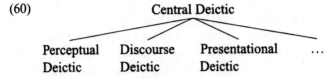

As Lakoff notes, the methodology of generative grammar is incompatible with this approach. The idea of a family of constructions radially structured around a prototype is not one provided by the language faculty in any generative framework of which I am aware. Indeed, models in the principles-and-parameters tradition regard even the notion 'construction' itself to be epiphenomenal (see below).

In the remainder of this appendix, I will examine three of the putatively noncentral constructions, namely, the Perceptual Deictic, the Presentational Deictic, and the Paragon Deictic. I will argue that no special statements are needed in the grammar to characterize these constructions that are not needed to characterize the Central Deictic. From this I will conclude that there is little evidence to regard the latter as a 'prototype' in any sense and, from this conclusion, go on to question the idea that constructions in general have a prototype structure.

A.2   The Perceptual Deictic

The Perceptual Deictic can be illustrated by sentences such as (61a–d), in which *there* seems to refer to a perceptual, rather than a spatial location:

(61) a. There's the beep.
     b. There goes the bell now!
     c. Here comes the beep.
     d. There goes that throbbing in my head again.

In Lakoff's analysis, the construction is given the representation in (62). Essentially, what this means is that it has all of the properties of the Central Deictic, except for those that follow from its being about nonvisual perception:

(62) *The Perceptual Deictic*
     Based on: The Central Deictic
     About: Nonvisual perception

The fact that it is about nonvisual perception guarantees that it will make use of those metaphors and metonymies that are relevant to that domain. These include the conceptual metaphors (63a–c) and a metonymy (63d):

(63) a. Nonvisual perceptual space is physical space; percepts are entities.
b. Realized is distal; soon-to-be-realized is proximal.
c. Activation is motion.
d. The thing perceived stands for the percept while the perception is in progress.

By means of (63a–d), the properties of sentences such as (61a–d) are said to be captured: *there* is understood in a nonvisual perceptual sense, *go* is used to denote activation, rather than motion, and so on.

I will offer instead an analysis that makes no reference whatsoever to a distinct Perceptual Deictic construction. Surely, in the absence of evidence to the contrary, the simplest assumption is that independently motivated principles of grammar, meaning, and use conspire to derive the formal and semantic properties of all the noncentral deictic *there* constructions. To be specific, the null hypothesis is that *there* and *here* are simply deictic locatives and that *come* and *go* are verbs of change, with nothing more required to be said (so far as our purposes are concerned). But, then, what about the fact that the deictics in (61) do not refer to literal physical location, but rather a metaphorical location in 'perceptual space'? I would follow Jackendoff (1983) in arguing that we do not have metaphor here at all, but rather thematic parallelism. Jackendoff, who posits a richer theory of the structure of mind than does Lakoff, argues that the structural parallels between our encoding of physical and perceptual space (for example) are part of our underlying mental resources, not a contingent by-product of metaphorical extension. In this view, Lakoff's 'invariance hypothesis', the idea that 'metaphorical mappings preserve the cognitive typology ... of the source domain' (Lakoff 1990: 54), is an epiphenominal by-product of these resources. As Jackendoff notes:

Thematic structure is the only means available to organize a semantic field of events and states coherently—it is an indispensable element of everyday thought. Moreover, the most remarkable aspect of metaphor is its variety, the possibility of using practically any semantic field for any other. By contrast, thematic relations disclose the same analogy over and over again: time is location, being possessed is location, properties are locations, events are locations. That is, the theory of thematic relations claims not just that some fields are structured in terms of other fields, but rather that all fields have essentially the *same* structure. (Jackendoff 1983: 209)

Jackendoff uses 'domain features' such as temporal, spatial, possessive, and identificational to state cross-domain generalizations—the same primitive conceptual function can appear in different domains. In other words, his hypothesis allows us at one and the same time to eliminate the need for a distinct Perceptual Deictic construction and to purge the syntax of the need to make appeal to metaphorical extension.

Lakoff does, however, put forward several independent arguments in support of a distinct Perceptual Deictic construction. The first is based on the contrast in (64) and (65) (I denote odd-sounding sentences with a cross-hatch, rather than with an asterisk, to emphasize that while these sentences might be unacceptable in certain contexts, they are not necessarily *ungrammatical*):

(64) a. There's Harry.
     b. Harry is there.

(65) a. There's the beep.
     b. #The beep is there.

Lakoff concludes that the deviance of (65b) shows that there must be a distinct Perceptual Deictic construction. In his view, (65a) with perceptual *there* is licenced because it meets the conditions for the construction. However, there is nothing to licence (65b) with perceptual *there*.

Lakoff fails, however, to consider that there might exist some construction-independent reason for the impossibility of (65b). One does come to mind. *Harry* and *the beep* in (64a) and (65a) respectively are focused; roughly, they serve to call attention to the hearer of a significant event (the location of Harry, the awaited sound of the beep). In the (b) sentences, however, the noun phrases are topical; Harry has been the subject of conversation, perhaps, in (64b) and the speaker wishes to point out his location to the hearer. The oddness of (65b) comes from the fact that it is difficult, for reasons having nothing to do with deictics per se, to construe transitory beeps as topical. Notice that one can create a scenario in which the acceptability of (65b) is dramatically improved. If one has finally identified the source of an annoying beeping sound, the following exchange is perfectly normal-sounding:

(66) a. Have you figured out where inside the wall that beep is coming from?
     b. As far as I can tell, the beep is *there*.

Lakoff's second argument that specific reference must be made to 'nonvisual perception' is based on the contrast in (67a–b):

(67) a.   There's the sound of the bell.
     b.   #There's the sight of the bell.

Lakoff writes:

The central deictic makes reference to entities, not to their visual percepts such as *the sight of the bell*. The noncentral deictic only makes reference to percepts and only to nonvisual percepts. This leaves visual percepts out in the cold, so far as *there*-constructions are concerned. (Lakoff 1987: 513)

I would suggest that the difference between (67a) and (67b) follows from independent facts about what can be conceptualized as occupying a location in one's spatial or perceptual field. In folk perceptual psychology, sounds are conceived of as existing independently (in space and time) from the perception of them, while sights are not. Notice that one can say *Where is that sound coming from?* but not *Where is that sight coming from?* Thus (67a) is fine, and (67b) is deviant. *Memories* of sights do occupy (mental) space, and so can be described using deictic *there*, as in (68):

(68) There's a sight that always gives me pleasure.

On the other hand, auditory *perceptions*, as opposed to the sounds themselves, are not conceived of as occupying space, and so (69) is impossible:

(69) #There's the auditory perception of the bell.

In short, the representation of the Perceptual Deictic need not refer specifically to nonvisual perception.

Lakoff's last argument for a specific Perceptual Deictic construction is a little bit more complicated and is based on 'metonymy' (63d). The conclusion that we need (62), which triggers this metonymy, is based on sentences like (70a–b):

(70) a. There goes the beep.
     b. There goes the alarm clock.

The alarm clock stands for the sound it makes. Or, similarly, consider (71a–b):

(71) a. There goes the pain in my knee.
     b. There goes my knee.

The knee stands for the pain in it. But, Lakoff argues, the perception has to be *in progress* for this to work. So, he says, (72a) is fine if the beep is *about* to happen, but not (72b):

(72) a.   Here comes the beep.
      b.   #Here comes the alarm clock.

Likewise, according to Lakoff, (73a) is good if we sense that the knee pain is on its way, but not (73b):

(73) a.   Here comes the pain in my knee.
      b.   #Here comes my knee.

So Lakoff concludes that a special construction is needed to trigger the metonymy, thereby ruling out (72b) and (73b).

   Again, Lakoff fails to consider a simple discourse explanation for the strangeness of these two sentences. Under normal every-day conditions, both alarm clocks and knees are in our field of awareness before they 'go beep' or cause us pain. So (72b) and (73b) have readings where they are *factually* contradictory—something can't be 'coming' if it is there all along. But notice how much better (72b) is than (73b). An alarm clock can be hidden from view—if it is, then (72b) is as good as (72a). But a knee can't be so dismissed; it is part of you! It is almost impossible to contextualize (73b) without a contradictory reading.

   In short, there is no reason to postulate a Perceptual Deictic construction, thereby undermining an argument for ranking two constructions in terms of degree of prototypicality.

A.3   The Presentational Deictic

Another 'nonprototypical' construction said to be based on the Central Deictic is the 'Presentational Deictic'. Some examples are given in (74):

(74) a.   There in the alley had gathered a large crowd of roughnecks.
      b.   There on the stage wearing an outrageous costume was standing one of our most distinguished public figures.
      c.   Here honored by thousands of her fellow citizens will be laid to rest our beloved former mayor, Sally Stanford.
      d.   There without a stitch on, staring at the ceiling, lay the beautiful KGB agent shot through the heart.
      e.   Here isolated from all the noise of the city will be built large, comfortable estates to house our former presidents.

Lakoff hypothesizes two uses for this construction. First, in a narrative, it can be used to indicate a discovery, thereby (re)introducing the referent of the noun phrase into the discourse:

(75) There in my favorite chair sat a fat man with a monocle.

Another suggested use is that of pointing out something the speaker considers extremely significant:

(76) If I am elected, I guarantee that here in this town will be built a multi-purpose athletic facility second to none!

A rather complex set of conditions form what Lakoff considers to be the 'minimal representation' of this construction (1987: 521–522):[27]

(77) *The Presentational Deictic*
Based on: The Central Deictic
Discourse conditions: Used in narratives or announcements when the speaker considers the entity coded by the noun phrase to be significant.
Lexical conditions: The verb designates a location, directly or indirectly.
Syntactic conditions:
(S-1) The verb may have a full auxiliary.
(S-2) The optional elements following the noun phrase may optionally occur before the verb.
(S-3) *There* or *here* may be null if the optional elements designate a location, directly or indirectly.

To illustrate the effects of the lexical condition, Lakoff notes that the verbs *come* and *go*, when used in this construction, cannot occur with a full auxiliary:

(78) a.   There goes the president.
     b.   #There is going the president.
     c.   #Here will come the president.

He remarks, 'Since the verb must pick out a location, rather than indicate motion, we can account for why *come* and *go* cannot occur [in these sentences] with a full auxiliary' (1987: 522). However, in keeping with syntactic condition (S-1), the full auxiliary is otherwise possible (see (74a–c, e)).

---

27. For ease of exposition, I have replaced Lakoff's symbols with English prose.

Sentences (79a–e) all illustrate syntactic condition (S-2). Note that the optional element of (74a–e) can occur finally:

(79) a. There had gathered a large crowd of roughnecks in the alley.
     b. There was standing on the stage one of our most distinguished public figures wearing an outrageous costume.
     c. Here will be laid to rest our beloved former mayor, Sally Stanford, honored by thousands of her fellow citizens.
     d. There lay the beautiful KGB agent shot through the heart without a stitch on, staring at the ceiling.
     e. Here will be built large, comfortable estates to house our former presidents, isolated from all the noise of the city.

As far as (S-3) is concerned, Lakoff points to the possible omission of *there* in (80a–b), where the optional elements designate a location relative to the speaker, but its obligatory presence otherwise ((81a–b), (82a–b), and (83a–b)):

(80) a. Behind the desk was sitting a bald-headed man.
     b. Strewn about the room were lying the victim's personal effects.

(81) a. There without a stitch of clothes on lay the victim.
     b. #Without a stitch of clothes on lay the victim.

(82) a. There, enjoying his solitude, can be found the country's most famous hermit.
     b. #Enjoying his solitude can be found the country's most famous hermit.

(83) a. There happy at last could be seen the smiling refugees.
     b. #Happy at last could be seen the smiling refugees.

If we subject to scrutiny the special conditions proposed for the Presentational Deictic, however, none turn out to be motivated.[28] To begin with the lexical condition, it is not clear in what sense (78a) can be said to designate a location, while (78b–c) cannot. All three sentences designate *both* location and motion. The aspectual distinction between them is not reducible to that of motion or lack of motion. But in any event, the facts reduce to independent facts governing the distribution of deictic *there* and *here*. The former can never occur with modals or aspectual elements, no

---

28. In this respect, I follow the conclusions arrived at in Denham (1996), though my specific analyses differ from hers on a number of points.

matter what deictic construction we are talking about. Indeed, Lakoff (1987: 506) lists 'occurs in the simple present tense' as one of the distinguishing characteristic of the Central Deictic. Note:

(84) a. #There is standing Harry on the table.
      b. #There will be Mary, thinking about going on vacation.

This property, as it turns out, is not specific to deictics; we find the same restriction with Directional Adverb Preposing (see Emonds 1976: 30–31):

(85) a. In ran John.
      b. #In was running John.

(86) a. Away they ran.
      b. #Away they didn't run.

But what about (74a–b, d) and (79a–b, d), which seem to illustrate Presentational Deictic *there* occurring in something besides the simple present tense? In fact, in the (a) and (b) sentences we do not have the Presentational Deictic. In (74a–b), *there* is in apposition to the following locative, with which it forms a constituent. These sentences, then, simply illustrate run of the mill preposed locative phrases. And in (79a–b), we have existential *there*, not the Presentational Deictic. Note that in neither of these sentences can *there* be stressed, thereby demonstrating that we are not dealing with the Presentational:

(87) a. #*There* had gathered a large crowd of roughnecks in the alley.
      b. #*There* was standing on the stage one of our most distinguished
          public figures wearing an outrageous costume.[29]

In other words, as far as the patterning of *there* is concerned, the Presentational behaves like the Central, obviating the need for the lexical condition.

Here behaves differently. *Here* patterns with preposed locatives and, as a consequence, allows the full range of aspectuals:

(88) Here / In the meadow / Under the municipal
      monument / etc., will be laid to rest our beloved former mayor, Sally
      Stanford, honored by thousands of her fellow citizens.

---

29. I am not sure what to make of (74d) and (79d). The past tense is unexpected, but seems possible with the Central Deictic as well, as in *There lay the beautiful KGB agent.*

The oddness of (78c) reflects the oddness of (89). For whatever reason, no preposed locative can occur before *will come;*

(89) #In the meadow will come the president.

The contrast between deictic *there* and *here* can be demonstrated by the following sentences:

(90) a. #There will be laid to rest our beloved former mayor, Sally
Stanford, honored by thousands of her fellow citizens.
   b. #There will be built large, comfortable estates to house our
former presidents, isolated from all the noise of the city.

(91) a. Here will be laid to rest our beloved former mayor, Sally
Stanford, honored by thousands of her fellow citizens.
   b. Here will be built large, comfortable estates to house our former
presidents, isolated from all the noise of the city.

Sentences (90a–b) are ill-formed, given the presence of overt verbal aspect, while sentences (91a–b) are fine.

Lakoff gives no other examples of why the Presentational Deictic would have to specify a verb referring to a location (that would not also have to be specified for the Central Deictic) and I can think of none. Hence the lexical condition can be dispensed with.

Let us turn now to the three syntactic conditions. As has already been suggested, (S-1) is simply false. The Presentational Deictic with *there* follows the Central in not allowing the full auxiliary; deictic *here* patterns with preposed locatives in allowing it.

Syntactic condition (S-2), while descriptively correct, is as much a property of the Central Deictic as the Presentational:

(92) a. There's Harry with the red jacket on.
   b. There with the red jacket on is Harry.

Thus no special statement need be made for the Presentational.

Turning to (S-3), Denham (1996) has pointed out that the initial phrases in sentences (80a–b) are preposed locatives. There is no reason to hypothesize a 'missing' deictic expression. (81b), (82b), and (83b), in fact, do not seem to me to be wholly unacceptable. To the extent that they do deviate from full acceptability, it would seem to be a function of the greater difficulty of preposing the particular modifying expressions than preposing locatives. I see no pertinence to the question of the Presentational Deictic at all.

Finally, let us consider the discourse conditions. Here, I disagree with Lakoff's generalizations. In sentences (75) to (76), it is not the noun phrase whose significance is signaled. Rather it is that of the locative phrases, *in my favorite chair* and *in this town*, respectively. Again, this is predictable from the discourse role played by preposed expressions in general and preposed locatives in particular.

In sum, there is no evidence that the grammar has to single out a distinct 'Presentational Deictic' construction.

A.4 The Paragon Deictic

Let's now look at another deictic construction discussed by Lakoff—the Paragon Deictic. Examples are given in (93):

(93) a. *There*'s a real cup of coffee!
      b. Now *here* is chicken soup the way Mama made it!
      c. Now *there* goes a great center fielder!

This construction has heavy stress on the deictic followed by pause. According to Lakoff, it is used when one wants to identify the entity referred to as the best case—the paragon—of a particular attribute. A person saying (93a) conveys the idea that he or she is enjoying the best cup of coffee imaginable; (93b) likewise for chicken soup; and by saying (93c), one conveys the idea that one is in the presence of a model center fielder.

Even in Lakoff's own terms, there is little reason to consider the Paragon Deictic as a separate construction in the grammar of English. As he notes, its special pragmatic properties fall out from those of another construction, which he calls the 'Paragon-Intonation Construction', and which is defined in (94):

(94) The Paragon-Intonation Construction
      Meaning: Expression of awe
      Form: The initial element is pronounced with extra heavy stress and breathiness.

Sentences (95a–c) illustrate the broader construction:

(95) a. *This coffee* is fantastic!
      b. *This chicken soup* is the way Mama made it!
      c. *Joe Dimaggio* was one great centerfielder!

Lakoff's only reason for calling the Paragon Deictic a separate construction is that 'such complex constructions have some cognitive status as speech formulas—special things one says on certain occasions' (1987: 529). But surely in Lakoff's way of looking at things, all constructions are, in some sense, 'special things one says on certain occasions'. The specialness may be minimal and the occasions may be frequent, as, for example, with a simple active declarative transitive clause. Nothing in principle distinguishes such basic constructions from more exotic species such as the Paragon Deictic, however.

In any event, there is no reason to attribute special cognitive status to the broader Paragon-Intonation construction either. The reason is that what Lakoff sees as its distinguishing characteristics—expression of awe and the pronunciation of the initial element with extra heavy stress and breathiness—fail to distinguish a linguistically distinct entity.

Support for this claim is provided in Gaines (1993). First, he notes that extra-heavy stress on the initial element is clearly optional. For example, when declaring *That's a real cup of coffee* or *This coffee is fantastic,* something as simple as the speaker's personality (painfully shy or bombastic) or attitude (relieved or enthusiastic) can determine the degree of stress on the deictic word and even its very presence.

Second, extra-heavy stress on the deictic word is not unique to 'paragon'-type utterances. Simple contrastive stress, for example, can produce exactly the same prosodic structure over exactly the same string as is found in the Paragon Deictic. For example, a rebuke to a person who has incorrectly identified an item on a café counter might well be *No,* HERE *is a cup of coffee!*

And third, although the possibility of extra-heavy stress is reasonable in the contexts that Lakoff observes, the limitation of the use of the construction to expressions of awe at a paragon is unmotivated. A wide-range of speaker attitudes and accompanying choice of predication can employ the prosody in question. After all, one can say:

(96) Now *there* is a pretty good centerfielder.

In other words, here as elsewhere in human language, we find a many-many relationship between form, meaning, and discourse function. Neither a Paragon Deictic construction nor a Paragon-Intonation construction appears to be theoretically motivated.

A.5 Conclusion and further discussion

We have examined three (purportedly) nonprototypical deictic constructions and have found that no principles are needed to characterize

them that are not already needed to characterize the (purportedly) prototypical Central Deictic construction or are not independently needed
elsewhere. In other words, these constructions provide no evidence for a
radial category structure, based around a prototypical central member.
I have, admittedly, not put the other deictic constructions to equal scrutiny, nor have I examined in depth other proposed radial categories.
Nevertheless, the failure of the prototype-construction model for central
instances of deictic constructions, where it has received the most extensive
motivation, naturally leads one to question whether such a model is *ever*
motivated.

A reasonable question to raise is whether the notion 'construction'
plays *any* role in grammatical theory. Chomsky, in fact, has argued that it
does not:

> Constructions in the traditional sense, may simply be an artifact, perhaps useful
> for descriptive taxonomy, but nothing more. If this proves to be correct, tradi-
> tional grammatical constructions are on a par with such notions as terrestrial
> animal or large molecule, but are not natural kinds. There is no passive con-
> struction, interrogative construction, etc. Rather, the properties of the relevant
> expressions follow from the interaction of language invariant principles, with
> parameters set. (Chomsky 1991: 24)

Defenders of traditional constructions (e.g. Zwicky 1987, 1994; Pullum
and Zwicky 1991), however, have pointed to a myriad of phenomena that
do not seem reducible to construction-independent interacting parameterized principles. Indeed, a framework of 'Construction Grammar'
has been developed on the basis of the presumed failure of the latter on
grounds of descriptive adequacy (Fillmore, Kay, and O'Connor 1988;
Goldberg 1995; Michaelis and Lambrecht 1996). To be candid, one could
even argue that the abandonment of constructions by principles-and-
parameters approaches to syntax is little more than rhetorical. Many
parameters proposed have been so language specific (indeed, *construction-
specific*) that constructions seem to be entering by the back door.

One thing does seem clear to me, however. That is that the methodological thrust of *focusing* on individual constructions runs one the risk of
overlooking valid generalizations whose formulation cannot easily be
accommodated to a construction-centered approach. I will close this
appendix with reference to one last example from Lakoff's book. This
example, I believe, illustrates well the dangers of a methodological focus
on constructions, rather than those broader principles from which many
properties of constructions can be derived.

Lakoff notes (1987: 503) that with deictic *there*, the noun phrase precedes the verb if it is a pronoun and follows the verb if it is not:

(97) a. There he goes.
  b. #There goes he.
  c. There goes Harry.

As he points out, (98a–b) show that this generalization extends beyond deictic *there*—it is characteristic of deictic adverbials in general:

(98) a. Away he ran.
  b. #Away ran he.

Lakoff (1987: 505) proposes the following construction-specific constraint to handle these facts:

(99) Ordering constraint on spatial deictic adverb constructions: In spatial deictic adverbial constructions, the noun phrase precedes the verb if it is a definite pronoun, and the verb precedes the noun phrase otherwise.

Exploring the matter further, however, we find that the generalization governing sentences (97) to (98) is quite a bit broader than (99) would suggest. Sentences (97b) and (98b) contain definite pronouns in the position of final daughter of VP. But we find that VP-final definite pronouns are disallowed with the double object construction and the 'particle movement' construction as well:

(100) a. John gave Mary the book / #it.
  b. I'll have to look up the answer / #it.

It appears that no VP can occur with a final definite pronoun if that VP has available an earlier NP position in which that definite pronoun can occur. Note that there is no problem with definite pronouns occurring as simple direct objects or, for that matter, as objects of prepositions. In such cases, the VP has only one NP daughter:

(101) a. I saw it.
  b. I can't write with it.

But the generalization is broader still. *No phrase* of English allows a final definite pronoun if there is another 'slot' in that phrase where the pronoun might be placed:

(102) a. the table's leg
  b. the leg of the table

(103) a.   its leg
      b.   #the leg of it

Hence we have a construction-independent fact about English. Whatever its ultimate explanation,[30] it would appear that a narrow focus on constructions and their properties has the effect of leading one to overlook generalizations of this type.

To conclude, the *there*-constructions form, for Lakoff, a typical example of a set of constructions radially organized around a central prototype. But as we have seen, there is little reason to posit the 'nonprototypical' constructions as entities with any theoretical status. A reasonable hypothesis is that the apparent radial nature of the set of constructions is a consequence of the fact that as one moves from what has been called the 'prototypical center', the number of implicatures and other pragmatic conditions on their use increases. Syntactic constructions, then, are similar to syntactic categories in that prototype effects fall out as a result of the interaction of independently needed principles from different domains.

30. It seems that what is going on here is a performance dispreference for phrase-final 'light' elements (Hawkins 1994). When speakers have the grammatical option of producing such elements early, they generally take it. Hawkins has argued, convincingly in my opinion, that generalizations such as these cannot be framed in terms of the positioning of focused or nonfocused items (as in Erteschik-Shir 1979).

Chapter 5
Deconstructing Grammaticalization

1 Overview

To a certain degree, the different research programs of functional and generative linguistics have led their practitioners to investigate—and attempt to explain—a different set of natural language phenomena.[1] Generativists, for example, have been consumed with such things as the intricacies of parasitic gap constructions, the precise conditions for the extraction of question elements, and the nuances of quantifier scope judgments. These problems have to a large extent been ignored in the functionalist literature.

On the other side of the fence, there are phenomena which functionalists have shown far more interest in than have generativists. Without any doubt, the foremost of these is *grammaticalization*. And just as many generativists would claim that, say, parasitic gaps defy functional explanation,[2] functionalists point to grammaticalization as presenting an equal challenge to generative grammar. Traugott and König, for example, feel that 'the study of grammaticalization challenges the concept of a sharp divide between *langue* and *parole* and ... also challenges the concept of categoriality' (1991: 189). In the view of Heine, Claudi, and Hünnemeyer (1991b: 1), 'grammaticalization theory' challenges what they see as the predominant conceptions of theoretical linguists since Saussure. Indeed, they feel that it calls for a 'new theoretical paradigm', counterposed to

1. This chapter owes a great debt to the work of, and electronic conversations with, Lyle Campbell, Alice Harris, Richard Janda, and Brian Joseph. However, I must stress that none of these individuals bears any responsibility for ideas expressed here that are not directly attributed to them, nor do I wish to imply that they are necessarily in agreement with the rest.

2. See for example, Chomsky (1982a: 51) and Engdahl (1983).

most post-Saussurean models of grammar [which] rely—explicitly or implicitly—
on the following tenets:

(a) Linguistic description must be strictly synchronic.
(b) The relationship between form and meaning is arbitrary.
(c) A linguistic form has only one function or meaning.

And Paul Hopper goes so far as to claim, 'There is, in other words, no
"grammar" but only "grammaticization"—movements toward structure'
(1987: 148).

In this chapter I will put grammaticalization under the microscope and
conclude that such claims are unwarranted. Indeed, I will conclude that
there is no such thing as grammaticalization, at least in so far as it might be
regarded as a distinct grammatical phenomenon requiring a distinct set of
principles for its explanation. Instead, I will attempt to demonstrate that
the set of phenomena that fall under its label are a simple consequence of
principles that any theory—whether formal or functional—would need to
posit anyway.

The chapter is organized as follows. Section 2 describes the diachronic
changes referred to as 'grammaticalization' in as theory-neutral means as
possible. In §3, I outline the two principal ways that it has been characterized, one as a distinct historical process that requires an independent
'theory' for its explanation and the other as an epiphenomenal result of
independent processes. Section 4 defends at some length the latter option,
arguing that the component parts of grammaticalization all occur—and
must be explained—independently of each other and of grammaticalization itself. The following §5 takes on the question of the 'unidirectionality'
of grammaticalization, demonstrating that it is falsified by the many
attested and reconstructed 'upgradings' from higher to lower degrees of
grammatical content. I attempt to explain why downgradings do greatly
eclipse upgradings in frequency. Section 6 raises two problems endemic
to functionalist studies of grammaticalization, one methodological and
one theoretical. The former involves the frequent use of reconstructed
forms as theoretical evidence. The latter is the postulation of 'panchronic
grammars', that is, grammars combining synchronic and diachronic
statements. Section 7 discusses generative work in grammaticalization,
while §8 is a brief conclusion.

2 Grammaticalization: A Capsule Description

This section will attempt to characterize the component parts of grammaticalization. These include morphosyntactic reanalysis (§2.1), certain

types of semantic change (§2.2), and phonetic reduction (§2.3). It will also call attention to certain structural and semantic changes above the level of the word, which are often, but not always, considered to fall under the rubric of 'grammaticalization' (§2.4).

2.1 Morphosyntactic reanalysis

The term 'grammaticalization' (or, equivalently, 'grammaticization') is used to describe a phenomenon observed in language change involving, roughly put, the loss of grammatical independence of a grammatical structure or element. A standard definition, and one which I will adopt throughout this chapter, may be found in the major theoretical contribution to the topic, Heine, Claudi, and Hünnemeyer (1991b). As they put it, we are dealing with grammaticalization 'where a lexical unit or structure assumes a grammatical function, or where a grammatical unit assumes a more grammatical function' (1991b: 2).[3] Such entails, of course, that we can characterize certain structural types as having more of a grammatical function or less of a grammatical function than others.[4] In fact, there is very little disagreement on this point. The list in (1) presents types of grammatical structures in order of increasing grammatical function:

(1) a. lexical categories
    b. functional categories and pronominal elements
    c. clitics
    d. derivational affixes[5]
    e. inflectional affixes

3. Heine et al.'s definition is essentially that put forward several decades ago by Jerzy Kurylowicz: 'Grammaticalization consists in the increase of the range of a morpheme advancing from a lexical to a grammatical or from a less grammatical to a more grammatical status, e.g. from a derivative formant to an inflectional one' (Kurylowicz 1965/1975: 52).

4. Occasionally we read of certain structural types as being 'more grammatical' or 'less grammatical' than others, meaning 'bearing more (or less) of a grammatical function than others'. I have avoided this usage, given its potential to create confusion. Especially in the early days of generative grammar, the notion 'degree of grammaticalness' was used to refer to the degree of well-formedness of a particular sentence (see, for example, Chomsky 1961).

5. Actually, there is disagreement on the relative positioning of derivational affixes and inflectional affixes. While I believe that most grammaticalization researchers posit that derivational affixes have a lower degree of grammatical content than inflectional (see Heine, Claudi, and Hünnemeyer 1991b: 213, 263), others (e.g. Harris and Campbell 1995: 337) posit the reverse.

In other words, the primary diagnostic of a grammaticalization is a *re-analysis* involving an increase in grammatical function. Here are some well-known illustrative examples of grammaticalization.

2.1.1 Lexical category to functional category In Old French sentences with negative force, the negative particle *ne* was often reinforced by the use of semantically appropriate independent nouns. With motion verbs, for example, *ne* was accompanied by the noun *pas* 'step'. Other negation-reinforcing nouns included *point* 'dot, point', *mie* 'crumb', *gote* 'drop', among others. As French developed, *pas* began to accompany *ne* even where no motion was taking place, displacing its rival negation-reinforcers; indeed since the seventeenth century *pas* has been virtually compulsory in the negative construction. In other words, *pas* underwent grammaticalization from noun to negative particle.

2.1.2 Functional category or pronoun to clitic Old Norse had a third person accusative reflexive pronoun *sik*. This pronoun developed into a enclitic -*sk*, which spread to other persons and developed into a voice marker as well.

2.1.3 Clitic to affix In the earliest Polish written records (prior to the sixteenth century), the copula existed in both tonic and clitic forms (the latter presumably being a grammaticalization of the former). In the transition to Modern Polish, the clitic form evolved into an inflected past tense.

2.1.4 Derivational affix to inflectional affix The Old High German (derivational) stem-forming suffix -*ir*, inherited from Proto-Germanic, was reanalyzed as an (inflectional) plural suffix. This survives as the -*er* plural in Modern German (cf. *Bücher, Eier, Häuser,* etc.).

2.2 Semantic change
Typically, reanalyses involving the increase of grammatical function do not occur in isolation, but are accompanied by a variety of other changes. The foremost are *semantic*. Indeed, in most functionalist accounts of grammaticalization, it is said that the semantic changes are the ultimate cause of the morphosyntactic reanalysis. All earlier accounts of grammaticalization, and some recent ones as well, tend to emphasize *loss* of

semantic value (otherwise known as 'bleaching' of meaning[6]) as a component part of grammaticalization:

> With the term 'grammaticalization' we refer essentially to an evolution whereby linguistic units *lose* in semantic complexity, pragmatic significance, syntactic freedom, and phonetic substance, respectively. (Heine and Reh 1984: 15; emphasis added)

The idea that grammaticalization is associated with semantic loss seems most evident where an erstwhile lexical meaning has evolved into a more purely grammatical meaning, e.g. in the development of dummy verbs (such as supportive *do* in English) from causatives, auxiliaries from full verbs, definite articles from demonstratives, and so on.

More recently, investigators have downplayed semantic 'loss' and pointed instead to positive forces, such as metaphor and metonymy, as central components of grammaticalization. Consider, by way of example, two accounts of the progressive grammaticalization of *have* in English, from its original use as a full verb expressing physical possession ('to hold in one's hand') to an auxiliary-like element expressing simple intention to perform an act.[7] Among other uses of *have* in Old English was the expression of possession, as in sentences corresponding to (2):

(2) I have a letter to mail.

At some point an implied sense of obligation came to the fore when sentences of the following type arose:

(3) I have a letter to write.

Later we find *have* as a simple marker of obligation (with the syntactic reanalysis of *to* as its adjunct) in:

(4) I have to write a letter.

---

6. The term 'bleaching' was apparently first used by Georg von der Gabelentz more than a century ago: 'Gabelentz (1891: 241) invites his readers to visualize linguistic forms as employees of the state, who are hired, promoted, put on half-pay, and finally retired, while outside new applicants queue up for jobs! Forms "fade, or grow pale" ("verblassen"); their colors "bleach" ("verbleichen"), and must be covered over with fresh paint. More grimly, forms may die and become "mummified," lingering on without life as preserved corpses (p. 242)' (Hopper and Traugott 1993: 19–20).

7. The example sentences are taken from Fleischman (1982).

And in recent times, *have* is attested, in colloquial speech, as simply conveying intent to engage in a future activity:

(5) What are you doing tonight? Oh, I have to go to a party.

Note that in the progression from (2) to (5), the original senses of *have* were not lost—(2) to (4) are all grammatical sentences in modern English. Thus the semantic changes observed in grammaticalization can result in polysemy. Meaning retention is not obligatory, however; *might* in its verbal (as opposed to nominal) use no longer conveys any sense of physical power.

Fleischman (1982: 58–59) describes the series of changes in the meaning of *have* in terms of a progressive weakening of meaning. But Bybee and Pagliuca regard the chain of events, not as a weakening or bleaching of meaning, but rather as a progressive series of metaphorical extensions: 'A concrete lexical item is recruited to express a more abstract concept, and while its use at first is understood as metaphorical, with continued use in abstract functions it itself is taken to encompass the abstract meaning.... [The development of the epistemic function of the *have to* construction] is a metaphorical extension of obligation to apply to the truth of a proposition' (1985: 72–73).[8]

Traugott and König (1991) give examples of semantic changes in grammaticalization that could not reasonably be said to involve loss of semantic content. Indeed, in certain cases the transition to a more grammatical use of a morpheme involves *strengthening* of informativeness. This takes place by means of the conventionalization of conversational implicatures, which they see as a type of metonymy. For example, many languages have subordinating conjunctions with a causal sense (English *since*, German *infolgedessen*, French *puisque*, and so on). Typically they derive from temporals, whose conversationally implicated causal sense has undergone conventionalization. Since there is no justifiable reason to consider 'causation' a 'weaker' semantic notion than 'temporality', it would be incorrect to say that in such cases grammaticalization was accompanied by bleaching.

----

8. Another issue is whether the meanings of the grammaticalized forms were present in the semantic structure of their lexical sources. For answers in the affirmative, see Givón (1973) and Fintel (1995). For answers in the negative, see Willett (1988) and Heine, Claudi, and Hünnemeyer (1991b).

2.3 Phonetic reduction

Generally speaking, the reanalysis to a structural type manifesting a more grammatical function and the accompanying semantic changes are accompanied by the phonetic reduction (or 'erosion') of the element involved. The English modal auxiliaries provide a case in point. In the earliest stages of English, they were full verbs with full lexical meaning (e.g. *will* 'desire'; *can* 'know how'; *shall* 'owe'; *might* 'have power'; and so on). In this capacity, they took full stress and never occurred in reduced form. In their current reanalyzed condition as auxiliaries, however, they take reduced stress and, in some cases, can be contracted to the preceding subject.

2.4 Grammaticalization above the level of the word

We also find the term 'grammaticalization' used to refer to changes that have taken place involving entire syntactic constructions. For example, an historical change from a paratactic (i.e. coordinating or appositional) construction to a hypotactic (i.e. grammatically dependent) construction is typically referred to as a grammaticalization. Examples are provided in Haspelmath (1997). He suggests that English (subordinating) relative clauses such as *the house that we built* derive from paratactic constructions such as *the house—that (one) we built*. Another example is a German sentence such as *Bist du müde, (so) mach eine Pause* ('If you are tired, take a break'), which Haspelmath suggests derives from *Bist du müde? Mach eine Pause.*

The incorporation into the grammar of a clausal or phrasal ordering favored by some principle external to grammar is also referred to as a 'grammaticalization'. Indeed, I have used the term in that regard already in this work, particularly in chapter 3. For example, when a particular ordering of syntactic elements favored by a discourse principle becomes obligatory, that ordering is said to be a 'grammaticalization' of that discourse principle or, as Hyman (1983: 73) put it, 'the harnessing of pragmatics by a grammar'. Hence one finds remarks in the literature such as: 'Subjects are essentially grammaticalized topics' (Li and Thompson 1976: 484). Likewise, the expression of a parsing preference in the grammar is often referred to as a 'grammaticalization' of that parsing preference. Consider, for example, the prior discussion (ch. 3, §4.2) of the grammaticalization of principles such as the Nested Dependency Constraint, Early Immediate Constituents, and so on.

In the remainder of this chapter I will have nothing to say about the grammaticalization of discourse or parsing principles, as mechanisms very different from those implicated in 'lower level' cases of grammaticalization appear to be involved and they have already been extensively discussed. I will, however, make a few remarks on the issue of parataxis giving rise historically to hypotaxis.

3   What Is the 'True Nature' of Grammaticalization?

While there is general agreement on what sorts of diachronic changes count as being instances of 'grammaticalization', we find inconsistency in the functionalist literature on whether grammaticalization is best regarded as a distinct historical process (i.e. as a distinct phenomenon requiring an inherent set of explanatory devices) or as an epiphenomenal result of other principles, mechanisms, theories, or whatever that need to be posited anyway. This section will review accounts of grammaticalization that take it to be an historical process requiring its own theory (§3.1 and §3.2), and an epiphenomenal result of other processes (§3.3).

3.1   Grammaticalization as a process

The term 'process' is often used informally to mean nothing more than 'phenomenon to be explained'. Many of the references to grammaticalization as a 'process' seem simply to have this use of the term in mind. Consider, for example, the major theoretical work devoted to grammaticalization, Heine, Claudi, and Hünnemeyer's *Grammaticalization: A Conceptual Framework* and the major introductory overview, Hopper and Traugott's *Grammaticalization*. Both begin by describing it as an historical process:

What is common to most definitions of grammaticalization is, first, that it is conceived of as a process. (Heine, Claudi, and Hünnemeyer 1991b: 4)

We define grammaticalization as the process whereby lexical items and constructions come in certain linguistic contexts to serve grammatical functions, and, once grammaticalized, continue to develop new grammatical functions. (Hopper and Traugott 1993: xv)

The description of grammaticalization as a process goes back to the first use of the term, by Antoine Meillet, who described it as a process of innovation (1912/1926: 133) that contrasts with the process of analogy:

Whereas analogy may renew forms in detail, usually leaving the overall plan of the system intact, the 'grammaticalization' of certain words creates new forms and introduces categories which had no linguistic expression, transforming the system as a whole. (1912/1926: 133)

For Meillet, it is a process of weakening whereby, through frequent use, a word or group of words ceases to be expressive (1912/1926: 136), that is, it loses some of its semantic value, while, at the same time, its pronunciation becomes less distinct. In this way, full lexical items become, over the course of time, auxiliaries. So, for example, *laissez* in *Laissez venir à moi les petits enfants* has become, to some extent, an auxiliary (1912/1926: 134). The process is held to be a gradual one: 'And there is every intermediate stage between full lexical items and auxiliaries' (1912/1926: 135).

A distinguishing characteristic of the process, in virtually all functionalist accounts of grammaticalization, is its purported *unidirectionality:*

An intrinsic property of the process is that grammaticalization is unidirectional, that is, that it leads from a 'less grammatical' to a 'more grammatical' unit, but not vice-versa. (Heine, Claudi, and Hünnemeyer 1991b: 4).

In Givón (1979a: 209) we find one attempt to characterize the sequence of unidirectional stages in grammaticalization (which he breaks down into 'syntacticization' and a 'morphologization' substages) as follows:

(6) Discourse → Syntax → Morphology → Morphophonemics → Zero

Given the discussion surrounding this diagram, it would be appropriate to connect 'Zero' to 'Discourse' with an arrow. The end point of grammaticalization—the total loss of inflection—leads to a greater determining role for speaker options provided by discourse principles and the 'cyclic wave' of grammaticalization begins anew.

In all functionalist accounts, unidirectionality is held to apply to every component of the process. For example, the meaning shift is always from the concrete to the abstract (Heine, Claudi, and Hünnemeyer 1991b: 31, 73, 75, 98), a shift that is 'never reversed' (1991b: 214). While, as noted above, Traugott and König reject the idea that grammaticalization always involves bleaching, the conventionalization of conversational meaning that they point to is also said to be unidirectional (Traugott and Heine 1991: 5). That is, we never find what one might call 'depragmaticization'—a shift from an implicated sense to that of an entailed one.

The term 'process' has another, stronger, use than as a mere synonym for 'phenomenon'. In this use, a process is a phenomenon *of a particular type*, namely, one driven by a distinct set of principles *governing the phenomenon alone*. Let us call such a type of phenomenon a 'distinct process'. Hopper and Traugott (1993) appear to view some aspects of grammaticalization as a distinct process in that sense. In their view, two components of grammaticalization, reanalysis and analogy, arise from independently needed mechanisms, but unidirectionality is said to be unique to grammaticalization:

> The subset of processes that are *particular to grammaticalization* are those that over time render more independent elements less independent. (Hopper and Traugott 1993: 62; emphasis added)

The many references in the literature to deterministic pathways of development in grammaticalization convey strongly the idea that it is an encapsulated phenomenon, governed by its own set of laws. The following quote seems to invite the conclusion that grammaticalization is a distinct process:

> Grammaticalization ... may be defined as the evolution of grammatical form and meaning from lexical and phrasal antecedents and the continued formal and semantic developments such material subsequently undergoes. The ... lexical sources of particular grammatical forms ... [undergo] formal and semantic changes which characterize their developmental histories.... As a lexical construction enters and continues along a grammaticalization pathway, it undergoes successive changes in meaning, broadly interpretable as representing a unidirectional movement away from its original specific and concrete reference and toward increasingly general and abstract reference.... The most advanced grammatical forms, in their travel along developmental pathways, may have undergone continuous reduction from originally free, unbound items, to affixes entirely dependent on their hosts. (Pagliuca 1994: ix)

3.2 Grammaticalization as a theory

Naturally, one would attempt, if possible, to account for the phenomena associated with grammaticalization within existing theoretical models. Failing that possibility, however, it would be necessary to construct a novel theory to explain them. Much wording in the functionalist literature suggests that it is the latter option that has been chosen. One frequently encounters references to a 'grammaticalization theory', which makes 'predictions' about its subject matter. The implication that there is a predictive theory *of* grammaticalization recurs repeatedly, for example, in the work of Bernd Heine and his colleagues:

> In the present paper it will be argued that these similarities are not coincidental, but that they can be accounted for within the framework of grammaticalization theory. (Heine 1990: 129)

Grammaticalization theory would be hard pressed to account for a conceptual shift from infinitive marker to tense category; what we are dealing with here is a restructuring process leading to the reinterpretation of morphological functions. (Heine, Claudi, and Hünnemeyer 1991b: 220)

Auxiliary reduction, or erosion, as we call it,... is in fact predicted by grammaticalization theory. (Heine 1993: 106).

The most detailed explication of what is referred to as 'grammaticalization theory' appears in Bybee, Perkins, and Pagliuca (1994: 9–22). In their view, the theory embodies the following eight hypotheses:

(7) a. *Source determination.* The actual meaning of the construction that enters into grammaticalization uniquely determines the path that grammaticalization follows and, consequently, the resulting grammatical meanings.

   b. *Unidirectionality.* The path taken by grammaticalization is always from less grammatical to more grammatical.

   c. *Universal paths.* From (a) and (b) it follows that there will be universal paths of grammaticalization.

   d. *Retention of earlier meaning.* Semantic nuances of the source construction can be retained long after grammaticalization has begun.

   e. *Consequences of semantic retention.* From (c) and (d) it follows that attested forms can be used to reconstruct earlier stages of the language.

   f. *Semantic reduction and phonological reduction.* Semantic reduction is paralleled by phonetic reduction.

   g. *Layering.* The rise of new markers is not contingent on the loss or dysfunction of its predecessors.

   h. *Relevance.* The more semantically relevant a grammatical category is to the stem the more likely that affixation will take place.

3.3 Grammaticalization as the result of other processes

The implication that grammaticalization is a distinct process whose workings are to be attributed to a distinct 'theory' contrast with many other references that suggest that it is essentially an epiphenomenal result of *independent* historical developments, each of which falls out of some independent theory. For example Bybee and Pagliuca's capsule scenario of the causes of grammaticalization suggests no process unique to it, much less the need for a distinct theory to explain the process:

We suggest that human language users have a natural propensity for making metaphorical extensions that lead to the increased use of certain items.... Thus the paths of development leading to grammatical meaning are predictable, given certain lexical meaning as the starting point. As the meaning generalizes and the range of use widens, the frequency increases and this leads automatically to phonological reduction and perhaps fusion (Pagliuca 1982). (Bybee and Pagliuca 1985: 75–76)

An older attempt to derive the phenomena observed in grammaticalization from independent principles appealed to the filling of language-specific (indeed, situation-specific) 'communicative needs':[9]

Grammatical subsystems and their attendant inflectional morphologies ('coding devices') arise when the specific communicative need arises, normally when the older system coding a particular function has eroded beyond a certain threshold of communicative coherence ('transparency'). (Givón 1982: 117)

In other words, frequent use triggers the loss by erosion of a grammatical item and the consequent loss of communicative expressiveness. In drag-chain fashion, a less reduced form is recruited to serve the function of the eroded item.

Bybee (1985b: 203–204) gives four cogent reasons why 'communicative need' cannot be invoked to explain the grammaticalization of free morphemes as inflectional affixes. First, there is little evidence that there is a cross-cultural set of such needs that languages have to fulfill. There is no 'need' for a language to code overtly for tense, for example; some languages do it and some do not. Second, if unfilled needs motivated grammaticalization, we would predict that there should never be multiple markers fulfilling the same function. This is not the case. As Bybee notes, English has grammaticalized three separate verbs for the function of expressing possibility—*may*, *might*, and *can*. Third, Givón's hypothesis is inconsistent with the redundancy of many inflections. And finally, the cause and effect relation is not that predicted by a need-based theory. No erosion is generally necessary of an old inflectional marker before a new one takes over.

As far as unidirectionality is concerned, there have been a number of attempts to derive it from the (putative) unidirectionality of independent

9. See also Heine, Claudi, and Hünnemeyer (1991b: 29), where it is claimed that 'the need for presenting a certain grammatical function ... in discourse leads to the recruitment of a lexical form for the expression of this function'.

mechanisms and processes. For example, Bybee and Pagliuca (1985), Heine, Claudi, and Hünnemeyer (1991b), and Haspelmath (1998) agree that part of the answer lies in the fact that certain cognitive processes, in particular the human tendency to conceptualize abstract notions in terms of concrete notions by means of metaphor, are both universal and unidirectional. Haspelmath adds 'the tendency for humans to associate pragmatic force with novelty (Lehmann 1985)' (1998: 55), which accounts for semantic changes in which no metaphor is involved, say, the reduction of full pronouns to agreement markers. He goes on to note that the phonetic reduction and merger aspect to grammaticalization is also the result of an independent process: the speaker's desire for ease of production. This desire is often counterbalanced by the hearer's need for perceptual clarity. But with familiar frequent items, clarity is less of an issue, so reduction wins out. Haspelmath concludes: 'The unidirectionality of grammaticalization is [thus] an indirect effect of general principles of human cognition and behavior' (1998: 58).

Finally, it should be mentioned that nonfunctionalists who have addressed the issue of grammaticalization have been virtually unanimous in agreeing that its effects are epiphenomenal (see, for example, Roberts 1993; Harris, and Campbell 1995; Joseph 1996; Janda 1996). Brian Joseph likens grammaticalization to lexical diffusion,

in that there is clearly a diffusionary effect in the way that sound change is realized in lexical material, but one need not privilege Lexical Diffusion with the status of a 'mechanism' of change—instead, the well-known mechanisms of analogy and dialect borrowing together can give the diffusionary effect that has been referred to as 'Lexical Diffusion'. (Joseph 1996: 20)

In the next section, I will argue that it is correct to view grammaticalization as an epiphenomenon.

4 The Epiphenomenal Nature of Grammaticalization

This section is devoted to arguing for the correctness of the view that the historical changes observed in grammaticalization are the product of well understood forces. Grammaticalization, as I will argue, is nothing more than a label for the conjunction of certain types of independently occurring linguistic changes.

We begin in §4.1 by showing that grammaticalization cannot sensibly be conceived of as a distinct process. Indeed, the very idea that there can be such a thing as a 'diachronic process' will be challenged. The following

§4.2 continues in the same vein, questioning whether there exists—or even
can exist—such a thing as 'grammaticalization theory'.

Section 4.3 addresses the relationship between grammaticalization and
reanalysis. I argue that it is simply not an empirical question to ask
whether the former demands the latter. The standard definition of grammaticalization incorporates the notion of reanalysis; no definition that
does not do so seems particularly useful. This section then goes on to
discuss the empirical question of the temporal ordering of reanalysis with
respect to the accompanying semantic and phonetic effects.

That still leaves open the question of the degree of independence of
the morphosyntactic reanalyses, the semantic changes and the phonetic
reductions associated with grammaticalization. I argue in §4.4 that each
can occur without the other; it is only when the latter two happen to
converge with a certain type of reanalysis that we speak of 'grammaticalization' having taken place.

4.1 On the notion 'diachronic process'
As noted in §3.1, the term 'process' is often used informally to mean
nothing more than 'phenomenon to be explained'. If such is all that is
implied in calling grammaticalization a 'process', then no harm is done.
But I feel that the term 'process' is dangerous when applied to set of *diachronic* developments. The reason for the danger is that it invites one to
conceive of such developments as being subject to a distinct set of laws
that are independent of the minds and behaviors of individual language
users. However, nothing transgenerational can be situated in *any* human
faculty. Children are not born with racial memories that fill them in with
the details of the history of the forms that they hear. They have no way of
knowing whether some particular clitic in their grammar, for example,
was once a full noun phrase or whether it is on its way to affixhood. If it
truly is the case that speakers *are* more likely to reanalyze an item as less
lexical, rather than as more lexical, then we need to look at *synchronic*
mechanisms, that is, at mechanisms that are rooted in the cognition and
behavior of living speakers. As Janda (1998) has noted, there can be no
'diachronic constraints' which prevent a later speaker from analyzing a
given linguistic item as more lexical than the corresponding item was for
an earlier speaker.

Several decades ago Paul Kiparsky warned against the practice, all too
common in historical linguistic studies, of disembodying language change
from language speakers:

The point is simply that a language is not some gradually and imperceptibly changing object which smoothly floats through time and space, as historical linguistics based on philological material all too easily suggests. Rather, the transmission of language is discontinuous, and a language is recreated by each child on the basis of the speech data it hears. (1968: 175)

But to read the functionalist-oriented grammaticalization literature, one has the impression that words, morphemes, affixes, and so on are literally driven to evolve in a particular way. Consider, for example, the quote from William Pagliuca in §3.1, which appears to conceptualize language change in such terms. There is some irony to the fact that Bernd Heine (1993) would open his book on the grammaticalization of auxiliaries with the following quotation from William Croft: 'Languages don't change; people change language' (Croft 1990: 257). The very definition provided by Heine of what auxiliaries are, namely, 'linguistic items located along the grammaticalization chain extending from full verb to grammatical inflection of tense, aspect, and modality' (1993: 131) invites one to think of grammars apart from the minds and activities of speakers. No actual speaker can be expected to know where some item might fall along a particular chain. The focus of the book on these unidirectional chains of auxiliary development and on cognitively incoherent 'panchronic' statements (see below, §6.2) effectively negates the force of Croft's aphorism, painting a picture in which languages are impelled to change regardless of what the people who speak them are disposed to do or think.

If the sequence of events characterizing grammaticalization were to some significant degree deterministic, then we would have more reason to speak of it as a distinct process. But, despite the frequent references encountered to 'universal paths' taken in grammaticalization (e.g. Bybee 1985b: 201), there is little evidence of determinism. For example, Heine, Claudi, and Hünnemeyer (1991b: 38) point to the fact 'that one source concept can give rise to more than one grammatical category and that, conversely, a given grammatical category may be historically derived from more than one source concept or structure'. In later work, Heine (1993: 91) gives no less than eight distinct possible grammaticalization outcomes for verbs whose meaning translates as 'come':

It has developed, for example, into

- A marker of future tense (Bybee, Pagliuca, and Perkins 1991);
- A marker of near past tense (e.g. French *venir de* 'come from');
- A venitive derivative extension (Heine and Reh 1984; Lichtenberk 1991);
- An ingressive/resultative marker (see preceding);

- A marker of relative closeness to the point of reference (see preceding);
- A marker of motion away from point of reference (Lichtenberk 1991);
- An agent marker of passive constructions (Lichtenberk 1991);
- A proximal (deictic) demonstrative (Frajzyngier 1987).

And as far as a particular category arising from a multitude of sources is concerned, Heine shows that tense-aspect markers can originate from full verbs, from adpositions, and from adverbs.

The following sections, as they unfold, will provide further evidence that grammaticalization lacks the distinguishing characteristics of what one might reasonably call a distinct process.

4.2 Grammaticalization is not a theory

As we have seen, references to 'grammaticalization theory' abound in the functionalist literature. But most such references do not appeal to any such theory; rather, they seem to have in mind something much less ambitious. 'Grammaticalization theory' seems to mean something like 'the set of independently-needed theories that are relevant to the explanation of the phenomena commonly associated with grammaticization'.[10]

Consider, for example, Bybee, Perkins, and Pagliuca (1994)'s enumeration of the hypotheses that are suggested to form the component parts of 'grammaticalization theory' (7a–h). The problem is that a theory is not a list of hypotheses. Rather, hypotheses to be tested and, hopefully, confirmed fall out from the internal structure of a theory. While, as noted above, some of the hypotheses follow as logical consequences of others, still others stand and fall independently (unidirectionality does not entail layering). In fact, none of the mechanisms that they later (ch. 8) propose to explain these hypotheses (metaphorical extension, inference, generalization, harmony, and absorption of contextual meaning) are specific to grammaticalization. In short, Bybee at al. do not put forward anything that might be referred to as 'grammaticalization theory', nor does any other work with which I am familiar.

---

10. Many references to 'grammaticalization theory' seem to reflect nothing more than carelessness of usage. For example, Bybee, Perkins, and Pagliuca write: 'Reduced to its essentials, grammaticization theory begins with the observation that grammatical morphemes develop gradually out of lexical morphemes or combinations of lexical morphemes with lexical or grammatical morphemes' (1994: 4). But theories don't begin with observations, though observations might provide puzzles that one needs a theory to explain.

4.3 Grammaticalization and reanalysis

Since in all accounts morphosyntactic reanalysis is central to grammaticalization, it is important to scrutinize this phenomenon. Section 4.3.1 describes the various types of reanalysis. In §4.3.2 I reject the idea that one can have grammaticalization without reanalysis—at least not without changing profoundly the standard definition of the former. And §4.3.3 takes on the question of the temporal ordering of reanalysis and the semantic and phonetic changes associated with grammaticalization. It argues that even when all three are attested in one overall change, there is no deterministic order of temporal precedence among them. This fact also serves to call into question the idea that grammaticalization is a distinct process.

4.3.1 On reanalysis The reanalysis of a syntactic pattern takes place when the abstract structure changes with no accompanying change in the order of the surface elements in that pattern. Harris and Campbell (1995: ch. 4) present several types of reanalyses, which I repeat below using some of their examples. No doubt, type (C) can be considered a subspecies of type (A), though this is of little consequence to what follows:[11]

(A) Reanalysis of constituency and hierarchical structure

In the English complementizer construction with *for + to*, both elements are constituents of the lower clause, as the preposibility of this clause attests:

(8) a. I would prefer ₛ'[for Mary to represent us]
      b. ₛ'[For Mary to represent us] would be the most desirable situation

However, at an earlier stage in the history of English, *for + NP* belonged to the higher clause, as in the following example from Chaucer:

(9) [It is bet for me] [to sleen myself than ben defouled thus]
     'It is better for me to slay myself than to be violated thus.'

In other words, $X + for + NP + $ infinitive was reanalyzed from $[X\ for + NP] + $ infinitive to $X[for + NP + $ infinitive$]$.

(B) Reanalysis of category label

---

11. Harris and Campbell also point to a distinct category of reanalysis involving change of grammatical relations. I assume that such cases can be derived from reanalysis of constituency and hierarchical structure.

In the Ancient Chinese serial verb construction, we find the word order pattern *S bǎ O V O*, where *bǎ* is the verb 'take hold of'. According to Li and Thompson (1974), *bǎ* was reanalyzed an an object marker. This change in category label had the attendant consequence of triggering a change in constituency as well—from SVO to SOV.

(C) Reanalysis of degree of cohesion

'Cohesion' in this usage refers to the degree of bondedness between linguistics elements, as reflected by the nature of the boundary (if any) that separates them. Thus there is more cohesion between two elements separated by a morpheme boundary than by a clitic boundary (if such exists as a separate species of boundary). Likewise there is more cohesion between two elements separated by a clitic boundary than by a word boundary. In the extreme case, an element which enjoyed morphemic status is reanalyzed as fully fused to the stem, resulting in complete cohesion.

Examples of reanalysis of degree of cohesion are familiar from the literature on grammaticalization. Hopper and Traugott (1993) cite the case of English *lets* as a typical case. Originally, *us* was a full-fledged pronominal object to the verb *let*. Later, it was reanalyzed as a clitic, as in *let's go*. And now we find instances where the degree of cohesion between *let* and *s* is total (i.e. there is no boundary at all separating them). For example, one individual can say to another *Lets give you a hand.*

What causes reanalysis? Or, otherwise put, what causes children to construct grammars where an element is assigned a different category label or a sequence of elements is assigned a different constituent structure from that of the grammars of their parents? David Lightfoot (1979a, 1981, 1986) has called attention to cases in which what he calls 'opacity' is responsible. Such occurs when other changes in the language have rendered it impossible for the child to assign the same analysis to a sentence type that it had formerly. For example, the verb *like* originally meant 'please' in one of its uses. Sentences with *like* often occurred in the productive [object ____ subject] frame in Middle English. Thus we found sentences like *Him liked the pears, The king liked the pears,* etc., where in both cases the initial NP was understood as object. As a result of a complex series of changes in this period of English (the loss of case endings, a change in order from SOV to SVO, and so on), the object-verb-subject analysis of the above sentences became opaque to the child language learner—there was nothing in the triggering experience to suggest such an analysis. *The king liked the pears* was therefore reanalyzed as subject-verb-object, while sentences such as *Him liked the pears* simply dropped out of the language.

Closely related to opacity-caused reanalyses are those in which regular phonological change leads to the loss of previously existing cues as to the structure, thereby triggering reanalysis of that structure. Harris and Campbell (1995: 316–317) give a number of examples. One is from Klokeid's (1978) study of Lardil. The loss of the ergative case marker in that language as a result of phonological change triggered reanalysis of the antipassive construction, leading to a change from ergative-absolutive to nominative-accusative structure.

Harris and Campbell stress (1995: 71f.) that not every case of reanalysis can be attributed to opacity. This is particularly true for many categorial reanalyses. For example, the Finnish noun-postposition unit meaning 'on the chest' was reanalyzed as a simple postposition meaning 'next to':

(10) lapse-n   rinna-lla
     child-GEN chest-On
     'on the child's chest'

(11) lapse-n   rinnalla
     child-GEN POSTPOSITION
     'next to the child'

There was nothing opaque about (10) that would demand a reanalysis as (11). Indeed, both (10) and (11) are still possible in modern Finnish. Reanalysis and the accompanying semantic change result simply from the fact that being on one's chest entails being next to the possessor of the chest.

Reanalyses also result, Harris and Campbell suggest, from the use of what they call 'exploratory expressions'. These are expressions that are permitted by the principles of the grammar and are introduced 'for emphasis, for reinforcement, for clarity, [or] for exploratory reasons' (1995: 73). For whatever reason, some may come to be used extraordinarily frequently, leading to reanalysis by the next generation of language learners.[12] They give the example of the *ne ... pas* negation

12. Harris (1996) suggests that frequency can trigger reanalysis even in cases where exploratory expressions are not involved. So the highly frequent use of the passive in Persian and (perhaps) some Polynesian languages led to its reanalysis as an ergative construction.

construction in French (see §2.1). *Pas* was originally a noun reinforcer of negation. But its use became so widespread in this respect that children acquiring the language took it to be an intrinsic part of negation, and hence effected a categorial reanalysis from Noun to a constituent of Negative Phrase.

4.3.2 Does grammaticalization depend upon reanalysis?   There is obviously a close relationship between grammaticalization and reanalysis. Indeed, the very *definition* of grammaticalization seems to imply a reanalysis, since we say that grammaticalization has taken place only if there has been a downgrading, that is a reanalysis, from a structure with a lesser degree of grammatical function to one with a higher degree. To repeat Heine, Claudi, and Hünnemeyer's characterization of grammaticalization, we find it 'where a lexical unit or structure assumes a grammatical function, or where a grammatical unit assumes a more grammatical function' (1991b: 2). Since 'assumes a (more) grammatical function' seems like a simple rephrasing of 'is reanalyzed categorially', grammaticalization would appear to entail reanalysis.

Later in the book, however, Heine et al. write, 'Typically, reanalysis accompanies grammaticalization' (1991b: 217). The hedge 'typically' is necessary, they feel, because of the frequent origins of definite articles from demonstratives and indefinite articles from numerals:

Grammaticalization need not be accompanied by reanalysis. Thus when a demonstrative is grammaticalized to a definite article (*this man* > *the man*), the definite article to a nongeneric article etc. (see Greenberg 1978), or the numeral 'one' to an indefinite article (*one man* > *a man*; cf. Givón 1981a), then we are dealing with grammaticalization of a demonstrative or numeral where no reanalysis is involved: the status of the determiner-head phrase remains unchanged. (Heine, Claudi, and Hünnemeyer 1991b: 219)

The assumption here is that demonstratives and definite articles share categorial status, as do indefinite articles and numerals. In fact, however, few generative linguists would accept the idea that we do have a sharing of categorial status in these cases. A current view of the demonstrative/determiner distinction is that the phrase containing the former has a more complex internal structure than the latter, perhaps embodying adjective-like elements (Chomsky 1995: 338). And a long-standing view of the numeral/article distinction is that the former belong to the category Q(uantifier), while the latter do not. In other words, the grammaticalizations pointed to by Heine et al. do indeed involve reanalysis. In fact I know of no convincing cases involving a lexical unit or structure assuming a (more) grammatical function in which reanalysis is not implicated.[13]

In later work, Heine appears to advocate a more profound separation between reanalysis and grammaticalization, writing that the 'relevance [of reanalysis] to grammaticalization theory is not entirely clear' (Heine 1993: 118). The problem seems to be that reanalyses can have, in relevant respects, opposite effects, particularly at the level of the clause. As we have seen, for example, a paradigm grammaticalization phenomenon is the shift from parataxis to hypotaxis, that is, the reanalysis of a main clause as a subordinate clause. But precisely the opposite sort of reanalysis is also attested. Heine and Reh (1984) and Lord (1989) argue that in a number of African languages, a proposition of the form 'It is X' that Y', where 'it is X' is the main clause and 'that Y' a subordinate clause has been reanalyzed as a structure where 'it is X' turns into a focus-marked constituent and 'that Y' into the main clause. From the surrounding discussion, it would appear that Heine has chosen to sidestep this seeming threat to unidirectionality by the tactic of expunging reanalysis from the definition of grammaticalization. But one is left wondering, then, how grammaticalization is to be defined. In any event, at the level of the lexical item and 'below', there seems to be no difficulty in defining grammaticalization in terms of reanalysis.

The major attempt of which I am aware to dissociate reanalysis from grammaticalization is Haspelmath (1998). However, his principal argument that grammaticalization can proceed without reanalysis is, as far as I can see, purely terminological. That is, he simply excludes category label changes from counting as reanalyses. So, for example, he calls attention to the grammaticalization of serial verbs as prepositions (12a) and complementizers (12b) in Ewe, discussed in Heine and Reh (1984). These authors depict the structural effects of the grammaticalization by the following trees (1984: 37–38):

13. Earlier treatments of *this* and *the* assign them to the same syntactic category, namely 'DET', but distinguish them according to their syntactic feature content. Under this conception, one would be faced with two options with regard to a historical change from *this* to *the*. Either it would not count as a grammaticalization or the definition of 'reanalysis' would have to be broadened to include a change in syntactic feature content. The latter option seems perfectly reasonable to me. To be fair to Heine et al., they do note that 'examples such as these are not fully satisfactory, especially since there exists a wide range of different opinions as to how "reanalysis" and "grammaticalization" are to be defined. For those, e.g., who treat the two terms as synonymous, the grammaticalization of a demonstrative as a definite article would also be an instance of reanalysis' (1991b: n. 12).

(12) a. From serial verb to preposition

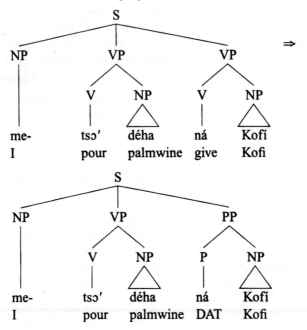

'I gave Kofi palmwine'

b. From serial verb to complementizer

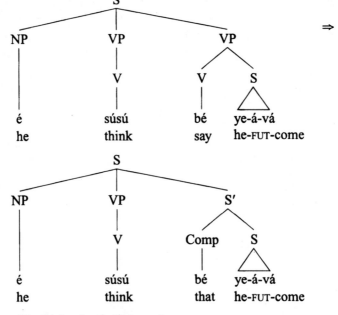

'He thinks that he'll come'

As the phrase markers indicate, category labels have changed, but not the gross structural configuration. Haspelmath chooses not to consider such changes as instances of reanalysis, thereby establishing that grammaticalization need not involve reanalysis. But I see no useful reason to restrict the definition of 'reanalysis' to exclude the types of structural changes depicted in (12a–b).

Haspelmath in fact does provide arguments for distinguishing re-assignment of category membership from cases of reanalysis involving changes in constituency and hierarchical structure. The most important is based on his belief that the former takes place gradually, while the latter is (necessarily) abrupt:

> Finally, the [categorial] changes in question are gradual rather than abrupt. Verbs do not turn into prepositions and complementizers overnight but lose their verbal properties and acquire the properties of their new word-class step by step. Givón 1975: 82ff distinguishes a number of semantic, morphological and syntactic criteria of verbal vs. prepositional status and notes that a verb is unlikely to change into a preposition by all criteria at once.... In discussions of syntactic change, thinking in discrete terms where the phenomena are gradient means that clear instances of grammaticalization are erroneously attributed to reanalysis because grossly oversimplified tree diagrams such as [(12a–b)] do not reflect the gradualness of the change. (Haspelmath 1998: 65)

This passage embodies two substantive claims. First, there is the claim that categorial changes are gradual. The second claim follows from the first: since the transition from category X to category Y is gradual, categories themselves must be gradient, rather than discrete. That is, instead of X and Y, we have 'degrees of Xness' and 'degrees of Yness'.

Chapter 4 of this book was devoted to defending the discreteness of syntactic categories, arguing that their apparent gradience is in fact attributable to gradiences of meaning and to pragmatic factors. But what about the historical dimension? Isn't there incontrovertible evidence that the transition from serial verbs to prepositions and complementizers in Ewe was gradual? Or, to give another much-discussed example, don't we now know that the transition from verbs to modal auxiliaries in the history of English took place gradually over a period of centuries? In fact, all that we know is that *aspects* of these changes were gradual, or, better put, did not take place all at once. In order to challenge the idea of discrete categories, one would have to demonstrate that each change had categorial consequences for the syntax. To claim that two elements are members of the category Verb, for example, is not to claim that their observed syntactic behavior will be in every way identical. The semantic properties of these elements will influence their distribution and behavior. So, the fact that *kick* in English passivizes, while *cost* does not is not a consequence of *cost* being less of a verb syntactically than *kick*, but rather is a consequence of properties independent of its categorial status (see ch. 4, §4.3.1). Nobody would wish to deny that over time the meaning of a linguistic element can change in a fairly gradual fashion. One must be careful to distinguish those aspects of the changed distribution of that element that are consequences of the semantic change from those that are the consequences of a categorial change.

We will return to the question of the gradualness of categorial change in §7.1 below.

4.3.3 Reanalysis, semantic change, and phonetic reduction—their temporal ordering in grammaticalization

I will assume then that without reanalysis, whatever it might be, it is not grammaticalization. But that still leaves us with the question of the diachronic relationship between the reanalysis and the other effects observed in grammaticalization. It is to this issue that we now turn.

The idea that grammaticalization is a distinct process is based in large part on its always passing through the same stages. However, there is no consensus on the question of what those stages are. Let us begin with the ordering of the semantic changes and the reanalysis. In the view of Heine (1993: 48), 'In the process of grammaticalization like the one considered here, conceptual shift precedes morphosyntactic shift.' Indeed, 'conceptual is the first obligatory step in grammaticalization' (1993: 51). Along these lines, Givón had written earlier:

In diachronic change, as has been widely suggested, structural adjustment [i.e. reanalysis] tends to lag behind creative-elaborative functional reanalysis (Givón 1971, 1975, 1979, ch. 6; Lord 1973; Heine and Reh 1984; Heine and Claudi 1986).... Our quantified methodology can probably detect the early, functional, onset of grammaticalization long before its more conventionalized structural correlates come on line. (Givón 1991b: 123)

But for Hopper and Traugott (1993: 207), the components occur side-by-side: 'In general it can be shown that meaning change accompanies rather than follows syntactic change' (see also Bybee, Pagliuca, and Perkins 1991).

Alice Harris and Lyle Campbell, two historical linguists working outside of the functionalist tradition, have been interpreted as taking a position opposite to that expressed by Heine and Givón. The wording in the following quotes suggests the possibility of semantic changes following reanalysis:[14]

Grammaticalization is one type of macro-change, consisting minimally of one process of reanalysis, but frequently involving more than one reanalysis.... Grammaticalization is often associated with 'semantic bleaching', and this 'bleaching' is the *result of reanalysis* or, perhaps better said, it is the essence of the reanalysis itself. (Harris and Campbell 1995: 92; emphasis added)

That grammaticalization is often associated with 'semantic bleaching' we see as hardly remarkable, since the semantic bleaching, the shift from more lexical to more grammatical content, is the *result of the reanalysis*.... Semantic bleaching follows from the essence of reanalysis. (Campbell 1997: §4.1; emphasis added)

As far as I have been able to determine, there is some degree of truth to all three of these positions. Sometimes the semantic changes precede the morphosyntactic changes, sometimes they accompany them, and sometimes they follow them. Since the position that semantic change is the result of reanalysis seems to be the most controversial, let me give a concrete example supporting it. Consider the development of English periphrastic *do* from its origins as an early Middle English causative verb. Kroch, Myhill, and Pintzuk (1982) argue that the rise of *do* in questions was a direct consequence of the shift of English word order to SVO—the use of *do* as a dummy allowed that order to be preserved even in questions. Evidence is provided by the fact that *do* was first used in this capacity where the inversion of the main verb with the subject produced the most extreme violations of SVO order. It then spread to other environments. But there is no evidence that the bleaching of the meaning of *do* played any role in the *causation* of this sequence of events. Quite the contrary, as it was only as *do* was coopted as a question marker that it lost its causative properties.[15]

14. Alice Harris and Lyle Campbell have informed me (personal communication) that the phrase 'result of reanalysis' implies simultaneous syntactic and semantic changes.

15. Traugott and König (1991: 190) agree that the bleaching of the meaning of *do* took place very late in its historical development. See Hopper and Traugott (1993: 89–90) for an account of the development of *do* that is somewhat different from that provided by Kroch et al. (1982). They argue that the semantic changes observed in grammaticalization occur in two stages—the pragmatic enrichment (metonymy) occurs very early and starts the other developments on their way. Bleaching, however, is very late.

Other reanalyses seem inextricably linked to their accompanying semantic changes. Consider, for example, the Finnish case, discussed above (§4.3.1), in which a noun-postposition unit meaning 'on the chest' was (optionally) reanalyzed as a simple postposition meaning 'next to'. Let us say that the original—and still possible—structure of this phrase was (13):

(13)

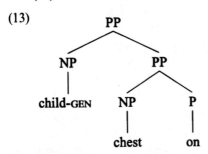

                         child-GEN   NP   P

What could it possibly mean to claim that the meaning of the PP 'on the chest' changed to 'next to' without an accompanying reanalysis of that PP as a postposition? Such would imply that at some stage the embedded PP consisted of a full NP followed by a postposition which somehow compositionally yielded the meaning 'next to'. That seems quite implausible. Semantic factors (a cognitive propensity for metaphorical extension or whatever) may have provided the ultimate *motivation* for the change, but the semantic change itself could have hardly taken place before the reanalysis.

If we look at a series of historically successive grammaticalizations involving the same element, then of course a semantic change at time T can precede a subsequent reanalysis at time $T + 1$. The semantic change involving the use of *have* in the sense of obligation preceded the grammaticalization of *have* and a following *to* as *hafta*. Marchese (1986) gives an example from Tepo, a Western Kru language of West Africa, of the same reanalysis being both a response to and a cause of semantic change. *Mu* 'go' can be used in its literal sense with a nominalized complement:

(14) ɔ mu ná wɔ́
     he go drink NOM
     'He went to drink'

Mu also occurs in semantically bleached form as a future marker, which (apparently) triggered the reduction and loss of the nominalizer:

(15) ʊ   mʊ n   cré   ∅
they FUT me shave ∅
'They will shave (my head)'

In other words, the following structural changes took place:

(16) S V$_1$ [(O) V$_{2nom}$] → S V$_1$ (O) V$_2$

This led in turn to the reanalysis of V$_1$ as AUX and of V$_2$ as a main verb: S AUX (O) V. But now, according to Marchese, the restructuring itself is setting into motion a *new* set of semantic changes.

As far as the relative ordering of phonetic erosion is concerned, the mainstream functionalist position is, I think, that it is a response to frequency of use, which itself is a response to the semantic changes (for an explicit statement to this effect, see Heine, Claudi, and Hünnemeyer 1991b). I certainly have no desire to question the idea that *in general* erosion comes late. But it is easy to see how the precise opposite chain of events might unfold. Phonetic erosion can be the result of natural phonological processes, say, the loss of unstressed final syllables. Such losses, as we saw with the Lardil case cited above (§4.3.1), can trigger profound morphosyntactic changes. So for example, Vennemann (1974) argues that shifts from SOV to SVO order have often been triggered by the loss of case markers due to phonological change. The word order change was a necessary functional response to allow the grammatical relations among the major sentential constituents to be unambiguously expressed. But this in turn led to the grammaticalization of distinct preverbal auxiliaries with the attendant semantic shifts. In other words, phonetic erosion was the (ultimate) cause of semantic change.

Finally, it should be pointed out that once the first steps of grammaticalization have taken place, there is no inevitability that the other steps will follow suit. As Hopper and Traugott (1993: 95) have noted:

There is nothing deterministic about grammaticalization and unidirectionality. Changes do not have to occur. They do not have to go to completion, in other words, they do not have to move all the way along a cline. A particular grammaticalization process may be, and often is, arrested before it is fully 'implemented'.

To summarize, grammaticalization fails to evince the most important distinguishing feature of a distinct process—the unfolding of its component parts in a determinate sequence in which one step of the sequence inevitably engenders the following one.

4.4   The independence of the component parts of grammaticalization
I will now provide evidence that the component parts of grammaticalization can occur *independently* of each other. We find the relevant
semantic changes without reanalysis or phonetic reduction (§4.4.1), phonetic reduction without semantic change (§4.4.2), and reanalysis without
semantic change or phonetic reduction (§4.4.3).

4.4.1   The independence of the semantic changes   Some functionalists
have attempted to characterize grammaticalization in terms of an increase
in metaphorical abstractness: 'Grammaticalization may also be viewed as
a subtype of metaphor.... Grammaticalization is a metaphorical shift
to the abstract' (Matisoff 1991: 384). But such a definition fails in both
directions. As we have seen, there are semantic shifts observed in grammaticalization that are not properly characterized as metaphoric. And
metaphorical shifts to the abstract are commonplace which are not
accompanied by the other components of grammaticalization. I will
illustrate by reference to (17), which has been proposed by Heine, Claudi,
and Hünnemeyer (1991a: 157; 1991b: 48) to represent a scale of metaphorical directionality: 'Any one of them may serve to conceptualize any
other category to its right' (Heine, Claudi, and Hünnemeyer 1991b: 49).
Thus, for example, an object may be conceptualized as a person, but not
vice-versa. Note that each position on the sequence (arguably) represents
a greater degree of abstractness than the position to its left:

(17)   PERSON > OBJECT > ACTIVITY > SPACE > TIME > QUALITY

Heine et al. illustrate with numerous examples. Consider the PERSON >
OBJECT > QUALITY progression of metaphors:

Many languages have a comitative adposition 'with' that is used to refer to
instruments with inanimate nouns and to manner with certain abstract nouns.
Metaphor, in this instance, has the effect of conceptualizing an instrument as
a companion and a quality as an instrument. (Heine, Claudi, and Hünnemeyer
1991b: 52)

The OBJECT > SPACE metaphor might be exemplified by the use of body
part terms to denote spatial orientation (cf. the extension of the meaning
of 'chest' to 'next to' in Finnish, as was discussed above); the SPACE >
TIME metaphor by the grammaticalization of adpositions meaning 'behind'
into subordinating conjunctions meaning 'after'; and so on.
   The problem is that these metaphors are rampant in all languages in
a variety of circumstances and seem only tangentially connected with

grammaticalization. Saying 'I've read a lot of Barbara Vine' instead of 'I've read a lot of Barbara Vine's novels' illustrates the PERSON > OBJECT metaphor. Calling an examination room a 'torture chamber' extends an object to a quality. The OBJECT > SPACE metaphor was presumably involved in the creation of expressions like 'the mouth of the river', 'the eye of the needle', and so on. We find the OBJECT > TIME metaphor in the derivation of *month* from 'moon', and possibly the SPACE > TIME metaphor is exemplified by Paul Theroux's Australian in *Riding the Iron Rooster* who measured time in terms of 'Kalgoorlies'. It appears to be the case, then, that there are no metaphorical extensions of meaning that are unique to grammaticalization.

The same point could be made with respect to the conversational implicatures identified with grammaticalization. As noted above, it is not uncommon to find an element with a temporal meaning taking on a conversationally implicated causal sense. But there is nothing specific to grammaticalization in such a development. As Traugott and König (1991: 194) themselves acknowledge, the classic fallacy of *post hoc ergo propter hoc* pervades our everyday use of language. Note that in the following examples, temporality has been strengthened to causation (for detailed linguistic and philosophical discussions of these and related cases, see Geis and Zwicky 1971; Atlas and Levinson 1981; Horn 1984):

(18) a. After we heard the lecture, we felt greatly inspired. (*Implicates* 'Because of the lecture, we felt greatly inspired'.)
      b. The minute John joined our team, things started to go wrong. (*Implicates* 'Because John joined our team, things started to go wrong'.)

I must agree with Sweetser (1988: 389) that one should attempt 'to treat the semantic changes attendant on grammaticalization as describable and explicable in terms of the same theoretical constructs necessary to describe and explain lexical semantic change in general'. Surely, that is the most parsimonious route to take and the one we should adopt in absence of any disconfirmatory evidence. Such a route leads inevitably to the rejection of the idea that grammaticalization is a distinct process.

4.4.2 The independence of phonetic reduction I do not disagree with the observation of Heine (1994: 267) that 'When a given linguistic unit is grammaticalized, its phonetic shape tends to undergo erosion'. But the question is *why* this should be the case. In this section I will argue that the phonetic reductions identified with grammaticalization are explicable by reference to forces that must be posited—and explained—independently of grammaticalization itself. These are essentially 'least-effort' forces that lead to more frequently used items being, in general, shorter than less frequently used ones.

Heine (1993: 109–111) provides four factors said to account for the erosion observed in grammaticalization (see also Heine, Claudi, and Hünnemeyer 1991b: 214). The first is the 'Quantity Principle' (Givón 1991a) according to which there is an iconic relationship between the amount of information conveyed and the amount of coding. The second is a 'least-effort' principle in the sense of Zipf (1935), leading people to shorten the linguistic expressions that are most commonly used. The third is based on the idea that there is a positive correlation between the 'information value' of a linguistic symbol and the amount of coding material employed to express it. And the fourth is a 'physical motivation', along the lines suggested by Gabelentz (1891). Since the more a physical entity is used, the more rapidly it is likely to wear out, it follows that the frequency of use of a grammatical element leads to a reduction of its phonetic substance.

Whatever the status of the Quantity Principle may be, I fail to see its general relevance to grammaticalization.[16] It is by no means obvious, for example, that an affix conveys less information than a full form or that an element with the status of a functional category conveys less information than one with the status of a lexical category. In some conversational situations, for example, the lexical material coding tense and aspect is wholly extractable from the context of the discourse; in others conveying clearly that the proposition expressed is in the past tense rather than in the present tense can make all the difference in the world. *Have* in the sense of 'perfect aspect' does not convey *less* information than *have* in the sense of 'possess'; it simply conveys *different* information. Sweetser makes the same point with respect to the development of future morphemes from words meaning 'go':

16. The quantity principle is presumably an instantiation of Grice's maxim of quantity: 'Make your contribution as informative as required (for the current purposes of the exchange)' (Grice 1975: 45). For other approaches to the grammatical correlates of predictability or familiarity of information content, see Prince (1981, 1985) and Gundel, Hedberg, and Zacharski (1990).

[In this development] we lose the sense of physical motion (together with all its likely background inferences). We gain, however, a new meaning of future prediction or intention—together with *its* likely background inferences. We thus cannot be said to have merely 'lost' meaning; we have, rather, exchanged the embedding of this image-schema in a concrete, spatial domain of meaning for its embedding in a more abstract and possibly more subjective domain. (1988: 392)

Furthermore, in a simple negation like *Mary doesn't study linguistics any more, does* surely conveys less information than *not* (does *does* convey *any* information?), yet it is the latter that is reduced, not the former. Perhaps there is some way that the notion 'amount of information conveyed' can be characterized precisely. Until then, I feel that we can safely dismiss the Quantity Principle as a factor contributing to phonetic reduction.

Heine's third and fourth motivations seem equally suspect. As for the third, I fail to distinguish it from the first—it seems no more than a restatement of the Quantity Principle. The fourth, if interpreted literally, is absurd—whatever words are, they are manifestly *not* physical entities. And if taken loosely, it seems simply to be a restatement of the least-effort principle.

We are thus left with the least-effort principle as the primary cause of the phonetic reductions that accompany grammaticalization. Well over a half century ago George Zipf observed that frequently used expressions and grammatical elements are, on the whole, shorter than rarely used ones:

High frequency is the cause of small magnitude.... A longer word may be truncated if it enjoys a relatively high frequency [either] throughout the entire speech community [or] if its use is frequent within any special group. (Zipf 1935: 31–32)

Zipf cited studies showing that the average length of both words and morphemes declines in proportion to the frequency of their use (for more recent findings along these lines, see Nettle 1995). Extending these results, I would predict that the following propositions are also true (though I know of no confirmatory studies):

(19) a. The average member of a lexical category tends to be both longer and less frequently used than the average member of a functional category.
   b. The average member of a functional category tends to be both longer and less frequently used than the average clitic.
   c. The average clitic tends to be both longer and less frequently used than the average affix.

If (19a–c) are true, then the erosion associated with reanalysis may simply be a least-effort response having nothing to do with grammatical-ization per se. That is, in order for the observed fact of phonetic erosion to bear on whether grammaticalization is a distinct process, one would have to demonstrate some special linkage between erosion and the other component parts of grammaticalization *not* attributable to frequency. That might involve, for example, showing that given two equally fre-quently used homophonous senses of a single morpheme, one grammati-calized and one not, the grammaticalized sense is the more reduced of the two. I know of no examples illustrating this. Indeed, as Heine himself notes, the English copula *be* reduces in its main verb usage as well as in its grammaticalized auxiliary sense (Heine 1993: 111):

(20) a. He's going.
     b. He's criticized every day.

(21) a. He's a farmer.
     b. He's sick.

Fidelholtz (1975) has confirmed the idea that erosion is at least in part a function of frequency, independent of grammaticalization effects. He demonstrated that the degree of stress reduction on a lax vowel in a pre-tonic syllable correlates with its frequency (I repeat his results as summa-rized in Horn 1993: 35):

(22) a. ăstronomy   gàstronomy
     b. mĭstake   mìstook
     c. ăbstain   àbstention
     d. mŏsquito   Mùskegon [city in Michigan]

And an empirical study by Johnson (1983) supports the idea that there is a correlation between the frequency of a word and the extent to which fast speech rules apply to it. Johnson analyzed several hours of recorded nat-ural speech and found the only systematic correlation between the appli-cation of optional fast speech processes and any other factor involved the frequency of the word operated on by the rule.

One good indication that the phonetic reductions observed in gram-maticalization are simply a subset of those at work in general in fast speech comes from the fact that they are just as likely to lead to marked syllable structures as those not implicated in grammaticalization. Con-sider, for example, the reductions that have taken place in *can't* and *won't we* (Forner et al. 1992: 87):

(23) a. *can't*   /kænt/   → [kæ̃nt]   → [kæ̃t]
    b. *won't we*   /wont wi/ → [wõntwi] → [wõʔwi]

Presumably if grammaticalization were a distinct process, guided by principles independent of those operative elsewhere, one would expect it to avoid the creation of such marked structures.

The frequent use of a form, it might also be pointed out, is no guarantee that it will set into motion other grammaticalization effects. Heine, Claudi, and Hünnemeyer (1991b: 39), citing a study by Bertoncini (1973), note that of the fifteen most frequently used words in Swahili, none has been a source for grammaticalization.

If, following Slobin (1977), the maximization of processibility has been an important factor in language change, it is clear that as a general trend frequency effects will manifest themselves as reductions. In short, one does not need a theory of grammaticalization to explain why unbound forms are more likely to become bound than vice-versa any more than one needs a 'theory of ice cream' to explain why it is easier to melt together a scoop of chocolate and a scoop of vanilla in the same bowl than to reconstitute the original scoops from the melted mass. In the former case, elementary facts about speech production and perception will suffice very well.

Finally, it should be pointed out that many phonetic reductions observed in grammaticalization are simply the effects of regular *phonological* change occurring elsewhere in the language and have no bearing on grammaticalization per se (in fact, this point is made in Hopper and Traugott 1993: 147). For example, the phonological reductions in the development of the Modern Greek future marker *tha* from the Classical and early Post-Classical Greek verb *thelo* 'want' are often cited as exemplifying the 'grammaticalization process'. But Joseph (1996) shows that some of these reductions were simply manifestations of regular sound change and hence lend no support to the idea that grammaticalization has an independent reality.

4.4.3 The independence of reanalysis   The fact that reanalysis is built into the definition of grammaticalization by no means implies that every case of reanalysis is accompanied by the other features that are typically associated with grammaticalization. Haspelmath (1998) gives several examples illustrating reanalysis without these accompanying changes, two of which I will now present.

In standard German, the complement of the verb *anfangen* 'begin'
is a sentential infinitival clause, obligatorily postposed after the finite
verb:

(24) Sie fängt an, zu singen.
     'She begins to sing.'

However in Haspelmath's own dialect of German, the infinitival phrase
precedes the finite verb and the verbal particle *an* precedes the infinitive,
as in (25a). This order is impossible with other verbs (25b–c):

(25) a. Wenn sie an zu singen fängt, ...
         'If she begins to sing, ...'
     b. *Wenn sie auf zu singen hört, ...
         'If she stops singing, ...'
     c. *Wenn sie ein zu heiraten willigt, ...
         'If she agrees to get married, ...'

Haspelmath makes the reasonable conjecture that (25a) originated as a
reanalysis of (24), as in (26b). In this reanalysis, *an* apparently became
part of the complex infinitival complementizer:

(26) a.

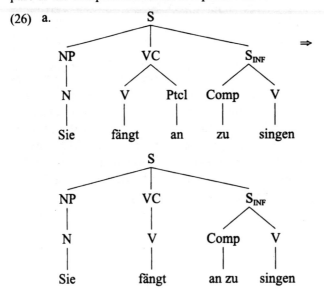

But this reanalysis does not qualify as a 'grammaticalization'—none of
the other effects associated with grammaticalization accompanied it.

Another example discussed by Haspelmath is from French. In colloquial speech, the postverbal 3rd person subject pronoun has been reanalyzed as an interrogative particle *ti:*

(27) a. Votre père [v[part- PRO[il]]?
          'Does your father leave?'
      b. Votre père v[par] PTCL[ti]?
          'Does your father leave?'

Here again, the other diagnostics for grammaticalization are missing.

One might object that the above examples do not illustrate categorial reanalysis—that type of reanalysis most germane to grammaticalization. It is true that semantic change is typically associated with categorial reanalysis. The reanalysis of a lexical category as a functional category, for example, is accompanied by a meaning shift. However, functional categories have a characteristic semantic value *regardless* of whether they represent downgradings from lexical categories. As Susan Steele has pointed out to me (personal communication), only a small percentage of auxiliaries and other functional category members are known to have originated as verbs or as other lexical category members. What this means is that the form-meaning association that we find with functional categories is not fruitfully regarded as an intrinsic part of the 'process' that grammaticalizes lexical categories.

4.5 Summary

We have examined the component parts of grammaticalization and found that they all are manifested independently. By a (not particularly useful) convention of usage, it has become customary to use the term 'grammaticalization' only when a downgrading reanalysis happens to coincide with certain independently occurring semantic and phonetic changes. Figure 5.1 gives a schematic illustration of how grammaticalization is simply the set union of the three historical changes.

Definitions are free for the making; one obviously has the right to use the term 'grammaticalization' to describe the conjunction of certain types of historical changes that are manifested independently. No harm is done as long as the use of the term in such a way does not invite the conclusion that some dynamic is at work in grammaticalization that cannot be understood as a product of these historical changes.

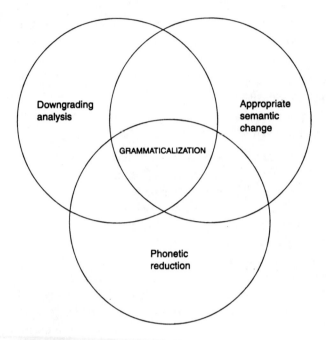

Figure 5.1
Grammaticalization as an epiphenomenon.

5 On Unidirectionality

This section probes further the question of the purported unidirectionality of the conjunction of effects associated with grammaticalization. In §5.1, I phrase the issue in such a way as to give unidirectionality the status of an empirical hypothesis. Section 5.2 makes the point that if grammaticalization were a distinct process, then unidirectionality would be expected as a natural consequence. The lengthy §5.3 provides numerous counterexamples to unidirectionality, while the concluding §5.4 is addressed to why categorial downgradings (and their associated effects) are much more common than upgradings.

5.1 Phrasing unidirectionality as an empirical hypothesis
Any attempt to evaluate the correctness of the unidirectionality principle must begin by making sure that it is phrased as an empirical hypothesis. Such is not always the case in functionalist accounts of grammaticaliza-

tion—often we find unidirectionality built into the very *definition* of grammaticalization, as the following quotations illustrate:

Where a lexical unit or structure assumes a grammatical function, or where a grammatical unit assumes a more grammatical function, we are dealing with grammaticalization. (Heine, Claudi, and Hünnemeyer 1991b: 2)

We define grammaticalization as the process whereby lexical items and constructions come in certain linguistic contexts to serve grammatical functions, and, once grammaticalized, continue to develop new grammatical functions. (Hopper and Traugott 1993: xv)

In other words, grammaticalization is defined as a unidirectional process. Suppose that in some particular case, directionality appeared to be reversed, that is, suppose we observed a lexical item or construction that had developed a *less* grammatical function. Such a circumstance would not bear in the slightest on whether grammaticalization is unidirectional or not, because *nothing* could bear on that question. The point is that definitions make no empirical claims. Setting aside for the moment the question of whether grammaticalization is a distinct process or not, one might feel that the above definitions are either useful (i.e. they pick out some segment of reality) or not useful (there are not enough instances of what they pick out to warrant such a definition), but, as is the case with definitions in general, they cannot be either right or wrong.

But elsewhere we find discussions of unidirectionality that can only be interpreted so as to suggest that it *is* taken to be an empirical hypothesis:

The strong *hypothesis* of unidirectionality *claims* that all grammaticalization involves shifts in specific linguistic contexts from lexical item to grammatical item, or from less to more grammatical item, and that grammaticalization clines are irreversible. Change proceeds from higher to lower, never from lower to higher on the cline. Extensive though the *evidence of unidirectionality is*, it cannot be regarded as an absolute principle. *Some counterexamples do exist.* (Hopper and Traugott 1993: 126; emphasis added)

In the remainder of this section, I will treat unidirectionality only as an empirical hypothesis. That is, I will take it as a claim about language change. I will assume that if unidirectionality is true, then grammatical elements may 'downgrade' (i.e. increase in degree of grammatical content morphosyntactically), but never 'upgrade' (i.e. decrease in degree of grammatical content morphosyntactically). As we will see, the claim is false.

5.2 If grammaticalization is a distinct process, then unidirectionality (if true) is uninteresting

The purported (near) unidirectionality of grammaticalization is typically presented in the functionalist literature as a remarkable fact, and one which would never have been uncovered by the standard methodology of generative grammar. But suppose that grammaticalization were, in fact, a distinct process. If so, then unidirectionality would be the most unremarkable fact imaginable.[17] The reason is that unidirectionality is a property of natural processes *in general*. Such processes are either entirely irreversible or reversible only given huge amounts of effort, time, unusual circumstances, and so on. Consider the aging process as a prototypical example![18] Or consider any chemical or physical process. Mountains are eroded and washed down to the sea; mountain-creating mechanisms in no way involve sand grains flowing upstream followed by 'de-erosion'. Sodium hydroxide and hydrochloric acid react to create table salt and water. Extreme amounts of energy—amounts never encountered under natural conditions on earth—are required to reverse the process. Biological evolution has never been known to recreate an ancestral form. And so on.

In short, given that unidirectionality is a general characteristic property of natural processes, we would expect it to hold of distinct grammatical processes as well. If grammaticalization were a distinct process, its unidirectionality should not merit more than a footnote. Indeed, it would be

17. I owe this observation to Richard Janda (personal communication).

18. Östen Dahl makes a pertinent point in an interesting *Linguist List* posting of 18 August 1996. He writes: 'I think grammaticalization is unidirectional in about the same sense as biological processes such as growth, maturation, and aging are. As we grow up, we become taller; in old age, we may shrink a little. However, we would not expect a child to start becoming shorter and finally return to its mother's womb. Similarly, eyesight generally deteriorates with age, but myopic persons may actually become less so due to their eye lenses getting more rigid and compensating the myopia. In other words, the biological processes that take place during our lives sometimes give rise to contradictory results but there can be no doubt that they are basically irreversible'. I agree. Growth, maturation, and aging are, in fact, *utterly* irreversible, as are all biological processes. The examples that Dahl cites show that the *effects* of this irreversibility can be masked by extraneous intervening factors. As we will see, however, the directionality of morphosyntactic change can itself be reversed. Hence grammaticalization cannot be a distinct process.

the *non*occurrences of unidirectionality that should occupy the bulk of the attention of those who subject it to study. But since, as we have seen, grammaticalization is *not* a distinct process, we have no a priori reason to expect rigid unidirectionality.

5.3 Unidirectionality is not true

Less than 20 years ago, Christian Lehmann (1982/1995: 19) could assert that 'no cogent examples of degrammaticalization [i.e. reversals of directionality] have been found'. More recently, Heine, Claudi, and Hünnemeyer have remarked, 'Although both degrammaticization and regrammaticization have been observed to occur, they are statistically insignificant' (1991b: 4–5). Unfortunately, however, they fail to provide any statistics to back up their claim. My sense is that such phenomena are rampant, though I would not hazard a speculation about their statistical breakdown. In this section, I will document some of the best known cases of upgrading and conclude with some remarks on their theoretical import. None of these cases will be presented in full detail; the reader might wish to consult the cited literature for a complete account.

First, however, I must stress an important methodological point. I take any example of upgrading as sufficient to refute unidirectionality. Occasionally, one reads of certain upgradings not really counting as counterexamples to unidirectionality because they are not genuine cases of 'grammaticalization reversing itself'. Rather, they are said to manifest some other process, such as, say 'lexicalization'. My feeling is that attributing upgradings to some process distinct from the inverse of grammaticalization is tantamount to covertly building unidirectionality into the definition of grammaticalization. Certainly it would have the effect of ruling out the great majority of potential counterexamples to unidirectionality.

In any event, it is certainly the case that *complete reversals* of grammaticalization are extremely rare, perhaps nonexistent. This should hardly be a cause of surprise; as noted by Janda (1995, 1998), given the predominant arbitrariness of the sound/meaning association in linguistic signs and the phonological deformations that accompany downgrading, it would be nothing less than a miracle if some aspect of the *precise* earlier stage of a language were recreated in degrammaticalization.

5.3.1 The problem posed by the lexicalization of affixes
The claim of unidirectionality in its strongest form is refuted by the phenomenon of

'lexicalization', which is widespread in the languages of the world. One manifestation of this phenomenon is the fusion of affixes to the root to create a new, morphologically opaque, lexical item. Many such examples are discussed in Ramat (1992). English *drench* derives from bimorphemic **drank-jan* 'cause to be wet'; the ancestors of English *wash* and German *forschen* 'to search, investigate' contained an inchoative morpheme (cf. Latin *rubesco, pallesco* 'to go red', 'to turn pale'); English *elder* and French *maire* once contained a causative morpheme; and so on.

   What these examples show is that there is an alternative developmental possibility for an affix than to weaken to zero, as Givón's diagram (6) suggests is the normal case. Now, none of these examples illustrate the upgrading of the affix in and of itself (for such examples, see below §§5.3.2–5.3.4) and in that sense do not refute the claim that a particular element may move only from the less grammatical to the more grammatical. However, they do indicate a 'recycling' process from morphology to lexicon and hence a more complex picture of linguistic evolution than is typically presented in the grammaticalization literature. The obvious consequence of this more complex state of affairs is for historical reconstruction. Contrary to what has become standard practice among grammaticalization theorists, internal reconstructions based on the assumption that full ungrammaticalized lexical items are 'starting points' in historical development must be viewed as methodologically illicit. The possibility that such items are themselves the result of a feeding process from the morphology must always be entertained.

5.3.2   From inflectional affix to derivational affix

An example of an inflectional affix upgrading to a derivational affix is provided in Lehmann (1989). The Latin inflectional present participle suffix *-nt* evolved into the French derivational adjectival suffix *-ant* (cf. Latin *currens* 'running' and French *courant* 'current').

   Greenberg (1991a) gives many examples of what he calls 'regrammaticalization', an important component of which involves an inflectional affix being upgraded to the status of derivational affix. Citing both attested and reconstructed forms, he outlines a common path of development from demonstrative to definite article to noun marker to a derivational affix of nominalization (as in some Bantu languages) or to one signaling transitivization or causativization (as in the Chibchan languages). A somewhat similar development is mentioned in Lehmann (1982/1995). Tok Pisin grammaticalized the English pronoun *him* as an inflectional object marker *-im*. This element subsequently upgraded to a derivational marker of verbal transitivity. Hopper and Traugott (1993: 166) regard such developments (whose historicity they do not dispute), 'not as examples of a radical shift in directionality but rather as natural examples of the sort of generalization, spread, and splitting into different functions that accompanies ongoing grammaticalization'. Natural or not, however, they *are* in fact incompatible with the strongest hypothesis of unidirectionality, which sees a relentless shift to the more grammatical.

5.3.3 From inflectional affix to clitic

Our first example of an affix upgrading to a clitic comes from Finno-Ugric (Nevis 1986a). Comparative evidence suggests Finno-Permic had an abessive case affix *-pta*, which it inherited from its Finno-Ugric ancestor. Indeed, all Finno-Permic languages spoken today have such an affix, which is unquestionably a reflex of this element. In Northern Saame (Lappish), however, one of the reflexes of *-pta* is a clitic postposition *taga*. Its clitic (as opposed to affixal) status is indicated by the fact that it governs the genitive on the preceding noun phrase, permits conjunction reduction, and attaches outside possessive enclitics, among other things. Furthermore, in the Enontekiö dialect of Northern Saame, *taga* has upgraded further to a freestanding adverb—it no longer requires a host for cliticization.

Still another case of an inflectional element upgrading to a clitic is motivated in Garrett (1990a) and discussed further in Joseph (1996). While most of the early attested Indo-European languages have object clitics (presumably inherited from PIE), most languages in the Anatolian branch of Indo-European have subject clitics as well. Garrett argues that their development in Hittite was based on a straightforward analogy with the preexisting object clitics, as follows (the analogical formula, using *antuhša-* 'man', is taken from Joseph 1996):

(28) antuḫšan : antuḫšaš :: an   *X*   *X* → aš
     NOUN/ACC   NOUN/NOM   CLIT:ACC CLIT.NOM

Joseph argues for a somewhat similar analogical development of the weak subject pronouns in Modern Greek. As he notes, these developments seem to refute the corollary to the principle of unidirectionality implicit in the following quotation:

> To date there is no evidence that grammatical items arise full-fledged, that is, can be innovated without a prior lexical history in a remote (or less remote) past. (Hopper and Traugott 1993: 128–129)

The fact that inflectional items can arise via analogy means that not all are reductions of forms that have 'a prior lexical history'.

Another example of an affix upgrading to clitic status was called to my attention by Martin Haspelmath and Anders Holmberg (personal communication) and is discussed in Fiva (1984). This involves the development of the Old Norse genitive affix -s to the modern Mainland Scandinavian -s, which, as in English, is a clitic marker on the full NP. Consider the following examples from Norwegian:

(29) a. NP[NP[den gamle mannen] s hus]
              the old   man-the 's house
         'the old man's house'
     b. NP[NP[den gamle mannen med skjegget]s   hus]
              the old   man-the with beard-the's house
         'the old man with the beard's house'

Unlike in English, however, there is no possibility that the clitic could be a reduction of *his* (see below, §5.3.4). We have a simple case of 'pure' upgrading from affix to clitic. Further evidence is provided by *wh*-movement. Norwegian has two possessive constructions, (30a) and (30b), the former with cliticized -s and the latter with *sin*, the usual possessive reflexive:

(30) a. Pers   bil
         Peter's car
     b. Per   sin   bil
         Peter his (refl) car
         'Peter's car'

The -s form is older in the sense that it goes back to the Old Norse genitive. The form with *sin* is said to have come into the language in the Middle Ages from Low German merchants in Bergen. Normally, under *wh*-movement, both *sin* and *s*- are extracted along with the *wh*-pronoun:

(31) a. Hvem sin   (bil) er det
         who   REFL (car) is that
         'Whose (car) is that?'
     b. Hvems (bil) er det
         who+s (car) is that
         'Whose (car) is that?'

Sin can regularly be stranded under *wh*-movement:

(32) Hvem er det sin (bil)
    who is that REFL (car)
    'Whose (car) is that?'

Remarkably, for many speakers, -s can be stranded as well, cliticizing to the element preceding it. Here, of course, an analysis as an affix is out of the question:

(33) Hvem er det's (bil)
    who is it+s (car)
    'Whose (car) is that?'

Holmberg has even observed forms like (33) in Swedish child language, where no equivalent of the *sin* form exists. It would appear, then, to be a spontaneous reanalysis independent of direct Low German influence.

Our last example is provided by developments in New Mexican and other nonstandard dialects of Spanish (Janda 1995). In standard Spanish, the regular first person plural forms of the first conjugation are as follows (stress marking is indicated, whether present orthographically or not). Forms of *cantar* 'to sing' are depicted:

(34) a. pres. indic.   cant-ámos
    b. pret. indic.   cant-ámos
    c. future   cantar-émos
    d. pres. subj.   cant-émos
    e. imperf. indic.   cant-ábamos
    f. imperf. subj.   cant-áramos
    g. conditional   cant-aríamos

At an earlier stage in the development of New Mexican Spanish the stress shifted on the present subjunctive (i.e. *cant-émos* > *cánt-emos*). A subsequent development was reanalysis involving the replacement of affixal -*mos* with clitic -*nos* (homophonous with the clitic of *nosotros*) in four tenses of the paradigm:

(35) d'. pres. subj.   cánt-emos > cánte-nos
    e'. imperf. indic.   cant-ábamos > cantába-nos
    f'. imperf. subj.   cant-áramos > cantára-nos
    g'. conditional   cant-aríamos > cantaría-nos

As inspection of these paradigms should make clear, the conditioning factor for cliticization was the placement of stress. Cliticization took place only where stress was not penultimate. The analogical replacement of affixal *-mos* by the independently existing clitic *-nos* involved (by the definition of cliticization) the insertion of a word boundary. With that word boundary in place, stress became regularized as penultimate throughout the paradigm.[19]

5.3.4 From inflectional affix to word Old English had a rich case system, which included the genitive case inflection *-(e)s*. Janda (1980, 1981) describes how this inflection was upgraded to a full lexical pronoun. By the Middle English period, *-(e)s* and the unstressed form of the possessive adjective *his* had become homophonous—in most dialects the initial orthographic 'h' of the possessive was not pronounced. As a result of this phonological accident, the former was reinterpreted as the latter; ME texts commonly show *his* as an invariant possessive marker, even with semantically female possessors, e.g. *my moder ys sake*. Interestingly, this usage still survives in precious archaisms, as in printed bookplates (e.g. *John Smith his book*). Janda goes on to argue that this pronoun was subsequently downgraded to the status of phrasal-bound enclitic.[20] Hence the fact that the NE supposed 'possessive inflection' need not appear on the possessor itself: *The linguist I was talking about's contribution.*

Bybee, Perkins, and Pagliuca (1994) give an example from the history of Irish of an inflectional affix becoming a pronoun. Earlier stages of the language had a rich set of person/number agreement suffixes on the verb. All but one of these have been lost and replaced by obligatory subject pronouns. The exception is the first person plural suffix *-mid/-muid*, which is now an independent pronoun (replacing the earlier first person pronoun *sinn*):

(36) Is muide a   rinne   é
      be 1P.EMP who do.PAST   it
      'It's we who did it.'

Bybee et al. remark that there was 'strong paradigmatic pressure for the reanalysis of [this] person/number suffix as a free pronoun' (1994: 13),

---

19. Lyle Campbell (personal communication) questions, however, whether *-nos-* is a clitic at all. As he points out, true clitics in Spanish attach to various word classes and come in different positions. The *-nos-* in question is always stuck in situ, showing up only where the older *-mos* showed up.

20. Some linguists (e.g. Carstairs 1987) have questioned whether there was a pronominal intermediary between affix and clitic. The upgrading of affix to clitic, however, is uncontroversial.

though they do not elaborate. But 'paradigm pressure' is hardly a rare motivating factor in historical change. If paradigm pressure is able to 'reverse unidirectionality', it suggests that pressure towards unidirectional change is perhaps not so overpowering as is sometimes claimed. In other words, we might expect to find many more cases where unidirectionality has 'lost out' to paradigm pressure.

A last example is taken from Rubino (1994). An inflectional suffix -*Vt* is reconstructed for Proto-Semitic to mark accusative case on nominals. It shows up in Akkadian only on pronouns (37) and in Kemant (Central Cushitic) on pronouns and definite nouns (38):

(37) yâti   1s.ACC
     k(u)âti   2s.ACC

(38) -yət   1s.ACC
     -kət   2s.ACC
     N+-t   definite accusative nouns

In Modern Hebrew this suffix has developed into a preposition, ʔet, which precedes nouns for which it specifies for definite accusativity:

(39) a. raʔíti ʔet   ha-iš
        I:saw DEF:ACC the:man
        'I saw the man.'
     b. sgór   ʔet   hadélet
        close DEF:ACC the:door
        'Close the door.'

5.3.5   From derivational affix to word   One area where we find rampant upgrading—and hence clear counterexamples to unidirectionality—is the relatively common development whereby a derivational affix is detached from its stem and lexicalized as an independent word. This has happened to the suffix -*ism*, for example, not just in English, but also in Finnish and Estonian (Nevis 1986b) and in German and Italian (Ramat 1992), in each case acquiring the meaning 'doctrine, theory'. In Italian, -*anta* (as in *quaranta* '40') has become used as a noun meaning 'older than 40': *ha passato gli anta* 'he is over 40' (Norde 1997, citing Anna Giacalone Ramat). *Ade, teen, ex, pro,* and many other words of English were at one time restricted to use as derivational affixes. And this type of diachronic change is productive—witness the title of the movie *Boyz N the Hood*, where *hood* is African-American slang for *neighborhood*.

A particularly interesting example is provided by Norde (1997). In Dutch, the derivational suffix *-tig* (cognate with English *-ty*) has developed into an indefinite numeral with the meaning 'umpteen, zillion':

(40) Ik heb het al tig keer gezegd
      'I have already said it umpteen times.'

In keeping with what one would expect of a reversal of grammaticalization, *tig* is pronounced with a full vowel, whereas as a suffix the vowel is generally reduced to schwa.

Trask (1997) reports on a series of upgradings of derivational affixes to words in the history of Basque. Due to lack of adequate records, we cannot be absolutely sure about cases like *ume* 'child' and *-kume* 'offspring', the latter of which appears in numerous formations like *katakume* 'kitten'; and *ohi* 'habit, custom' and *-koi* 'fond of'. But the Bizkaian dialect has recently converted the suffix into a noun *kume* (or, really, *kuma*, with dialectal final-vowel lowering) 'young animal'. Clearer cases are *talde* 'group' and *toki* 'place'. These derive from the synonymous word-forming suffuxes *-alde* and *-oki*. We may be sure of this order of development, since, first, the suffixes are archaic—the latter is confined to place names—and, second, no native Basque word of any antiquity begins either with a voiceless plosive or with a coronal plosive (apart from three or four puzzling cases with initial /k/). More recent still is the noun *tasun* 'quality', derived from the common noun-forming suffix *-(t)asun* '-ness'. The noun is not even attested before the late nineteenth century, but today it is moderately frequent and has given rise to derivatives like *tasunezko* 'qualitative'.

5.3.6 From clitic to word The upgrading of clitic pronouns to full lexical pronouns seems to have happened repeatedly. Kroch, Myhill, and Pintzuk (1982) give an example from the history of English. In the sixteenth century, inverted subject pronouns such as those in (41) were encliticized to the verb:

(41) a. Where dwellyth she?
      b. Why bewaylest thou thus soore, O Pelargus?

Their clitic status is indicated by the spellings of the period, in which the verb and pronoun are represented as orthographic units: *hastow*, *wiltow*, and *wille* for 'hast thou', 'wilt thou' and 'will he' respectively, as well as the spelling of *ye* as 'y'. But there is considerable evidence that the pronoun underwent decliticization after 1550. For example, *not* appears for the first time between the inverted main verb and the pronoun, instead of occurring after the subject. Also at this time *you* began to displace *ye* as the second person subject pronoun. This is important, since before that time the strong form *you* was not used in this construction, except for emphasis. In other words, as decliticization took place, a preexisting strong pronoun was coopted to replace the clitic.

Consider free-standing relative / indefinite / interrogative words in Indo-European languages, such as Latin *quis, quod,* Greek *hos,* Sanskrit *yas,* and Hittite *ku-is, ku-it.* It is, I believe, uncontroversial among Indo-Europeanists that they derive etymologically from PIE enclitic particles. These particles followed the first accented word in a clause in PIE and were themselves followed by one or more clitics (for details, see Watkins 1963, 1964; Gonda 1971; Jeffers and Pepicello 1979). In the course of a discussion of these developments, Jeffers and Zwicky (1980: 224) conclude that 'the tacit assumption that clisis is invariably one stage in an inexorable development toward the status of an affix, or toward ultimate oblivion, is simply false'.

A somewhat similar development took place in the development of Estonian, according to Nevis (1986b, 1986c) and Campbell (1991). In this language, interrogative *es* and emphatic *ep* are full words, showing no phonological interaction with a preceding word. However, in the other Balto-Finnic languages they are second position clitics. There is both attested historical evidence from the history of Estonian and comparative evidence from other Balto-Finnic languages that *es* and *ep* derive from the Proto-Baltic-Finnic clitics **s* and **pa* respectively. As a result of a sequence of phonological developments in Estonian, no evidence presented itself to the language learner that *es* and *ep* formed a single phonological word with the base. They were therefore upgraded to independent words and later shifted to sentence-initial position.

Rubino (1994) gives an Ilokano example of the development of a clitic to a free word. This Austronesian language spoken in the Philippines has a future enclitic *-to*, with two allomorphic variants *-to*, after consonants, and *nto*, after vowels:

(42) a. Mapan-ak-to
          INTR:go-1S.ABS-FUT
          'I'll go.'
      b. Mapan-ka-nto
          INTR:go-2S.ABS-FUT
          'You'll go.'

This clitic is attested even in pre-Hispanic times, with no traces of it in noncliticized form. In the modern language, however, it occurs unbound in colloquial speech, usually in an affirmative response to a question or request for an action to be done in the future:

(43) Um-ay-ka   no bigat,   a
     INTR-come-2S.ABS FUT morning PART
     'Come tomorrow. Okay?'

     To
     'I'll do that.'

Rubino provides a parallel case from Hungarian (he cites Robert Hetzron, p.c., for the data). This language has a versatile enclitic particle *-is*, which can be glossed as 'also' and as an emphatic marker, among other things:

(44) a. Jancsi-is   tudja   ezt
       Johnny also knows:it this:ACC
       'Johnny also knows this.'
     b. Tudja-is   a választ
       know:PAST the answer:ACC
       'He did indeed know the answer.'

In Modern Hungarian *is* can be used as a separate word with the sense of 'indeed' (as in (45), where evidence from stress indicates that it is not a clitic) and, in reduplicated form, as an affirmation of both conjuncts of 'or' questions (46):

(45) Jancsi meg- is   érkezett
     Johnny did   indeed arrive

(46) Külföldröl hozzák   vagy itt gyártják
     abroad:from they:bring or   here they:manufacture:it
     'Do they import it or manufacture it here?'

     Is-ís
     REDUP PART
     'both'

5.3.7 From functional category to lexical category (and from pronoun to noun) The history of English *for* (Van Gelderen 1996) shows that even what appears at first glance to be a 'unidirectional' change can be more complex than meets the eye. Superficially, the development of this item fulfills the standard grammaticalization scenario. In Old English, *for* was a preposition indicating location, translatable roughly as 'in front of' (cf. German *vor*). By the late Old English period it had grammaticalized to causative and benefactive senses. Its first use as a complementizer (indicating further grammaticalization) is attested around 1200. In this use it is never separated from the infinitive marker *to*. It is only more than a century later that *for* and *to* could be separated by a pronoun in the objective case (*for him to reade*). In other words, *for actually regained* 'prepositional' case-assigning properties. While still functioning as a clause subordinator, it became less of a grammatical item than it had been previously.

A rather different case is discussed in Van Gelderen (1997). The origin of Modern English expletive *there* lies not in the locative adverb, as is sometimes claimed, but in the Old English demonstrative *þære*. The progression taken by *þære* (and by demonstratives *þara* and *þæt* as well) was from demonstrative to relative pronoun to expletive pronoun. But by many criteria, *there* is a noun head of a NP (for discussion, see ch. 4, §4.3.2). If *there* is a lexical noun, then we have an example of an upgrading from determiner to noun, that is, from a functional category to a lexical category.

As Van Gelderen (1997) shows, the history of the word *man* also presents challenges for any sweeping claims about unidirectionality. In Old English its predominant use was as an indefinite pronoun (cf. German *man*). Subsequently it seems to have swung back and forth from pronoun to full lexical noun and back again. In any event, it is the *less* grammaticalized use that has survived into Modern English.

The upgrading of prepositions to full verbs is widely attested. For example, the Spanish verb *sobrar* 'to be extra, leftover' derives from the preposition *sobre* 'over, on, above'. Harris and Campbell (1995) note that in Central American Spanish the preposition *dentro* 'inside' has undergone the same development, becoming the root of *dentrar* 'to insert'. We find similar developments in English:[21] *up the ante, down three drinks, off the pigs* (1960s student protester slogan). Pronouns as well can upgrade to verbs as the German *duzen* and French *tutoyer* 'to use the familiar form' attest.

---

21. Martin Haspelmath has suggested to me (personal communication) that many of the preposition-to-lexical category examples that I cite from English are actually examples of adverbs changing category. The etymological sources that I consulted have not, in general, been explicit on this point. One must bear in mind, in any event, that a well accepted analysis of many 'adverbs' that are homophonous with prepositions takes them in fact *to be* (intransitive) prepositions (Emonds 1972b).

Prepositions and conjunctions may be lexicalized as adjectives, as *an iffy situation* (Ramat 1987). We also find English adjectives *for* and *against* (*How many of you are against?*), *through* in the sense of 'finished', and *on* and *off* (*I'm just not on today*). Also note that German *zu* developed an adjectival meaning 'closed' (*eine zuene Tür* 'a closed door'), ultimately from *zugemacht* 'closed' (Janda 1998).

Prepositions and conjunctions can upgrade to nouns, as is illustrated by *inn* (from preposition *in*), *bye* (from preposition *by*), and *out* (as in *I have an out*). Note also the *ups and downs* and *the ifs and buts,* and the French *derrière* 'behind' and *devant* 'in front of', which have developed the meaning 'buttocks' and 'front' respectively. There also seem to be cases of prepositions that derive historically from nouns, and have later reconverted to nounhood: *inside, outside,* and *front* (in certain uses).

5.3.8 From hypotaxis to parataxis At the level of the clause, not all changes have proceeded in unidirectional fashion toward increased hypotaxis. As Matsumoto (1988) has shown, in Japanese the precise opposite has happened. In the modern language, there are two ways of expressing the proposition 'Although Taro is young, he does a good job', one by the simple conjunction of the two main propositions (47a), the other by use of the adversative subordinating suffix -*ga* (47b):

(47) a. Taro-wa   wakai(-yo). Ga, yoku yar-u(-yo)
        Taro-TOP young.   But well do-PRES
        'Taro is young. But he does a good job.'
     b. Taro-wa   wakai-ga, yoku yar-u(-yo)
        Taro-TOP young,   well do-PRES
        'Although Taro is young, he does a good job.'

The principle of unidirectionality would predict that sentences of the form of (47a) should be historically antecedent to those of the form of (47b). But this is not the case. According to Matsumoto, paratactically-formed sentences such as (47a) have been recorded only since the seventeenth century, while the hypotaxis manifested in (47b) is observed much earlier.[22]

---

22. For more examples of this sort from the history of Japanese, see Onodera (1995) and for general discussion of their theoretical importance, see Traugott (1997). Traugott points out in this paper and in Tabor and Traugott (forthcoming) and Traugott (forthcoming) that the transformation of construction-internal elements into discourse particles is very common diachronically, thereby contradicting the scenario that 'decrease in syntactic freedom' is an essential ingredient of grammaticalization.

Harris and Campbell (1995: ch. 10) is an extended argument against the idea that hypotactic constructions *in general* develop out of paratactic ones. They attribute the widespread belief that such is the case to what they call the 'Marker/Structure Fallacy'. This fallacy begins with the observation that some marker that was originally present in a paratactic construction began to be used as a marker of subordination in a hypotactic construction. It then concludes on this basis that the latter construction must have originated from the former.

Harris and Campbell argue that there is very rarely historical evidence for such a development. A case in point is the development of English relative clause markers, *who, which, where,* etc. Given their homophony with *wh*-question words, it is often suggested that relative clauses developed from free-standing questions along the lines *The house. Which (one) is yours? > The house which is yours.* But as Harris and Campbell note, the earliest attested occurrences of *wh*-relatives give no indication that the relative clause itself developed from a question:

(48) Ðis   waes swiðe gedeorfsum gear her   on lande ðurh
     This was   very grievous   year here in land   through

     gyld   ðe   se cyng nan for his dohter   gyfte &   ðurh
     money that the king took for his daughter's dowry and through

     ungewaedera *for whan* eorðwestmas wurdon swiðe amyrde
     unweather   for which harvests   became very spoiled

     'This was a very grievous year in the land because of the money
     which the king took for his daughter's dowry and because of the bad
     weather, on account of which the crops were badly spoiled.'
     (Peterborough Chronicle 1111.23; Harris and Campbell 1995: 285,
     cited from Allen 1980: 198)

All that appears to have taken place was that the original relative marker *ðe*, which derived from the demonstrative, was gradually replaced by markers derived from question pronouns. As the passage above illustrates, both could even occur in the same text.

5.4 Why unidirectionality is *almost* true

While unidirectionality is false—every conceivable type of upgrading that one can imagine has actually occurred—it is not *all that* false. Again, nobody is in a position to offer statistics on the matter, but a rough impression is that downgradings have occurred at least ten times as often

as upgradings. So we have two questions to answer. The first, posed by
Paolo Ramat, is why upgradings occur at all:

It may be that degrammaticalization is statistically insignificant when compared
with the large number of grammaticalization processes . . . , but its examples are by
no means uninteresting, and not as scanty as one would prima facie incline to
admit. The question we have to deal with is therefore, why is it that grammaticalization and degrammaticalization coexist in natural languages? (Ramat 1992:
553)

And the second question is why the latter are so much rarer than the
former.

We have already seen a glimmer of the answer to these questions in the
discussion in §4.1.2 of the phonetic reductions that accompany affixation.
Less effort is required on the part of the speaker to produce an affix than
a full form. Add the element of frequency-caused predictability to the
extreme amount of redundancy in grammatical codings, and it is not
difficult to see why the quick-and-easy option of affixation is frequently
chosen. Other downgradings can readily be interpreted as least-effort
effects as well. Functional categories require less coding material—and
hence less production effort—than lexical categories. As a result, the
change from the latter to the former is far more common than from the
former to the latter (for more discussion of this point, see §7.2). All other
things being equal, a child confronted with the option of reanalyzing a
verb as an auxiliary or reanalyzing an auxiliary as a verb will choose the
former.

But all things are not always equal. There are other, conflicting, pressures that might lead the child to do the precise opposite. Analogical
pressure might result in the upgrading of an affix to a clitic or in the
creation of a freestanding verb from an affix. Paradigm regularization,
as we have seen, can lead to the reanalysis of an affix as a free-standing
pronoun. Now it would appear to be the case that the 'savings' in production effort generally outweigh the 'savings' that would lead to an
upgrading reanalysis. For that reason, we find downgradings greatly
exceeding upgradings in frequency. Hence, just as with grammaticalization itself, unidirectionality is an epiphenomenal result of the interaction
of other factors.

Joseph and Janda (1988) provide a different sort of explanation (i.e. one
not based on least-effort considerations) for why diachronic changes
involving the morphologization of syntactic elements are far more wide-

spread than those of demorphologization into the syntax. As they note, the morphologization of *phonological* processes also tends to be far more widespread than the reverse. One of the most common attested changes is for a rule that at one point was subject only to phonological conditions to become subject to the properties of morphemes and their boundaries. They point out that some of the best-studied phenomena in the history of our field attest to this fact: consider German umlaut, Grassman's Law in Sanskrit, consonant mutations in Celtic, accent shifts in Modern Greek, among other developments. The preference for morphological over phonological solutions is so strong that speakers will choose a fragmented morphological analysis involving considerable allomorphy over a simple purely phonological solution. Joseph and Janda cite the Maori example discussed in Hale (1973) and Kiparsky (1971) in support for this idea. This language replaced an across-the-board phonological rule deleting word-final consonants with a large set of suffixal allomorphs and a requirement that verb stems be lexically marked for their choice of allomorph.

We also cannot exclude the possibility that purely *sociological* factors are partly responsible for the general trend toward an increased degree of grammatical content. Janda (1998) puts forward a scenario under which such might be expected to take place. We have known since the work of Labov in the late 1960s that a central motivation for younger speakers to generalize a sound change to a new context is that this allows them 'to show their solidarity with older members (by sharing participation in the change via use of common innovative forms) and yet also to set themselves apart (by extending a variant to unique new contexts where it is not in fact phonetically motivated)' (Janda 1998: 25). As Labov put it:

> Succeeding generations of speakers within the same subgroup, responding to the same social pressures, carried the linguistic variable further along the process of change, beyond the model set by their parents. (Labov 1972b: 178)

Janda suggests an analogous effect in grammaticalization:

> There is no inherent reason why an analog of such socially functioning phonological extensions could not also be at work in grammaticization. That is, once a form has been initially grammaticalized, its further downgrading could ... be at least partly conditioned by the social function of age-group marking. (Janda 1998: 25)

I consider the possibility that Janda raises to be a promising direction for grammaticalization research to take. Its primary obstacle as a *general* explanation of unidirectionality is the often painfully slow pace of the changes involved. Clearly if a form has remained stable over many generations before undergoing further downgrading, the younger members of the speech community would not be 'showing their solidarity with older members' by downgrading it still further. Nevertheless, I would hope that empirical studies would be undertaken to see if Janda's scenario can be documented in the progress of some attested historical change.

As we have seen, many reconstructions of historical antecedents to grammaticalized forms are based on assumptions about the unidirectionality of *semantic change*, as well as on the assumption of the unidirectionality of the other parts of grammaticalization. Recall that it is assumed that change is always from the concrete to the abstract, that conversationally implicated meanings are conventionalized, but not the reverse, and so on. I suspect that, for whatever reason, there is a *general* directionality to the semantic changes observed in grammaticalization. But strict unidirectionality appears to be incorrect. One of the longest and most intricately detailed studies of grammaticalization is Frajzyngier (1996), which focuses its attention on the Chadic languages. On the basis of comparative evidence, Frajzyngier reconstructs for some of these languages less abstract sequential markers as deriving from more abstract complementizers and temporal markers as deriving from conditional markers. He draws explicitly methodological conclusions from his findings:

Thus the unidirectionality hypothesis with respect to grammaticalization from one grammatical morpheme to another is shown to be factually incorrect and certainly should not be used as a tool in grammaticalization research. In fact, bidirectionality appears to be the most likely possibility for those grammaticalization processes that involve metaphor and metonymic extensions. (Frajzyngier 1996: 467)

Let us conclude this section with a general observation about the methodological consequences of the fact that unidirectionality is not true across the board. Many reconstructions are based, implicitly or explicitly, on the reliable unidirectionality of every aspect of grammaticalization. For example, given the observation that in some (normally unwritten) language we find homophonous V and P with related meanings, it is assumed that the directionality of historical change was V > P. Assumptions of unidirectionality have led without exception to the P being taken to represent the later development. Perhaps such claims are not as secure as one might wish them to be.

6   Two Issues in Grammaticalization Research

In this section, I will address two prominent themes in functionalist-oriented research on grammaticalization, one methodological and one theoretical. The first involves the disturbing trend to use reconstructed forms as evidence, that is, to take reconstructions as 'results' that can be accorded the same methodological status as attested historical changes. The second is the hypothesis of a 'panchronic grammar', in which synchronic and diachronic statements find equal place.

6.1   Using reconstructions as evidence

Uncontroversially, one of the principal goals of historical linguistics is to hypothesize what unattested antecedent forms of a particular language or group of related languages might have looked like. Certainly one of the major goals of the field of linguistics over the past two centuries has been to attempt to sharpen the picture of the phonological system of Proto-Indo-European. But since this language was spoken perhaps 6000 years ago and more than two thousand years before its oldest attested descendent, we have no right to call our latest version of this picture an established 'result'. Rather, it is a simple hypothesis, awaiting improvement, perhaps based on new data that have to date eluded our attention, or perhaps on improved theoretical conceptions pertinent to the technique of reconstruction.

A large share of grammaticalization research is devoted to historical reconstruction. Routinely in this literature hypotheses are put forward about the origins of some grammatical marker or construction or, in more theoretically oriented work, about the general origins of particular types of elements. There is nothing pernicious about such reconstructions to the extent that they are based on the sorts of internal and comparative evidence commonly appealed to in historical linguistics. That does not guarantee that they are *correct*, of course, but, in principle, the reconstruction of a verb of possession as the historical antecedent of a perfective marker is no more or less dubious than that of a sequence of a vowel and nasal consonant as the antecedent of a nasalized vowel.

Methodological problems *do* arise, however, with certain *uses* to which these reconstructions might be applied. It would be unthinkable in mainstream historical linguistics, for example, to take some *reconstructed* sequence of vowel and nasal consonant and add it to a data base which included *attested* changes, say for the purpose of arguing for a particular theory of language change. However, in the functionalist-oriented research on grammaticalization, we find exactly that sort of methodology. That is, we find reconstructions based on the hypothesis of unidirectionality in grammaticalization being used as *evidence* to support the principle of unidirectionality.[23]

The following subsections illustrate my claim with reference to two of the best regarded lines of research in grammaticalization. The first (§6.1.1) is drawn from the work of Bernd Heine on the origins of grammatical markers in African languages. The second (§6.1.2) is the much-cited work of Joan Bybee and her colleagues on the origin of grammatical markers denoting 'futurity'.

6.1.1   Heine on progressives and locatives   Heine (1994) notes that in the West African language Ewe there are formal parallels between progressives and locatives. One means of forming progressives involves the free morpheme *le* and an *-ḿ* suffix on the verb:

(49) Kofí le   xɔ   tu-ḿ
     Kofi PROG house build-PROG
     'Kofi is building a house'

As it turns out, *le* is synchronically also a locative auxiliary verb ('be at') and *me* (the presumptive source of-*ḿ*) exists as a locative preposition. On the basis of the hypothesis that 'spatial expressions are metaphorically employed to conceptualize temporal notions' (Heine 1994: 269) and that the direction taken by the metaphor is unidirectional, Heine reconstructs progressives such as (49) as deriving historically from locative expressions.

I have no problem with this reconstruction per se—it may very well be correct. I do have a problem, however, with the next step that Heine takes, namely that of using this very reconstruction as *evidence for* 'grammaticalization theory'. In his concluding remarks (1994: 277–281), Heine asserts that this theory is able to *explain* the sequence of developments that led to the development of the locative into the progressive. But a (unidirectional) sequence of developments was *assumed* in the very recon-

23. Curiously, as central as the use of reconstructions are to mainstream work in grammaticalization, grammaticalization theorists are not beyond criticizing the use of even well accepted reconstructions, if they lead to unacceptable conclusions. For example, Bybee, Perkins, and Pagliuca (1994: 13) dismiss the reconstruction of a clitic upgrading to a word in Indo-European (discussed in Jeffers and Zwicky 1980 and §5.3.6 above) as being 'reconstructed and thus hypothetical'.

struction. There is no known sense of 'explanation' in which the assumption of X to demonstrate Y can legitimately allow one to conclude that X has been confirmed.

Such a use of a reconstructed form as evidence goes well beyond acceptable practice in historical linguistics. It's a little bit like reconstructing the Indo-European consonantal system on the basis of notions about the naturalness of sound systems in general and then including that reconstruction in a sample of sound systems in order to argue that some particular systems are more natural than others!

At least in the Ewe reconstruction, Heine points to a variety of factors in the current language that can be taken as independent evidence for the correctness of his reconstruction. But after finishing his discussion of Ewe, he goes on to discuss progressive constructions in a number of other languages, most of which have no significant written history (these include Diola Fogny, Usarufa, Umbundu, Tyurama, and Maninka). Here he reconstructs diachronic ancestors for the progressive in the absence of any independent evidence. The reconstructions are based solely on the assumption of unidirectionality of semantic change. Yet these reconstructions as well are appealed to as confirmation of the idea that there are natural paths of development for progressive morphemes.[24]

6.1.2 Bybee et al. on the origins of future morphemes We find similar methodological problems in the extensive writings of Joan Bybee and her colleagues on the origins of morphemes denoting 'future tense' in the world's languages (Bybee and Pagliuca 1987; Bybee, Pagliuca, and Perkins 1991; Bybee, Perkins, and Pagliuca 1994). A case in point is Bybee, Pagliuca, and Perkins (1991), whose goal is to test the following hypotheses:

(1) That futures in all languages develop from a small set of lexical sources and that all future morphemes from a given source go through similar stages of development;
(2) That the semantic change in grammaticization is accompanied by formal reduction, whereby the morpheme loses its independence and may fuse to contiguous material. (1991: 17)

24. Implicit in Heine's analysis (and in the thinking of many grammaticalization theorists) is the assumption that there is an isomorphism between diachronic development of clines of grammaticalization and the synchronic relations among polysemous items. For reasons to doubt this assumption, see Tabor and Traugott (forthcoming).

After a lengthy discussion, the paper claims that these hypotheses have been confirmed:

There is, as predicted, a highly significant correlation between the semantic classification we have imposed on the future grams [grammatical morphemes] and their formal properties. Moreover, these correlations are in the predicted direction—the semantic properties hypothesized to belong to older grams correlate with the formal properties that are accrued in the process of grammaticization. We conclude, then, that there is good reason to believe that future grams develop in very similar ways across unrelated languages, and that semantic and formal changes move in parallel in grammaticization. (1991: 41)

Unfortunately, however the authors motivate hypothesis (1) partly on the basis of an untested assumption and partly by appealing to the correctness of hypothesis (2). They motivate hypothesis (2), in turn, primarily by assuming the correctness of hypothesis (1)! Let me illustrate.

Since Bybee, Pagliuca, and Perkins (1991) draws heavily on Bybee and Pagliuca (1987), I will begin with a description of the earlier paper. The authors examined 50 languages and found that the future morphemes in most of those languages bear an unmistakable resemblance to one or more morphemes with a fairly circumscribed set of meanings, including 'desire', 'movement', possession', 'obligation', 'existence', and 'becoming'. On the basis of virtually no discussion, they assume that the historical 'sources' (1987: 111) for the future are verbs bearing these meanings, rather than vice-versa or considering the possibility that the shared meanings might have arisen from a common source.[25] The *only* examples they give of attested stages in the development of any future morphemes in any language are English *will*, *shall*, and *be going to*, from 'desire', 'obligation', and 'movement', respectively, and as far as *will* is concerned, they acknowledge that a future meaning was present even in *Beowulf*.

They give one argument that 'these modal flavors do not develop from the future meaning, but rather, when present, must be interpreted as retentions' (1987: 118), which I repeat in its entirety:

The inflectional future paradigm in Quechua is heterogeneous—the first person singular and plural exclusive inflections are based on an old movement morpheme (i.e. 'going to'); the second person is identical to the present, and the third person suffix appears to have evolved from an obligation marker. The evidence for this is that in most dialects its reading is prediction, but in the dialect of Cajamarca, it is used for obligation ('must'), probability, and future (Felix Quesada, personal

25. In this respect, they follow Ultan (1978).

communication). The crucial point is that the movement-derived first singular and plural exclusive can have readings with prediction and intention but *not* readings with obligation and necessity. Only the third person—that is, the form derived from an obligation source—can obligation or necessity be present as modal flavors. (Bybee and Pagliuca 1987: 118)

The nature of the argumentation in the above passage is not clear to me. Given the (reasonable) assumption that we are not dealing with accidental homophony, we find a first person future that shares a common source with 'movement' and a third person future that shares a common source with 'obligation'. In the absence of further relevant information bearing on the directionality of developments, we have no more reason to think that the future senses derived from the 'movement' and 'obligation' senses than vice-versa, or that (quite reasonably, in my opinion) in one person the future is historically basic and in the other historically derivative. No principles of language change of which I am aware dictate that all forms in a suppletive paradigm are necessarily semantically innovative.

Armed with the assumption of common origins of future morphemes in a small set of lexical sources, Bybee et al. propose the following set of developments for those that develop from a 'modality' sense (1991: 29):

(50) a. *Stage 1.* The youngest future morphemes (i.e. the most recent to develop) have a sense of obligation, desire, or ability.
   b. *Stage 2.* The next oldest future morphemes have a sense of intention or 'root possibility'.
   c. *Stage 3.* The next oldest future morphemes have a future sense only.
   d. *Stage 4.* The very oldest future morphemes have a probability sense or are used as imperatives.[26]

In other words, they propose a model instantiating hypothesis (1). But what is the evidence for this model? Based on a survey of 75 languages, they show that the stages correlate with the future morpheme's degree of reduction of form, as measured in terms of degree of fusion with the verb, morphophonological autonomy, and length. Given the assumption that semantic change is accompanied by formal reduction, they conclude that

26. Bybee, Perkins, and Pagliuca (1994: 280) revise their earlier views on imperatives and remark that 'futures that have not undergone a lot of formal grammaticalization can have an imperative function'.

the age of a future morpheme can be measured in this manner. But this assumption is none other than hypothesis (2).

As we have seen, hypothesis (2) was also claimed to have been tested and confirmed. But the only evidence that they present in this paper to support the idea that semantic change goes hand-in-hand with formal reduction demands the assumption that futures in all languages develop from a small set of lexical sources and that all future morphemes derived from a given source go through similar stages of development. That is, it demands the assumption of hypothesis (1).

In short, Bybee and her colleagues are trapped in a vicious circle. Hypothesis (2)—a central assumption of the great bulk of work dealing with grammaticalization—might well be correct independently of the evidence for it provided by Bybee et al. But the only way that they can be said to have provided *independent* evidence for it is by assuming the correctness of hypothesis (1), which is given little support beyond that contributed by hypothesis (2).

6.2 Panchronic grammar

There is just a short step from the notion that there can be distinct diachronic processes to the rejection of the synchrony-diachrony distinction. At least rhetorically, Heine, Claudi, and Hünnemeyer take this step, arguing that 'for a theory of grammaticalization it is both unjustified and impractical to maintain a distinction between synchrony and diachrony' (1991b: 258). Since '[grammaticalization] phenomena exhibit simultaneously a synchronic-psychological and a diachronic relation', they advocate instead 'panchronic grammar' capable of integrating the two domains.[27]

It is not clear to me, however, that the call for a blurring of the synchrony-diachronic distinction is more than rhetorical. For example, they note that there are two ways that grammaticalization can be viewed:

on the one hand as a cognitive activity mapped onto language structure. This activity *is accessible to a diachronic analysis* once it is 'structuralized', that is, ends up in a conventionalized or 'frozen' form. It is *also accessible to synchronic analysis* in the form of language use patterns or in assessments of conceptual/semantic relation. (1991b: 259; emphasis added)

27. As Heine et al. (1991b) note, the notion of 'panchrony' goes back to Saussure (1916/1966: 134–135) and Hjelmslev (1928). However, they fail to mention Bailey's (1973) 'dynamic paradigm', which develops the idea at some length.

While I am not sure what it means for an activity to map onto structure, this above passage seems to presuppose the possibility of a (strictly) synchronic analysis. Heine et al. continue:

> On the other hand, grammaticalization can be viewed as a continual movement toward structure or a structure that 'comes out of discourse and is shaped by discourse as much as it shapes discourse as an on-going process' (Hopper 1987: 142). (1991b: 259)

But here again, there is nothing to challenge the synchrony-diachrony distinction. Hopper's remarks, phrased in the language of his theory of Emergent Grammar (see ch. 2, §4.2.1), question whether one can separate knowledge of language from use of language. They do not address directly the question of panchronicity.

Heine et al. do, to be sure, give two sets of examples in support of panchronic grammar. The first involves the concept 'back' in So, a Kuliak language spoken in Eastern Uganda. As in many languages, it appears to have undergone grammaticalization from a 'body part' sense to a 'spatial' sense. First consider (51a–c), all of which can be translated 'He is behind the mountain'. We note that there are options for ablative case marking—it can be marked on the word for 'back' in (51a), on both 'back' and 'mountain' in (51b), and on 'mountain' in (51c):

(51) a. néke íca   cú-o   sóg
        be   he/she back-ABL mountain
     b. néke íca   sú-o   sóg-o
     c. néke íca   sú   sóg-o
        'He is behind the mountain.'

We also find the opposite situation, where several forms correspond to only one meaning. So in (52), 'back' can denote either a body part (52a) or a spatial concept (52b):

(52) néke cúc sú-o   ím
     be   fly back-ABL girl
     a. 'There is a fly on the girl's back.'
     b. 'There is a fly behind the girl.'

Heine et al. remark that 'a grammar of So has to account for ... why there are three optional variants in [(51)] expressing much the same meaning' and 'why [(52)] is semantically ambiguous', among other things (1991b: 249). In their view, this can be accomplished only by appeal to the diachronic situation that the sentences of (51) and (52) 'represent different stages of this process [of conceptual manipulation]' (1991b: 250). Hence the need to build diachronic statements into synchronic descriptions.

The problem is that Heine et al. confuse what a *grammar of a language* has to account for and what a comprehensive theory of *language in general* has to account for. The grammar of So—that is, what a speaker of So knows about the structure of So—simply represents the fact that (51a–c) are paraphrases and that (52) is ambiguous. But no learner of the language could possibly possess the information about what point on a cline of grammaticalization the word for 'back' might happen to fall, for the simple reason that clines of grammaticalization represent neither innate knowledge (and surely they will agree with me there!) or knowledge that can be induced from the environment.[28]

Now, then, why are the facts of So as they are? Let us assume that they are correct in attributing the observed meaning shift to:

a categorial metaphor of the OBJECT-TO-SPACE type, according to which a concrete object, such as a body part 'back', serves as a metaphorical vehicle to conceptualize a spatial notion, the prepositional meaning 'at the back of, behind'. (1991b: 250)

If human cognition is such that we are predisposed to such metaphorical extensions of meaning, then we have a (partial) explanation for why some speaker or group of speakers, at some point or points in the history of So, extended the meaning of 'back' from a purely physical sense to a derivative spatial one. Subsequent learners of the language acquired the extended meaning along with the original one.

It is true, of course, that we have not provided a full explanation of why there are three optional variants in (51) expressing much the same meaning and why (52) is semantically ambiguous. That is, the ungrammaticality of (51a) would be consistent with the account that I have offered so far, as would a situation in which (52a) was not a possible translation of *nɛ̀ke cúc sú-o ím*. But such situations would be equally compatible with the account provided by Heine, et al. Perhaps if adequate records of the history of this language were available to us, we might have an insight into the data serving as input to successive generations of learners of So. Such data, in conjunction with our understanding of universal grammar and grammar-independent cognitive processes at work in language acquisition would lead to greater detailed understanding of specific changes (and nonchanges) in the grammar and lexical semantics of the language.

---

28. The remarks in note 24 seem particularly appropriate here.

The second set of examples offered by Heine et al. involves German. They note that prepositions in this language exhibit a great deal of homophony. *Für* 'for', for example, can mark benefaction (53a), time (53b), purpose (53c), and manner (53d):

(53) a. Er kaufte Blumen für Maria.
        'He bought flowers for Maria.'
     b. Er ging für zwei Jahre nach Afrika.
        'He went to Africa for two years.'
     c. Er kaufte den Schlüssel für die Haustür.
        'He bought the key for the house door.'
     d. Es ist für die Katz.
        'It's all a waste.'

Along the same lines, *an* 'at' can mark space, time, causation, and progressive aspect; *mit* 'with' can mark comitatives, condition, instruments, and manner; and *zu* 'to' can mark allatives, manner, reason, and dative. Heine et al. made two interesting discoveries: first, dictionaries invariably take one sense of each preposition as 'basic', that is, they list that sense first in the entry. For example, the benefactive sense of *für* is given before any of the others. Second, *speakers* of German also agree that one particular sense for each preposition is the basic one and their judgments are in accord with those of the dictionary writers. Now as in turns out, this intuited basic sense happens to coincide with the least grammaticalized sense, that is, with what is assumed (or, in some cases, known) to be the historically prior sense.

Since 'the parameters underlying grammaticalization are essentially the same as those used by native speakers intuitively when making judgments on "genuine meanings" or by grammarians when ordering the functions of prepositions' (Heine et al. 1991b: 257), the line between synchrony and diachrony is said to be blurred. Only a panchronic grammar, it would seem, can unify these three facts.

Such is not the case, however. Again, let us assume that humans are endowed with cognitive propensities to make certain metaphoric transfers and that these propensities are an active part of cognition. This propensity might be reflected in a variety of ways in language use. For example, a speaker will, as we have seen, report that the nonmetaphorical meaning of a word is more basic than the metaphorical. Likewise, a speaker will be more likely to *extend* the meaning of a word in a metaphorical direction than in a nonmetaphorical one. It is much easier, say, to imagine somebody describing the beams, joists, studs, etc. of a house as the 'ribs' of the house than referring to part of their bodily skeleton as their 'joists'. For reasons that are surely based as much in personal and sociological factors as in linguistic ones, some of these metaphorical extensions will 'stick' and become incorporated into the lexical meaning of the word. Hence the next generation of language learners will be exposed to a different set of input data than their parents were exposed to. The language, that is, will have changed.

Nothing in this account suggests that the strict distinction between synchrony and diachrony need be abandoned in favor of a panchronic grammar. Mentally real and active cognitive propensities lead speakers to extend the senses of certain words. The next generation acquires these extensions along with the rest of the language and—in some cases—is led by these same propensities to extend the senses still further.

Let me summarize this section with a succinct statement by Joseph and Janda on why we must abandon any appeal to 'panchrony' in linguistic explanation:

> In denying [the sharp distinction between] synchrony and diachrony, the view that there is only a panchronic or achronic dynamism in language suggests that there exist grammatical principles or mechanisms which direct speakers to change their languages in certain ways other than through cross-generational and cross-lectal transmission. To the best of our knowledge, however, there is absolutely no evidence suggesting that this kind of asocial individual causation of linguistic change really exists. But such questionable devices can be dispensed with on the usual view, taken here, that language change occurs solely via two independently motivated entities: the present (synchrony) and time (a succession of presents, i.e. diachrony). (Joseph and Janda 1988: 194)

7 Grammaticalization and Generative Grammar

We will now turn to the relationship between grammaticalization and the principles of generative grammar. Section 7.1 rebuts the idea that there is something intrinsic to grammaticalization that threatens generative approaches to language. In §7.2 I discuss the rather limited attempts to account for some of the phenomena associated with grammaticalization within the generative framework.

7.1 Does grammaticalization refute generative grammar?

As noted above in §1, it is a common belief among functionalists that the historical changes observed in grammaticalization challenge the core

ideas of generative grammar. Traugott and König (1991), as we have
seen, point to an undermining of the *langue-parole* dichotomy and refutation of the idea that grammatical distinctions can be expressed categorially. The former conclusion is apparently drawn from the fact that many
of the important diachronic changes associated with grammaticalization
have their root in performance. But that fact in and of itself threatens only
an extreme form of the dichotomy that no generativist (to my knowledge)
advocates. None would deny that *parole* can have profound effects upon
langue (or, in more current parlance, that performance can affect competence). Competence changes ultimately based on performance factors
are, to be sure, particularly evident in the case of grammaticalization. But
as argued at length earlier in this work, such a circumstance no more
challenges the dichotomy than the fact that environmental factors can
affect the structure of our bodily organs challenges the fact that they too
are structural systems.

An extensive discussion of the question of categoriality was undertaken
in the previous chapter, arguing on the basis of synchronic data that
the major challenges to the idea that grammatical categories are discrete
are simply based on misanalyses. When the proper balance among principles of syntax, semantics, and pragmatics is taken into account, there
ends up being little support for an abandonment of such categories. As
far as diachronic grammaticalization-relevant data is concerned, I again
see little in the way of a challenge to categoriality. Such challenges, as
argued persuasively by Steele (1994), are invariably based on a confusion
between analysis and data. Typically, a functionalist will take some historical development, such as that from full verb to auxiliary or to preposition, and show that various properties typically associated with auxiliaries
or prepositions appeared over a course of centuries. From this it is concluded that the verb-auxiliary and verb-preposition distinctions are not
clear cut; rather there are said to be clines of categoriality.

Such claims, however, are always made with respect to unanalyzed
data, not with respect to *grammars* proposed to account for the data. That
is, we do not find supporters of nondiscrete categories writing grammars
(or even partial grammars) for some stage of English and demonstrating
that certain elements generated by those grammars should have neither
the category label 'V', nor 'AUX', but rather are something 'in between'
that defies a discrete category label. Instead, they simply assume that such
is true based on a small set of examples illustrating that a given grammatical element lacks certain properties associated with verbs in some

language (or earlier stages of the same language) and also lacks certain
properties associated with auxiliaries. But in order to refute the idea that
the element is either a verb or an auxiliary, it would be necessary to *write
a better grammar* of the language than one in which the element has discrete categorial status. This has never been done for any language, to my
knowledge. Until it is, there is nothing for a defender of the traditional
view that grammatical elements are discrete to respond to.

No generativist questions the idea that there are purely syntactic changes
that are not reflections of a change in categorial status. The categorial
change of the modals in English from V to AUX could well have been
abrupt, even if it was preceded by centuries of changes in their distribution in which morphosyntactic properties generally associated with verbs
were lost and morphosyntactic properties generally associated with
auxiliaries were gained (see Lightfoot 1991: 141f. and Kemenade 1993).
Describing what has happened to modals primarily in terms of a progressive grammaticalization along a V-AUX continuum (e.g. as Plank 1984
would have it) obscures the complex interplay of factors that led to the
categorial change and is, for that reason, ultimately unexplanatory.

Heine, Claudi, and Hünnemeyer (1991b: 1) agree with Traugott and
König that grammaticalization poses a challenge to formal linguistics. As
we have seen, it is said to challenge

most post-Saussurean models of grammar [which] rely—explicitly or implicitly—
on the following tenets:

(a) Linguistic description must be strictly synchronic.
(b) The relationship between form and meaning is arbitrary.
(c) A linguistic form has only one function or meaning.

I have a hard time associating *any* of these three tenets with generative
grammar, which is presumably a 'post-Saussurean model of grammar' *par
excellence*. As far as (a) is concerned, if taken literally, it is nonsense.
There is a plethora of 'descriptions' of language change by advocates of
generative grammar. Perhaps Heine et al. mean that generativists believe
that synchrony and diachrony can be *understood* in total isolation from
each other. But this too is incorrect. A particular synchronic stage of a
language is, in part, a product of children's reanalyses of an earlier synchronic stage. In that way, synchrony and diachrony are inseparable. No
generativist model holds tenet (b) either, since all assume very direct links
between form and meaning. Finally, I am more puzzled than anything
else about the attribution of tenet (c) to generative grammar (assuming

that Heine et al. have this in mind as a prototypical post-Saussurean approach). This tenet has always been a mainstay of *functionalist* thinking, as is evidenced by Dwight Bolinger's remark that 'The natural condition of language is to preserve one form for one meaning' (1977b: x). Indeed, generativists have often used the many-many relation between forms and meanings and between forms and functions as support for the autonomy hypothesis (see ch. 2, §3).

To be sure, not all functionalists dismiss generativist theory as irrelevant to grammaticalization research. Haspelmath (1992), for example, is encouraged by Baker (1988)'s proposal that the same principles apply word-internally as apply sentence-internally. He notes that clines of grammaticalization would suggest that should be the case. In a subsequent paper (Haspelmath 1994), he points approvingly to the development of the distinction between lexical category and functional category in generative grammar, which has led to a certain degree of theoretical convergence between the two approaches. As he points out, the principal characteristics of functional categories dovetail well with those of grammaticalized elements. One could easily substitute 'grammaticalized element' for 'functional element' in list provided in Abney (1987: 64–65) of the principal properties of the latter:

(54) a. Functional elements constitute closed lexical classes.
   b. Functional elements are generally phonologically and morphologically dependent. They are generally stressless, often clitics or affixes, and sometimes even phonologically null.
   c. Functional elements permit only one complement, which is in general not an argument.
   d. Functional elements are usually inseparable from their complement.
   e. Functional elements lack 'descriptive content'.

Haspelmath goes on to point out that in recent generative work, functional elements need not be words and that the categories COMP and INFL are analyzed as heads. Such facts he sees as representing a turn in generativist research toward positions that had been taken earlier in functionalist grammaticalization studies.[29] While Haspelmath remains

---

29. As to the latter point, Haspelmath (1992) had argued that head-dependent relations are preserved in grammaticalization.

critical of the generative program in general and of particular analyses put forward within it, he regards this particular convergence between the two traditions as a positive development.

Despite the above, it cannot be denied that generative grammar per se has had little to contribute to an understanding of most of the historical changes that fall under the rubric of grammaticalization. In particular, the semantic changes and phonetic reductions are explained by theories of meaning and processing respectively, not by the set of theoretical conceptions identified with the generative enterprise. For that reason, obviously, studies of grammaticalization have not loomed large in the generativist literature. But crucially, there is nothing that we find in grammaticalization that is *incompatible* with any well established principle of generative grammar.

In fact, there is one component of grammaticalization that generative grammar might be expected to have something useful to say about. As we have seen, grammaticalization, by definition, involves reanalysis, that is, the reallocation of preexisting structure. It seems reasonable, then, that generativist theory might help to characterize the circumstances in which reanalysis can take place, and, in that manner, help to narrow down the possible grammaticalization-related changes. Indeed, some generative research has taken precisely that position. It is to this work that we now turn.

7.2 Generative accounts of grammaticalization

Ian Roberts is the linguist who has devoted the most effort to explaining grammaticalization in terms congenial to generative linguistic theory.[30] He starts from the observation that the two most common manifestations of grammaticalization, the change from a full lexical item to that of an auxiliary-like item and the change from the latter to an affix, lend themselves to ready characterization in the vocabulary of generative syntax. The former change, which can also be characterized as the change from a lexical category to a functional category, is illustrated in (55a–b) with respect to the first stages of evolution of the Romance future (see Roberts 1993):

30. See also Fintel (1995) for interesting discussion of how the semantic changes observed in grammaticalization might be handled by semantic mechanisms interfacing with formal syntax.

(55) a.

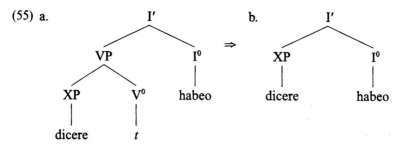

But what would *cause* such a reanalyis? Roberts points to language learners following a 'Least Effort Strategy' (1993: 228–229):[31]

(56) *Least Effort Strategy (LES)*
Representations assigned to sentences of the input to acquisition should be such that they contain the set of the shortest possible chains (consistent with (a) principles of grammar, (b) other aspects of the trigger experience).

In other words, LES led to the elimination of the *habeo* ... *t* chain and consequent reanalysis of *habeo* as an auxiliary.[32]

At first blush, this would appear to be a straightforward case of grammaticalization being driven by reanalysis and reanalysis being driven by strategies followed by child language learners. However, things are not quite so simple. While, given Roberts' discussion, LES appears to be necessary for reanalysis, it is clearly not sufficient. After all, not all verbs (nor even all verbs with auxiliary-like properties) develop into true auxiliaries. Three other conditions had to be met in the development of the Romance future, and two of them reflect a strong degree of convergence between Roberts' account and the accounts that we find in the mainstream grammaticalization literature.

The first involved changes in the Late Latin complementation system from one which relied largely on infinitival and subjunctive complementation to one which relied on CPs formed by *quod* and an embedded

31. The idea that grammaticalization is primarily due to simplification-driven reanalysis is also expressed in Battye and Roberts (1995: 11). Such an idea is the essence of the account of the origins of the English modal auxiliaries discussed in Lightfoot (1979a).

32. Later in the paper (1993: 243f.) Roberts argues that the reanalysis from auxiliary to affix also was a consequence of LES.

clause. This change led ultimately from the change of the XP in (55a–b) from a DP to a VP, facilitating the renalysis of *habeo* as an auxiliary.

The other two ingredients for reanalysis, however, were not 'structural' ones and therefore presumably fall under '(b) other aspects of the trigger experience'. One was semantic. Roberts notes that before reanalysis, *habere* lacked the ability to assign a θ-role to its complement (i.e. it was, in Roberts' terminology, a 'lexical auxiliary'). Hence it already shared semantic properties with true functional auxiliaries. Prior to reanalysis, '*habere*'s temporal meaning ... was that of a neutral future by the end of the Imperial period. Temporal notions are among those notion which are naturally associated with functional heads' (Roberts 1993: 235) (for more discussion of this point, see Roberts 1992: §3.3). In other words, semantic changes—bleaching of meaning, to be specific—both preceded the reanalysis and were partly responsible for it. If I understand Roberts correctly, he is assuming that children follow a strategy that leads them to expect certain correlations between meaning and grammatical category. Specifically, he is following Grimshaw (1991) in assuming that functional categories lack the power of 'semantic selection', roughly the power to select for the thematic properties of their specifiers and complements. Hence it follows that a dethematizing semantic change might have the effect of engendering a downgrading of categorial status, as the grammar adjusts itself to conform to the 'expected' form-meaning correlation.[33]

Second, Roberts points to '*habere*'s reduced form, which made it distinct from the progressive' (1993: 235) as a factor in triggering the reanalysis. While he does not go into detail on this point, it would appear that he accepts the idea that learners also expect a 'natural' correlation between the degree of reduction of a phonological form and the degree of 'lexicalness' of a syntactic category. So it would appear that Roberts accepts the idea that what are generally considered two central ingredients of the grammaticalization phenomenon—semantic bleaching and phonetic reduction—are temporal precursors to reanalysis and partial causes for it.

---

33. For discussion of the formal semantic properties of functional categories, see Fintel (1995). Based in part on prior work by Chierchia (1984), Partee (1987), and May (1991), he suggests that functional meanings are permutation-invariant, of high semantic type, and subject to universal semantic constraints.

Campbell (1997: §4.2.2) suggests that LES is too restrictive to account for the bulk of reanalyses that have been implicated in grammaticalization. In his view, few if any of the following changes are plausibly derived by simplification of the number of chain-positions in a phrase-structure tree:

(57) a. The reanalysis of grammatical affixes as independent words.
b. The development of definite articles from demonstrative pronouns.
c. The development of third person pronouns from demonstratives.
d. The development of relative pronouns from interrogative pronouns.
e. The development of switch reference markers from contrastive conjunctions.
f. The development of partitive constructions from ablative or genitive markers; the development of genitive markers from ablative or locative markers.
g. The development of copulas from demonstratives or third person pronouns.
h. Shifts in irrealis forms either from or to futures, subjunctives, optatives, potential/conditionals, or imperatives.
i. The development of existential/presentational constructions from 'have', 'give', 'be' or from locative pronouns.
j. The development of coordinate conjunctions from 'with'.

It remains to be seen whether some or all of these grammatical changes can be derived from least-effort considerations internal to grammar. In any event, as we have seen, Roberts does not demand a wholly syntactically-based treatment of grammaticalization.

8 Conclusion

We have examined the associated set of diachronic changes that fall under the rubric of 'grammaticalization' and have found that no new theoretical mechanisms, nor mechanisms unique to grammaticalization itself, are needed to explain them. Far from calling for a 'new theoretical paradigm', grammaticalization appears to be no more than a cover term for a conjunction of familiar developments from different spheres of language, none of which require or entail any of the others.

Chapter 6
Language Typology and Its Difficulties

1 Overview

There is an important sense in which the previous chapters have put the cart before the horse. Each in its own way has taken one or more cross-linguistic generalizations and discussed the ins and outs of how they might be best explained. But what is obviously methodologically prior is establishing that such generalizations are *valid* ones. How can we be sure, for example, that the rarity of indefinite subject NPs is more than a mere artifact of some nonrepresentative sampling of languages? Or how do we know that the correlation between having verb-final order in the clause and having postpositions is theoretically significant? This chapter takes on the problem of establishing valid cross-linguistic generalizations. To be specific, it examines the subfield of language typology, broadly, the study of the distribution of the world's languages in terms of their structural features. My purpose is to deal in some depth with what I consider to be the most pressing foundational questions of the enterprise, not to survey the field as a whole. As a result, numerous important contributions to language typology will receive no mention, and many debates in the field will be dealt with only cursorily or ignored altogether.

Section 2 gives a brief historical sketch, followed by an introduction to the major school of typology today, namely, that which considers the uncovering of typological generalizations and providing external explanations for them to be linked enterprises. But §3 raises doubts as to whether the generalizations that have come out of typological research point us to 'real' phenomena in need of explanation, or are merely artifacts of a less than optimal sampling method. It also suggests that quite possibly ill-founded assumptions about the operation of functional forces underlie many of the attempts to use typological generalizations in a predictive manner. Furthermore, a lack of consistency in identifying the grammatical elements that enter into typological statements might have the effect of rendering them valueless. In §4, I concede that there is no alternative but to provisionally accept the validity of the more robust-seeming typological generalizations. Section 5 argues that even if the most pessimistic possibilities raised in the previous sections are not motivated, there are nevertheless important measures that should be taken as prerequisites to typological investigation. Most important is a thorough formal analysis of the phenomena to be investigated. Section 6 scrutinizes an argument for functionalism based on typological analysis, while §7 puts generative approaches to typology under the microscope. Section 8 is a short summary.

2   The Field of Language Typology

In this section I briefly outline the history of the field of language typology (§2.1), discuss the 'functional-typological approach' (§2.2), and explain why typological generalizations should be of interest to all linguists (§2.3).

2.1   Historical background

The roots of modern language typology are co-extensive with those of genetic classification; indeed, for a good part of the nineteenth century it was assumed that genealogy and typology coincided. That is, it was taken for granted that if two languages share typological features then they are genetically related, and vice-versa.

Until the middle years of the twentieth century, most major typological classification schemes were morphologically, rather than syntactically, based. The first important one was devised by Friederich von Schlegel (1808/1977), who divided languages into two types: flectional and flectionless. His brother August Wilhelm Schlegel (1818) soon expanded the classes to the tripartite one which, in one form or another, was dominant for a century and still finds its way into introductory text books and lectures. These three classes are 'those without grammatical structure' (later 'isolating'), 'affixing' (later 'agglutinative'), and inflectional.[1] His scheme is represented in Koerner (1995) as in figure 6.1 (with the last-named class further subdivided into 'synthetic' and 'analytic').

---

1. Humboldt (1836) added a fourth type, 'incorporating', a term which also is encountered in modern textbooks.

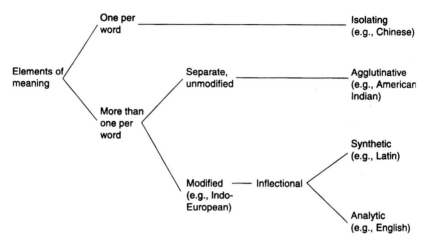

Figure 6.1
The tripartite morphological classification of languages.

August Schleicher was apparently the first linguist of the past century, or one of the very first, who considered it a *theoretical* possibility that typological and genealogical classification might be distinct (on this point, see Davies 1975: 635). Nevertheless, he did not think that there was any empirical support for such an idea:

All languages which have so far been recognized as belonging to a single family agree also in their morphological form. The splitting-up of the parent language must thus have begun only after the evolution of the morphological form had already been completed. (Schleicher 1869: 31; translation in Bynon 1986: 141–142)

It was only later in the century, after a larger number of languages had been studied and after the Neogrammarian program had cleared the air of much of the speculative metaphysics that demanded that the evolution of a people be reflected in the outward forms of its language that it became commonly accepted that the genealogical and the typological classification of a language might not be in step.

The most elaborate scheme of morphological typology is surely that presented in Sapir's *Language* (1921). Sapir categorized languages in terms of three largely independent factors: first, whether particular types of conceptual relations are manifested overtly; second, the method for modifying roots; and third, the degree of fusion between the root and the

Table 6.1
Correlations between word order and adposition order

	VSO	SVO	SOV
Preposition	6	10	0
Postposition	0	3	11

From Greenberg 1963.

affix. This leads to a more than a dozen subtypes of languages. Despite the importance Sapir seems to have accorded to his classification scheme (two of the book's eleven chapters are devoted to elaborating it) and its refinement in Greenberg (1960), it is largely ignored in current typological work.[2]

Only a fairly limited number of typological generalizations and classification schemes involving syntax were put forward before the second half of the twentieth century (see, for example, Weil 1844/1887; Schleicher 1848: 6–7; Lepsius 1880; Grasserie 1889, 1890; Wundt 1900; Schmidt 1926). All agree that it was Greenberg's seminal 1963 paper that laid the basis for modern syntactic typology. Inspired by Jakobson's call for an 'implicational typology' (Jakobson 1957/1971), Greenberg, working with a sample of 30 languages, presented the implicational relationships between their dominant form of word order (VSO, SVO, SOV, etc.) and such properties as whether they are prepositional or postpositional, their adjective-noun ordering, their determiner-noun ordering, and their numeral-noun ordering. For example, his sample of 30 languages contained 6 with VSO order, all of which were prepositional; 13 SVO languages, which were overwhelmingly prepositional; and 11 SOV languages, all postpositional (see table 6.1). Such striking correlations were widely regarded as being inconceivably the result of coincidence. As a result of Greenberg's paper, few linguists remained who regarded the genetic approach as 'the only linguistic classification having both value and usefulness' (Meillet 1931: 53).

2. Martinet writes that Sapir's typological endeavor, 'for all its perspicuity, . . . stands as a nearly tragic illustration of the pitfalls of psychologism' (1962: 94) and that Greenberg simply 'translates Sapir's scheme into currently fashionable jargon' (1962: 67). The only current approach to morphological theory that I have found, functionalist or formalist, that gives Sapir's scheme more than passing reference, is Anderson (1992).

2.2 The functional-typological approach

Very few linguists with typological interests are content merely to state descriptive generalizations governing the distribution of linguistic elements in the languages of the world. Typically, they wish to go beyond description and to *explain* this frequency and distribution. Indeed, many consider the tasks of ascertaining and explaining typological variation as inseparable:

> In our view, language typology lies at the very center of linguistics in that it serves directly the goals of the discipline itself: to explain, as well as describe, the facts of natural language structure. Language typology not only provides a description of the range of variation among natural languages, but also addresses itself to the *explanatory* task. (Hammond, Moravcsik, and Wirth 1988: 1; emphasis in original)

Greenberg appears to have shared that opinion. For example, his 1963 paper went further than merely to point out the typological correlations among linguistic elements. Its last section, 'Conclusion: Some general principles', attempts to explain why certain typological patterns exist. For example, the predominance of noun-adjective and subject-verb order is attributed to 'a general tendency for comment to follow topic' (1963: 100). And three universals that exemplify a 'general tendency to mark the ends of units rather than the beginning' are 'probably related to the fact that we always know when someone has just begun speaking, but it is our sad experience that without some marker we don't know when the speaker will finish' (1963: 103).

Following Greenberg's lead, the great majority of the work devoted to explaining cross-linguistic patterns attempts to do so in terms of linguistic function, in particular communicative function. That is, such work has been carried out to an overwhelming degree within the functionalist tradition. The three major English-language overviews of syntactic typology of the past two decades, Mallinson and Blake (1981), Comrie (1989), and Croft (1990) share this general approach. Indeed, Croft considers a functional approach to language and a commitment to explaining typological patterns as inextricably linked, as is manifested by his reference to 'the functional-typological approach' (1990: 2). He notes that this approach 'is primarily associated with Talmy Givón, Paul Hopper, and Sandra Thompson, though it has well established historical antecedents.'

Broadly speaking, there are three interconnected types of typological patterns that functionalists have attempted to account for. The first is the patterning of grammatical elements with respect to each other (both paradigmatically and syntagmatically) without regard to their meanings. The second and third have to do with meaning-form relations: the patterning of particular types of grammatical elements with respect to their meanings and functions; and the manifestation of particular meanings and functions as grammatical elements. I will give brief exemplifications of each in turn.

The first type of account is illustrated by the plethora of word order studies that have followed on the heels of Greenberg's seminal work. For example, consider the grammatical elements 'subject' and 'verb'. It is widely accepted that in their basic ordering,[3] the overwhelming majority of languages place the subject before the verb. Why should this be? Functionalists have provided a number of possible explanations; an important one regards this ordering as an iconic reflection of principles of information flow (see Du Bois 1985, 1987; Lambrecht 1987; and chapter 3, §4.5). To put it fairly crudely, the sequence of grammatical elements mirrors the sequential flow of information.

The second type of account identifies a grammatical construct (or interrelated set of constructs) as being cross-linguistically widespread and attempts to account for its frequency in terms of its meaning or function. For example, it has been observed that many languages have the syntactic categories 'noun', 'verb', and 'adjective'. This tripartite division has been explained on the basis of their enabling the efficient expression of the three central functions of reference, predication, and modification, respectively (see chapter 4).

The third type of account is illustrated by studies that take a linguistic function (comparison, focusing, modification, and so on), study the means by which it is coded cross-linguistically, and attempt to explain why some types of coding predominate over others. Consider relativization, for example. The languages of the world form relative clauses (or their functional equivalents) in a number of different ways: by complete nonreduction of the clause, by gapping the coreferent noun phrase, by changing word order, by nominalization, by use of a resumptive pronoun, by use of a relative pronoun, and by special coding on the verb. Why do some strategies predominate over others and why would a particular language choose a particular strategy? In the view of Givón (1979a), a language will choose a strategy which allows most easily (all other things

---

3. I will return to discuss this notion in §3.4.2.

being equal) the recovery of the semantic roles of the arguments involved. Thus one can, to a certain extent, predict how relatives will be formed in a particular language in terms of efficient strategies for recovery.

We will return in §6 to examine an interesting argument *for* functionalism that has arisen on the basis of typological investigation.

As is demonstrated in the collection of papers edited by Shibatani and Bynon (1995), however, functionalists do not have a monopoly on the field of language typology. In particular, more and more generative-oriented studies have been devoted to explaining typological patterns. As might be expected, they have been concerned more with the distribution of, and correlations among, the formal elements of language in and of themselves, rather than with their meanings and functions. A full discussion of generative typological studies will be deferred until §7.

Before proceeding any further, it may prove useful to ask why one might expect anything of theoretical importance to come out of typological research.

2.3   Why care about typology?

It is not self-evident that knowing how languages are distributed in terms of their structural features should have broader implications for linguistic theory. That is, it is not obvious that typological patterns, whatever their intrinsic interest may be, point in some direct way to the organization of the language faculty. It is easy to find in the natural world any number of morphological features of plants and animals that can be classified and compared, but which bear but little on any branch of biological theory. For example, species of placental mammals vastly outnumber those of nonplacentals, the latter having achieved great ecological success only in Australia. This fact has played a role in understanding the history of the earth, but has little bearing on foundational questions in biology. Furthermore, morphological features of plants and animals that seem virtually dysfunctional in certain circumstances can help them to achieve great success in others, while a species that is barely hanging on in its native continent can become ecologically predominant when introduced into another. Such facts suggest that factors unrelated to the biochemistry of life have played an important role in the distribution of species and in the distribution of the structural (i.e. anatomical) and functional (i.e. physiological) traits that they manifest.

One might ask then whether the same could be true of the features that languages manifest. Why should the frequency of occurrence of some formal linguistic feature lead to any more insight about the nature of the language faculty than the frequency of occurrence of some biological feature is likely to lead to insight about, say, the genetic mechanisms responsible for life? While the natural historian, of course, is greatly interested in biological 'typology', genetic theory has based its theoretical formulations on the detailed investigation of only a few organisms. Might it not be the case, then, that linguistic theory is wholly analogous? Might it not be the case that an in-depth study of a few languages, or conceivably even of just one, could lead to the discovery of all that we need to know about the human language faculty? Chomsky has been interpreted as taking just such a position. For example, he concludes a discussion of some rather complex aspect of universal grammar with the comment:

I have not hesitated to propose a general [i.e., universal] principle of linguistic structure on the basis of observation of a single language. The inference is legitimate, on the assumption that humans are not specifically adapted to learn one rather than another human language.... Assuming that the genetically determined language faculty is a common human possession, we may conclude that a principle of language is universal if we are led to postulate it as a 'precondition' for the acquisition of a single language. (Chomsky 1980c: 48)

If all normal humans are born with the same capacity to acquire language, what is there to be gained in terms of understanding this capacity, one might ask, by studying more than one language? Again, without disparaging their intrinsic interest, what *theoretical* value might typological studies be expected to have?

In fact, however, virtually every linguist agrees that there is value to comparative and typological studies. Consider the continuation of the Chomsky quote above:

To test such a conclusion, we will naturally want to investigate other languages in comparable detail. We may find that our inference is refuted by such investigation. (1980c: 48)

In other words, any claim about universals based on a single language makes a testable falsifiable hypothesis. The more languages that are studied, the better the hypothesis is tested.

There is a more profound reason why typological studies are more relevant to linguistic theory than to biology. The genome of any biological organism is directly responsible for all of the structural features of that organism (allowing for some variation due to environmental factors). But languages are not organisms. All linguists assume that *some* features of language are genetically-determined, and most generative grammarians assume that a highly specific and complex set of features are provided by the genome. No linguist, however, would attribute the *differences* between any two languages to genetic differences between the speakers of those languages. Even if the structural differences between two languages could be wholly attributed to differences in their parameter settings and the set of possible settings is innate, typological investigation is still called for to ascertain the set of possible settings.

Furthermore, most generativists would agree that the principles of UG are underdetermined by the phenomena evident from even the most detailed analysis of any one single language. In English one finds rather permissive properties of extraction and rather restrictive properties of anaphor binding. These were mistakenly regarded as the norm before such processes were investigated in a wide variety of languages. And not every language provides evidence for every theoretically important construct. For example, no amount of intensive investigation of a single language will lead to an answer to the question of whether adjectives are proper governors or Case assigners, if that language happens to lack a distinct category of adjectives.

And finally, it is self-evident that one cannot hope to uncover cross-linguistic implicational relationships among linguistic features if one focuses only on a single language. Consider, for example, a hierarchy pertaining to noun incorporation motivated in Mithun (1984) (see also the discussion in Croft 1995a). If we look at many languages with this incorporation process, we find a robust hierarchy: Nonreferential nouns are the most incorporable of all, followed by demoted NPs, then by backgrounded NPs, followed at the extreme end of the scale by fully referential NPs. If a NP at one point in the hierarchy is incorporable, then an NP to its left in the hierarchy will be as well:

(1) *Hierarchy of morphological incorporability*
     Nonreferential Ns < Demoted NPs < Backgrounded NPs < Fully
     Referential NPs

So, Lahu, a language at the left end of the hierarchy, allows only nonreferential nouns to be incorporated. But Mohawk, at the right end, allows the incorporation of all four types of nominal structures.

If this hierarchy is indeed valid, rather than being simply an artifact of the examination of a small or nonrepresentative sample of languages, it represents a generalization in need of explanation. It goes without saying that such a generalization could never have been uncovered by the investigation, however intensive, of a single language.[4] The same point can be made about the dozens of other implicational hierarchies that have been uncovered in typological research.

Let us now turn to a discussion of some of the special problems that arise in putting into practice the research program with the goals outlined in this section.

3 Barriers to Language Typology

A recent edition of *Ethnologue* lists 6170 languages spoken in the world today (Grimes 1988: vii). Three centuries ago, before the advance of Western civilization led to the extinctions of languages that we have witnessed in the Americas and in Australia, the total must have been a great deal higher. We have historical knowledge pointing to the existence of perhaps another 500 to 1000 languages and we can assume that many thousands more have been spoken throughout the time span of *Homo sapiens*.

Of the languages existing today and those whose past existence we have record of, there are probably no more than a few hundred that have been subjected to a morphosyntactic study large enough to fill a medium-sized grammar book. Many of these studies (say, grammars written by missionaries a couple centuries ago) are close to being useless for linguistic typology, since they omit discussion of those topics now considered theoretically central.

Furthermore, the (tens of thousands of?) languages that have ever existed may just be a small percentage of *possible* human languages, among which are certainly those which chance, rather than principle, has decreed should never have a native speaker.

---

4. Mithun herself proposes a functional explanation for the hierarchy; formal explanations for part of the hierarchy's effects are found in Sadock (1986) and Baker (1988, 1996). Jerry Sadock (personal communication) points out that Mithun's statement of the hierarchy is problematic, in that it mixes in rather unsystematic fashion syntactic notions (demoted vs. nondemoted), semantic notions (reference vs. nonreference), and pragmatic notions (backgrounded vs. not backgrounded).

The question, then, is whether the materials that we have at our disposal, or are likely to have in the reasonably near future, are sufficient to form a basis for making typological generalizations that linguistic theory need address. This section takes up that question and concludes on a note somewhere between cautious optimism and reluctant skepticism.

3.1 Problems of sampling and bias

The basic problem is this: we want to ensure that, for some sample, generalizations such as 'Of the languages in the sample 73% have feature x' or 'Of the languages in the sample 83% that have feature x also have feature y' point to some inherent property of language in need of explanation. Let us examine some of the factors that raise the possibility that *no attainable sample* might have such properties.

3.1.1 On the representativeness of available languages What reason might we have to conclude that the distribution of features that any possibly available sample manifests represents anything more than some accidental product of the vicissitudes of human history? That is, what reason might we have to conclude that any implicational relationships we might find among these features represent some linguistically significant fact to be explained? One fact is certain: the distribution of peoples on the earth (and thus their languages) has been shaped by forces that have nothing to do with universal grammar or any *non*universal aspect of grammar for that matter. The steady diminution of the number of Australian languages and their sure, but tragic, ultimate extinction is not due one iota to their nonconfigurationality. And German has not been on the retreat in Eastern Europe in the post-war period due to its inconsistency in placement of heads and complements.

To take a somewhat clichéd example, suppose that a nuclear war wiped out most of humankind and its written history, but spared the Amazonian region of Brazil. Some centuries later, a carefully constructed sample of the world's languages would in all probability show those with OVS order to be relatively common. Now, of course, such a nuclear war hasn't happened, but there is every reason to think that there were mass extinctions of languages in the past. Long before Columbus paved the way, the Indo-European, the Sino-Tibetan, the Niger-Congo, the Altaic, and other large families diffused over near-continental sized land masses. What languages were spoken on these land masses before? What theoretically-interesting properties might these languages have revealed to us? In most cases we simply do not know and, in all probability, will never know.[5]

One might object that this problem is no more serious than that faced in biology, where only a small percentage of extant species and a minuscule percentage of ever-existing species have been subject to minute analysis. But what is the analogue in biology to linguistic typology? Biologists do not assume that some sample of leaf shape, digestive system organization, or whatever will provide insights into the nature of life. What they do, in fact, is to study individual life forms at microscopic depth (literally and figuratively), by way of making testable generalizations about how life processes are organized. Again, linguistics is not biology and I agree that the multitude of factors that work to shape grammars *does* make typological investigation in principle a useful tool for ascertaining the nature and interplay of these factors. The central question then is whether the language base we have available to us transforms 'useful in principle' into 'useful in reality'. The answer, as we will see, is 'possibly'.

3.1.2 The problem of sample size   How large a sample of languages do we need to insure that the statistical breakdown that we find of some grammatical feature or relationship among features is of theoretical significance? There is, of course, no answer to that question. If it is only a quirk of history that has consigned object-before-subject languages or languages with clicks to marginal status, then the answer might be 'No sample will be big enough'. But let us make the simplifying assumption that a large enough random sample of languages will yield the statistically meaningful relationships that we seek. How large would a sample have to be just for us to be confident that our sample has not missed some rare— but possibly theoretically important—feature? Bell (1978) has addressed this question; table 6.2 represents his calculation of the likelihood that a sample contains *no* instance of a language type.

For example, if one percent of languages are of a particular type, there is better than one chance out of three that a sample of 100 languages would not contain that language type. But one percent still represents

---

5. For such reasons I find it difficult to be confident in the truth of James Hurford's claim that 'practically, there are enough languages left in the world for us to hazard the assumption that any class of structure that the innate LAD [Language Acquisition Device] is capable of acquiring will be found in at least one extant language somewhere in the world' (Hurford 1992: 279).

Table 6.2
Likelihood that a sample contains no instance of a language type

Rarity of type	Sample size (based on a random sample)									
	1	5	10	20	30	50	100	200	300	500
10%	.90	.59	.35	.12	.04	.005	.0003	even less		
1%	.99	.95	.90	.82	.74	.60	.36	.13	.05	.0006

From Bell 1978: 143.

dozens of languages. Clearly very large samples are called for! But are they achieved? Only very rarely. As a leading typologist, Russell Tomlin, has pointed out:

Yet the empirical basis for many typological claims is weak; generalizations are regularly made on untested convenience samples of *fewer than 50 languages (and usually considerably fewer)*. Even the most appealing work in syntactic typology, for example, Hopper and Thompson (1980) and Givón (1981b), would be strengthened by a more systematic discussion of the database used in the research. This criticism by no means implies that the generalizations are false ones, or that no insight into the nature of language is to be drawn from the work; but it does mean that the reliability and the validity of their claims is compromised to some extent. (Tomlin 1986: 17–18; emphasis added)

If Tomlin is right—and I have no reason to doubt him—then a large percentage of theoretical conclusions based on typological studies must be viewed with extreme suspicion. And in particular, one must be wary of researchers' claiming 'statistical significance' for particular typological generalizations. Unfortunately, such claims are more frequently made than defended. Consider, for example, the discussion in Comrie (1984a: 90), where it is asserted that there is a 'statistically significant bias in the direction of adherence to [a] functionally explainable universal', namely Greenberg's 'Universal 15':

Universal 15 In expressions of volition and purpose, a subordinate verbal form always follows the main verb as the normal order except in those languages in which the nominal object always precedes the verb. (Greenberg 1963: 84)

As far as the reader is able to determine, Comrie's only basis for attributing statistical significance to this purported universal is Greenberg's (undocumented) claim that in his 30 language convenience sample he did not find it counterexemplified.

3.1.3 Genetic and areal sources of bias We have no hope of ever ascertaining what percentage a particular grammatical feature would represent in a random sample of possible human languages. However, we can take measures to control for bias in any sample that draws on known human languages. Among the most evident are genetic and areal bias. That is, we want to make sure that neither particular language families nor particular regions of the world are overrepresented in the sample. Since it is well known that genetically-related languages (i.e. members of the same family) tend to share more typological characteristics than do unrelated languages and that many typological features are area-wide (and can encompass more than one genetic family spoken in that area), steps need to be taken to ensure that no family nor area is over- or underrepresented in the sample.

Language contact is a particularly serious source of potential bias in typological studies. Mallinson and Blake (1981), citing the work of Masica (1976) and Heath (1978), say that 'As work on language contact continues, it is becoming clear that practically any feature of language can be borrowed' (1981: 425).[6] Word order patterns aptly illustrate this point. It is very often the case that a language will develop the word order patterns manifested by those languages that history has decreed will surround it. For example, it has been suggested that Amharic developed SOV order from an earlier VO as a result of the influence of the neighboring Cushitic languages (Comrie 1989: 208, based on studies by E. G. Titov); being surrounded by SVO Indo-Europeans may have been a factor in Hungarian and Finnish developing that order; the Munda languages of India seem to have acquired SOV order as a result of contact with Dravidian and Indic; while some of the Austronesian languages of Papua New Guinea changed from VO to OV after contact with non-Austronesian Papuan languages (these last examples from Matthew Dryer, personal communication).

If it is the case, as is often asserted, that in contact situations it is the features of the more culturally-dominant language that are more likely to be borrowed than those of the less dominant, then it follows that in any particular area (however 'area' is to be defined), the typological breakdown of particular features might be more revealing of geopolitical forces than linguistic ones. True, one might expect, or at least hope, that skewing

---

6. See Moravcsik (1978) for interesting discussion on universal patternings of borrowing.

factors of such a nature would even out when enough languages from enough areas are investigated. Nevertheless, such factors do point to the absolute necessity of large geographically diverse samples.

And finally there is the distorting influence of creole languages, virtually all of which share SVO word order and many other syntactic properties. The number of creoles that exist at any point in time, as well as their geographical distribution, are due entirely to nonlinguistic factors. This fact presents a dilemma for the typologist. Should creoles be included in the sample, thus perhaps distorting the prevalence of SVO? Or should they be excluded, a move that could easily be regarded as arbitrary, given the fact that no other attempt is generally made to adjust for the effects of historical circumstance (say by excluding those languages that have been massively influenced by some Indo-European colonial language in the past few centuries). In any event, since the process of decreolization is gradual, any number of SVO languages might have that property as a result of their now untraceable descent from a creole.

Tomlin (1986) undertook a typological study of an important typological feature, basic word order, which employed a large sample—402 languages—and attempted to control for both genetic and areal bias. As for the former, he was careful to ensure that all language families be represented. His method was to choose languages from each family proportionally to the number of languages in that family. Since there are 792 Austronesian languages in the world, he chose 57 for his sample; 209 Afroasiatic languages led to 19 in the sample; 154 Indo-European languages led to 13 in the sample. The net result was that about eight percent of the world's languages formed his sample, and thus about eight percent of the members of each family. The final sample, however, was adjusted to correct for areal bias as well. Tomlin divided the world into 26 areas and made sure that languages were proportionally represented according to their numbers in each area. Correcting for areal bias in this way required only minor adjustment in the genetically-proportional sample.

As table 6.3 illustrates, Tomlin found approximately equal percentages of SVO and SOV languages, with VSO order a distant third and the other orders lagging much farther behind (1986: 22).

Dryer (1989b), however, pointed out that genetic and areal bias do still lurk in Tomlin's methodology. The basic problem with the latter's method of proportional sampling is that the number of languages in a particular family or in a particular area is due to historical and cultural

Table 6.3
The frequencies of basic constituent orders in Tomlin's sample

Constituent order	Number of languages	Frequency in final sample
SOV	180	44.78
SVO	168	41.79
VSO	37	9.20
VOS	12	2.99
OVS	5	1.24
OSV	0	0.00
Total	402	100.00

factors, rather than to linguistic ones. The fact that there are over 1000 Niger-Kordofanian languages but only a few dozen in the Khoisan family represents, in part, the geopolitical success of speakers of the former in displacing speakers of the latter. Yet Tomlin's sampling technique results in the inclusion of 82 Niger-Kordofanian languages and 3 Khoisan, skewing the typological importance of the properties of the former at the expense of those of the latter.

As Dryer notes, this sampling technique has probably resulted in SOV languages being underrepresented, and SVO and VSO overrepresented. About 40% of the SVO languages in the world are in the Niger-Congo branch of Niger-Kordofanian and about 71% of VSO languages are Austronesian. Since we do not find families with enormous numbers of SOV languages, controlling for the vicissitudes of history would probably reflect a greater preference for that ordering than is found in Tomlin's survey.

A further problem pointed out by Dryer is that linguistic areas—that is, areas 'in which at least one linguistic property is shared more often than elsewhere in the world to an extent which is unlikely to be due to chance, but which is probably due either to contact or remote genetic relationships' (Dryer 1989b: 266)—can cover continental-sized land masses. For example, drawing on Nichols (1986), he notes a distinct preference for head-marking (e.g. pronominal affixes on verbs indicating subject and/or object) as opposed to dependent marking (e.g. case markers) among the languages of North America. Nichols herself, in her impressive book *Linguistic Diversity in Space and Time* (Nichols 1992), finds a number of other grammatical features which tend to be concentrated in some large geo-

Table 6.4
Genera by language area in Dryer (1989b)

Africa	Eurasia	Australia, New Guinea	North America	South America	Total
45/59	52/56	30/80	60/70	31/57	218/322

graphical areas, but not in others. These include having numeral classifiers, an inclusive/exclusive opposition, and an ergative-absolutive distinction.

Dryer attempts to correct for the genetic and areal bias implicit in surveys such as Tomlin's by taking several steps.[7] The first is to divide the languages of the world into 'genera', that is, genetically determined groups comparable to the subfamilies of Indo-European. Since languages within genera tend to be fairly similar typologically, the more blatant forms of genetic bias are thus controlled for. The second step is to assign each genus to one of five large continental areas, areas which are assumed to be independent of each other in terms of typological features. They are Africa, Eurasia, Australia-New Guinea, North America, and South America. Table 6.4 (from Dryer 1989b: 269) represents the breakdown of areas in terms of number of genera (the figure to the left of the slash indicates the number in Dryer's sample; the figure to the right indicates his estimate of the total number of genera, including those not in his sample).

The third step is to determine how the five areas conform to the hypothesis being tested. So, consider the three most-attested basic word orders: SOV, SVO, and VSO. Dryer determined how many genera in his sample from each area manifest that order and came up with the results in table 6.5. In all five areas there is a preference for SOV over SVO and in all areas but Africa, there is a very strong preference. Thus Tomlin's conclusion that the two are preferred equally is called into doubt. Interestingly, in North America the preference for VSO is double that for

7. For two attempts to minimize genetic bias (while paying less attention to areal bias), see Bell (1978) and Rijkhoff et al. (1993). The proposal in Perkins (1988) for controlling for culture area is criticized in Dryer (1989b). Perkins (1989) suggests that a sample of 100 languages, or even fewer, suffice for the investigation of most linguistic variables, but I feel that he greatly underestimates the degree of areal influences on typology.

Table 6.5
A breakdown of genera in terms of basic word order, by area

	Africa	Eurasia	Australia, New Guinea	North America	South America	Total
SOV	22	26	19	26	18	111
SVO	21	19	6	6	5	57
VSO	5	3	0	12	2	22

SVO, as measured by the number of phyla manifesting that order. Nevertheless, the results still point to a trend favoring SVO over VSO.

Dryer's methodology is not problem-free, however. Croft (1995b) argues that all Dryer has accomplished is to push back whatever bias there might be in the sample of languages by the time depth of a genus—roughly between 2500 and 3500 years. That is, the sample reflects that distribution of languages (and their features) that by chance existed in the second millennium BC. Croft concludes, rather disconcertingly, 'This is an inescapable problem, and can only be surmounted by obtaining evidence for typological explanations from other sources of data (e.g. direct or comparative historical evidence, child language development, and intralinguistic variation)' (1995b: 91).

Also, Dryer's methodology crucially demands that the five areas are independent of each other in terms of mutual influence. But are they? As he poses the question:

An obvious question to ask, if there can exist linguistic areas as large as continents, is whether the entire world might not constitute a single large linguistic area. How do we know that certain language types are more common throughout the world, not because of any truly linguistic preference but simply because the entire world forms a single linguistic area and certain language types are more common in all five areas simply because of remote genetic and areal factors? In fact, in general we have no way of knowing that such is not the case. (Dryer 1989b: 284)

Thanks to Nichols (1992), we are in a better position to answer this question today than Dryer was a decade ago. As noted above, Nichols has demonstrated that influences can extend half-way around the globe. Oversimplifying a bit, we find a gradual increase or decrease in the appearance of certain grammatical features, such as whether a language is head-marking or dependent-marking, as we travel eastward from Europe, into Asia, and even into North and South America. This gives us even less

Table 6.6
A breakdown of genera in terms of correlations of basic word order and
adposition order, by area

	Africa	Eurasia	Australia, New Guinea	North America	South America	Total
OV & Po	13	27	15	20	12	87
OV & Pr	2	2	1	0	0	5
VO & Pr	14	23	5	15	5	62
VO & Po	4	1	0	2	2	9

confidence that any statistical breakdown of the world's languages gives
us an insight into the human language faculty.

As far as basic word order is concerned, then, the predominance of
SOV could simply be a function of the possibility of an original SOV
word order, which, as a result of descent and diffusion, was able to
maintain its numerical superiority over the other orders.

If we cannot be confident that *any* sample is free of areal bias, how
confident can we be that any typological study presents findings that have
relevance for linguistic theory? So much could be the result of historical
accident on the one hand and contact and descent on the other, rather
than the product of external functional forces or the design of UG. And
the more reason we have to think that there are a lot of typologically
possible but—purely by chance—nonexisting languages. In the next two
sections we will look at proposals for salvaging significance from the
results of typological studies.

3.2 Correlations of factors and tests for significance

Dryer (1989b: 285) suggests that 'associations or correlations between
typological parameters are more difficult to explain by appealing to the
idea that the entire world might be a single linguistic area'. So, consider
his findings with respect to the correlation between basic word order and
adposition order (table 6.6). In all five areas, there is a clear preference for
the correlations of OV order with postpositions, and VO order with
prepositions, correlations that Dryer regards as 'immune to explanation
in terms of a single world-wide linguistic area' (1989b: 285). While he does
not elaborate, his reasoning seems to be as follows: As far as we know, the
correlation between word order and adpositionality has existed from time
immemorial. In every linguistic area, however, there are VO languages

that developed diachronically from OV languages and OV languages that developed diachronically from VO languages. How could an appeal to a 'world-wide linguistic area' explain why the correlation managed to survive these diachronic changes? The only conclusion is that there is something 'natural' about VO languages 'wanting' prepositions and OV languages 'wanting' postpositions.

Indeed, even if we make the nonuniformitarianist assumption (see below, §3.3) that the distribution of typological features has changed over time, we end up concluding that the correlation is a natural one. Suppose, for example, that the language of all very early human communities was OV and postpositional. As this language evolved over time, breaking up into ever more remote daughter branches, OV order would, in many cases, turn into VO order. But why would this change be accompanied by what seems a virtual lock step change involving the loss of postpositions and the gain of prepositions, unless there was something 'linguistically natural' about the correlation? A different nonuniformitarianist scenario makes the contrary assumption that in the earliest linguistic communities, there was no correlation whatever between the two variables. Now then, one would have to ask why the correlation exists today. Only, it would seem, by the postulation that the 'sorting out' was dictated by some pressure to put word order and adpositionality in line with each other.

The pressure would not necessarily have to be of the sort of interest to grammatical theory of course. One could imagine that the same 'cultural' factors predispose a speaker to prefer putting the verb at the end of the sentence and the adposition after the noun. That is logically possible, but, in absence of any cultural mechanism that would lead to such a correlation, quite implausible.

In short, Dryer is probably right that the correlation of word order and adpositionality is something that requires explanation—*if* we can be confident about claims as to basic word order (see below §3.4.2) There is no reason to think that this correlation is an artifact of areal or genetic bias and it has been tested on a larger number of languages than most. Clearly, we have here a candidate for 'exemplary' typological generalization.

All other things being equal, the more complex the implicational relationships among independent linguistic variables, the more difficult to attribute them to chance or sampling bias. Along these lines Simon Kirby (*Linguist List* posting 15 May 1996) makes the reasonable suggestion that the accessibility hierarchy (AH) of Keenan and Comrie (Keenan and

Comrie 1977, 1979; Comrie and Keenan 1979) is just the sort of typological generalization that could never have arisen 'by accident'. These linguists propose a hierarchy governing the ability of NP positions to be relativized in simple main clauses as follows (Comrie and Keenan 1979: 650):

(2) SU > DO > IO > OBL > GEN > OCOMP

Here '>' means 'is more accessible than'. 'SU', 'DO', IO', 'OBL', 'GEN', and 'OCOMP' stand for 'subject', 'direct object', 'indirect object', 'major oblique case NP', 'genitive', and 'object of comparison', respectively. The relevant constraints for accessibility are stated as follows (pp. 652–653):

(3) *Subject relative universal*
  All languages can relativize subjects.

(4) *Accessibility hierarchy constraint*
  a. If a language can relativize any position on the accessibility hierarchy (AH) with a primary strategy, then it can relativize all higher positions with that strategy.
  b. For each position on the AH, there are possible languages which can relativize that position with a primary strategy, but cannot relativize any lower position with that strategy.

A strategy is considered primary if it is the one used to form relative clauses on *subjects* for that language. The sets of positions in (5) are those that AH predicts to be relativizable (and are illustrated with an actual language manifesting them taken from Keenan and Comrie's sample), but not those sets of positions in (6).

(5) a. SU, DO, IO, OBL, GEN, OCOMP (Urhobo)
  b. SU, DO, IO, OBL, GEN (French)
  c. SU, DO, IO, OBL (Korean)
  d. SU, DO, IO (Roviana)
  e. SU, DO (Tongan)
  f. SU (Tagalog)

(6) a. *SU, DO, GEN
  b. *SU, OBL, OCOMP
  c. *SU, DO, OBL
    And 55 others

In other words, of 64 language types (= 2^6), only 6 are compatible with AH. Surely, one would think that if AH is indeed consistent with the facts, it must reflect a real generalization about language in need of explanation.

AH might well turn out to be right. However, it provides us with an object lesson in the care that must be taken in making typological generalizations that have any solid claim to validity. Let us look at some problems. First, subject position cannot be considered an independent variable, as far as testing the claim is concerned. AH is formulated with respect to whether other positions relativize in the same manner as do subjects, which are postulated *always* to relativize (3). Thus AH is really making the claim that 5 out of 32 language types exist, not 6 out of 64. Furthermore, many now agree that the lowest position on the hierarchy, OCOMP, has to be excluded. As Hawkins (1994: 447) notes, the expression of this grammatical relation is too variable across languages (see Stassen 1985) to lend itself to adequate investigation of the AH—even Keenan and Comrie leave this position blank for many languages. Eliminating OCOMP, AH predicts that 4 out of 16 possible language types exist. This is still a very interesting claim, of course, and, if correct, one in need of explanation.

However, there are a number of studies that point to what appear to be counterexamples to AH, or at least to cases problematic for it (Manaster-Ramer 1979; Cinque 1981; Fox 1987), none of which, to my knowledge, have been addressed by supporters of the hierarchy.[8] Of course, typological generalizations are not, in general, absolutes. The fact that there are a few prepositional verb-final languages hardly threatens the extremely robust generalization that verb-finality and postpositionality tend to go together. Nevertheless, the problems raised in these studies are disconcerting and raise the question about the possible existence of many more counterexemplifying languages.

A deeper uncertainty about the validity of AH is whether the sample on which it was based can be considered representative enough of the world's languages for it to be at this point anything more than an intriguing idea whose correctness needs to be verified by further sampling. Keenan and Comrie examined only 49 languages, i.e. less that one percent of the

8. Cinque points out that one consequence of the Empty Category Principle (see Chomsky 1981 and ch. 2, §3.5.3) is that in many languages subject extraction will be *more* difficult than extraction of other arguments, a fact totally contrary to AH. For more discussion of this point, see McCloskey (1996).

Table 6.7
Breakdown of languages in Keenan and Comrie's sample, by area

Area	No. of languages
Africa	9
Eurasia	40
Australia, New Guinea	0
North America	0
South America	0

world's total. But even worse, these 49 represented what is called a 'convenience sample', that is, one based on the ease of data collection, not on any attempt to correct for areal and genetic bias. As far as the former is concerned, all 49 languages belong to only 2 of Dryer's 5 areas (see table 6.7).

The danger of genetic bias in Keenan and Comrie's sample is also very real: 86% of the languages in the sample are from just 4 language families: Indo-European (21 languages), Austronesian (12), Niger-Kordofanian (5), and Afro-Asiatic (4). In other words, we cannot rule out the possibility that AH effects are the result of common descent or areal contact.

A rebuttal to such a possibility would no doubt point out that even very closely related languages in the sample (Dutch and North Frisian; German and Zurich German; Malay and Toba Batak) exemplify the hierarchy in different ways. Thus, it might be argued, the hierarchy effects could not have been 'inherited' from a common ancestor language. However, we have no theory that tells us, for any particular formal feature, how that feature might change over time. We therefore have no basis for ruling out a common-descent explanation for the shared features of two closely related languages simply because the sharing is not absolute. Take preposition stranding, for example. All Germanic languages allow preposition-like elements to be 'stranded' sentence finally and nobody doubts that stranding was an early Germanic feature, passed down into the daughter languages. Yet, there are major differences in stranding from language to language (cf. German separable prefixes and English true prepositions). The same might well be true of the slightly different mechanics of relativization in, say, Dutch and North Frisian.

Furthermore, extremely abstract aspects of grammars can be borrowed from one language to the next. For example, Mallinson and Blake (1981:

425) note that the English passive is being imitated in Chinese and some southeast Asian languages. Given the standard generative view that there is no passive rule per se, but only a constellation of parameter settings that 'conspire' to create the illusion of a distinct passive construction, it means that features of language far removed from speakers' conscious awareness can be borrowed.[9]

So is AH a robust typological generalization in need of explanation? My deep instincts tell me that there is indeed something there to be explained.[10] But a great deal more sampling of languages from diverse areas and genetic groups is necessary before I will have total confidence in the matter.

To summarize, typological correlations among distinct features are in general far better candidates for significance than are the mere presence or absence of features. The more robust the implicational relationships among features, the more secure the generalization. But the potential problems of sampling bias are as serious here as elsewhere and—to the extent that it is possible to do so—need to be corrected for.

3.3 Trends in language change as tests of typological significance and the question of uniformitarianism

Let us now turn to the question of whether trends in language change can be used to test claims of typological significance. Suppose that a typologist finds that in some sample, feature A occurs in 67% of all languages and feature B (where no language can possess simultaneously A and B) occurs 33% of the time. If our typologist has confidence in the representativeness of the sample, he or she will postulate that there is something twice as 'natural' about having A than B, and perhaps go on to posit some set of formal or functional principles from which the 2-to-1 ratio follows.

There is a potential independent way to corroborate such a conclusion. If the 2-to-1 ratio is natural *and* the balance of functional forces affecting language has remained constant throughout history, then that ratio should have remained constant throughout history. This means that the

---

9. Consider also the loss of the infinitive, presumably through areal contact, in many Balkan languages. Again given current generativist assumptions, this points to the borrowing of a number of abstract parameter settings.

10. And, indeed, Hawkins (1994: ch. 2) shows that its effects follow from the parsing principle Early Immediate Constituents.

raw counts of changes from A to B and B to A should be approximately the same (in order to maintain the 'natural' balance between the two), though at any given time the proportion of B languages changing to A will be double the proportion of A languages changing to B.[11]

To make matters more concrete, consider the question of the relative naturalness of VO versus OV order. All other things being equal, if the latter order is functionally favored over the former, then the former should be more unstable diachronically. That is, if the historical record were complete, we would expect to find a considerably higher number of VO languages becoming OV than vice versa (thus guaranteeing that the proportions of the two orderings remain the same).

The historical record is, of course, woefully incomplete. As noted above, there are very few languages for which we have records for more than a century. All that can be said is that given the data available to us, there is little support for the idea that OV is more natural than VO. The ancient Indo-European languages of which we have record were, by and large, SOV, and their descendants are, by and large, SVO. I am not aware of any attested change in the Indo-European (or any other) family from VO to OV.[12]

But before we jump to the conclusion on the basis of (the tiny number of) attested changes that OV is less 'natural' than VO, we need to examine an unstated assumption underlying the idea that the typological patterns that we observe today should manifest themselves in historical

11. If A and/or B can arise from a third source, then we would predict greater stability for the newly arisen As than for the newly arisen Bs. In particular, we might expect B to change rapidly to A. Haspelmath (1993) gives an example of such a circumstance from the history of Latin. There appears to be a universal (functionally motivated?) preference for derivational morphology to occur inside inflectional morphology. Old Latin developed a reinforcing particle to a suffix-inflecting demonstrative, leading to derivation occurring outside inflection. But changes soon took place that resulted in the reversal of the ordering of the two types of suffix.

12. There are, of course, many reconstructed changes in the languages of the world from SVO (or VSO) to SOV, two of which are cited above in §3.1.3. For another view on the matter, Nichols (1992: 249–251) offers the opinion that verb-final order is more stable than other orders and more likely to be borrowed in a language-contact situation, while Croft (1990: 274) writes, 'Although basic word order has changed significantly in Indo-European, a wider examination of language families suggests that SOV and SVO orders are quite stable'.

change. This is the assumption of 'uniformitarianism', namely the idea
that the typological universals discovered in contemporary languages
should also apply to ancient and reconstructed languages. Croft (1990)
notes that uniformitarianism is the dominant hypothesis in typological
work today, and goes on to observe:[13]

The uniformitarian hypothesis, like other hypotheses of diachronic typology, is a
general assumption about the nature of language and language change that can be
considered a defining characteristic of diachronic-typological theory, in the same
way that the innateness hypothesis of generative grammar ... is a general
assumption that can be only quite indirectly verified or falsified. (1990: 204)

But what if uniformitarianism is a mistaken assumption, and, as a
result, the typological breakdown among the world's languages has
changed over the years? What would that mean for typology and the
formal and functional principles designed to explain typological patterns?
There are actually two ways that uniformitarianism might be a mistaken
assumption. The first would be if the functional forces responsible for the
observed properties of language (and the correlations among them) have
remained constant throughout human history but are, so to speak, 'lop-
sided', that is, if they are propelling language—slowly, to be sure!—in
particular overall directions as far as its distribution of typological features are concerned. Let us call this possibility 'non-U_1'. The correctness
of non-U_1 would have fairly drastic implications for typology as it is now
practiced. For one thing, we could not use even well-documented ancient
languages in the same sample with presently spoken languages. That is,
the typological features of, say, Homeric Greek or Ancient Egyptian
could be relevant only to an accounting of the relative weighting of functional forces at work at the time these languages were spoken, not their
relative weighting today.

A more serious consequence of non-U_1 would be that reconstructions
of proto-forms and proto-languages, in so far as they are based on what
seems natural today, would be all but worthless. According to Croft
(1990), it was Jakobson (1957/1971) who first suggested a typological
naturalness constraint on reconstructions. Jakobson called attention to
the typological peculiarity of the standard reconstruction of the Proto-
Indo-European stop series, comprising for each point of articulation a
voiceless unaspirated stop, a voiced unaspirated stop, and a voiced

13. See also Comrie (1989: 9) for a similar statement.

aspirated stop and suggested that their analysis be revised to make them in line with the typological features of known consonant inventories. Jakobson's challenge was taken up by Emonds (1972a), Hopper (1973), and Gamkrelidze and Ivanov (1973), among others. The latter, for example, replaced the standard reconstruction with a series of simple voiceless stops and voiceless glottalized and aspirated stops—an attested consonant inventory in some languages. But given non-U_1, we have no firm way of knowing whether the classical reconstruction was or was not a natural one 6,000 years ago.

In other words, if non-U_1 is correct, two features that are correlated typologically today might not have been correlated in the past. Therefore, it would not be legitimate to propose a reconstruction appealing to that correlation. So, for example, consider Lehmann's (1973) reconstruction of Proto-Indo-European as SOV. This order was hypothesized by Lehmann to a large extent on the basis of PIE's putatively possessing traits that are common among currently spoken SOV languages, such as agglutinative morphology and the absence of relative pronouns. But again, these correlations might well have developed over historical time, and have no bearing on the structure of PIE.[14]

Some evidence for non-U_1 is provided by Hombert and Marsico (1996), who argue that complex vowel systems are fairly recent historical developments. In particular, they present evidence that seems to suggest that front rounded vowels and nasalized vowels have shown a tendency to increase over the centuries; few reconstructed proto-systems show any evidence of having had them. Non-U_1 appears in the literature of syntactic typology in terms of claims that languages are more likely to 'drift' to one type of syntactic pattern than to another. Consider, for example, a series of papers published by Theo Vennemann in the 1970s (Vennemann 1973, 1974, 1975). They address the question of why, given the conclusion that 'SOV is the most natural [i.e. functionally motivated] serialization of S, O, and V' (Vennemann 1973: 28), diachronic changes *from* this ordering of elements seem to be more common than changes *toward* this ordering. Vennemann speculates that while in some global sense functional forces prefer the SOV ordering, more local immanent forces present ready

---

14. On the other hand, Hawkins (1983) finds that the oldest *attested* Indo-European languages manifest the same word order correlations as are found in languages spoken today.

opportunities for reanalysis of an SOV pattern to an SVO one, but not vice-versa. More recently, Bichakjian (1991) has revived the idea of a general drift to VO order and its typological correlates.

There is a second, more drastic, way that uniformitarianism might be an incorrect assumption (let us call this 'non-U_2'). Under the non-U_2 scenario, the functional forces *themselves* have changed indeterminately throughout human history. Now almost certainly, this could not be true of those aspects of language that form part of our biological inheritance. The same innate mechanisms for representing and processing language must have been available to humans, say, 10,000 years ago as are available today—it is hard to imagine that UG or the neural wiring that makes production and comprehension of language possible could have changed significantly in that short period of time. But consider other factors, say sociocultural ones. Suppose that such factors affect the surface shape of language far more pervasively—and far more selectively—than we normally assume. If that turned out to be the case, then standard approaches to historical typology would be in even deeper trouble.

Under non-U_1, the forces shaping typology are unbalanced, but at least they are determinate. That is, it is in principle imaginable that one might work out their relative weighting and calculate on that basis what sorts of systems they might have favored at some arbitrary point of historical time. But, setting aside the crudest versions of Marxism, there is no disagreement that sociocultural factors are *in*determinate. Under non-U_2, virtually no hope remains for reconstructing proto-systems. Even more troubling is the fact that non-U_2 casts a dark cloud over synchronic typology as well, or at least over the nature of external explanations for typological patterns. One common thread in external explanation is that the explanans appealed to are attributes of *humans taken as a group*: the nature of their cognitive faculties, their common need to achieve successful communication, and so on. Now, these attributes are complex and, to some extent, exert conflicting pressures. Hence we find a great diversity of language types, but also tremendous systematicity within that diversity. If some feature or correlation of features is rare, for example, typologically minded functionalists assume that the rarity is a consequence of the difficulty for humans *in general* to process sentences of a particular type, to interpret material in a particular position as playing some particular discourse-communicative role, and so on. What they do not do is to attribute that rarity to sociocultural facts about the speakers of the languages with those rare features. Thus one might say that even functionalists, following in the footsteps of Franz Boas, have adopted a version of the autonomy thesis. Non-U_2 would appear to entail the rejection of even that version of autonomy.

If non-U_2 is correct, then the explanation of typological patterns becomes more complex by an order of magnitude. Is there any evidence supporting non-U_2? We find a suggestion along these lines in Givón (1979a: ch. 7). Givón speculates that 'early-hominid communication' employed SOV order. This order would, in his opinion, have followed naturally from adding verb-coding to pre-existing argument coding. In support of the proto-SOV hypothesis, he advances the opinion that the majority of languages that are SOV today were always SOV and that 'the overwhelming majority of languages and language families which do not show actual SOV syntax currently, can be nevertheless reconstructed via internal and comparative methods back to an earlier SOV stage' (1979a: 275):

[But SOV order] represent[s] a likely instance of a *relic* of an earlier evolutionary stage of human language which has survived into the present era.... Put another way, somehow the SOV word order, though seemingly the *earliest* attested [*sic*] in human language, is *not* the one most *compatible* with the currently extant discourse-pragmatic evolutionary stage of human language. (Givón 1979a: 275–276; emphasis in original)

What is the 'currently extant discourse-pragmatic evolutionary stage' that we find ourselves in? One in which, according to Givón, discourse is 'topic-oriented' and 'multipropositional', and which, he claims, is more readily coded by SVO order than by SOV (see esp. p. 309). While I do not pretend to follow Givón's reasoning here (the Japanese, for example, seem to manage 'multipropositional discourse' quite well, despite the handicap of an SOV order that shows no signs of transforming itself), his views do clearly represent a rejection of both non-U_1 and non-U_2.[15] In fact, he further speculates that the use of indefinite subjects without existential verbs is to be found 'mostly in literate, more complex societies' and that languages which have only coordination but no subordination are found only in 'preliterate "societies of intimates"' (1979: 306). And more

15. Though ironically many of Givón's reconstructions of the purported ancestral SOV order are based on the uniformitarianist assumption that the word order correlations that we find today *did* hold in earlier stages of language evolution. See Lightfoot (1979b) and Van Valin (1981) for discussion of some problems with Givón's reconstruction of a proto-human SOV word order.

recently, Perkins (1992) has devoted over 200 pages to arguing that less complex cultures tend to have more complex deixis systems

I am not sure how much weight to accord to the possibility that uniformitarianism might be incorrect. But I am sure that the *possibility* that it might be incorrect casts yet another shadow on the enterprise of language typology as currently practiced.

3.4   On the data base for typological generalizations
Another serious foundational problem exists for language typology: the lack of consistency in identifying the grammatical elements that enter into typological statements. If this problem is as widespread as I believe it to be, we have another reason to be skeptical whenever we come across a typological generalization that is presented as a 'result' in need of explanation.

3.4.1   The problem of using secondary data sources
The following two statements are truisms: Solid typological generalizations require reference to a detailed analyses of many languages; No individual linguist is capable of providing first-hand information regarding the detailed analysis of many languages. Thus typologists are dependent on consultants and published materials. As far as the former is concerned, nobody has either the time or the opportunity to work with dozens of consultants, each speaking a different native language. That leaves published materials. Unfortunately, the sorts of published materials that we have at our disposal all too often fail to provide us with the information that is most relevant for the investigation that we are undertaking. As Leon Stassen has noted:

I assume that every universalist researcher [i.e. 'typologist'] will have encountered the frustrating situation that a grammar fails to state some detailed pieces of information which are vital to the problem under investigation; in such a case, there is no other choice than to cancel that language from the sample. (Stassen 1985: 12–13)

Stassen's frank remarks underscore a major barrier to the achievement of a properly representative sample for typological generalization. What reason might we have for believing that languages are 'canceled' from samples in proportion to their manifestation of whatever trait is under investigation? None at all, I would suggest. To aggravate matters, we are virtually never told in the finished publication presenting the typological generalization what the canceled languages are. Thus if the relevant information from those languages does become available, no scholar other than the one who was responsible for the initial publication has the means to see how that information might alter the generalization.

Furthermore, even where we do seem to find the information we seek in a published grammar, there is often no reason to be confident in either its accuracy or its usefulness. Part of the problem is terminology and its cross-linguistic applicability and consistency. Is one grammarian's 'particle' another grammarian's 'clitic'? Is one grammarian's 'conjunction' another grammarian's 'complementizer'? The typologist has to answer such questions as well as he or she can, even though often presented with limited means for deciding (an alternative, of course, is to cancel the relevant languages from the sample). But more seriously, no grammatical terms are theory-neutral. Even the most seeming 'visible' constructs of morpho-syntax, say 'noun' or 'suffix', can be identified only after certain analytic assumptions are made (though they are not always made consciously or called attention to in print). I have to agree with the following assessment:

Although the quest for universals makes dependence on secondary sources inevitable, relying on extant grammars of individual languages is a little like trying to make an omelet out of hard-boiled eggs: the data have already been 'cooked' by the theoretical preconceptions of the grammarians who tend to supply examples which fit their hypotheses and ignore those which do not. (Contini-Morava 1983: 252, quoted in Tobin 1990: 89)

If somebody claims, say, that in a sample of 102 languages, pronominal clitics are formed from indirect objects in 46 of them, we want to be sure that the same criteria were applied for each language in identifying pronominal clitics and indirect objects. But by what means could we *ever* be sure that such might be true? And since we cannot be sure, why should we trust the typological generalization employing the constructs?

Even worse are *successive* references to secondary sources, which hearken back to the undesirable features of hand-copied manuscripts of pre-Gutenberg days: Each one has the potential to introduce a new source of error, which is passed on to the next scholar, who then might introduce yet a new error, and so on, and so forth. Mallinson and Blake give a somewhat amusing example of something along these lines having actually taken place:

There is also a tendency for secondary sources to use other secondary sources as primary material and the most obvious danger here is the perpetuating of errors. A good example of this appears in Keenan (1978: 185). He cites data on Dalabon from Comrie (1978: 386–387), who cites it from Silverstein (1976: 129), who cites it from the original source, Capell (1962). Keenan repeats part of a point made by Silverstein that the subject of a transitive verb is marked if it is equal to or below the patient on a [particular] hierarchy. Silverstein's point is not supported by the data, contains an incorrect page reference to the source (102-3 for 111), and omits some diacritics. Ironically, Silverstein's incorrect reference is to a page of Capell's grammar that contains a counter-example to his hierarchical explanation for the distribution of case-marking in Dalabon. (Mallinson and Blake 1981: 14–15)

One might think that a partial solution to the problem of appeal to secondary sources might lie in replacing individual typological studies citing many secondary sources with anthological compilations of a particular topic, where each contribution is based on primary research. The compiler of the anthology, ideally, would be able to 'enforce terminological consistency' on the contributors.

Unfortunately, I know of no typology-oriented anthology where such has actually happened. A case-in-point is a 700-page collection of papers on passive and voice (Shibatani 1988). Despite the editor's assurance in the Introduction that the typological approach opens up insights into the understanding of voice phenomena that the generative approach cannot, there is, in fact, no consistency from contributor to contributor even on how passives might be identified in a particular language (on this point, see Andersen 1990). Since constructions that would be identified as 'passives' in a particular language by one author would not be so identified by another, one feels, after reading the contributions, that little headway has been gained in achieving the kinds of robust typological generalizations about voice phenomena that might serve as input to an explanatory theory of voice.

I will close this section with a concrete example of some of the problems that the use of secondary sources leads one to, focusing attention on Leon Stassen's 1985 book *Comparison and Universal Grammar*. I choose this book not because it is notably deficient with respect to other works in the typological genre, but for precisely the opposite reason. Given that it is one of the most exhaustive and well-researched typological studies of which I am aware,[16] any of its deficiencies resulting from the use of secondary sources will, I feel, carry over *mutatis mutandis* to less adequate studies of this type.

---

16. Typologists themselves appear to have a high opinion of Stassen's book. For example, Croft writes that it contains 'one of the more lucid and complete explications of typological theory and method in the literature' (1990: 260).

Stassen presents an impressive investigation of comparative constructions in 110 languages, for all but two of which he relied on secondary sources. (The two are Dutch, his native language, and English, for which he used native speaker consultants.) The main results of the book are the formulation of a set of statements designed to predict the range of variants of the comparative construction in the languages of the world and to account for the attested distribution of languages over these variants. Six distinct types of comparative construction are identified:

(7) a. *The Separative Comparative.* Comparison is expressed in one single surface clause; the standard NP is encoded as a constituent of an adverbial phrase with a separative interpretation.

    b. *The Allative Comparative.* Comparison is expressed in one single surface clause; the standard NP is encoded as a constituent of a goal phrase.

    c. *The Locative Comparative.* Comparison is expressed in one single surface clause; the standard NP is encoded as a constituent of an adverbial phrase with a locative interpretation.

    d. *The Exceed Comparative.* The standard NP is constructed as the direct object of a special transitive verb meaning 'exceed' or 'surpass'.

    e. *The Conjoined Comparative.* Two clauses are conjoined by means of adversative coordination.

    f. *The Particle Comparative* (which partly overlaps with properties of (7a–e) and is considered separately). A special comparative particle is used.

Stassen proceeds to point out some fairly detailed typological correlations between the type of comparative and other structural features (including basic word order) and to propose external explanations for those correlations. In the sample 26 languages are said to exemplify the Exceed Comparative, on which Stassen comments: 'As for word order, we can observe that for this set of languages *SVO order appears to be mandatory*' (1985: 44; emphasis in the original), a generalization that his external principles are in part designed to account for.

Specialists in these languages have pointed out to me, however, that Classical Greek, Latin, and Classical Tibetan, all SOV languages, manifest a wide range of comparatives of the 'Exceed' type. How could Stassen have missed noting this fact about the two former languages, which are both in his sample? Reliance on secondary sources is to blame—the existence of the Exceed Comparative in these languages is virtually never mentioned in their published grammars. The reasons for their omission are not difficult to understand: for one thing, verbal constructions such as '*X* exceeds/surpasses *Y* (in *Z*)' are not traditionally even regarded as a type of comparative; for another, comparative constructions are quite often discussed exclusively in the context of the adjective. What this means is that Stassen probably greatly underestimates the full range of possibilities for comparison in the world's languages.

Now Stassen cannot be faulted personally for not having taken the time to actually learn all the languages in his sample, instead of merely thumbing through the odd grammars. *Nobody* has that kind of time. But if he had done so, one feels that he would have ended up with a radically different set of statements concerning the universals of comparative constructions from that which he proposes in his book.

In sum, reference to secondary sources and reliance on consultants in typological research may be more than a necessary evil—it may point to the shaky foundations of the entire enterprise.[17]

3.4.2 Claims about 'basic word order'   No typological feature has been subject to more discussion than that of the 'basic word order' in a particular language of the subject, the verb, and the object. One could easily find hundreds of publications, generativist as well as functionalist, that assume that all, or virtually all, languages can be 'typed' with respect to this feature, and routinely will classify a language as 'SVO', 'VSO', and so on. In the words of Susan Steele:[18]

All languages have a dominant word order, a surface ordering of subject, object, and verb relative to one another that is at least more common than other possible orders. (*Note*: This is an assumption, of course, but one which is justified. Even grammars which talk about the absolute freedom of position for the elements of the sentence will note that certain orders are more common than others.) (Steele 1978: 587)

17. For the most scathing critique of the effects of the use of secondary sources of which I am aware, see Andersen (1994). Andersen focuses primarily on the typological studies of passive voice in Klaiman (1991) and middle voice in Kemmer (1993).

18. Steele (personal communication) has informed me that she no longer holds this position.

Indeed, the terms 'SVO language', 'SOV language', etc. are as familiar to most linguists as are the terms 'subject', 'verb', or 'object' themselves, and, outside of introductory texts, never appear in their unabbreviated form.

The broader importance of the V-S-O typing comes from the fact that basic word order is by far the typological feature that is most frequently correlated with other typological features.[19] This practice has its roots in Greenberg (1963), which set the tone for later typological studies by considering basic word order as the primary means of classifying languages typologically; about half of the 45 universals proposed in that paper are correlations with basic word order.

If all languages manifested only one ordering, there would be no problem. But there are few, if any, languages, in which the three major 'participants' in a clause occur in a fixed order. Greenberg took note of this fact, but seemed to find it unproblematic. In his view: 'The vast majority of languages have several variant orders but a single dominant one' (1963: 76). One would think, then, that there would be widespread agreement on the means for identifying that dominant order. Nothing could be farther from the truth. Leaving aside the fact that there is not even agreement on how to identify subjects and objects, there are more than half a dozen distinct ways that basic word order has been identified in the literature, among which are the following (for a more detailed discussion of these and other criteria for determining basic order, see Brody 1984 and Siewierska 1988):

(8) a. It is the order with the highest text frequency.
   b. It is the order in which S and O are full NPs.
   c. It is the order that carries the fewest special presuppositions (say, the order one would find in answer to the question *What happened?*).
   d. It is the order that one finds in main clause declaratives.

19. Strictly speaking, this is true only of typological research carried out in North America and Western Europe. A long-standing Czech tradition generalizes from morphological type assignments to aspects of syntax and semantics (for recent overviews, see Skalička and Sgall 1994 and Sgall 1995). And the Russian linguist G. A. Klimov takes the division of the languages of the world into 'ergative', 'active', and 'nominative/accusative' as fundamental and presents the typological correlations of those categories (see Klimov 1983 and the English-language overview in Nichols 1992).

    e. It is the order associated with the most basic intonation contour.

    f. It is the order associated with the least overall syntactic or morphological elaboration.

    g. It is the order at a motivated underlying level of syntactic structure.

Criteria (8a) through (8g) no doubt give identical results for some languages. But for many, if not most, at least one of the criteria will give results that contradict one of the other criteria (again, for a more detailed discussion, see Brody and Siewierska[20]). Test (8g) in particular often leads to a basic order that conflicts with (8a–f). For example, Bach (1970) argued that Amharic, an SOV language by most of these latter criteria, is VSO by test (8g). And more recently, Everett (1987) has argued that the basic (underlying) order of Yagua is SVO, despite the fact that (8c) and other tests point to a VSO order.[21] The great bulk of typological work in linguistics, however, pays attention only to surface structure patterns in language and therefore would not even consider criterion (8g) in determining basic order. For example, there is no recognition in Comrie (1984b) or Croft (1990) that any syntactic level other than the most 'observable' might be relevant to typological generalization.

It appears, however, that criterion (8a) also conflicts with many of the others in a significant number of cases. By criteria (8b–f), Sacapultec, like other Mayan languages, is VSO. Givón (1995), drawing on the results of Du Bois (1987) challenges this classification. He reports that in actual Sacapultec narratives, VSO order is almost never found; in 86% of transitive clauses the subject is missing and the verb and object therefore appear contiguous. This state of affairs is apparently the norm for VSO languages, from which Givón draws explicit typological conclusions:[22]

---

20. Siewierska distinguishes between 'basic', 'dominant', and 'unmarked' word order, all of which can differ for a particular language.

21. The arguments provided by Bach and Everett were purely language-internal. For example, in Everett's account, word order variation in Yagua results from the fact that both clitics and arguments compete for a single Case. The conflict is resolved by moving the head of the phrase to the phrase-internal AGR position and allowing the clitic to acquire morphological visibility via incorporation into the head. This movement analysis is supported by the distribution of reflexives in the language.

22. Interestingly, Emonds (1980), using criterion (8g), also concludes that VSO languages are basically SVO.

Functionally oriented typologists would thus tend to suspect that the typological difference between VSO, VOS and SVO, and therefore also between OVS and SOV, is relatively shallow at the level that really counts—actual speech production and comprehension. Typological variability, and its import for both language acquisition and language processing, is only relevant when it translates into actual 'performance' facts. (Givón 1995: 195)

Even well-studied languages are assigned conflicting basic word orders by different linguists. For example, Croft (1990: 204), following a long-standing tradition, refers to 'French's rigid SVO order'. But for Nichols (1992), French is a VSO language, presumably due to the fact that, especially in colloquial speech, the subject is typically cliticized to the verb. German and Dutch are SVO for Greenberg (1963), I assume because that is the most common ordering in main clause declaratives (test (8d)). But for most generative grammarians, these languages are SOV (see Koster 1975), since that ordering simplifies the statement of the formal grammatical processes operating in those languages (test (8g)). Mallinson and Blake (1981), on the other hand, have a separate classification for German, 'V2', because in main clauses the inflected element occurs in second position (a variant of test 8d).

Of the 174 languages in the sample used in Nichols (1992), 11 are given a basic word order assignment different from that in Hawkins (1983) and/ or Tomlin (1986) and 11 more are not assigned a basic word order at all, even though the other two works do assign them one. If we look at other sources, we find further disparities with Nichols' assignments. For example, Nichols, Hawkins, and Tomlin all agree that Papago is verb-initial. But Hale (1992) argues that a variety of converging tests show that this language has a grammaticalized basic OV order. Likewise, the three agree that Basque is SOV, while Bybee, Pagliuca, and Perkins (1990) classify it as primarily SVO and Aske (1998) rejects any classification of that language based on grammatical relations. They agree that Chontal is VSO and Songhai SVO, but these languages are typed SVO and SOV respectively by Hawkins and Gilligan (1988). Hawkins and Gilligan call Georgian SOV, Nichols types it SVO/SOV, and Tomlin SVO. For Hawkins and Gilligan, Karok is SVO, for Nichols it is 'Free', and for Tomlin SOV. Hawkins and Gilligan type Kutenai VSO, while for Nichols and Tomlin it is VOS.[23] Nichols' classification of Mandinka as SOV is challenged by

23. Hawkins and Gilligan cite (apparently unpublished) work by Gary Gilligan for Chontal; by Joan Bybee and Revere Perkins for Georgian, Kutenai, and Songhai; and by Leon Stassen for Karok.

Claudi (1994: 195) on the grounds that 'it is not even possible to define in a clear-cut manner what constitutes a verb in Mande [languages]'. And while for Nichols and Tomlin, Luiseño is SVO, Steele (1978) classifies it as a SOV language.

The disconcerting fact, then, is that there is open controversy about the basic word order assignment of 18% of the languages in Nichols' sample. I suspect that a literature search will lead to this figure being elevated to well over 20%, particularly if we follow Givón in dismissing the typological relevance of the difference between SVO and VSO. In other words, a quarter of the basic word order assignments in Nichols' book may be 'tainted'. How confident can one be about the reliability of *any* purported correlations of grammatical features when there is such a degree of disagreement over what is perhaps the best studied of them all?

Some linguists are comfortable with the idea of excluding from the data base languages which do not clearly (by their preferred standards) manifest an unambiguous basic word order. Comrie, for example, remarks that lack of a basic order should be no more worrisome than the fact that not all languages are tonal and not all languages have a passive construction (1989: 36). So he excludes Dyirbal on the basis of the fact that 'all permutations of major constituents give rise to grammatical sentences, and if there is any preference for one word order over another, it is so slight as to be almost imperceptible' (1989: 88); he excludes Philippine languages, such as Tagalog, on the basis of the fact that classical 'subject properties' are split between two noun phrases. But other linguists are not at all happy about the idea of a language with no basic word order. Mallinson and Blake (1981), for example, classify Dyirbal as a (qualified) OSV language on the basis of sentences with nonpronominal nouns more frequently manifesting that ordering, while for Tomlin (1986), Tagalog is VSO on the basis of his identification of the subject with that NP most frequently carrying thematic information.

Thus it is commonplace to find typological studies appealing to the basic word order of different languages where different criteria have been applied to determine that basic order. One would, of course, like to compare languages in a particular sample only where the assignments were based on identical criteria. But this is impossible, since the typologist, who must rely heavily on secondary sources, has in general no means for ascertaining which criteria were applied. It is a fact of life that many sources are insufficiently explicit on that point or take as self-evident some categorization that another would take as controversial or simply wrong.

We are forced to conclude, then, that any typological generalizations that crucially incorporate or appeal to the notion of 'basic word order' must be considered suspect.

3.5 Summary

This section has identified four serious problems for the field of language typology as it is currently practiced. First, the set of presently existing languages may not point to deep properties of the human language faculty. Second, the set of languages that has *ever* existed may suffer from the same defect. Third, the samples used by linguists might not be representative of the set of existing languages. And fourth, the secondary data that are used by typologists may introduce further distortion because of errors and inconsistency. The next section will discuss some steps that might be taken to help remediate the situation.

4   What Is to Be Done?

In the previous two sections, I presented a number of reasons to lack confidence in the relevance of any typological generalizations for linguistic theory. It may simply not be possible to design *any* language sample that unequivocally points to facts that a theory of grammar has to explain. The languages of the world today might be so skewed in their features as a result of linguistically irrelevant sociohistorical factors that no sample, however carefully constructed, bears directly on universal grammar. If that is the case—and we really do not know whether it is or not—then the 'single language in depth' approach of generative grammar becomes a preferred methodological strategy virtually by default. The parallel commitment of formalists and functionalists to language typology could come to nothing if typological research leads to inherently unreliable generalizations.

But of course we do not *know* that the more extensively motivated typological generalizations are unreliable; we only have reason to suspect that they might be. Rather than at this point to throw out the baby with the bath water, I will continue to assume that the more robust-seeming typological generalizations really are facts to be explained. I could live to regret my decision, but it is a decision that I willingly make. Many of these generalizations are *interesting* and there are interesting explanations that have been proposed to account for them. Now, I would be the last to equate 'interest' with 'truth'. Nevertheless, the fact that we do find a quite striking pairing of generalization and explanation might well provide indirect evidence that there really is something to the former after all.

I will, however, recommend some precautions. One is to limit ones discussions to generalizations that have been constructed with very large samples that have, at least to some degree, been adjusted to correct for genetic and areal bias. And furthermore to take as explananda only those typological generalizations expressed in the form of implications and correlations. As we have seen, in principle such generalizations are freer from the possibility of sampling bias than those stated in terms of only one linguistic feature.

What about basic word order? Unfortunately, since the notion is so central to language typology, it is hard to see how appeal to it might be avoided. One possibility might be to construct typological generalizations incorporating as many different constellations of word order patterns as are actually found in individual languages. Thus one could attempt to reformulate existing generalizations as statements such as 'If SVO and SOV and OVS, then X' and 'If SOV and VSO and VOS and OSV, then Y'. But that approach would surely create more problems than it would solve. First, one could never be sure that one had included all patterns for any particular language. The average descriptive grammar, I am sure, fails to record the rarer patterns—how many grammars of English, for example, would make note of the OSV pattern in sentences like *Beans he likes*? Second, this strategy flies in the face of our intuitions that for most languages some orderings *are* more basic than others. The fact that Japanese, Turkish, and many other languages typically classified as SOV also allow an SVO ordering strikes one, quite reasonably I feel, as less important in terms of broader generalizations than their essential 'SOVness'. And third, the more categories of languages there are, the fewer languages will be placed in each category. Most generalizations relating two or more categories, therefore, will have little claim to statistical significance.

Another possibility would be to be avoid referring to any typological study appealing to basic order without a guarantee that the same criteria had been used for assigning that label to every language in the sample. But that would perhaps entail the immediate elimination of 90% of all such studies that have appeared in print. In the long run, perhaps that is a consequence that typologists should be willing to accept. If it is necessary to reconstitute the methodology of language typology from the ground up, practitioners of that discipline should be willing to make a commitment to do just that. But, again, for the immediate purposes of the present work, it is simply not practical to avoid reference to 'basic word order'. For better or worse, I will continue to refer to the 'basic word order' assignments and correlations that have come out of typological research. And hope for the best.

5 Formal Prerequisites to Typological Analysis

This section argues that formal analysis of language is a logical and temporal prerequisite to language typology. That is, if one's goal is to describe and explain the typological distribution of linguistic elements, then one's first task should be to develop a formal theory.

5.1 Identifying grammatical elements in a single language

Let us say that we wish to account for the distribution of grammatical elements with respect to each other and with respect to the functions that they carry out. What is a logical prerequisite to such an activity? It should hardly even need stating that our first task must be to *identify* these features. Given this truism, it follows that at least *some* formal analysis has to be done before a functional analysis can begin. One can hardly expect to say anything sensible about the functions of word order or of the cognitive grounding of syntactic categories, say, until one has identified the relevant units whose ordering is to be explained and determined which grammatical elements belong to which categories. So the only question is *how much* formal analysis is a prerequisite. I will suggest that the answer is a great deal more than many functionally-oriented linguists would acknowledge.[24]

To read the literature of the functional-typological approach, one gets the impression that the task of identifying the grammatical elements in a

---

24. Unfortunately, there is a tendency among some functionalists to regard functional (or cognitively based) explanations for typological facts as somehow the 'default', with formal analysis requiring the assumption of special 'models'. For example, Stassen, in his typological study of the comparative construction, remarks, 'My general approach should be conceived of as being *model neutral*' (1985: 21; emphasis in original). But by this he merely seems to mean that he is not adopting some generative model such as Government-Binding Theory or Relational Grammar. In fact, his explanations of typological patterns explicitly make a rich set of assumptions about the grammatical interaction of syntax, semantics, and pragmatics, though not assumptions compatible with most generative models (see especially chapter 11 of that work).

particular language is considered to be fairly trivial. The reader is often given no explicit indication why one element is identified as a subject, or a verb, or a relative marker, or whatever, while another element is not so identified. And where such an indication is given, it seems to be based, more often than not, on some loose semantic or pragmatic criteria. This practice is fundamentally misguided. Take the identification of subjects and objects, for example. Surely it is a mistake to identify such items based on the semantic roles that they play (that is, whether they are agents, patients, or whatever) or on their discourse functions (that is, whether they encode topics or new participants). Since one holds out the hope of *explaining* their nature on a semantic or discourse basis, it is methodologically illicit to define subject and objects on semantic or discourse grounds. To do so would be to reason in the most viciously circular fashion. In other words, we need a formal characterization of subject and object.

Or consider syntactic category membership, that is whether a particular item is a noun, a verb, or whatever. Scores of functionalist publications have been devoted to arguing that category membership can be grounded in semantics or discourse. But if such studies are to avoid circularity, the *identification* of syntactic categories and categorial assignment of particular lexical items demands a formal specification of the set of categories in the language. It would hardly do to identify nouns on the basis of some assumed semantic or pragmatic property, and then to announce that one has 'discovered' that nouns have a consistent semantic or pragmatic property! Yet such a practice is all too common.

Assigning category membership is often no easy task. Consider, for example, the drastic revisions in the inventory of categories that have been proposed in the past decade. Is Inflection the head of the category Sentence, thus transforming the latter into a Inflection Phrase? Is Complementizer the head of the old S', thereby transforming it into a Complementizer Phrase? Is every Noun Phrase dominated by a Determiner Phrase? Is there really a veritable ocean of functional categories, such as Tense Phrase, Subject Agreement Phrase, Object Agreement Phrase, Negative Phrase, and so on along with their lower-level projections? Where do quantifiers fit in? Are they a separate category or part of some other projection? There are no settled answers to these questions. Given the fact that we are unsure precisely what the inventory of categories for any language is, it is clearly premature to make sweeping claims about their semantic or discourse roots. Yet much functionalist-based typological work does just that.

Finally, consider the matter of surface constituent structure. Here again, we would like to know the extent to which such structure reflects semantic structure or external functional factors. So the worst move we could possibly make would be to *assume* that formal levels of structure correspond to semantic levels (as is done, as I understand it, in the theory of 'Functional Grammar' of Dik 1981, 1989). Rather, the relationship between the two levels must be left as an open question for investigation.

Neither casual inspection nor one's intuition as a native speaker or as a trained linguist suffices to establish what the constituent structure of a particular sentence is. As Hawkins has observed:

Only detailed argumentation drawing on numerous rules and structures within a given language can provide decisive evidence about the grouping of words into phrases. Mere observation of surface structures is not enough. Simple substitution tests based on surface structures are also not enough; witness the inadequacies of structuralist Immediate Constituent (IC) analysis (cf. Palmer 1971) and its replacement by rule-based arguments for constituency (cf. e.g. Radford 1981) and more recently by principle-based arguments (cf. e.g. Riemsdijk and Williams 1986). Only in the context of explicitly formulated rules and principles within a precise formal theory can such issues be resolved. (Hawkins 1988b: 93)

No amount of reflection, for example, will give a definitive answer to whether in the sentence *Mary expected John to leave early, John* belongs to the higher clause or to the lower clause. But that is a relatively easy case. Let me cite two examples from recent work on English to illustrate how difficult it is to be sure of a sentence's constituent structure. First, there is the question of the structure of embedded propositions missing both complementizers and auxiliary elements: an example like (9) is typical. Is the VP triple-branching, as in (10a) (see Emonds 1976, 1985), or should we adopt a small clause analysis (10b), as suggested in Chomsky (1981) and Stowell (1981)? There are arguments in both directions, some wholly theory-internal, but others based on traditional tests for constituency (for an overview of the issues involved, see Hoekstra 1988):

(9) I consider John intelligent.

(10) a.

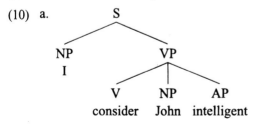

b.
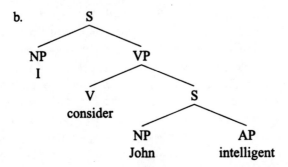

The English double object construction is another case in point. There are at least three popular constituent analyses of sentences like (11). In (12a), the VP triple-branches to the verb, the direct object, and the indirect object (Oehrle 1976); in (12b), the verb and the direct object form a constituent (Chomsky 1981); and in (12c), the verb and the indirect object do so (Larson 1988):

(11) John sent Mary a letter.

(12) a.

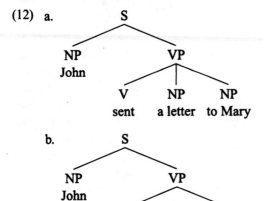

c.

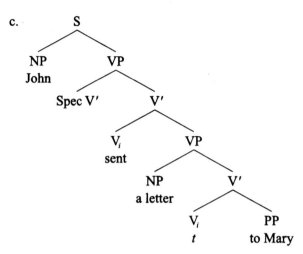

It is not my wish here to take a position on which of the three is correct; indeed, there are other plausible analyses, any one of which might be correct. But the point is that any external function-based account of why particular structures cross-linguistically carry the semantic and/or pragmatic functions associated with indirect objects had better have a compelling characterization of just what those structures *are*. In other words, formal analysis precedes functional explanation.

To conclude, if we are interested in the semantic or pragmatic function or motivation of the categories and constituents in a particular language, our first task is to identify them. Clearly, to avoid circularity, this identification cannot be based on semantic or pragmatic criteria. As we have seen, this identification demands a sophisticated formal theory.

5.2 Identifying grammatical elements cross-linguistically

Croft (1990: §1.3) raises the question of cross-linguistic comparability, that is, how one might 'identify the "same" grammatical phenomenon across languages' (1990: 11) and points out that 'this problem has commanded remarkably little attention relative to its importance'. He suggests, following the discussion in Greenberg (1963), that variation in structure across languages makes it impossible to use purely structural criteria, consistently applicable across languages, for identifying the grammatical units of one language with those of another. As a consequence, 'the ultimate solution is a semantic one, or to put it more generally, a functional solution' (1990: 11). For example, Croft devotes several pages to arguing for the impossibility of equating subjects in one language with subjects in another by purely formal means. As he notes, 'The grammatical relation of "subject" is expressed structurally in several different ways: by case/adposition marking, by indexation or agreement, or by a combination of both of these' (1990: 13). Croft concludes:

Whatever solution is taken to this problem must refer at some level to the actual semantic relations that hold between the 'subject' and the verb. Thus a cross-linguistically valid definition of 'subject' referring extensively to external properties appears to be unavoidable. (1990: 16)

When all else fails, we can resort to 'our pretheoretic intuitions about grammatical categories [which] strongly suggest that some external definitions are better cross-linguistic criteria than others' (Croft 1990: 17).

I believe that Croft's appeal to semantic criteria in the cross-linguistic identification of grammatical units is seriously flawed, first because it suffers from the same methodological difficulties as using semantic criteria to identify grammatical elements in an individual language. We cannot hope to understand the relationship between syntactic categories and meaning, for example, if we have used semantic criteria in identifying those categories.

But more seriously, Croft proposes a false dichotomy. He implies that *either* we propose some invariable observable criterion for identifying the same element from language to language *or* we are forced to resort to semantic (or intuitive) criteria. From the failure of the first, he concludes the necessity for the second. But there is a third possibility, namely that linguistic theory itself provides the means for identification, though not necessarily one that can be read directly off the surface.[25] There are, in fact, cross-linguistic structural definition of 'subjects': a currently popular view is what is called the 'Internal Subject Hypothesis': the subject is that element underlyingly occupying the highest argument position within VP.[26] In most, but not all, languages, that element will raise to the position of specifier of Inflection Phrase in S-structure ([Spec, IP]). Many of

25. There is also a fourth possibility: to reject any possibility of a theoretically meaningful crosslinguistic approach to grammatical relations. This is precisely the position taken on semiotic grounds in Tobin (1990) and on functionalist grounds in Dryer (1997).

26. For discussion and motivation of the Internal Subject Hypothesis, see Kitagawa (1994), Koopman and Sportiche (1991), Rosen (1990), Speas (1986), Woolford (1991), and Zagona (1988).

the common typological properties of what are called 'subjects' in the languages of the world are consequences of their all having originated in this lower VP position; other more restricted typological properties correlate well with their having raised or not raised (for extensive discussion, see McCloskey 1996).

But one cannot casually observe a set of sentences in a language to determine where precisely the highest argument position within VP is or what structural configuration identifies [Spec, IP]. These determinations require deep grammatical *analysis*. But again, this reinforces the conclusion at which we have already arrived: the explanation of typological patterns in language requires, as a first step, the construction of a formal theory.

5.3 Semantic criteria and missed generalizations

There is an even more fundamental reason for the typologist to ensure that the grammatical elements that form the explananda for grammatical theory be characterized on a purely formal basis: doing so leads to more profound generalizations about how language works. That is, typological generalizations themselves are often more robust when the bases for them are formally defined categories, rather than semantically or functionally defined ones. Dryer (1992: 120) has noted that 'the standard practice in word order typology since Greenberg (1963) has been to identify different categories largely on the basis of semantic criteria'. But he then goes on to show that such practice is gravely in error. Many of the word order correlations that he has devoted so much research to explaining are inexplicable if one appeals to semantic categories such as 'negative word' or 'tense/aspect word'. However, if statements are based on their *formal* properties, interesting generalizations fall nicely into place.

Dryer's paper in no way obviates the serious foundational problems of language typology that were discussed above. The general methodological concerns are no less profound here than elsewhere. One can raise the same questions about the representativeness of the sample and the criteria by which languages are pigeon-holed with respect to particular features. But given that it is legitimate to suspend those concerns when evaluating two contrasting approaches that are in relevant respects *methodologically identical*, Dryer provides what is possibly the most impressive demonstration to date for the necessity of formal constituent analysis. Using a corpus of 625 languages, he examines the correlations between the order of verb and object and a multitude of other properties, such as having prepositions or postpositons, the order of relative clause and head noun, the order of adjective and noun, and so on.

Dryer points out that most prior explanations of the correlations have been semantically-based. In particular, most have appealed to some version of semantically based head-dependent theory, in which it is claimed that there is pressure to maximize the parallelism between heads and dependents. It is well accepted among typologists that languages in which verbs precede objects tend to have prepositions; languages in which objects precede verbs tend to have postpositions. Why should such a correlation exist? According to head-dependent theory, because verbs and adpositions are heads of their associated object phrases. In VO languages, relative clauses are said to tend to follow their head nouns, and in OV languages to precede them. Why? Again, according to head-dependent theory, because nouns are heads and relative clauses are dependents.

Dryer argues that this explanation is incorrect. What is relevant is not what is a head and what is a dependent, but rather the *branching direction* of the elements involved. According to the branching-direction theory, languages tend toward one of two ideals: right-branching languages, in which phrasal categories follow nonphrasal categories, and left-branching languages, in which phrasal categories precede nonphrasal categories. The two types of languages are illustrated in (13):

(13)

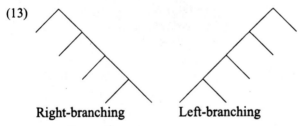

Right-branching   Left-branching

Now, of course, for many pairs, head-dependent theory and branching-direction theory make the same prediction. Relative clauses follow their heads in VO languages. Head-dependent theory predicts this ordering because both objects and relatives are complements. Branching-direction theory makes the same prediction because both VO structures and noun-relative structures are right branching. But the two theories are not equivalent; where they make different predictions, it is the branching-direction theory that is correct.

Let us begin by examining auxiliary-verb and determiner-noun order. Traditionally, auxiliaries have been considered to be dependents of verbal heads—their specifiers in many early versions of generative grammar (see, for example Akmajian, Steele, and Wasow 1979). Precisely the same can be said for articles with respect to nouns (Jackendoff 1977). To be specific, auxiliaries were considered part of the maximal projection of V, modifying their verbal head, while articles were part of the maximal projection of N, modifying their nominal head. Phrase structure (14a–b) illustrates:

(14) a.   VP   b.   NP

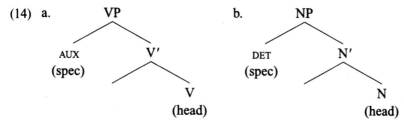

    AUX   V′   DET   N′
   (spec)   (spec)

            V   N
       (head)   (head)

Head-dependent theory, then, would predict that the order between verb and auxiliary in most languages should parallel that between noun and article and that both should parallel the order between verb and object. But typological research has concluded that such is not the case. VO languages show a near universal tendency for auxiliaries to precede verbs, not to follow them, while in OV languages auxiliaries follow verbs, rather than precede them. For determiners and nouns, the typological correlations are less robust, but there is a general tendency for determiners to precede nouns in VO languages and to follow them in OV languages.

Branching-direction theory, however, makes the correct predictions.[27] Auxiliary-verb and article-noun structures are overwhelmingly right-branching in VO languages and left-branching in OV languages. Hence we derive the ordering correlations verb-object, auxiliary-verb, and determiner-noun on the one hand, and object-verb, verb-auxiliary, and noun-determiner on the other.

It is quite interesting that in recent years many generativists have abandoned the idea that auxiliaries and determiners are specifiers of verbs and nouns respectively. Instead, it has become widely accepted that verbs (or, more properly verb phrases) are *complements* to auxiliary heads and

27. And, again, branching-direction theory falls out from EIC (see Hawkins 1994: ch. 4).

that nouns are *complements* to determiners (see especially Pullum and
Wilson 1977 for the former, Abney 1987 for the latter). Phrase structure
(15a–b) gives a schematic illustration:

(15) a.   IP   b.   DP

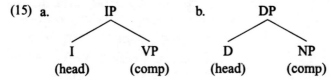

          I   VP   D   NP
       (head)   (comp)   (head)   (comp)

In a sense then, we have seen head-dependent theory and branching-
direction theory converging, in that they now make identical predictions
with respect to auxiliary-verb ordering and determiner-noun ordering.
Importantly, these revisions in phrase-structure were arrived at without
any typological considerations in mind and did not appeal to the semantic
relationship between the elements involved. Thus recent research in generative grammar has provided *empirical support* for a homology between
formal relations and semantic relations whose correctness had only been
assumed in the functional-typological approach.

   This homology is not complete, however. There are cases in which
head-dependent theory fails, while branching-direction theory does not.
Consider the following three examples. First, many languages have a
category 'Demonstrative' that is distinct from Determiner. In such languages, there is no robust correlation between the order of demonstrative
and noun, even though in relevant respects demonstratives parallel determiners semantically. Second, tense-aspect *particles* do not show a consistent ordering with respect to the verb, even though semantically parallel
auxiliaries do so. And, third, there is no robust correlation between the
ordering of adjective and noun and that of dependents and heads.

   Branching-direction theory explains why these correlations do not hold.
In each of the three cases, a reasonable phrase-structure analysis involves
the concatenation of two nonphrasal categories (e.g. A and N within NP).
There is no dominant branching direction and hence no correlation with
the order of verbs and adpositions, auxiliaries and verbs, and so on.[28]

   Another limitation of the practice of typological comparison of semantically or functionally defined categories across languages is that it

28. Dryer (1992: 99) points out that in most principles-and-parameters accounts
of inflectional elements, tense/aspect particles, as well as auxiliary verbs, are
heads. Thus such accounts predict, incorrectly, that particle-verb order should
parallel auxiliary-verb order.

occludes the uncovering of any purely *structural* principles at work in particular languages or in language in general. But the elaboration of such principles seems self-evidently relevant to typology, since they limit the typological variation possible among linguistic elements. Furthermore, since (as we saw in chapter 2) there is a many-many relation between functionally-defined construction types and structural principles, elaboration of the latter is relevant for understanding the degree of possible variation of the former (for more development of this point, see Hoekstra and Kooij 1988).

Coopmans (1984) has given an interesting example along these lines. A category that appears frequently in the typological literature is that of 'genitive'. That is, one tries to elucidate the order of genitives with respect to the nouns they modify, whether they parallel adjectives in their distribution, and so on. But immediately a problem arises with English: as we can see in (16a–b), genitives can occur *both* before and after the noun. Hence, the perennial difficulty about whether to classify English as a noun-genitive language or a genitive-noun language:

(16) a. the table's leg
     b. the leg of the table

Coopmans questions whether much is to be learned by having to make decisions about which pigeon hole a language fits into, as far as genitive-noun order is concerned. As he notes, 'genitive' is a purely *descriptive* category, based loosely on the notion of semantic possession. The *structures* involved in coding semantic possession in English are used to code other semantic relationships as well. Expressions (16a) and (16b) are structurally parallel to (17a) and (17b) respectively, even though the latter are not possessives:

(17) a. Tuesday's lecture, Fermat's theorem, Rome's destruction
     b. a piece of cake, the dog in the window, the destruction of Rome

So, an important question to ask, from a typological point of view, is not just what the order of genitive and noun is in English and other languages, but what *structures* are available to express possession and what their correlation is with structures encoding other semantic concepts.[29] But again, step one in such an undertaking is a rigorous structural analysis.

---

29. See Andersen (1982) for a parallel argument based on the structures involved in comparative constructions.

6 Implicational Hierarchies and a New Argument for Functionalism

Croft (1995a), in his discussion of autonomy and functional linguistics, presents what I consider to be an intriguing argument for functionalism, and one which depends heavily on typological analysis. He suggests that the arbitrary and nonarbitrary (i.e. externally motivated) aspects of syntax might be distinguishable along the following lines: All universal aspects of language are externally motivated and representable by implicational hierarchies, arrived at through typological investigation. That which is arbitrary is language-specific. However, any arbitrary element, rather than partaking of a grammar-internal autonomous system, represents some point in one of the universal hierarchies. Hence, the 'balance' between what is language-particular and what is arbitrary is very different from what is posited in generative models—a balance that cannot even begin to be appreciated without a wholesale commitment to typology. Croft calls any approach embodying such an idea 'typological functionalism', and implies that the great majority of functionalists qualify to be labeled as 'typological functionalists'.

Let me illustrate concretely. Recall the Hierarchy of Morphological Incorporability, repeated below:

(1) *Hierarchy of Morphological Incorporability*
    Nonreferential Ns < Demoted NPs < Backgrounded NPs <
    Fully Referential NPs

As far as incorporability is concerned, all that the grammar of any language need do is specify what at point that language falls along the hierarchy. All elements to the left of that particular cut-off point will automatically be predicted to incorporate. What is especially attractive about such an approach, according to Croft, is that what might appear to be exceptional from the point of view of the grammar of a single language turns out from a functional-typological perspective to be consistent with universal principles. Hence Mohawk at first glance seems extraordinary in that it allows referential NPs to be incorporated. But in fact the only (relevant) property that makes that language differ from any other is its position on the hierarchy. As predicted, other types of NPs will incorporate as well. Croft goes on to remark that such a generalization is not stateable within a generative approach to language, in which syntax is autonomous.

I suspect that few of the hierarchies that have been proposed in the functionalist literature are robust enough to allow one to reliably derive the generalizations that Croft would wish to derive. As we saw in chapter 4, for example, the prototypicality hierarchy is quite suspect. Furthermore, I am skeptical that any more than a few hierarchies have been formulated carefully enough (see note 4) or nonredundantly enough to form the basis for deriving these generalizations. But let us put such reservations aside and assume that Croft is right. Let us assume that all arbitrary language-specific properties can be characterized by reference to a point on a functionally-determined universal hierarchy. If so, what would then follow about the adequacy of the generativist program vis-à-vis that of the functionalist program? The answer is 'Absolutely nothing'.

If we share the goal of characterizing the language-particular and universal knowledge that speakers have about grammars, then there is no place *in grammar itself* for the kinds of generalizations that Croft attributes to typological functionalism. And the reason for that is simple: speakers have no knowledge of hierarchies. How, in any reasonable sense of the term 'know', could a speaker be expected to 'know' the Hierarchy of Morphological Incorporability or where their language falls on it? Surely, such knowledge is neither provided innately nor, given the absence of evidence to the language learner, could it be learned inductively.

But that does not mean that the generalization expressed by the hierarchy is not (or, better, could not be) a 'real' one. Consider an analogy. The United States Department of Agriculture divides the 48 contiguous states into 11 'climate zones', each defined by its average annual minimum temperature. 'Zone 1' designates the area of the United States with the lowest minimum average, and '11' the highest. The listing for any particular plant in a nursery catalogue gives one zone number only, namely the lowest-numbered zone in which that plant can survive. That is, if a plant is designated 'zone 5', it can also survive in zones 6–11; if it is designated 'zone 10', it can survive only in that zone and in zone 11; etc. In other words, what is 'arbitrary' is the zone number of any individual plant; what is 'universal' is the hierarchy of hardiness.

The question, then, is what the 'theoretical significance' is of the fact that *Daphne odora*, say, is a 'zone 7' species. I would say 'Very little indeed'. That is not to deny that its zone ranking is a true generalization about the species, nor that the zone hierarchy is a true generalization about plant hardiness. And it is certainly not to deny the *usefulness* of the ranking, say, to gardeners. But no botanist would consider either the zone hierarchy or the zone rating of an individual plant as central to theoretical questions in botany. Rather, they follow from independent facts about types of cells found in plants and their ability to withstand cold temperatures.

As far as the Hierarchy of Morphological Incorporability is concerned, one could make an analogous point. Surely any functionalist would agree that it is not a primitive of theory, but has its basis in something external to grammar. And the fact that Blackfoot, say, falls somewhere in the middle of the hierarchy is even of *less* theoretical interest than is the zone ranking of *D. odora*. The latter can be derived from the plant's molecular and cellular structure; the former is, as far as I know, a *wholly* arbitrary fact about the language.

In summary, we have had a look at the attempt to equate language universals with functionally-determined hierarchies and to equate language-particular facts with points on these hierarchies. I am skeptical that its project is likely to be any more than partially successful. To the extent that it is successful, it will have provided a wealth of interesting generalizations that might bear on the external shaping of grammars. However, there is nothing in the enterprise that challenges the generative commitment to construct a theory of language as a cognitive faculty, that is, a theory of what speakers of a language know about the structure of their language.

7   Typology and Generative Grammar

In this section, we will examine the approach to language typology taken within generative grammar. Section 7.1 argues that the search for statistical regularities and that for structural principles are wholly complementary. In §7.2 I explain the reasons for an increased interest in typology among generativists, while §7.3 presents a critique of the current generative approach to typology.

7.1   'Statistical tendencies' and grammatical theory

Chomsky had the following comments to offer on Greenberg's paper two years after its publication:

It is commonly held that modern linguistic and anthropological investigations have conclusively refuted the doctrines of classical universal grammar, but this claim seems to me very much exaggerated. Modern work has indeed shown a great diversity in the surface structure of languages. However, since the study of deep structure has not been its concern, it has not attempted to show a corresponding diversity of underlying structures, and, in fact, the evidence that has been accumulated in modern study of language does not appear to suggest anything of this sort.... Insofar as attention is restricted to surface structures, the most that can be expected is the discovery of statistical tendencies, such as those presented by Greenberg (1963). (Chomsky 1965: 118)

This passage was embedded in a long discussion of how at a deep levels of analysis, languages are more similar to each other than they are at a surface level. That is, Chomsky was combating the tendency, manifest in both earlier structuralist models and the nascent functional-typological approach, to *restrict attention* to surface structure.

Nevertheless, it was hard for many linguists to avoid reading a dismissive tone into his remarks about the usefulness of typological investigations. The wording of the last sentence, intentionally or not, conveyed the impression that 'the discovery of statistical tendencies' is of no particular interest. Surely, Chomsky's own apparent lack of interest in either ascertaining the nature of such tendencies or in explaining them gave credence to such an interpretation. I would not hesitate to pinpoint that passage as the major rhetorical factor in leading many linguists whose goal was to explain typological facts about language to view that goal as incompatible with the goal set by generative grammarians for linguistic theory.

Such a conclusion, while perhaps understandable, was unfortunate. There is no imaginable reason why there should be any incompatibility between the two sets of goals—after all, in many sciences the uncovering of fundamental principles and the explanation of statistical tendencies take place side-by-side. Statistical tendencies, to the extent that they are reliable, are, after all, data in need of explanation by whatever principles. In the remainder of this section, I will develop this point, arguing that the program of searching out and explaining typological generalizations about language is fully compatible with the generativist program.

To begin with, it seems a priori highly plausible (though not, by any means, logically necessary) that a full explanation of the statistical tendencies of human language surface structures would involve appeal to *both* structural (i.e. generative) and functional principles. In other areas of investigation it is commonplace to find partial functional explanations for typological generalizations where the existence of contributory structural systems can hardly be in doubt.[30] Take another bio-medical analogy, for

30. For more discussion of this point, see Nettle (1998).

example. One researcher might describe the physiology of John Smith's lung cancer and investigate the extent to which it can be attributed to a genetic predisposition. Another might investigate the entire constellation of factors at work in causing lung disease and the percentages of various populations that will succumb to one of these diseases. There is no incompatibility between these two enterprises.

Analogously in linguistics, a generativist, in analyzing a particular language, might specify the values of the relevant parameterized universal principles interacting to permit the various word order possibilities in that language. He or she might also attempt to specify the full range of principles permitted by UG that interact to derive the possible word orders in the languages of the world. Another linguist, more directly interested in, say, why statistically SV order seems to predominate over VS, might appeal to principles of attention, information packaging, and so on, which lead to a general preference for SV order. The former mode of theorizing in no way precludes the latter, nor the latter the former.

To put it concisely, there is no principled incompatibility between the search for autonomous principles of grammar and the desire to understand why grammatical forms have the statistical distribution that they do in the languages of the world. Why should there be *perceived* incompatibility, then? This perception arises, I believe, only because of the belief of many functionalists that a generativist perspective precludes the possibility of *any* external explanation and the manifest willingness of many generativists (in practice, if not always in principle) to encourage functionalists in their belief by ignoring even obvious external factors as part of a complete explanation for whatever phenomenon they might be investigating. But the functionalists' beliefs and the generativists' attitudes are equally unfortunate, in that they polarize the field unnecessarily.

There will, of course, be many cases in which an external and a structural explanation for some typological generalization will be, to whatever extent, in conflict. But that should cause no more grief, nor be the object of any more interest, than two rival structural explanations being in conflict or two rival external explanations. The only way to resolve any two conflicting purported explanations for a given phenomenon, whatever their nature may be, is by intensive empirical investigation and standard approaches to theory construction and evaluation.

More and more generative grammarians appear to be arriving at the conclusion that typological generalizations do have relevance for their theoretical concerns. Two factors have triggered an interest among generative grammarians in typological questions in recent years that was missing in the past. The first is the greatly increased numbers of languages that have been studied intensively. It is now possible for a generativist to approach the question of binding domains from a typological angle (see, for example, Manzini and Wexler 1987), simply because there have been so many in-depth studies of binding in different languages. The second is the approach to cross-linguistic variation that has come to characterize generative theorizing in the past 15 years, which has encouraged contrasting features of different languages. The next section will outline these developments.

7.2   Typology and 'the second conceptual shift' in generative grammar

Chomsky (1986b) refers to two major conceptual shifts in the recent history of linguistics.[31] The first, ushered in by the advent of generative grammar, 'shifted the focus of attention from actual or potential behavior to the system of knowledge that underlies the use and understanding of language, and more deeply, to the innate endowment that makes it possible for humans to attain such knowledge' (1986b: 24). The second conceptual shift is represented by the principles-and-parameters approach of Chomsky (1981), in which the idea that language is an elaborate rule system is abandoned. Rather, the internal structure of the grammar is modular; syntactic complexity results from the interaction of grammatical subsystems, each characterizable in terms of its own set of general principles. The central goal of syntactic theory now becomes to identify such systems and to characterize the degree to which they may vary (be 'parameterized') from language to language.

One consequence of the principles-and-parameters approach to linguistic theory has been to spur investigation of a wide variety of languages, particularly those with structures markedly different from some of the more familiar Western ones. The explanation for this is straightforward. In earlier transformational grammar (oversimplifying somewhat), one wrote a grammar of English, a grammar of Thai, a grammar of Cherokee, and so on, and attempted to extract universal properties of grammars from the principles one found in common among these constructed grammars. But now the essential unity of all grammars, within the limits of parametric variation, is taken as a *starting point*. One cannot

---

31. The following few paragraphs are condensed from Newmeyer (1995: 332–334) and Newmeyer (1996: 85–87).

even begin to address the grammar of some language without asking the question of how principles of Case, binding, bounding, and so on are parameterized in that language. But this is impossible unless one has a rough feel for the degree of parameterization possible for the principle. As Chomsky notes, to delimit the domain of core grammar, we 'rely heavily on grammar-internal considerations and *comparative evidence*, that is, on the possibilities for constructing a reasonable theory of UG *and considering its explanatory power in a variety of language types*, with an eye open to the eventual possibility of adducing evidence of other kinds' (Chomsky 1981: 9; emphasis added).

The need to base a theory of parametric variation on a wide variety of languages has resulted in what Bernard Comrie has referred to approvingly as 'one of the most interesting recent developments in linguistic typology ..., the entry of generative syntax into the field' (Comrie 1988: 458). Comparative studies of the null-subject parameter, binding domains, configurationality, and so on are now routine and provide a generative interpretation of the kind of cross-linguistic study that was initiated by the work of Greenberg.

In this regard, it is instructive to observe Chomsky's changing attitude to Greenbergian typological work.[32] In 1981, Chomsky offered what was perhaps his first favorable reference to this line of research:

Universals of the sort explored by Joseph Greenberg and others have obvious relevance to determining just which properties of the lexicon have to be specified in this manner in particular grammars—or to put it in other terms, just how much has to be learned as grammar develops in the course of language acquisition (Chomsky 1981: 95)

By 1982 he was writing that 'the Greenberg universals ... are ultimately going to be fairly rich.... They have all the difficulties that people know, they are "surfacy," they are statistical, and so on and so forth, but nevertheless they are very suggestive' (Chomsky 1982b: 111). And in 1986, they are 'important, ... yielding many generalizations that require explanation' (Chomsky 1986b: 21).

How, then, might typological generalizations be accounted for in the principles-and-parameters approach? Chomsky puts it succinctly:

32. Greenberg (1991b) offers an interesting (if somewhat personal) picture of the historical tension between the generative and the functionalist approaches to typology.

Within the P&P approach the problems of typology and language variation arise in somewhat different form than before. Language differences and typology should be reducible to choice of values of parameters. A major research problem is to determine just what these options are, and in what components of language they are to be found. (1995: 6)

Language acquisition in this approach consists of the child's setting the values for the parameters provided by UG, which themselves are now subject to markedness relationships (see Chomsky 1981: 7). Such a model has the potential to contribute to an explanation of typological patterns if implicationally-linked typological features are an automatic product of a particular parameter setting.

The 1980s and 1990s have seen numerous attempts to put this idea into practice. In *Lectures in Government and Binding*, where the parametric approach to typology was first articulated in detail, Chomsky suggested that a rich set of typological facts follows from whether an affix-movement rule applies in the syntax or in the mapping from S-Structure to Phonetic Form. The former characterizes 'pro-drop' (or 'null subject') languages, which are claimed to have the typological properties of allowing null thematic subjects in tensed clauses, free inversion in simple sentences, long *Wh*-Movement of subjects, empty resumptive pronouns in embedded clauses, and apparent violations of the *that*-trace filter (Chomsky 1981: 253–254). We will return to examine some of these typological predictions in §7.3.

Another important parameter with direct implications for typology was introduced in Hale (1982). Hale proposed that X-bar theory be para-meterized to allow for what he called 'nonconfigurational languages' (in Hale 1983 he suggested a parameterization of the Projection Principle instead). Such languages are characterized by the use of a rich case sys-tem, free word order, lack of NP movement, lack of pleonastic NPs, use of discontinuous expressions, complex verb words, and free or frequent 'pronoun drop'.[33]

A third early (and continuing) issue in parametric-typological syntax is that of the word order correlations that have been subject to so much attention by the functional-typological approach. Stowell (1981), for example, proposed a parameter of phrase structure with two possible values: heads precede complements or heads follow complements. Thus

---

33. Edith Moravcsik (personal communication) has pointed out that, as they are stated above, the null subject and configurationality parameters are not indepen-dent—pro-drop and free word order are part of both.

the correlation, noted by Greenberg, that VO languages tend to be prepositional, while OV languages tend to be postpositional, follows automatically.

As Stowell was aware, the one parameter setting approach to head-complement ordering is too strong—there exist quite a few 'mixed' languages, in which heads of some categories precede their complements and heads of other categories follow them. He suggested several possible solutions to this problem, but came to no firm conclusion. The standard way of dealing with this case, I believe, would be two assume that there are two parameters, one regulating the order of verb and object, the other adposition and object, which are linked by a principle of markedness, thereby predicting the general correlation.

The problem is even more complex, however. There is tremendous language-particular variation just within the verb phrase. Travis (1989: 271) calls attention to eight possible orderings of the verb, direct object NP, complement PP (PP_1), and adjunct PP (PP_2):

(18) *Word orders*
      a. PP_2 PP_1 NP V
      b. PP_2 PP_1 V NP
      c. PP_2 NP V PP_1
      d. PP_2 V NP PP_1
      e. PP_1 NP V PP_2
      f. PP_1 V NP PP_2
      g. NP V PP_1 PP_2
      h. V NP PP_1 PP_2

As Travis noted, three separate parameters are needed to allow for the possibilities in (18a–h), which she designated 'headedness', 'direction of theta-role assignment', and 'direction of case assignment' (see also Koopman 1984 for a very similar proposal). If these three parameters were independent, then all eight orderings would be predicted to exist, by virtue of the combinations of settings illustrated in table 6.8. However, no language manifesting (c) and (f) appears to exist, nor is there evidence that such a language ever existed. Travis therefore proposed implicational relations among these 3 parameters whose effect is to predict that (c) and (f) are impossible.

To summarize, the second conceptual shift in generative grammar has opened up the possibility of explaining typological facts about language in ways that would have been impossible in earlier models.

Table 6.8
Combinations of the headedness, direction of theta-role assignment, and direction of case assignment parameters

	Headedness	Theta	Case	Language[34]
a	final	left	left	Japanese
b	final	left	right	Chinese (future)
c	final	right	left	*
d	final	right	right	Chinese (present)
e	initial	left	left	Kpelle (past)
f	initial	left	right	*
g	initial	right	left	Kpelle (present)
h	initial	right	right	English

7.3   Criticisms of the generativist approach to typology

The program of attempting to capture implicational relationships among linguistic features in a parameter-setting model has led many generativists to accept in principle the importance of cross-linguistic comparison of languages. And indeed we do find impressively detailed studies of parametric differences among some closely related languages and dialects, particularly in the Romance and Germanic families (see, for example, Jaeggli 1981 and Haider, Olsen, and Vikner 1995 respectively). However, wide-scale in-depth comparisons of even a single feature involving dozens of languages from diverse families have been few and far between. Such is perhaps understandable, given what is involved in a generative analysis of even one language. Nevertheless, I think that it is fair to say that most generativists have not paid sufficient attention to the typological literature, even when it bears on claims with typological implications that they themselves have put forward.

I will illustrate my point with respect to what is probably the *best* studied parameter in the principles-and-parameters approach—the null subject parameter, mentioned above in §7.2 (for an overview of the issues involved, see the papers collected in Jaeggli and Safir 1989).[35] Four of the

34. Travis speculates that Chinese will have parametric system (b) in the future and that Kpelle had system (f) in the past. I would guess that there are attested languages that manifest these systems, though I am not aware of them.

35. The discussion that follows draws heavily on a pre-publication version of Croft (1995a). Croft's discussion of these issues was omitted from the final version of the paper.

Table 6.9
The null-subject parameter and its predicted correlations

	Language types				Predictions and attestations	
	Null thematic subjects	Null nonthem. subjects	Subject inversion	*That*-trace filter violations	Predicted	No. in sample
a	+	+	+	+	LR, KS	7
b	+	+	+	−	no	4
c	+	+	−	+	no	6
d	+	+	−	−	KS	2
e	+	−	+	+	no	0
f	+	−	+	−	no	0
g	+	−	−	+	no	0
h	+	−	−	−	no	0
i	−	+	+	+	LR, KS	1
j	−	+	−	+	no	2
k	−	+	−	−	no	1
l	−	+	+	−	no	0
m	−	−	+	+	KS	0
n	−	−	−	+	no	3
o	−	−	+	−	no	0
p	−	−	−	−	LR, KS	3

typological features that have been claimed to be associated with this parameter are the possibility of null thematic subjects in tensed clauses, null nonthematic (expletive) subjects, subject inversion, and *that*-trace violations. Thus as is shown in the 'language types' section of table 6.9, there are 16 ways that these 4 properties might in principle be distributed in a particular language.

Two major proposals for handling null subjects and associated phenomena are Rizzi (1982) and Safir (1985). Rizzi predicts the existence of three of these types a, i, p. Safir, who proposes three parameters, also predicts types a, i, p, and, in addition, types d, m. These predictions are indicated in the left column of the 'Predictions and attestations' section of table 6.9 ("LR' refers to Rizzi's predictions and 'KS' to Safir's).

Rizzi's and Safir's predictions were put to the test by Gilligan (1987), who worked with a 100 language sample, which he attempted to correct for areal and genetic bias. Of these 100, there were 10 with data for all four properties. To these he added 19 more languages, for which data on these properties was available in the literature. As the right column of the 'Predictions and attestations' section of table 6.9 illustrates, neither Rizzi's nor Safir's predictions appear to be borne out. All three of the language types that Rizzi predicts to exist are attested, as are four of the five Safir predicts (and the missing one could easily be a function of the small sample). But disconcertingly, five types that neither theory predicts are attested.

Now, one must be clear that these results in and of themselves do not necessarily refute either Rizzi or Safir. It is possible that the cases of nonpredicted subject inversion, for example, are the result of something other than the null subject parameter. As Gilligan himself points out: 'Perhaps the Rizzi hypothesis is correct but its effects are obscured in [Brazilian Portuguese and Mandarin—two languages with a cluster of properties predicted not to exist] because of some as yet unanalyzed aspect of these languages' (1987: 90). Or, perhaps we have another example of a sampling problem, which, if corrected, would bear out Rizzi or Safir. Or, again, perhaps the null subject parameter itself is an epiphenomenon, whose effects are to be attributed to other parameters. Nevertheless, the fact that even the most extensively investigated generative parameter appears to lack typological support makes one wonder what the status would be of the myriad of others, were they put to a similar test.

Another example of a sweeping typological claim that has been put forward on the basis of meager evidence is found in Richard Kayne's important recent book *The Antisymmetry of Syntax* (1994). Kayne proposes underlying SVO order for *all* languages, partly on the basis of his belief that there is a typological generalization that specifier-head-complement order predominates in the world's languages:

We are now left with two constituent order possibilities, specifier-head-complement and complement-head-specifier. A rapid look at (a small subset of) the world's (presently existing) languages reveals that of the two orders, the former is a significantly more plausible universal than is the latter. (1994: 35)

The literature in language typology, however, which Kayne does not cite, gives little credence to the idea that specifier-head-complement order predominates. The results of Dryer (1989b) suggest that SOV order is more frequent than SVO and VSO put together (see table 6.5). But in

SOV languages the complements of verbs and adpositions *precede* their
heads. What about specifiers? Here we get into the question of what elements occupy specifier position. If genitive phrases are specifiers within
NP (or DP), then there is still less support for Kayne. In OV languages,
typologists agree that genitives precede their heads (so complement-head
order for V and P is matched by specifier-head order for N), while in VO
languages, genitives are said to follow their heads (so head-complement
order for V and P is matched by head-specifier order for N).

Kayne makes it clear, however, that his generalization is based on the
view (now widely accepted within generative syntax) that both subjects
and preposed *wh*-phrases are specifiers:

In fact, CP is a category whose specifier, the typical landing site for moved *wh*-
phrases, is visibly initial to an overwhelming degree. Spec, IP (i.e. subject position)
is clearly predominantly initial in its phrase. That is straightforwardly true for
SVO and SOV languages, and almost as obviously true for VSO languages,
assuming the by now usual analysis of VSO order as deriving from SVO order by
leftward V-movement. (1994: 35)

But all that means for OV languages is that within *IP* we find specifier-
head-complement order. Complements still precede their heads within VP
and PP. And furthermore, since OV languages rarely have *Wh*-Movement,
and, in any event, they have their complementizers on the right (i.e. within
CP, the complement precedes the head), there appears to be no general
typological support whatsoever for Kayne's purported universal.[36]

Any claim that one's theory has typological implications entails a
commitment to provide wide-ranging typological evidence in its support.
It would be unfair to single out Rizzi, Safir, and Kayne for not having
done so; there are very few generative proposals with implications for
typology that carry out the kind of cross-linguistic sampling that Gilligan
carries out, or even refer to such a sample carried out by someone else.

The question of the adequacy of a parameter-setting approach to
typology cannot be wholly separated from the question of the ontological
status of parameters and their interrelationships. In the 1980s, Chomsky
left no doubt that he believed the set of possible parameter settings to be
innate. To repeat his views on this issue (see ch. 3, §4.1):

36. But see Cinque (1996), where it is argued that, given a couple assumptions
congenial to Kayne's general approach, one can derive the typological generalizations about the ordering of N, Det, Adj, and Num that are discussed in Greenberg (1963) and Hawkins (1983).

What we 'know innately' are the principles of the various subsystems of S_0 [the initial state of the language faculty] and the manner of their interaction, and the parameters associated with these principles. What we learn are the values of these parameters and the elements of the periphery (along with the lexicon, to which similar considerations apply). The language that we then know is a system of principles with parameters fixed, along with a periphery of marked exceptions. (Chomsky 1986b: 150–151)

It is an undeniable fact that only a tiny, perhaps insignificantly tiny, percentage of the set of proposed principles and parameters have been subjected to poverty of the stimulus (or other) arguments to support their putative innateness. Yet for many, it does not seem too far-fetched to speculate that they might very easily have been learned inductively. To take what seems to me to be a fairly clear example, consider the acquisition of the order of heads and complements within each phrasal category for a particular language. Given the remarks in the above quote by Chomsky, the child would be presumed to be born knowing that it has to scan phrasal domains for information relevant to the determination of head-complement order, as well as be born knowing what the possible parametric values are for each relevant principle. (The precise nature of the innate knowledge would depend on the precise nature of the relevant determining principles.) Yet, given that the child has a mental representation of phrase structure and syntactic categories (whether learned or innate), it seems plausible, as is argued in Hawkins (1988b: 91), that it could figure out 'on its own' whether verbs, prepositions, and so on precede or follow their objects.[37]

The relevance of this issue to the explanation of typological patterning should be clear. If such patterning is wholly or largely a function of parameter setting, and the parameters, their possible settings, and their implicational relationships are innate, then typological generalizations have an innate basis. Why are OV languages usually postpositional? Why do languages that have null subjects tend to allow *that*-trace violations? Why do inflectional morphemes tend to appear outside derivational morphemes? Because innately fixed relationships among parameter settings determine that such should be the case.

Now I certainly have no objection to appeals to innateness in the abstract, nor do I feel that there is something in principle suspect about

37. But see Gibson and Wexler (1994) and J. D. Fodor (1998) for a full discussion of the complexity of the problem.

hypothesizing that a particular feature of language exists because it is innate. If the evidence leads in that direction, well and good. But often there are plausible explanations for a typological pattern that do not involve appeal to an innate UG principle. In such cases, harm *is* done by assuming innateness. What we would then have are two contrasting explanans: one that says that the pattern results from such-an-such motivated principle or force, the other that says that it is merely a genetic quirk.[38] All other things being equal, we should choose the former.

A concrete example of what I have in mind is discussed in Hawkins (1994). He contrasts Travis's and Koopman's theory of the ordering of verb phrase constituents, discussed above, with his own theory that attempts to ground many facts about constituent order in Early Immediate Constituents, a parsing preference to identify the major constituents of a phrase as early as possible (see ch. 3, §4.2.2). As he shows, EIC is *descriptively* better than the Travis-Koopman theory, in that it accounts for orderings for which the latter theory makes no prediction at all. For example, a head noun does not assign Case or θ-role to a modifying sentence, so their theory (as opposed to EIC) makes no predictions about N-S order.

Suppose that the Travis-Koopman parameter-based approach and the Hawkins parsing preference model made identical predictions. Which should we choose? One reasonable answer is 'both'. That is, it might turn out that at a certain level, both theories are correct. In such a scenario, our mental grammars encode parameters for directionality of Case and θ-role assignment, along the lines that Travis and Koopman suggest. The existence of these parameters is attributed to the effects of the parsing principle, say as a grammaticalization of it. In fact, Hawkins hints that something along these lines might be right: 'Languages of all these types [discussed by Travis and Koopman] clearly exist, and grammars need to be written for them, possibly in [their] terms' (Hawkins 1994: 109). However, as he goes on to stress: 'Generative rule types and principles such as directionality of case- and theta-role assignment may still be useful at the level of describing particular languages ... and in predicting all and only the sentences in the relevant domain, but they are no longer a part of UG itself' (Hawkins 1997: 746).

---

38. There is still the possibility that an innate feature of language might have been shaped functionally. For discussion of this possibility, see Kirby and Hurford (1997) and Newmeyer (in preparation).

Now contrast Hawkins' theory with a Travis-Koopman theory that, following Chomsky, says that 'we "know innately" ... the principles ... and the manner of their interaction, and the parameters associated with these principles'. In such an event, the Hawkins model is preferable, on grounds of generality. His parsing principle is of wide applicability and ties together many diverse phenomena. But any unelaborated appeal to innateness is, by its very nature, ad hoc.

Interestingly for our concerns, the nature of parameters has undergone a change with the transition from the Government-Binding theory of the 1980s to the Minimalist Program of the 1990s. In the MP, the computational system (that is, the derivational aspect of the grammar) is held to be subject to unparameterized economy principles, with parameters confined to morphological features in the lexicon, the particular choice of which has consequences for syntactic behavior (Borer 1984; Wexler and Chien 1985; Manzini and Wexler 1987).[39] Are the possible settings of these parameters held to be provided innately? There has not been a great deal of discussion of that topic. However, it seems to me that the idea that placing parameters in the lexicon further strengthens the case for individual parameter settings being learnable without demanding that the child literally choose form an innately-specified set. In this respect I agree with Pinker and Bloom, who write:

Parameters of variation, and the learning process that fixes their values for a particular language, as we conceive them, are not individual explicit gadgets in the human mind.... Instead, they should fall out of the interaction between the specific mechanisms that define the basic underlying organization of language ('Universal Grammar') and the learning mechanisms, some of them predating language, that can be sensitive to surface variation in the entities defined by these language specific mechanisms. (1994: 183)

39. The most detailed approach to parametric variation (and indirectly to typology) in the Minimalist Program of which I am aware is Wu (1994). See also Fukui (1995) and Roberts and Roussou (1997) for theoretical discussion of parametric variation in the MP. A rather different approach to typology within generative grammar is taken by Optimality Theory (Prince and Smolensky 1993). In this theory, language particular differences are captured, not by alternative parameter settings, but by the different ranking of universal constraints. Optimality Theory has been applied specifically to typological questions in several works: Prince and Smolensky for phonology; Legendre, Raymond, and Smolensky (1993) for case and voice systems; and Grimshaw (1997) for Wh-Movement and inversion.

It is important to conclude this discussion by stressing that there is no *logical* necessity for the set of parameters of variation to be innate; one can imagine the possibility of a theory in every respect like recent principles-and-parameters models, but in which the parameters are arrived at inductively by the child. Or one can imagine an intermediate theory, in which some, but not all, parameters are innate. If one's goal is to explain typological patterning, one is not forced to choose between a principles-and-parameters theory and a version of functionalism that denies the existence of an autonomous grammatical system. However, it does seem clear that one does have to reject the idea that all principles, and their range of possible parametric variation, are innate.

8 Summary

This chapter has taken on the difficult questions of the relevance for linguistic theory of typological generalizations and the means by which one might go about arriving at such generalizations. Virtually all functionalists and a majority of formalists feel that explaining such generalizations is a central task for linguistic theory. However, the former underestimate the need for formal analysis as a prerequisite to typological analysis, while the latter, by a rhetorical emphasis on innate parameter settings, are drawn away from investigating possible external explanations for typological patterns. Both of these circumstances are unfortunate. There is nothing in the program of external explanation of typological facts that is incompatible with the existence of an autonomous structural system. And there is nothing in the generative program that demands that all typological facts be attributed to the setting of innately specified parameters.

A more difficult foundational question is whether, given the current distribution of available languages, any attainable typological generalization is of a level of significance to require explanation by linguistic theory. Much of this chapter has been devoted to casting doubt on the significance of the generalizations that have been achieved in language typology. However, the best strategy is to assume, for want of evidence to the contrary, that the more robust-seeming of them are valid and to pursue whatever combination of formal and functional explanatory mechanisms seem appropriate to explaining them.

Chapter 7

Conclusion

This work opened with an imaginary dialogue between Sandy Forman, the archetypal generative grammarian, and Chris Funk, the archetypal functional linguist. Distilled into one summarizing line each, their conversation ran as follows:

Forman: The grammatical properties of human language are best characterized in terms of autonomous formal systems.
Funk: The grammatical properties of human language have been shaped by external pressure.

I hope to have presented a convincing case that both Forman and Funk are absolutely correct. Forman is right in believing that grammars are autonomous systems. And Funk is correct in the belief that grammars are not immune from external influence.

Chapters 2 and 3 were devoted to arguing these central points and to demonstrating that they are not contradictory. Chapter 2 took on the different versions of the autonomy thesis. As far as the autonomy of syntax is concerned, I stressed that its correctness has nothing whatever to do with how close the link might be between syntax on the one hand and meaning and/or discourse on the other. Indeed, even if every syntactic construct had a unique and invariable meaning, the autonomy of syntax could still be well motivated. The only issue, as far as this conception is concerned, is whether there is evidence for a system of interrelated elements best described in a syntax-internal vocabulary. As we saw, there is such evidence.

In chapter 2, we also looked at some challenges to the autonomy of knowledge of language with respect to use of language, that is, challenges to the competence-performance dichotomy. The most important posits that language structure is shaped to such a profound degree in the process of speaking that there is no hope of compartmentalizing grammatical knowledge. There is little evidence for such a position, however. Indeed, it is entirely possible that our mental grammars are fully shaped in childhood, and in principle are unable to change in later life. I argued that challenges to the autonomy of grammar as a cognitive system have tended to become intertwined with the distinct issue of 'innateness', that is, whether particular grammatical entities are provided by the human genome. I agreed with critics that innateness is far more often assumed than defended, but questioned whether such an assumption has had any effect on actual grammatical analysis. I went on to argue that the existence of inherited grammatical deficits supports the idea that grammar does form an autonomous cognitive system.

Just as the second chapter supported Forman's position, the third supported Funk's. I went through the long list of external factors that have been claimed to affect grammatical structure and found that two of them—real-time pressure to process language rapidly and pressure to keep form and meaning in some sort of alignment—have left their mark on grammars. Functionalists have pointed to these pressures, to be sure, and have also accorded importance to a third, namely, pressure for grammar to reflect iconically the structure of information flow in discourse. I gave several reasons why information flow has played little or no role in shaping grammars, two of which are the following. First, most proffered explanations along these lines are deficient in fundamental ways. Second, such explanations attribute to speakers and hearers more knowledge, whether overt or covert, than they actually are likely to have. It seems implausible that we have access to own information state, much less that of our addressee.

In chapter 3, I proposed three criteria by which a convincing external explanation might be identified. First, it must lend itself to precise formulation. Second, we have to be able to identify a linkage between cause and effect. And third, it must have measurable typological consequences. I argued that parsing pressure and pressure for structure-concept iconicity fare well by these criteria, while several other intuitively plausible types of external explanation do not.

The central question, of course, is *how* grammar can be both autonomous and externally motivated. Many functionalists and some generativists have dismissed the possibility that it can be both, but such dismissals are premature. As we saw, many systems, both natural and contrived, lend themselves to characterization in terms of their own internal algebra. There is no reason that such an algebra could not have been shaped—and continue to be shaped—in part by forces external to it. In this respect, grammar is no different from, say, the game of baseball, which is governed by a set of discrete rules. Just as the team owners can and have changed those rules (generally with the very 'functional' goal of increasing their profits), the 'rules' of grammar can and have responded to external pressure as well.

A considerable portion of chapter 3 was devoted to exploring the consequences of the fact that external pressures can *conflict* with each other. Functionalists have long been aware of functions in conflict, but have not, I feel, fully appreciated the implications of that fact. One such implication that I pointed out is that it undercuts the popular functionalist idea that synchronic grammars should link structures and external motivations. To illustrate my point, it is well known that parsing pressure and pressure for iconicity can conflict. Let's say that the structure of relative clauses in language *A* reflects the former and their structure in language *B* the latter. Linking structures and motivations in the respective grammars themselves does nothing to explain why the languages differ. Indeed, it is no more than a cumbersome way of saying *that* they differ. Competing motivations provide another argument for characterizing structures independently of those motivations, that is, another argument for autonomy.

The next three chapters addressed issues believed by many functionalists to challenge the core of generative theorizing. In each case, I argued that they do not do so. At most, they challenge the narrow-minded *outlook* of mainstream generative grammarians, who have in general shown no interest in addressing them. The first, which I took on in chapter 4, revolved around the fact that, at first glance, syntactic categories appear to be structured in terms of prototypes and deviations from the prototype. Functionalists have concluded from this observation that the algebraic nature of categories posited in generative theory is fundamentally misguided. The second, the topic of chapter 5, was grammaticalization. Functionalists point out that generativists have no mechanisms for dealing with the cluster of common diachronic changes—some syntactic, some semantic, and some phonetic—that seem to propel grammatical elements unidirectionally toward a certain end point. And, finally, chapter 6 discussed the subfield of language typology. Functionalists have been more committed than generativists to typological investigation in part because they believe that the hierarchies that such investigation reveals are central to grammatical analysis. In particular, they have suggested that all universal aspects of language are externally motivated and representable by implicational hierarchies, arrived at through typological investigation. That which is arbitrary is language-specific and represents some point in one of the universal hierarchies. If this is correct, it would seem that typology has a more central place in linguistic theory than most generativists are wont to believe.

As far as prototypes are concerned, I argued that, while their *effects* for syntactic categories are real, they themselves have no place in syntactic theory. In case after case, I demonstrated that one can derive their effects by appeal to discrete categories in interaction with independently needed principles from syntax, semantics, and pragmatics. For example, expletive *there* in English fails to undergo many syntactic processes that other NPs do undergo. One does not need to label *there* a 'nonprototypical NP' to account for this fact, however. Rather, given the meaning of *there*, it follows from simple pragmatic principles that this item will not occur felicitously in a wide variety of structures. The great majority of prototype effects—for syntactic constructions as well as for categories—can be handled in like manner.

I took a somewhat similar tack in my discussion of grammaticalization. My strategy was to demonstrate that the cluster of diachronic changes characterizing this phenomenon does not represent a distinct grammatical process. We find the syntactic reanalyses, the semantic bleaching (and other changes), and the phonetic erosion that are said to constitute grammaticalization all occurring independently of each other. Grammaticalization, then, is an epiphenomenon in the truest sense of the word—it is nothing more than a cover term for the intersection of these changes. There is no aspect of this phenomenon that challenges basic generative conceptions.

Finally, I argued that the argument for functionalism based on implicational hierarchies is fundamentally flawed. Even if the generalizations behind the argument are correct (which I doubt), they would have no bearing on the generative program. After all, as I pointed out, no speaker could possibly mentally represent most of the hierarchies that have been proposed, or be expected to know, for any particular grammatical construct, where that construct falls on some implicational hierarchy.

Much of chapter 6 was devoted to defending a rather pessimistic (though, I think realistic) appraisal of the possibility of successful typological investigation. There is the very real possibility that the set of presently existing languages—indeed, those that have *ever* existed—may not point to deep properties of the human language faculty. Furthermore, the samples used by linguists might not be representative of the set of existing languages. And finally, the secondary data that are used by typologists almost surely introduce further distortion because of errors and inconsistency.

The chapter continued in a pessimistic vein, only the object of criticism turned to the work of generativists, rather than functionalists. I argued that facile conclusions of innateness have had the effect of downplaying the search for external explanations for the nature of grammatical structure, and I gave a couple examples of negative effects of such conclusions.

To return one last time to Sandy Forman and Chris Funk, I hope that both have found something of value in this book. I hope that Sandy's horizons have been broadened with the realization that functionalists have enriched the field with many important generalizations regarding the influence of function upon form. And I hope that Chris now appreciates the fact that such explanations in many cases rely crucially on the theoretical apparatus arrived at in the last few decades of generative theorizing.

References

Abney, Steven P. (1987). The English noun phrase in its sentential aspect. Unpublished Ph.D. dissertation, MIT.

Adger, David (1992). The licencing of quasi-arguments. *Proceedings of ConSole I,* ed. by Peter Ackema and Maaike Schoorlemmer, pp. 1–18. Utrecht: Utrecht University.

Adger, David (1994). Functional heads and interpretation. Unpublished Ph.D. thesis, University of Edinburgh.

Akmajian, Adrian, and Frank Heny (1975). *An Introduction to the Principles of Transformational Syntax.* Cambridge: MIT Press.

Akmajian, Adrian, Susan Steele, and Thomas Wasow (1979). The category AUX in universal grammar. *Linguistic Inquiry* 10: 1–64.

Allen, Cynthia (1980). *Topics in Diachronic English Syntax.* New York: Garland.

Andersen, Henning (1973). Abductive and deductive change. *Language* 49: 765–793.

Andersen, Paul K. (1982). On Universal 22. *Journal of Linguistics* 18: 231–244.

Andersen, Paul K. (1990). Typological approaches to the passive. Review of *Passive and Voice,* ed. by M. Shibatani. *Journal of Linguistics* 26: 189–202.

Andersen, Paul K. (1994). *Empirical Studies in Diathesis.* Münster: Nodus Publikationen.

Anderson, John R. (1983). *The Architecture of Cognition.* Cambridge: Harvard University Press.

Anderson, Mona (1983). Prenominal genitive NPs. *Linguistic Review* 3: 1–24.

Anderson, Stephen R. (1977). On the mechanisms by which languages become ergative. In *Mechanisms of Syntactic Change,* ed. by Charles Li, pp. 317–363. Austin: University of Texas Press.

Anderson, Stephen R. (1988). Morphological change. In *Linguistic Theory: Foundations,* ed. by Frederick J. Newmeyer, pp. 324–362. Cambridge: Cambridge University Press.

Anderson, Stephen R. (1992). *A-morphous Morphology.* Cambridge: Cambridge University Press.

Aoun, Joseph, Norbert Hornstein, David Lightfoot, and Amy Weinberg (1987). Two types of locality. *Linguistic Inquiry* 18: 537–578.

Aoun, Joseph, and David Lightfoot (1984). Government and contraction. *Linguistic Inquiry* 15: 465–473.

Ariel, Mira (1998). Mapping so-called pragmatic phenomena according to a linguistic-nonlinguistic distinction: interpreting accessible propositions. In *Functionalism and Formalism in Linguistics*, vol. 2, *Case Studies*, ed. by Michael Darnell, Edith Moravcsik, Frederick J. Newmeyer, Michael Noonan, and Kathleen Wheatley, pp. 11–38. Amsterdam: John Benjamins.

Ariel, Mira (forthcoming). *Linguistic Pragmatics.*

Armstrong, Sharon Lee, Lila Gleitman, and Henry Gleitman (1983). What some concepts might not be. *Cognition* 13: 263–308.

Aske, Jon (1998). *Basque Word Order and Disorder: Principles, Variation, and Prospects.* Amsterdam: John Benjamins.

Atlas, Jay D., and Stephen C. Levinson (1981). *It*-clefts, informativeness, and logical form. In *Radical Pragmatics*, ed. by Peter Cole, pp. 1–61. New York: Academic Press.

Babby, Leonard H. (1987). Case, prequantifiers, and discontinuous agreement in Russian. *Natural Language and Linguistic Theory* 5: 91–138.

Babby, Leonard H. (forthcoming). The morpholexical foundations of Russian syntax. Cambridge: Cambridge University Press.

Bach, Emmon (1970). Is Amharic an SOV language? *Journal of Ethiopian Studies* 8: 9–20.

Bach, Emmon (1974). Explanatory inadequacy. In *Explaining Linguistic Phenomena*, ed. by David Cohen, pp. 153–172. Washington: Hemisphere Publishing Corporation.

Bach, Emmon (1980). In defense of passive. *Linguistische Berichte* 70: 38–46.

Bailey, Charles-James N. (1973). *Variation and Linguistic Theory.* Arlington, Va.: Center for Applied Linguistics.

Baker, Mark C. (1988). *Incorporation: A Theory of Grammatical Function Changing.* Chicago: University of Chicago Press.

Baker, Mark C. (1996). *The Polysynthesis Parameter.* New York: Oxford University Press.

Bar-Lev, Zev, and Arthur Palacas (1980). Semantic command over pragmatic priority. *Lingua* 51: 137–146.

Barlow, Michael, and Suzanne Kemmer (1994). A schema-based approach to grammatical description. In *The Reality of Linguistic Rules*, ed. by Susan D. Lima, Roberta L. Corrigan, and Gregory K. Iverson, pp. 19–42. Amsterdam: John Benjamins.

Bartsch, Renate, and Theo Vennemann (1972). *Semantic Structures: A Study in the Relation between Syntax and Semantics.* Frankfort am Main: Athenaum.

Bates, Elizabeth, and Brian MacWhinney (1982). Functionalist approaches to grammar. In *Language Acquisition: The State of the Art*, ed. by Eric Wanner and Lila Gleitman, pp. 173–218. Cambridge: Cambridge University Press.

Bates, Elizabeth, and Brian MacWhinney (1989). Functionalism and the competition model. In *The Crosslinguistic Study of Sentence Processing*, ed. by Brian MacWhinney and Elizabeth Bates, pp. 3–73. Cambridge: Cambridge University Press.

Battistella, Edwin (1990). *Markedness: The Evaluative Superstructure of Language*. Albany: State University of New York Press.

Battye, Adrian, and Ian Roberts (1995). Introduction. In *Clause Structure and Language Change*, ed. by Adrian Battye and Ian Roberts, pp. 3–28. Oxford: Oxford University Press.

Bazell, C. E. (1953). *Linguistic Form*. Istanbul: Istanbul Press.

Becker, A. L. (1991). Language and languaging. *Language and Communication* 11: 33–35.

Beckman, Mary (1988). Phonetic theory. In *Linguistic Theory: Foundations*, ed. by Frederick J. Newmeyer, pp. 216–238. Cambridge: Cambridge University Press.

Behagel, Otto (1932). *Deutsche Syntax: Eine geschichtliche Darstellung*, vol. 4, *Wortstellung: Periodenbau*. Heidelberg: Carl Winters Universitätsbuchhandlung.

Bell, Alan (1978). Language samples. In *Universals of Human Language*, vol. 1, *Method and Theory*, ed. by Joseph H. Greenberg, Charles A. Ferguson, and Edith A. Moravcsik, pp. 123–156. Stanford, Calif.: Stanford University Press.

Berlin, Brent (1978). Ethnobiological classification. In *Cognition and Categorization*, ed. by Eleanor Rosch and Barbara B. Lloyd, pp. 9–26. Hillsdale, N.J.: Erlbaum.

Bertoncini, Elena (1973). A tentative frequency list of Swahili words. *Annali dell'Istituto Orientale di Napoli* 33: 297–363.

Berwick, Robert C., and Amy Weinberg (1984). *The Grammatical Basis of Linguistic Performance*. Cambridge: MIT Press.

Bever, Thomas G., and D. Terence Langendoen (1971). A dynamic model of the evolution of language. *Linguistic Inquiry* 2: 433–461.

Bichakjian, Bernard H. (1991). Evolutionary patterns in linguistics. In *Studies in Language Origins, II*, ed. by Walburga von Raffler-Engel and Jan Wind, pp. 187–224. Amsterdam: John Benjamins.

Bickerton, Derek (1996). A dim monocular view of universal-grammar access. *Behavioral and Brain Sciences* 19: 716–717.

Bird, Charles, and Timothy Shopen (1979). Maninka. In *Languages and Their Speakers*, ed. by Timothy Shopen, pp. 59–111. Cambridge, Mass.: Winthrop.

Bishop, Dorothy V. M. (1987). The causes of specific development language disorder ('developmental dysphasia'). *Journal of Child Psychology and Psychiatry* 28: 1–8.

Bishop, Dorothy V. M. (1988). Language development in children with abnormal structure or function of the speech apparatus. In *Language Development in Exceptional Circumstances*, ed. by Dorothy V. M. Bishop and Kay Mogford, pp. 230–238. Edinburgh: Churchill Livingstone.

Bishop, Dorothy V. M., T. North, and C. Donlan (1995). Genetic basis of specific language impairment: evidence from a twin study. *Developmental Medicine and Child Neurology* 37: 56–71.

Bley-Vroman, Robert D. (1989). What is the logical problem of foreign language learning? In *Linguistic Perspectives on Second Language Acquisition*, ed. by Susan M. Gass and Jacqueline Schachter, pp. 41–68. Cambridge: Cambridge University Press.

Bloom, Paul (1990). Syntactic distinctions in child language. *Journal of Child Language* 17: 343–355.

Bloom, Paul (1994). Possible names: the role of syntax-semantics mappings in the acquisition of nominals. In *The Acquisition of the Lexicon*, ed. by Lila Gleitman and Barbara Landau, pp. 297–329. Cambridge: MIT Press.

Bloomfield, Leonard (1933). *Language*. New York: Holt.

Bock, J. Kathryn (1986). Syntactic persistence in language production. *Cognitive Psychology* 18: 355–387.

Bock, J. Kathryn, and Anthony S. Kroch (1989). The isolability of syntactic processing. In *Linguistic Structure in Language Processing*, ed. by Greg N. Carlson and Michael K. Tanenhaus, pp. 157–196. Dordrecht: Reidel.

Bolinger, Dwight (1966). Adjectives: attribution and predication. *Lingua* 18: 1–34.

Bolinger, Dwight (1977a). Another glance at main clause phenomena. *Language* 53: 511–519.

Bolinger, Dwight (1977b). *Meaning and Form*. London: Longmans.

Bolinger, Dwight (1982). Intonation and its parts. *Language* 58: 505–533.

Borer, Hagit (1984). *Parametric Syntax: Case Studies in Semitic and Romance Languages*. Studies in Generative Grammar 13. Dordrecht: Foris.

Borsley, Robert D. (1991). *Syntacic Theory: A Unified Approach*. London: Edward Arnold.

Bouchard, Denis (1991). From conceptual structure to syntactic structure. In *Views on Phrase Structure*, ed. by Katherine Leffel and Denis Bouchard, pp. 21–36. Dordrecht: Kluwer.

Brent, Michael (1993). From grammar to lexicon: Unsupervised learning of lexical syntax. *Computational Linguistics* 19: 243–262.

Bresnan, Joan W. (1978). A realistic transformational grammar. In *Linguistic Theory and Psychological Reality*, ed. by Morris Halle, Joan Bresnan, and George Miller, pp. 1–59. Cambridge: MIT Press.

Bresnan, Joan W., ed. (1982). *The Mental Representation of Grammatical Relations*. Cambridge: MIT Press.

Brody, Jill (1984). Some problems with the concept of basic word order. *Linguistics* 22: 711–736.

Brody, Michael (1995). *Lexico-logical Form: A Radically Minimalist Theory.* Cambridge: MIT Press.

Brugman, Claudia M. (1988). *The Story of Over: Polysemy, Semantics, and the Structure of the Lexicon.* New York: Garland.

Bybee, Joan L. (1985a). Diagrammatic iconicity in stem-inflection relations. In *Iconicity in Syntax*, ed. by John Haiman, pp. 11–48. Amsterdam: John Benjamins.

Bybee, Joan L. (1985b). *Morphology: A Study of the Relation between Meaning and Form.* Typological Studies in Language 9. Amsterdam: John Benjamins.

Bybee, Joan L. (1998). Usage-based phonology. In *Functionalism and Formalism in Linguistics*, vol. 1, *General Papers*, ed. by Michael Darnell, Edith Moravcsik, Frederick J. Newmeyer, Michael Noonan, and Kathleen Wheatley, pp. 209–240. Amsterdam: John Benjamins.

Bybee, Joan L., and Jean E. Newman (1995). Are stem changes as natural as affixes? *Linguistics* 33: 633–654.

Bybee, Joan L., and William Pagliuca (1985). Cross-linguistic comparison and the development of grammatical meaning. In *Historical Semantics and Historical Word Formation*, ed. by Jacek Fisiak, pp. 59–83. Berlin: de Gruyter.

Bybee, Joan L., and William Pagliuca (1987). The evolution of future meaning. In *Papers from the Seventh International Conference on Historical Linguistics*, ed. by Anna G. Ramat, Onofrio Carruba, and Giuliano Bernini, pp. 109–122. Amsterdam: John Benjamins.

Bybee, Joan L., William Pagliuca, and Revere D. Perkins (1990). On asymmetries in the affixation of grammatical material. In *Studies in Typology and Diachrony: Papers Presented to Joseph H. Greenberg on His 75th Birthday*, ed. by William Croft, Keith Denning, and Suzanne Kemmer, pp. 1–42. Amsterdam: John Benjamins.

Bybee, Joan L., William Pagliuca, and Revere D. Perkins (1991). Back to the future. In *Approaches to Grammaticalization*, vol. 2, *Focus on Types of Grammatical Markers*, ed. by Elizabeth C. Traugott and Bernd Heine, pp. 17–58. Amsterdam: John Benjamins.

Bybee, Joan L., Revere D. Perkins, and William Pagliuca (1994). *The Evolution of Grammar: Tense, Aspect, and Modality in the Languages of the World.* Chicago: University of Chicago Press.

Bynon, Theodora (1986). August Schleicher: Indo-Europeanist and general linguist. In *Studies in the History of Western Linguistics in Honour of R. H. Robins*, ed. by Theodora Bynon and F. R. Palmer, pp. 129–149. Cambridge: Cambridge University Press.

Campbell, Lyle (1991). Some grammaticalization changes in Estonian and their implications. In *Approaches to Grammaticalization*, vol. 1, *Focus on Theoretical and Methodological Issues*, ed. by Elizabeth C. Traugott and Bernd Heine, pp. 285–299. Amsterdam: John Benjamins.

Campbell, Lyle (1997). Approaches to reanalysis and its role in the explanation of syntactic change. In *Papers from the 12th International Conference on Historical Linguistics*, ed. by Linda van Bergen and Richard M. Hogg. Amsterdam: John Benjamins.

Cann, Ronnie (1993). *Formal Semantics: An Introducton.* Cambridge: Cambridge University Press.

Capell, Arthur (1962). *Some Linguistic Types in Australia.* Sydney: Oceania Linguistic Monographs.

Carstairs, Andrew (1987). Diachronic evidence and the affix-clitic distinction. In *Papers from the Seventh International Conference on Historical Linguistics*, ed. by Anna G. Ramat, Onofrio Carruba, and Giuliano Bernini, pp. 151–162. Amsterdam: John Benjamins.

Carston, Robyn (1993). Conjunction, explanation, and relevance. *Lingua* 90: 27–48.

Carston, Robyn (1995). Quantity maxims and generalised implicature. *Lingua* 96: 213–244.

Chafe, Wallace (1970). *Meaning and the Structure of Language.* Chicago: University of Chicago Press.

Chafe, Wallace (1976). Givenness, contrastiveness, definiteness, subjects, topics, and point of view. In *Subject and Topic*, ed. by Charles Li, pp. 25–55. New York: Academic Press.

Chafe, Wallace (1982). Integration and involvement in speaking, writing, and oral literature. In *Spoken and Written Language: Exploring Orality and Literacy*, ed. by Deborah Tannen, pp. 35–53. Norwood, N.J.: Ablex.

Chao, Yuen Ren (1968). *A Grammar of Spoken Chinese.* Berkeley: University of California Press.

Chierchia, Gennaro (1984). Topics in the syntax and semantics of infinitives and gerunds. Unpublished Ph.D. dissertation, University of Massachusetts.

Chierchia, Gennaro, and Sally McConnell-Ginet (1990). *Meaning and Grammar.* Cambridge: MIT Press.

Chomsky, Noam (1955/1975). *The Logical Structure of Linguistic Theory.* Chicago: University of Chicago Press.

Chomsky, Noam (1957). *Syntactic Structures.* Janua Linguarum Series Minor 4. The Hague: Mouton.

Chomsky, Noam (1961). Some methodological remarks on generative grammar. *Word* 17: 219–239. Reprinted under the title "Degrees of grammaticalness" in *The Stucture of Language: Readings in the Philosophy of Language*, ed. by J. A. Fodor and J. Katz, pp. 384–389. Englewood Cliffs, N.J.: Prentice-Hall, 1964.

Chomsky, Noam (1962). Explanatory models in linguistics. In *Logic, Methodology, and Philosophy of Science*, ed. by E. Nagel, P. Suppes, and A. Tarski, pp. 528–550. Stanford, Calif.: Stanford University Press.

Chomsky, Noam (1965). *Aspects of the Theory of Syntax*. Cambridge: MIT Press.

Chomsky, Noam (1970). Remarks on nominalization. In *Readings in English Transformational Grammar*, ed. by Roderick Jacobs and Peter Rosenbaum, pp. 184–221. Waltham, Mass.: Ginn.

Chomsky, Noam (1971). Deep structure, surface structure, and semantic interpretation. In *Semantics: An Interdisciplinary Reader in Philosophy, Linguistics, and Psychology*, ed. by Danny Steinberg and Leon Jakobovits, pp. 183–216. Cambridge: Cambridge University Press.

Chomsky, Noam (1972). *Language and Mind*. Enlarged edition. New York: Harcourt Brace Jovanovich.

Chomsky, Noam (1973). Conditions on transformations. In *A Festschrift for Morris Halle*, ed. by Steven Anderson and Paul Kiparsky, pp. 232–286. New York: Holt Rinehart and Winston.

Chomsky, Noam (1975a). Questions of form and interpretation. *Linguistic Analysis* 1: 75–109. Reprinted in N. Chomsky, *Essays on Form and Interpretation*, pp. 25–59. Amsterdam: North Holland, 1977.

Chomsky, Noam (1975b). *Reflections on Language*. New York: Pantheon.

Chomsky, Noam (1976). Conditions on rules of grammar. *Linguistic Analysis* 2: 303–351.

Chomsky, Noam (1977). Introduction. In his *Essays on Form and Interpretation*, pp. 1–21. New York: North-Holland.

Chomsky, Noam (1979). *Language and Responsibility: Based on Conversations with Mitsou Ronat*. New York: Pantheon.

Chomsky, Noam (1980a). On binding. *Linguistic Inquiry* 11: 1–46.

Chomsky, Noam (1980b). *Rules and Representations*. New York: Columbia University Press.

Chomsky, Noam (1980c). On cognitive structures and their development: a reply to Piaget. In *Language and Learning: The Debate between Jean Piaget and Noam Chomsky*, ed. by Massimo Piattelli-Palmarini, pp. 35–54. Cambridge: Harvard University Press.

Chomsky, Noam (1981). *Lectures on Government and Binding*. Studies in Generative Grammar 9. Dordrecht: Foris.

Chomsky, Noam (1982a). *Some Concepts and Consequences of the Theory of Government and Binding*. Cambridge: MIT Press.

Chomsky, Noam (1982b). *The Generative Enterprise: A Discussion with Riny Huybregts and Henk van Riemsdijk*. Dordrecht: Foris.

Chomsky, Noam (1986a). *Barriers*. Cambridge: MIT Press.

Chomsky, Noam (1986b). *Knowledge of Language: Its Nature, Origin, and Use*. New York: Praeger.

Chomsky, Noam (1988). *Language and Problems of Knowledge: The Managua Lectures*. Current Studies in Linguistics 16. Cambridge: MIT Press.

Chomsky, Noam (1990). On formalization and formal linguistics. *Natural Language and Linguistic Theory* 8: 143–147.

Chomsky, Noam (1991). Linguistics and adjacent fields: a personal view. In *The Chomskyan Turn: Generative Linguistics, Philosophy, Mathematics, and Psychology*, ed. by Asa Kasher, pp. 3–25. Oxford: Blackwell.

Chomsky, Noam (1993). A minimalist program for linguistic theory. In *The View from Building 20: Essays in Honor of Sylvain Bromberger*, ed. by Kenneth Hale and Samuel Jay Keyser, pp. 1–52. Cambridge: MIT Press.

Chomsky, Noam (1995). *The Minimalist Program*. Cambridge: MIT Press.

Chomsky, Noam, and Howard Lasnik (1977). Filters and control. *Linguistic Inquiry* 8: 425–504.

Chung, Sandra (1978). *Case Marking and Grammatical Relations in Polynesian*. Austin: University of Texas Press.

Churchward, Clerk M. (1940). *Rotuman Grammar and Dictionary*. Sydney: Australasian Medical Publishing Co.

Cinque, Guglielmo (1981). On Keenan and Comrie's primary relativization constraint. *Linguistic Inquiry* 12: 293–308.

Cinque, Guglielmo (1996). The 'antisymmetric' program: theoretical and typological implications. *Journal of Linguistics* 32: 447–465.

Clahsen, Harald (1988). Parameterized grammatical theory and language acquisition. In *Linguistic Theory in Second Language Acquisition*, ed. by Suzanne Flynn and Wayne O'Neil, pp. 47–75. Reidel: Kluwer.

Clahsen, Harald, and Pieter Muysken (1986). The avaliability of universal grammar to adult and child learners. *Second Language Research* 2: 93–119.

Clark, Herbert H., and Susan E. Haviland (1974). Psychological processes as linguistic explanation. *Explaining Linguistic Phenomena*, ed. by David Cohen, pp. 91–124. Washington: Hemisphere Publishing Corporation.

Clark, Robin, and Ian Roberts (1993). A computational theory of language learnability and language change. *Linguistic Inquiry* 24: 299–345.

Claudi, Ulrike (1994). Word order change as category change: the Mande case. *Perspectives on Grammaticalization*, ed. by William Pagliuca, pp. 191–232. Amsterdam: John Benjamins.

Claudi, Ulrike, and Bernd Heine (1986). On the metaphorical base of grammar. *Studies in Language* 10: 297–335.

Coleman, Linda, and Paul Kay (1981). Prototype semantics. *Language* 57: 26–44.

Comrie, Bernard (1978). Ergativity. In *Syntactic Typology*, ed. by Winfred P. Lehmann, pp. 329–394. Sussex: Harvester Press.

Comrie, Bernard (1984a). Form and function in explaining language universals. In *Explanations for Language Universals*, ed. by Brian Butterworth, Bernard Comrie, and Östen Dahl, pp. 87–104. Berlin: Mouton.

Comrie, Bernard (1984b). Language universals and linguistic argumentation: a reply to Coopmans. *Journal of Linguistics* 20: 155–164.

Comrie, Bernard (1988). Linguistic typology. In *Linguistic Theory: Foundations*, ed. by Frederick Newmeyer, pp. 447–461. Cambridge: Cambridge University Press.

Comrie, Bernard (1989). *Language Universals and Linguistic Typology*. Second Edition. Chicago: University of Chicago Press.

Comrie, Bernard, and Edward L. Keenan (1979). Noun phrase accessibility revisited. *Language* 55: 649–664.

Contini-Morava, Ellen (1983). Tense and non-tense in Swahili grammar: semantic asymmetry between affirmative and negative. Unpublished Ph.D. dissertation, Columbia University.

Coopmans, Peter (1984). Surface word-order typology and universal grammar. *Language* 60: 55–69.

Corbett, Greville G. (1978). Numerous squishes and squishy numerals in Slavonic. *International Review of Slavic Linguistics* 3: 43–73.

Corrigan, Roberta, Fred Eckman, and Michael Noonan, eds. (1989). *Linguistic Categorization*. Amsterdam: John Benjamins.

Crago, Martha B., and Shanley E. M. Allen (1996). Building the case for impairment in linguistic representation. In *Toward a Genetics of Language*, ed. by Mabel L. Rice, pp. 261–296. Mahwah, N.J.: Erlbaum.

Crain, Stephen (1991). Language acquisition in the absence of experience. *Behavioral and Brain Sciences* 14: 597–650.

Crain, Stephen, and Janet D. Fodor (1993). Competence and performance in child language. In *Language and Cognition: A Developmental Perspective*, ed. by Esther Dromi and Sidney Strauss, pp. 141–171. Norwood, N.J.: Ablex.

Crain, Stephen, and Cecile McKee (1986). Acquisition of structural restrictions on anaphora. *North Eastern Linguistic Society* 16: 94–110.

Crain, Stephen, and Mineharu Nakayama (1987). Structure dependence in grammar formation. *Language* 63: 522–543.

Crazzolara, J. Pasquale (1955). *A Study of the Acooli Language*. London: Oxford University Press.

Croft, William (1988a). Agreement vs. case marking and direct objects. In *Agreement in Natural Language: Approaches, Theories, Descriptions*, ed. by Michael Barlow and Charles A. Ferguson, pp. 159–179. Stanford, Calif.: Center for the Study of Language and Information.

Croft, William (1988b). Review of *Basic Word Order: Functional Principles*, by R. Tomlin. Linguistics 26: 892–895.

Croft, William (1990). *Typology and Universals*. Cambridge: Cambridge University Press.

Croft, William (1991). *Syntactic Categories and Grammatical Relations*. Chicago: University of Chicago Press.

Croft, William (1995a). Autonomy and functionalist linguistics. *Language* 71: 490–532.

Croft, William (1995b). Modern syntactic typology. In *Approaches to Language Typology*, ed. by Masayoshi Shibatani and Theodora Bynon, pp. 85–144. Oxford: Clarendon Press.

Croft, William (1996a). Bringing chaos into order: mechanisms for the actuation of language change. Unpublished manuscript, University of Manchester.

Croft, William (1996b). Linguistic selection: an utterance-based evolutionary theory of language change. *Nordic Journal of Linguistics* 19: 99–139.

Croft, William (1998). What (some) functionalists can learn from (some) formalists. In *Functionalism and Formalism in Linguistics*, vol. 1, *General Papers*, ed. by Michael Darnell, Edith Moravcsik, Frederick J. Newmeyer, Michael Noonan, and Kathleen Wheatley, pp. 85–108. Amsterdam: John Benjamins.

Cromer, Richard F. (1978). The basis of childhood dysphasia: a linguistic approach. In *Developmental Dysphasia*, ed. by M. Wyke, pp. 85–134. London: Academic Press.

Cruse, D. Alan (1992). Cognitive linguistics and word meaning: Taylor on linguistic categorization. *Journal of Linguistics* 28: 165–184.

Culicover, Peter W. (1988). Autonomy, predication, and thematic relations. In *Thematic Relations*, ed. by Wendy Wilkins, pp. 37–60. Syntax and Semantics 21. New York: Academic Press.

Culicover, Peter W., and Wendy Wilkins (1984). *Locality in Linguistic Theory*. New York: Academic Press.

Dalalakis, Jenny (1994). Familial language impairment in Greek. *McGill Working Papers in Linguistics* 10: 216–228.

Davies, Anna Morpurgo (1975). Language classification in the nineteenth century. In *Historiography of Linguistics*, ed. by Thomas A. Sebeok, pp. 607–716. The Hague: Mouton.

Deane, Paul D. (1991). Limits to attention: a cognitive theory of island phenomena. *Cognitive Linguistics* 2: 1–64.

Deane, Paul D. (1992). *Grammar in Mind and Brain: Explorations in Cognitive Syntax*. Cognitive Linguistics Research 2. The Hague: Mouton de Gruyter.

Deane, Paul D. (1996). On Jackendoff's conceptual semantics. *Cognitive Linguistics* 7: 35–91.

DeLancey, Scott (1985). The analysis-synthesis-lexis cycle in Tibeto-Burman: a case study in motivated change. In *Iconicity in Syntax*, ed. by John Haiman, pp. 367–390. Amsterdam: John Benjamins.

Denham, Kristin (1996). The presentational deictic in generative and cognitive grammar. Paper presented at Conference on Functionalism and Formalism in Linguistics, Milwaukee.

Dik, Simon C. (1981). *Functional Grammar*. Publications in Language Sciences 7. Dordrecht: Foris.

Dik, Simon C. (1989). *The Theory of Functional Grammar. Part 1: The Structure of the Clause*. Functional Grammar Series 9. Dordrecht: Foris.

Diver, William (1995). Theory. In *Meaning as Explanation: Advances in Linguistic Sign Theory*, ed. by Ellen Contini-Morava and Barbara S. Goldberg, pp. 43–114. Berlin: De Gruyter.

Dixon, R. M. W. (1977). Where have all the adjectives gone? *Studies in Language* 1: 1–80.

Dixon, R. M. W. (1979). Ergativity. *Language* 55: 59–138.

Dowty, David R. (1972). Studies in the logic of verb aspect and time reference in English. Unpublished Ph.D. dissertation, University of Texas.

Dowty, David R. (1979). *Word Meaning and Montague Grammar*. Dordrecht: Reidel.

Dressler, Wolfgang U. (1990). The cognitive perspective of 'naturalist' linguistic models. *Cognitive Linguistics* 1: 75–98.

Dressler, Wolfgang U., Willi Mayerthaler, Oswald Panagl, and Wolfgang U. Wurzel, eds. (1987). *Leitmotifs in Natural Morphology*. Studies in Language Companion Series 10. Amsterdam: John Benjamins.

Dryer, Matthew S. (1980). The positional tendencies of sentential noun phrases in universal grammar. *Canadian Journal of Linguistics* 25: 123–195.

Dryer, Matthew S. (1989a). Discourse-governed word order and word order typology. *Belgian Journal of Linguistics* 4: 69–90.

Dryer, Matthew S. (1989b). Large linguistic areas and language sampling. *Studies in Language* 13: 257–292.

Dryer, Matthew S. (1992). The Greenbergian word order correlations. *Language* 68: 81–138.

Dryer, Matthew S. (1995). Frequency and pragmatically unmarked word order. In *Word Order in Discourse*, ed. by Pamela Downing and Michael Noonan, pp. 105–136. Amsterdam: John Benjamins.

Dryer, Matthew S. (1997). Are grammatical relations universal? In *Essays on Language Function and Language Type*, ed. by Joan Bybee, John Haiman, and Sandra A. Thompson, pp. 115–143. Amsterdam: John Benjamins.

Du Bois, John (1985). Competing motivations. In *Iconicity in Syntax*, ed. by John Haiman, pp. 343–365. Amsterdam: John Benjamins.

Du Bois, John (1987). The discourse basis of ergativity. *Language* 63: 805–855.

Emonds, Joseph E. (1972a). A reformulation of Grimm's law. In *Contributions to Generative Phonology*, ed. by Michael K. Brame, pp. 108–122. Austin: University of Texas Press.

Emonds, Joseph E. (1972b). Evidence that indirect object movement is a structure-preserving rule. *Foundations of Language* 8: 546–561.

Emonds, Joseph E. (1976). *A Transformational Approach to English Syntax*. New York: Academic Press.

Emonds, Joseph E. (1980). Word order in generative grammar. *Journal of Linguistic Research* 1: 33–54.

Emonds, Joseph E. (1985). *A Unified Theory of Syntactic Categories*. Studies in Generative Grammar 19. Dordrecht: Foris.

Emonds, Joseph E. (1986). Grammatically deviant prestige constructions. In *A Festschrift for Sol Saporta*, ed. by Michael Brame, Heles Contreras, and Frederick J. Newmeyer, pp. 93–131. Seattle: Noit Amrofer.

Engdahl, Elisabet (1983). Parasitic gaps. *Linguistics and Philosophy* 6: 5–34.

Epstein, Samuel D., Suzanne Flynn, and Gita Martohardjono (1996). Second language acquisition: theoretical and experimental issues in contemporary research. *Behavioral and Brain Sciences* 19: 677–714.

Erteschik-Shir, Nomi (1979). Discourse constraints on dative movement. *Discourse and Syntax*, ed. by Talmy Givón, pp. 441–468. Syntax and Semantics 12. New York: Academic Press.

Erteschik-Shir, Nomi (1995). The dynamics of focus structure. Unpublished manuscript, Ben Gurion University of the Negev, Israel.

Estival, Dominique (1985). Syntactic priming of the passive in English. *Text* 5: 7–21.

Everett, Daniel L. (1987). Clitic doubling, reflexives, and word order alternations in Yagua. *Language* 65: 339–372.

Fauconnier, Gilles (1985). *Mental Spaces*. Cambridge: MIT Press.

Ferguson, Charles A., and Michael Barlow (1988). Introduction. In *Agreement in Natural Language: Approaches, Theories, Descriptions*, ed. by Michael Barlow and Charles A. Ferguson, pp. 1–22. Stanford, Calif.: Center for the Study of Language and Information.

Fidelholtz, James L. (1975). Word frequency and vowel reduction in English. *Chicago Linguistic Society* 11, 200–213.

Fillmore, Charles J. (1968). The case for case. In *Universals in Linguistic Theory*, ed. by Emmon Bach and Robert Harms, pp. 1–90. New York: Holt, Rinehart and Winston.

Fillmore, Charles J. (1982). Frame semantics. *Linguistics in the Morning Calm*, ed. by Linguistics Society of Korea, pp. 111–138. Seoul: Hanshin.

Fillmore, Charles J., and Paul Kay (1993). *Construction Grammar Coursebook*. Berkeley: Copy Central.

Fillmore, Charles J., Paul Kay, and Mary Catherine O'Connor (1988). Regularity and idiomaticity in grammatical constructions: the case of 'let alone'. *Language* 64: 501–538.

Finer, Daniel L., and Ellen I. Broselow (1986). Second language acquisition of reflexive binding. *North Eastern Linguistic Society* 16: 154–168.

Fintel, Kai von (1995). The formal semantics of grammaticalization. *North Eastern Linguistic Society* 25 (part 2): 175–190.

Firbas, Jan (1964). On defining the theme in functional sentence analysis. *Travaux Linguistique de Prague* 1: 267–280.

Firbas, Jan (1966). On the concept of communicative dynamism in the theory of functional sentence perspective. *Sbornik Praci Filosoficke Fakulty Brnenske University* A-19: 135–144.

Firbas, Jan (1987). On the operation of communicative dynamism in functional sentence perspective. *Leuvense Bijdragen* 76: 289–304.

Fiva, Toril (1984). NP-internal chains in Norwegian. *Nordic Journal of Linguistics* 8: 25–47.

Fleischman, Suzanne (1982). *The Future in Thought and Language: Diachronic Evidence from Romance*. Cambridge: Cambridge University Press.

Fletcher, Paul (1990). Untitled scientific correspondence. *Nature* 346.

Fletcher, Paul (1996). Language impairment in a British family: characteristics and interpretation. Paper presented to the Evolution of Human Language Conference, Edinburgh.

Fletcher, Paul, and Richard Ingham (1995). Grammatical impairment. *The Handbook of Child Language*, ed. by Paul Fletcher and Brian MacWhinney, pp. 603–622. Oxford: Blackwell.

Flynn, Suzanne (1987). *A Parameter-Setting Model of L2 Acquisition*. Dordrecht: Reidel.

Fodor, Janet D. (1978). Parsing strategies and constraints on transformations. *Linguistic Inquiry* 9: 427–473.

Fodor, Janet D. (1984). Constraints on gaps: is the parser a significant influence? *Explanations for Language Universals*, ed. by Brian Butterworth, Bernard Comrie, and Östen Dahl, pp. 9–34. Berlin: Mouton.

Fodor, Janet D. (1998). Unambiguous triggers. *Linguistic Inquiry* 29: 1–36.

Fodor, Jerry A. (1983). *The Modularity of Mind*. Cambridge: MIT Press.

Fodor, Jerry A., and Ernest Lepore (1996). The red herring and the pet fish: why concepts still can't be prototypes. *Cognition* 58: 253–270.

Foley, William A., and Robert D. Van Valin (1984). *Functional Syntax and Universal Grammar*. Cambridge Studies in Linguistics 38. Cambridge: Cambridge University Press.

Forner, Monika, Jeanette K. Gundel, Kathleen Houlihan, and Gerald Sanders (1992). On the historical development of marked forms. *Explanation in Historical Linguistics*, ed. by Garry W. Davis and Gregory K. Iverson, pp. 95–104. Amsterdam: John Benjamins.

Fortescue, Michael (1980). Affix ordering in West Greenlandic derivational processes. *International Journal of American Linguistics* 46: 259–278.

Fox, Barbara A. (1987). The noun phrase accessibility hierarchy revisited. *Language* 63: 856–870.

Fox, Barbara A., and Sandra A. Thompson (1990). A discourse explanation of the grammar of relative clauses in English conversation. *Language* 66: 297–316.

Frajzyngier, Zygmunt (1987). Encoding locative in Chadic. *Journal of West African Languages* 17: 81–97.

Frajzyngier, Zygmunt (1996). *Grammaticalization of the Complex Sentence: A Case Study in Chadic*. Studies in Language Companion Series 32. Amsterdam: John Benjamins.

Frazier, Lyn (1985). Syntactic complexity. *Natural Language Parsing: Psychological, Computational, and Theoretical Perspectives*, ed. by David Dowty, Lauri Karttunen, and Arnold M. Zwicky, pp. 129–189. Cambridge: Cambridge University Press.

Fukuda, Suzy E., and Shinji Fukuda (1994). Developmental language impairment in Japanese: a linguistic investigation. *McGill Working Papers in Linguistics* 10: 150–177.

Fukui, Naoki (1995). The principles-and-parameters approach: a comparative syntax of English and Japanese. *Approaches to Language Typology*, ed. by Masayoshi Shibatani and Theodora Bynon, pp. 327–372. Oxford: Clarendon Press.

Gabelentz, Georg von der (1891). *Die Sprachwissenschaft: Ihre Aufgaben, Methoden und bisherigen Ergebnisse*. Leipzig: Weigel.

Gaines, Philip (1993). A generative phonology account of Lakoff's 'paragon intonation' construction. Unpublished manuscript, University of Washington.

Gamkrelidze, T. V., and V. V. Ivanov (1973). Sprachtypologie und die Rekonstruktion der gemeinindogermanischen Verschlüsse. *Phonetika* 27: 150–156.

García, Erica (1979). Discourse without syntax. In *Discourse and Syntax*, ed. by Talmy Givón, pp. 23–49. Syntax and Semantics 12. New York: Academic Press.

Garrett, Andrew (1990a). Hittite enclitic subjects and transitive verbs. *Journal of Cuneiform Studies* 42: 227–242.

Garrett, Andrew (1990b). The origin of NP split ergativity. *Language* 66: 261–296.

Gazdar, Gerald (1979). *Pragmatics: Implicature, Presupposition, and Logical Form*. New York: Academic Press.

Gazdar, Gerald, and Ewan Klein (1978). Review of *Formal Semantics of Natural Language*, ed. by E. L. Keenan. *Language* 54: 661–667.

Gazdar, Gerald, Ewan Klein, Geoffrey Pullum, and Ivan Sag (1985). *Generalized Phrase Structure Grammar*. Cambridge: Harvard University Press.

Geeraerts, Dirk (1991). Review of *Linguistic Categorization*, by J. Taylor. *Linguistics* 29: 161–167.

Geeraerts, Dirk (1993). Vagueness's puzzles, polysemy's vagaries. *Cognitive Linguistics* 4: 223–272.

Geis, Michael L., and Arnold M. Zwicky (1971). On invited inferences. *Linguistic Inquiry* 2: 561–566.

Gibson, Edward, and Kenneth Wexler (1994). Triggers. *Linguistic Inquiry* 25: 407–454.

Gilligan, Gary M. (1987). A cross-linguistic approach to the pro-drop parameter. Unpublished Ph.D. dissertation, University of Southern California.

Givón, Talmy (1971). Historical syntax and synchronic morohology: an archaeologist's field trip. *Chicago Linguistic Society* 7: 394–415.

Givón, Talmy (1973). The time-axis phenomenon. *Language* 49: 890–925.

Givón, Talmy (1975). Serial verbs and syntactic change: Niger-Congo. *Word Order and Word Order Change*, ed. by Charles N. Li, pp. 47–112. Austin: University of Texas Press.

Givón, Talmy (1979a). *On Understanding Grammar*. New York: Academic Press.

Givón, Talmy (1979b). Preface. In *Discourse and Syntax*, ed. by Talmy Givón, pp. xiii–xx. Syntax and Semantics 12. New York: Academic Press.

Givón, Talmy (1980). The binding hierarchy and the typology of complements. *Studies in Language* 4: 333–377.

Givón, Talmy (1981a). On the development of the numeral 'one' as an indefinite marker. *Folia Linguistics Historica* 2: 35–53.

Givón, Talmy (1981b). Typology and functional domains. *Studies in Language* 5: 163–193.

Givón, Talmy (1982). Tense-aspect-modality: the creole prototype and beyond. In *Tense-Aspect: Between Semantics and Pragmatics*, ed. by Paul J. Hopper. Amsterdam: John Benjamins.

Givón, Talmy (1983). Topic continuity and word order pragmatics in Ute. In *Topic Continuity in Discourse: A Quantitative Cross-Language Study*, ed. by Talmy Givón, pp. 141–214. Amsterdam: John Benjamins.

Givón, Talmy (1984). *Syntax: A Functional-Typological Introduction*. Vol. 1. Amsterdam: John Benjamins.

Givón, Talmy (1985). Iconicity, isomorphism, and non-arbitrary coding in syntax. In *Iconicity in Syntax*, ed. by John Haiman, pp. 187–220. Amsterdam: John Benjamins.

Givón, Talmy (1986). Prototypes: between Plato and Wittgenstein. In *Noun Classes and Categorization*, ed. by Colette Craig, pp. 77–102. Amsterdam: John Benjamins.

Givón, Talmy (1988). The pragmatics of word order: predictability, importance, and attention. In *Studies in Syntactic Typology*, ed. by Michael Hammond, Edith Moravcsik, and Jessica Wirth, pp. 243–284. Amsterdam: John Benjamins.

Givón, Talmy (1989). *Mind, Code, and Context: Essays in Pragmatics.* Hillsdale, N.J.: Erlbaum.

Givón, Talmy (1990). *Syntax: A Functional-Typological Introduction.* Vol. 2. Amsterdam: John Benjamins.

Givón, Talmy (1991a). Isomorphism in the grammatical code: cognitive and biological considerations. *Studies in Language* 15: 85–114.

Givón, Talmy (1991b). Serial verbs and the mental reality of 'event': grammatical vs. cognitive packaging. In *Approaches to Grammaticalization*, vol. 1, *Focus on Theoretical and Methodological Issues*, ed. by Elizabeth C. Traugott and Bernd Heine, pp. 81–127. Amsterdam: John Benjamins.

Givón, Talmy (1995). *Functionalism and Grammar.* Amsterdam: John Benjamins.

Gleitman, Lila, and Barbara Landau, eds. (1994). *The Acquisition of the Lexicon.* Cambridge: MIT Press.

Goad, Heather, and Myrna Gopnik (1994). Phoneme discrimination in familial language impairment. *McGill Working Papers in Linguistics* 10: 10–15.

Goad, Heather, and Myrna Gopnik (1997). Three models for the description of SLI. Unpublished paper, McGill University.

Goldberg, Adele E. (1989). A unified account of the semantics of the English ditransitive. *Berkeley Linguistics Society* 15, 79–90.

Goldberg, Adele E. (1995). *Constructions: A Construction Grammar Approach to Argument Structure.* Chicago: University of Chicago Press.

Goldberg, Adele E. (1996). Jackendoff and construction-based grammar. *Cognitive Linguistics* 7: 3–19.

Goldsmith, John, and Eric Woisetschlaeger (1982). The logic of the English progressive. *Linguistic Inquiry* 13: 79–89.

Gonda, Jan (1971). *Old Indian.* Leiden: Brill.

Goodman, Morris (1985). Review of *Roots of Language*, by D. Bickerton. *International Journal of American Linguistics* 51: 109–137.

Gopnik, Myrna (1990). Dysphasia in an extended family. *Nature* 344: 715.

Gopnik, Myrna (1992). Theoretical implications of inherited dysphasia. In *Other Children, Other Languages*, ed. by Yonata Levy, pp. 331–358. Hillsdale, N.J.: Erlbaum.

Gopnik, Myrna (1994a). The articulatory hypothesis: production of final alveolars in monomorphemic words. *McGill Working Papers in Linguistics* 10: 129–134.

Gopnik, Myrna (1994b). The family. *McGill Working Papers in Linguistics* 10: 1–4.

Gopnik, Myrna (1994c). Impairments of tense in a familial language disorder. *Journal of Neurolinguistics* 8: 109–133.

Gopnik, Myrna (1994d). The perceptual processing hypothesis revisited. *McGill Working Papers in Linguistics* 10: 135–141.

Gopnik, Myrna, and Martha Crago (1991). Familial aggregation of a developmental language disorder. *Cognition* 39: 1–50.

Gopnik, Myrna, Jenny Dalalakis, Shinji Fukuda, Suzy Fukuda, and E. Kehayia (1996). Genetic language impairment: unruly grammars. *Proceedings of the British Academy* 88: 223–249.

Gopnik, Myrna, and Heather Goad (1997). What underlies inflectional error patterns in genetic dysphasia? *Journal of Neurolinguistics* 10: 109–137.

Gordon, Peter (1985). Level-ordering in lexical development. *Cognition* 21: 73–93.

Grasserie, Raoul de la (1889). De la classification des langues (part 1). *Internationale Zeitschrift für allgemeine Sprachwissenschaft* 4: 374–387.

Grasserie, Raoul de la (1890). De la classification des langues (part 2). *Internationale Zeitschrift für allgemeine Sprachwissenschaft* 5: 296–338.

Green, Georgia M. (1976). Main clause phenomena in subordinate clauses. *Language* 52: 382–397.

Green, Georgia M. (1980). Some wherefores of English inversions. *Language* 56: 582–602.

Green, Georgia M. (1989). *Pragmatics and Natural Language Understanding.* Hillsdale, N.J.: Erlbaum.

Greenberg, Joseph H. (1960). A quantitative approach to the morphological typology of language. *International Journal of American Linguistics* 26: 192–220.

Greenberg, Joseph H. (1963). Some universals of language with special reference to the order of meaningful elements. In *Universals of Language*, ed. by Joseph Greenberg, pp. 73–113. Cambridge: MIT Press.

Greenberg, Joseph H. (1966). *Language Universals, with Special Reference to Feature Hierarchies.* The Hague: Mouton.

Greenberg, Joseph H. (1978). How does a language acquire gender markers? In *Universals of Human Language*, vol. 3, *Word Structure*, ed. by Joseph H. Greenberg, Charles A. Ferguson, and Edith A. Moravcsik, pp. 47–82. Stanford, Calif.: Stanford University Press.

Greenberg, Joseph H. (1991a). The last stages of grammatical elements: contractive and expansive desemanticization. In *Approaches to Grammaticalization*, vol. 1, *Focus on Theoretical and Methodological Issues*, ed. by Elizabeth C. Traugott and Bernd Heine, pp. 301–314. Amsterdam: John Benjamins.

Greenberg, Joseph H. (1991b). Two approaches to language universals. In *New Vistas in Grammar: Invariance and Variation*, ed. by Linda R. Waugh and Stephen Rudy, pp. 417–435. Amsterdam: John Benjamins.

Grice, H. P. (1975). Logic and conversation. In *Speech Acts*, ed. by Peter Cole and Jerry Morgan, pp. 41–58. Syntax and Semantics 3. New York: Academic Press.

Grimes, Barbara F., ed. (1988). *Ethnologue: Languages of the World.* 11th ed. Dallas: Summer Institute of Linguistics.

Grimshaw, Jane (1981). Form, function, and the language acquisition device. In *The Logical Problem of Language Acquisition*, ed. by C. L. Baker and John J. McCarthy, pp. 165–182. Cambridge: MIT Press.

Grimshaw, Jane (1990). *Argument Structure*. Cambridge: MIT Press.

Grimshaw, Jane (1991). Extended projection. Unpublished manuscript, Brandeis University.

Grimshaw, Jane (1993). Minimal projection, heads, and optimality. Technical report 4. Piscataway, N.J.: Rutgers Center for Cognitive Science.

Grimshaw, Jane (1997). Projection, heads, and optimality. *Linguistic Inquiry* 28: 373–422.

Gundel, Jeanette (1985). 'Shared knowledge' and topicality. *Journal of Pragmatics* 9: 83–107.

Gundel, Jeanette, Nancy Hedberg, and Ron Zacharski (1990). Givenness, implicature, and the form of referring expressions in discourse. *Berkeley Linguistics Society* 16, 442–453.

Hagège, Claude (1976). *La grammaire générative: réflexions critiques*. Paris: Presses Universitaires de France.

Haider, Hubert, Susan Olsen, and Sten Vikner, eds. (1995). *Studies in Comparative Germanic Syntax*. Studies in Natural Language and Linguistic Theory 31. Dordrecht: Kluwer.

Haiman, John (1978a). A study in polysemy. *Studies in Language* 2: 1–34.

Haiman, John (1978b). Conditionals are topics. *Language* 54: 565–589.

Haiman, John (1980a). Dictionaries and encyclopedias. *Lingua* 50: 329–357.

Haiman, John (1980b). The iconicity of grammar: isomorphism and motivation. *Language* 56: 515–540.

Haiman, John (1983). Iconic and economic motivation. *Language* 59: 781–819.

Haiman, John, ed. (1985a). *Iconicity in Syntax*. Typological Studies in Language 6. Amsterdam: John Benjamins.

Haiman, John (1985b). *Natural Syntax: Iconicity and Erosion*. Cambridge: Cambridge University Press.

Haiman, John (1985c). Symmetry. In *Iconicity in Syntax*, ed. by John Haiman, pp. 73–96. Amsterdam: John Benjamins.

Hale, Kenneth (1973). Deep-surface canonical disparities in relation to analogy and change: an Austrialian example. In *Diachronic, Areal, and Typological Linguistics*, ed. by Thomas A. Sebeok, pp. 401–458. The Hague: Mouton.

Hale, Kenneth (1982). Preliminary remarks on configurationality. *North Eastern Linguistic Society* 12: 86–96.

Hale, Kenneth (1983). Warlpiri and the grammar of nonconfigurational languages. *Natural Language and Linguistic Theory* 1: 5–47.

Hale, Kenneth (1992). Basic word order in two 'free word order' languages. In *Pragmatics of Word Order Flexibility*, ed. by Doris Payne, pp. 63–82. Amsterdam: John Benjamins.

Hale, Kenneth, and Samuel Jay Keyser (1993). On argument structure and the lexical expression of syntactic relations. In *The View from Building 20: Essays in Honor of Sylvain Bromberger*, ed. by Kenneth Hale and Samuel Jay Keyser, pp. 53–110. Cambridge: MIT Press.

Hale, Kenneth, and Paul Platero (1986). Parts of speech. In *Features and Projections*, ed. by Pieter Muysken and Henk van Riemsdijk, pp. 31–40. Dordrecht: Foris.

Halle, Morris (1962). Phonology in generative grammar. *Word* 18: 54–72. Reprinted in *The Stucture of Language: Readings in the Philosophy of Language*, ed. by J. A. Fodor and J. Katz, pp. 344–352. Englewood-Cliffs, N.J.: Prentice-Hall, 1964.

Halle, Morris, and Alec Marantz (1993). Distributed morphology and the pieces of inflecton. In *The View from Building 20: Essays in Honor of Sylvain Bromberger*, ed. by Kenneth Hale and Samuel Jay Keyser, pp. 111–176. Cambridge: MIT Press.

Halliday, M. A. K. (1985). *An Introduction to Functional Grammar*. London: Edward Arnold.

Hammond, Michael, Edith Moravcsik, and Jessica Wirth (1988). Language typology and linguistic explanation. In *Studies in Syntactic Typology*, ed. by Michael Hammond, Edith Moravcsik, and Jessica Wirth, pp. 1–24. Amsterdam: John Benjamins.

Harré, Rom (1970). *The Principles of Scientific Thinking*. Chicago: University of Chicago Press.

Harris, Alice C. (1996). Diachronic syntax: lectures presented in Trondheim. Unpublished manuscript, Vanderbilt University.

Harris, Alice C., and Lyle Campbell (1995). *Historical Syntax in Cross-Linguistic Perspective*. Cambridge Studies in Linguistics 74. Cambridge: Cambridge University Press.

Harris, Zellig S. (1941). Review of *Grundzüge der Phonologie*, by N. Trubetzkoy. *Language* 17: 345–349.

Harris, Zellig S. (1951). *Methods in Structural Linguistics*. Chicago: University of Chicago Press.

Haspelmath, Martin (1992). Grammaticalization theory and heads in morphology. In *Morphology Now*, ed. by Mark Aronoff, pp. 69–82, 194–198. Albany: SUNY Press.

Haspelmath, Martin (1993). The diachronic externalization of inflection. *Linguistics* 31: 279–309.

Haspelmath, Martin (1994). Functional categories, X-bar theory, and grammaticalization theory. *Sprachtypologie und Universalienforschung* 47: 3–15.

Haspelmath, Martin (1997). Review of *Historical Syntax in Cross-Linguistic Perspective*, by A. Harris and L. Campbell. *Linguistic Typology*.

Haspelmath, Martin (1998). Does grammaticalization need reanalysis? *Studies in Language* 22: 49–85.

Haviland, John (1980). Guugu Yimidhirr brother-in-law language. *Language and Society* 8: 365–393.

Hawkins, John A. (1983). *Word Order Universals*. New York: Academic Press.

Hawkins, John A. (1985). Complementary methods in universal grammar: a reply to Coopmans. *Language* 61: 569–587.

Hawkins, John A. (1988a). Explaining language universals. In *Explaining Language Universals*, ed. by John A. Hawkins, pp. 3–28. Oxford: Basil Blackwell.

Hawkins, John A. (1988b). On generative and typological approaches to universal grammar. *Lingua* 74: 79–83.

Hawkins, John A. (1994). *A Performance Theory of Order and Constituency*. Cambridge Studies in Linguistics 73. Cambridge: Cambridge University Press.

Hawkins, John A. (1996). Morphological hierarchies, frequency effects, and grammaticalization. Unpublished manuscript, University of Southern California.

Hawkins, John A. (1997). Some issues in a performance theory of word order. In *Constituent Order in the Languages of Europe*, ed. by Anna Siewierska. Berlin: De Gruyter.

Hawkins, John A., and Gary Gilligan (1988). Prefixing and suffixing universals in relation to basic word order. *Lingua* 74: 219–260.

Heath, Jeffrey (1978). *Linguistic Diffusion in Arnhem Land*. Canberra: Australian Institute of Aboriginal Studies.

Heim, Irene (1988). *The Semantics of Definite and Indefinite Noun Phrases*. New York: Garland.

Heine, Bernd (1990). The dative in Ik and Kanuri. In *Studies in Typology and Diachrony: Papers Presented to Joseph H. Greenberg on His 75th birthday*, ed. by William Croft, Keith Denning, and Suzanne Kemmer, pp. 129–149. Amsterdam: John Benjamins.

Heine, Bernd (1993). *Auxiliaries: Cognitive Forces and Grammaticalization*. New York: Oxford University Press.

Heine, Bernd (1994). Grammaticalization as an explanatory parameter. In *Perspectives on Grammaticalization*, ed. by William Pagliuca, pp. 255–287. Amsterdam: John Benjamins.

Heine, Bernd, and Ulrike Claudi (1986). *On the Rise of Grammatical Categories: Some Examples from Maa*. Berlin: Dieter Reimer.

Heine, Bernd, Ulrike Claudi, and Friederike Hünnemeyer (1991a). From cognition to grammar: evidence from African languages. In *Approaches to Grammaticalization*, vol. 1, *Focus on Theoretical and Methodological Issues*, ed. by Elizabeth C. Traugott and Bernd Heine, pp. 149–188. Amsterdam: John Benjamins.

Heine, Bernd, Ulrike Claudi, and Friederike Hünnemeyer (1991b). *Grammaticalization: A Conceptual Framework*. Chicago: University of Chicago Press.

Heine, Bernd, and Mechthild Reh (1984). *Grammaticalization and Reanalysis in African Languages*. Hamburg: Helmut Buske Verlag.

Hempel, Carl (1965). *Aspects of Scientific Explanation*. New York: Free Press.

Hengeveld, Kees (1989). Layers and operators in functional grammar. *Journal of Linguistics* 25: 127–158.

Henry, Alison (1995). *Belfast English and Standard English: Dialect Variation and Parameter Setting*. New York: Oxford University Press.

Herring, Susan C. (1989). Verbless presentation and the discourse basis of ergativity. *Chicago Linguistic Society* 25, *Parasession on Language in Context*, 123–137.

Higginbotham, James (1987). The autonomy of syntax and semantics. In *Modularity in Knowledge Representation and Natural-Language Understanding*, ed. by Jay L. Garfield, pp. 120–131. Cambridge: MIT Press.

Hinds, John (1979). Organizational patterns in discourse. *Discourse and Syntax*, ed. by Talmy Givón, pp. 135–158. Syntax and Semantics 12. New York: Academic Press.

Hjelmslev, Louis (1928). *Principes de grammaire générale*. Copenhagen: A. F. Host and Son.

Hoekstra, Teun (1988). Small clause results. *Lingua* 74: 101–139.

Hoekstra, Teun, and Jan G. Kooij (1988). The innateness hypothesis. In *Explaining Language Universals*, ed. by John A. Hawkins, pp. 31–55. Oxford: Blackwell.

Holm, John (1986). Substrate diffusion. In *Substrata versus Universals in Creole Genesis*, ed. by Pieter Muysken and Norval Smith, pp. 259–278. Amsterdam: John Benjamins.

Hombert, Jean-Marie, and Egidio Marsico (1996). Do vowel systems increase in complexity? Paper presented to the Evolution of Human Language Conference, Edinburgh.

Hooper, Joan, and Sandra A. Thompson (1973). On the applicability of root transformations. *Linguistic Inquiry* 4: 465–498.

Hopper, Paul J. (1973). Glottalized and murmured occlusives in Indo-European. *Glossa* 7: 141–166.

Hopper, Paul J. (1987). Emergent grammar. *Berkeley Linguistics Society* 13: 139–157.

Hopper, Paul J. (1988). Emergent grammar and the apriori grammar postulate. In *Linguistics in Context: Connecting Observation and Understanding*, ed. by Deborah Tannen, pp. 117–134. Norwood, N.J.: Ablex.

Hopper, Paul J., and Sandra A. Thompson (1980). Transitivity in grammar and discourse. *Language* 56: 251–299.

Hopper, Paul J., and Sandra A. Thompson (1984). The discourse basis for lexical categories in universal grammar. *Language* 60: 703–752.

Hopper, Paul J., and Sandra A. Thompson (1985). The iconicity of the universal categories 'noun' and 'verb'. In *Iconicity in Syntax*, ed. by John Haiman, pp. 151–186. Amsterdam: John Benjamins.

Hopper, Paul J., and Elizabeth C. Traugott (1993). *Grammaticalization*. Cambridge: University of Cambridge Press.

Horn, Laurence R. (1984). Toward a new taxonomy of pragmatic inference: q- and r-based implicature. In *Meaning, Form, and Use in Context: Linguistic Applications*, ed. by Deborah Schiffrin, pp. 11–42. Washington: Georgetown University Press.

Horn, Laurence R. (1988). Pragmatic theory. *Linguistic Theory: Foundations*, ed. by Frederick J. Newmeyer, pp. 113–145. Cambridge: Cambridge University Press.

Horn, Laurence R. (1989). *A Natural History of Negation*. Chicago: University of Chicago Press.

Horn, Laurence R. (1993). Economy and redundancy in a dualistic model of natural language. *SKY 1993 (Suomen kielitieteellisen yhdistyksen vuosikirja 1993)*: 33–72.

Hornstein, Norbert, and David Lightfoot (1991). On the nature of lexical government. In *Principles and Parameters in Comparative Grammar*, ed. by Robert Freidin, pp. 365–391. Cambridge: MIT Press.

Hudson, Richard A. (1984). *Word Grammar*. Oxford: Blackwell.

Hudson, Richard A. (1990). *English Word Grammar*. Oxford: Blackwell.

Hudson, Richard A. (1997). Inherent variability and linguistic theory. *Cognitive Linguistics* 8: 73–108.

Hudson, Richard A., Andrew Rosta, Jasper Holmes, and Nikolas Gisborne (1996). Synonyms and syntax. *Journal of Linguistics* 32: 439–446.

Humboldt, Alexander von (1836). *Über die Verschiedenheit des menschlichen Sprachbaues*. Vol. 1 of *Über die Kawisprache auf der Insel Java*. Berlin: Königliche Akademie der Wissenschaften.

Hurford, James R. (1992). An approach to the phylogeny of the language faculty. In *The Evolution of Human Languages*, ed. by John A. Hawkins and Murray Gell-Mann, pp. 273–304. New York: Addison-Wesley.

Hyams, Nina M. (1986). *Language Acquisition and the Theory of Parameters*. Dordrecht: Reidel.

Hyams, Nina M. (1998). Underspecification and modularity in early syntax: a formalist perspective on language acquisition. In *Functionalism and Formalism in Linguistics*, vol. 1, *General Papers*, ed. by Michael Darnell, Edith Moravcsik, Frederick J. Newmeyer, Michael Noonan, and Kathleen Wheatley, pp. 385–414. Amsterdam: John Benjamins.

Hyman, Larry M. (1983). Form and substance in language universals. *Linguistics* 21: 67–86. Reprinted in *Explanations for Language Universals*, ed. by Brian Butterworth, Bernard Comrie, and Östen Dahl, pp. 67–86. Berlin: Mouton, 1984.

Jackendoff, Ray (1972). *Semantic Interpretation in Generative Grammar*. Cambridge: Cambridge University Press.

Jackendoff, Ray (1977). *X-Bar Syntax: A Study of Phrase Structure*. Cambridge: MIT Press.

Jackendoff, Ray (1983). *Semantics and Cognition*. Cambridge: MIT Press.

Jackendoff, Ray (1987). *Consciousness and the Computational Mind*. Cambridge: MIT Press.

Jackendoff, Ray (1990). *Semantic Structures*. Cambridge: MIT Press.

Jackendoff, Ray (1992). Mme. Tussaud meets the binding theory. *Natural Language and Linguistic Theory* 10: 1–32.

Jackendoff, Ray (1996). Conceptual semantics and cognitive linguistics. *Cognitive Linguistics* 7: 93–129.

Jackendoff, Ray (1997). *The Architecture of the Language Faculty*. Cambridge: MIT Press.

Jackendoff, Ray, and Fred Lerdahl (1981). Generative music theory and its relation to psychology. *Journal of Music Theory* 25: 45–90.

Jaeggli, Osvaldo (1980). Remarks on *to* contraction. *Linguistic Inquiry* 11: 239–246.

Jaeggli, Osvaldo, ed. (1981). *Topics in Romance Syntax*. Studies in Generative Grammar 12. Dordrecht: Foris.

Jaeggli, Osvaldo, and Kenneth J. Safir, eds. (1989). *The Null Subject Parameter*. Studies in Natural Language and Linguistic Theory 15. Dordrecht: Reidel.

Jakobson, Roman (1932/1971). Zur Struktur des russischen Verbums. In his *Selected Writings*, vol. 2, *Word and Language*, pp. 3–16. The Hague: Mouton.

Jakobson, Roman (1957/1971). Typological studies and their contribution to historical comparative linguistics. In his *Selected Writings*, vol. 1, *Phonological Studies*, pp. 523–532. The Hague: Mouton.

Jakobson, Roman (1963). Implications of language universals for linguistics. In *Universals of Language*, ed. by Joseph Greenberg, pp. 263–278. Cambridge: MIT Press.

Janda, Richard D. (1980). On the decline of declensional systems: the overall loss of OE nominal case inflections and the ME reanalaysis of *-es* as *his*. *Papers from the 4th International Conference on Historical Linguistics*, ed. by Elizabeth C. Traugott, Rebecca Labrum, and Susan Shapherd, pp. 243–252. Amsterdam: John Benjamins.

Janda, Richard D. (1981). A case of liberation from morphology into syntax: the fate of the English genitive-marker *-(e)s*. *Syntactic Change*, ed. by Brenda D. Johns and David R. Strong, pp. 59–114. Ann Arbor, Mich.: University of Michigan, Department of Linguistics.

Janda, Richard D. (1995). From agreement affix to subject 'clitic'—and bound root—*-mos* > *-nos* vs. (-)*nos*(-) and *nos-otros* in New Mexican and other regional Spanish dialects. *Chicago Linguistic Society* 31, vol. 2, *The Parasession on Clitics*, 118–139.

Janda, Richard D. (1998). Beyond 'pathways' and 'unidirectionality': on the discontinuity of language transmission and the reversibility of grammaticalization. Unpublished ms., University of Chicago.

Jeffers, Robert J., and William Pepicello (1979). The expression of purpose in Indo-European. *Indogermanische Forschungen* 84: 1–16.

Jeffers, Robert J., and Arnold M. Zwicky (1980). The evolution of clitics. *Papers from the 4th International Conference on Historical Linguistics*, ed. by Elizabeth C. Traugott, Rebecca Labrum, and Susan Shepherd, pp. 221–231. Amsterdam: John Benjamins.

Jespersen, Otto (1921/1964). *Language: Its Nature, Development, and Origin.* New York: W. W. Norton.

Johnson, Jacqueline S., and Elissa L. Newport (1991). Critical period effects on universal properties of language. *Cognition* 39: 215–258.

Johnson, Theodore C. (1983). Phonological free variation, word frequency, and lexical diffusion. Unpublished Ph.D. dissertation, University of Washington.

Joseph, Brian D. (1996). Where can grammatical morphemes come from? Greek evidence concerning the nature of grammaticalization. Paper presented to the Formal Linguistics Society of Mid-America.

Joseph, Brian D., and Richard D. Janda (1988). The how and why of diachronic morphologization and demorphologization. In *Theoretical Morphology: Approaches in Modern Linguistics*, ed. by Michael Hammond and Michael Noonan, pp. 193–210. New York: Academic Press.

Kaisse, Ellen M. (1985). *Connected Speech: The Interaction of Syntax and Phonology.* Orlando: Academic Press.

Kalmár, Ivan (1979). *Case and Context in Inukitut (Eskimo).* National Museum of Man Mercury Series 49. Ottawa: National Museums of Canada.

Kamp, Hans (1981). A theory of truth and semantic representation. In *Formal Methods in the Study of Language*, ed. by Jeroen Groenendijk, Theo M. V. Janssen, and Martin B. J. Stokhof, pp. 277–322. Amsterdam: Mathematical Centre Tracts.

Kamp, Hans, and Barbara H. Partee (1995). Prototype theory and compositionality. *Cognition* 57: 129–191.

Katz, Jerrold J. (1981). *Language and Other Abstract Objects.* Totowa, N.J.: Rowman and Littlefield.

Kayne, Richard S. (1994). *The Antisymmetry of Syntax.* Cambridge: MIT Press.

Kearns, Katherine S. (1991). The semantics of the English progressive. Unpublished Ph.D. dissertation, MIT.

Keating, Patricia (1988). The phonology-phonetics interface. In *Linguistic Theory: Foundations*, ed. by Frederick J. Newmeyer, pp. 281–302. Cambridge: Cambridge University Press.

Keenan, Edward L. (1972). On semantically based grammar. *Linguistic Inquiry* 3: 413–462.

Keenan, Edward L., ed. (1975). *Formal Semantics of Natural Language*. London: Cambridge University Press.

Keenan, Edward L. (1978). On surface form and logical form. In *Linguisitcs in the Seventies: Directions and Prospects*, ed. by Braj B. Kachru, pp. 163–204. Urbana, Ill.: Department of Linguistics, University of Illinois.

Keenan, Edward L., and Bernard Comrie (1977). Noun phrase accessibility and universal grammar. *Linguistic Inquiry* 8: 63–99.

Keenan, Edward L., and Bernard Comrie (1979). Data on the noun phrase accessibility hierarchy. *Language* 55: 333–352.

Keenan, Edward L., and Elinor Ochs (1979). Becoming a competent speaker of Malagasy. In *Languages and Their Speakers*, ed. by Timothy Shopen, pp. 113–158. Cambridge, Mass.: Winthrop.

Keil, Frank C. (1989). *Concepts, Kinds, and Cognitive Development*. Cambridge: MIT Press.

Kemenade, Ans van (1993). The history of English modals: a reanalysis. *Folia Linguistica Historica* 13: 143–166.

Kemmer, Suzanne E. (1993). *The Middle Voice*. Amsterdam: John Benjamins.

Kempson, Ruth M. (1986). Ambiguity and the semantics-pragmatics distinction. In *Meaning and Interpretation*, ed. by C. Travis, pp. 77–83. Oxford: Blackwell.

Kim, Karl H. S., Norman R. Relkin, Kyoung-Min Lee, and Joy Hirsch (1997). Distinct cortical areas associated with native and second languages. *Nature* 388: 171–174.

Kiparsky, Paul (1968). Linguistic universals and linguistic change. In *Universals in Linguistic Theory*, ed. by Emmon Bach and Robert Harms, pp. 170–202. New York: Holt, Rinehart, and Winston.

Kiparsky, Paul (1971). Historical linguistics. In *A Survey of Linguistic Science*, ed. by William O. Dingwall, pp. 576–649. College Park, Md.: University of Maryland Linguistics Program.

Kiparsky, Paul (1982). From cyclic phonology to lexical phonology. *The Structure of Phonological Representations*, vol. 1, ed. by Harry van der Hulst and Norval Smith, pp. 131–175. Dordrecht: Foris.

Kirby, Simon (1998a). *Function, Selection and Innateness: The Emergence of Language Univerals*. Oxford: Oxford University Press.

Kirby, Simon (1998b). Constraints on constraints, or the limits of functional adaptation. In *Functionalism and Formalism in Linguistics*, vol. 2, *Case Studies*, ed. by Michael Darnell, Edith Moravcsik, Frederick J. Newmeyer, Michael Noonan, and Kathleen Wheatley, pp. 151–174. Amsterdam: John Benjamins.

Kirby, Simon, and James Hurford (1997). Learning, culture, and evolution in the origin of linguistic constraints. In *Proceedings of the Fourth, European Conference on Artificial Life*, ed. by Phil Husbands and Harvey Inman, pp. 493–502. Cambridge: MIT Press.

Kitagawa, Yoshihisa (1994). *Subjects in Japanese and English*. Hamden, Conn.: Garland.

Klaiman, M. H. (1991). *Grammatical Voice*. Cambridge: Cambridge University Press.

Klimov, Georgi A. (1983). *Principy kontensivnoj tipologii*. Moscow: Nauka.

Klokeid, Terry J. (1978). Nominal inflection in Pamanyungan: a case study in relational grammar. In *Valence, Semantic Case, and Grammatical Relations*, ed. by Werner Abraham, pp. 577–615. Amsterdam: John Benjamins.

Koerner, E. F. K. (1995). History of typology and language classification. In *Concise History of the Language Sciences: From the Sumerians to the Cognitivists*, ed. by E. F. K. Koerner and R. E. Asher, pp. 212–217. Cambridge: Pergamon.

Koopman, Hilda (1984). *The Syntax of Verbs: From Verb Movement Rules in the Kru Languages to Universal Grammar*. Studies in Generative Grammar 15. Dordrecht: Foris.

Koopman, Hilda, and Dominique Sportiche (1991). The position of subjects. *Lingua* 75: 211–258.

Koster, Jan (1975). Dutch as an SOV language. *Linguistic Analysis* 1: 111–136.

Koster, Jan (1986). *Domains and Dynasties: The Radical Autonomy of Syntax*. Studies in Generative Grammar 30. Dordrecht: Foris.

Kroch, Anthony, John Myhill, and Susan Pintzuk (1982). Understanding *do*. *Chicago Linguistic Society* 18, 282–294.

Kuno, Susumu (1973). Constraints on internal clauses and sentential subjects. *Linguistic Inquiry* 4: 363–385.

Kuno, Susumu (1974). The position of relative clauses and conjunctions. *Linguistic Inquiry* 5: 117–136.

Kuno, Susumu (1980). Functional syntax. *Current Approaches to Syntax*, ed. by Edith A. Moravcsik and Jessica R. Wirth, pp. 117–136. Syntax and Semantics 13. New York: Academic Press.

Kuno, Susumu (1987). *Functional Syntax: Anaphora, Discourse, and Empathy*. Chicago: University of Chicago Press.

Kuno, Susumu, and Ken-ichi Takami (1993). *Grammar and Discourse Principles: Functional Syntax and GB Theory*. Chicago: University of Chicago Press.

Kurylowicz, Jerzy (1965/1975). The evolution of grammatical categories. *Esquisses linguistiques II*, ed. by Jerzy Kurylowicz, pp. 38–54. Munich: Fink.

Labov, William (1966). The linguistic variable as a structural unit. *Washington Linguistics Review* 3: 4–22.

Labov, William (1972a). *Language in the Inner City*. Philadelphia: University of Pennsylvania Press.

Labov, William (1972b). *Sociolinguistic Patterns*. Philadelphia: University of Pennsylvania Press.

Labov, William (1982). Building on empirical foundations. In *Perspectives on Historical Linguistics*, ed. by Winfred Lehmann and Yakov Malkiel. Amsterdam: John Benjamins.

Labov, William (1994). *Principles of Linguistic Change*, vol. 1, *Internal Factors*. Language in Society 20. Oxford: Blackwell.

Lakoff, George (1970). *Irregularity in Syntax*. New York: Holt, Rinehart, and Winston.

Lakoff, George (1972a). Hedges: a study in meaning criteria and the logic of fuzzy concepts. *Chicago Linguistic Society* 8: 183–228.

Lakoff, George (1972b). Linguistics and natural logic. In *The Semantics of Natural Language*, ed. by Donald Davidson and Gilbert Harmon, pp. 545–665. Dordrecht: Reidel.

Lakoff, George (1973). Fuzzy grammar and the performance/competence terminology game. *Chicago Linguistic Society* 9: 271–291.

Lakoff, George (1977). Linguistic gestalts. *Chicago Linguistic Society* 13: 236–287.

Lakoff, George (1984). Performative subordinate clauses. *Berkeley Linguistics Society* 10: 472–480.

Lakoff, George (1987). *Women, fire, and dangerous things: what categories reveal about the mind*. Chicago: University of Chicago Press.

Lakoff, George (1990). The invariance hypothesis: is abstract reasoning based on image-schemas? *Cognitive Linguistics* 1: 39–74.

Lakoff, George (1991). Cognitive versus generative linguistics: how commitments influence results. *Language and Communication* 11: 53–62.

Lakoff, George, and Claudia Brugman (1987). The semantics of aux-inversion and anaphora constraints. Unpublished paper presented to the Linguistic Society of America.

Lambrecht, Knud (1987). On the status of SVO sentences in French discourse. In *Coherence and Grounding in Discourse*, ed. by Russell Tomlin, pp. 217–262. Amsterdam: John Benjamins.

Langacker, Ronald W. (1969). On pronominalization and the chain of command. In *Modern Studies in English*, ed. by David Reibel and Sanford Schane, pp. 160–186. Englewood Cliffs, N.J.: Prentice Hall.

Langacker, Ronald W. (1985). Observations and speculations on subjectivity. In *Iconicity in Syntax*, ed. by John Haiman, pp. 109–150. Amsterdam: John Benjamins.

Langacker, Ronald W. (1987a). *Foundations of Cognitive Grammar*, vol. 1, *Theoretical Prerequisites*. Stanford, Calif.: Stanford University Press.

Langacker, Ronald W. (1987b). Nouns and verbs. *Language* 63: 53–94.

Langacker, Ronald W. (1988). An overview of cognitive grammar. In *Topics in Cognitive Linguistics*, ed. by Brygida Rudzka-Ostyn, pp. 3–48. Amsterdam: John Benjamins.

Langacker, Ronald W. (1991). *Foundations of Cognitive Grammar*, vol. 2, *Descriptive Application*. Stanford, Calif.: Stanford University Press.

Langacker, Ronald W. (1993). Universals of construal. *Berkeley Linguistics Society* 19: 447–463.

Langendonck, Willy van (1986). Markedness, prototypes, and language acquisition. *Cahiers de l'institut de linguistique de Louvain* 12: 39–76.

Lapointe, Steven (1986). Markedness, the organization of linguistic information in speech production, and language acquisition. In *Markedness*, ed. by Fred Eckman, Edith Moravcsik, and Jessica Wirth, pp. 219–240. New York: Plenum.

Larson, Richard K. (1988). On the double object construction. *Linguistic Inquiry* 19: 335–392.

Lascarides, Alex, and Nicholas Asher (1991). Discourse relations and defeasible knowledge. *Proceedings of the Association for Computational Linguistics*, 55–62.

Lasnik, Howard (1976). Remarks on coreference. *Linguistic Analysis* 2: 1–22.

Lasnik, Howard (1998). On the locality of movement: formalist syntax position paper. In *Functionalism and Formalism in Linguistics*, vol. 1, *General Papers*, ed. by Michael Darnell, Edith Moravcsik, Frederick J. Newmeyer, Michael Noonan, and Kathleen Wheatley, pp. 31–52. Amsterdam: John Benjamins.

Lass, Roger (1980). *On Explaining Language Change*. Cambridge: Cambridge University Press.

Lebeaux, David (1986). The interpretation of derived nominals. *Chicago Linguistic Society* 22: 231–247.

Lee, Michael (1988). Language, perception, and the world. In *Explaining Language Universals*, ed. by John A. Hawkins, pp. 211–246. Oxford: Basil Blackwell.

Lees, Robert B., and Edward Klima (1963). Rules for English pronominalization. *Language* 39: 17–28. Reprinted in *Modern Studies in English*, ed. by D. Reibel and S. Schane, pp. 145–159. Englewood-Cliffs, N.J.: Prentice-Hall, 1969.

Legendre, Géraldine, William Raymond, and Paul Smolensky (1993). An optimality-theoretic typology of case and grammatical voice systems. *Berkeley Linguistics Society* 19: 464–478.

Lehmann, Christian (1982/1995). *Thoughts on Grammaticalization*. Revised and expanded version. LINCOM Studies in Theoretical Linguistics 1. Munich: LINCOM Europa.

Lehmann, Christian (1985). Grammaticalization: synchronic variation and diachronic change. *Lingua e Stile* 20: 303–318.

Lehmann, Christian (1989). Grammatikalisierung und Lexicalisierung. *Zeitschrift für Phonetik* 42: 11–19.

Lehmann, Winfred P. (1973). A structural principle of language and its implications. *Language* 49: 47–66.

Leonard, Laurence B. (1989). Language learnability and specific language impairment in children. *Applied Psycholinguistics* 10: 179–202.

Leonard, Laurence B. (1992). Specific language impairment in three languages: some cross-linguistic evidence. In *Specific Speech and Language Disorders in Children: Correlates, Characteristics, and Outcomes*, ed. by Paul Fletcher and David Hall, pp. 118–126. San Diego: Singular Publishing.

Leonard, Laurence B. (1994). Some problems facing accounts of morphological deficits in children with specific language impairment. In *Specific Language Impairments in Children*, ed. by R. V. Watkins and Mabel L. Rice, pp. 91–106. Baltimore: Paul H. Brookes.

Leonard, Laurence B., Umberta Bortolini, M.-Cristina Caselli, Karla K. McGregor, and Letizia Sabbadini (1992). Morphological deficits in children with specific language impairment: the status of features in the underlying grammar. *Language Acquisition* 2: 151–179.

Lepsius, Richard (1880). *Nubische Grammatik*. Berlin.

Leroy, Maurice (1963/1967). *Main Trends in Modern Linguistics*. Berkeley: University of California Press. Translation of *Les grands courants de la linguistique moderne*.

Levelt, W. J. M., and S. Kelter (1982). Surface form and memory in question answering. *Cognitive Psychology* 14: 78–106.

Levin, Beth (1993). *English Verb Classes and Alternations: A Preliminary Investigation*. Chicago: University of Chicago Press.

Levinson, Stephen (1983). *Pragmatics*. Cambridge: Cambridge University Press.

Lewis, Barbara A., and Lee A. Thompson (1992). A study of developmental speech and language disorders in twins. *Journal of Speech and Hearing Research* 35: 1086–1094.

Lewis, G. L. (1967). *Turkish Grammar*. Oxford: Oxford University Press.

Li, Charles N., ed. (1976). *Subject and Topic*. New York: Academic Press.

Li, Charles N., and Sandra A. Thompson (1974). An explanation of word order change SVO → SOV. *Foundations of Language* 12: 201–214.

Li, Charles N., and Sandra A. Thompson (1976). Subject and topic: a new typology of language. In *Subject and Topic*, ed. by Charles N. Li, pp. 457–490. New York: Academic Press.

Lichtenberk, Frank (1991). Semantic change and heterosemy in grammaticalization. *Language* 67: 475–509.

Lightfoot, David W. (1976). Trace theory and twice-moved NPs. *Linguistic Inquiry* 7: 559–582.

Lightfoot, David W. (1979a). *Principles of Diachronic Syntax*. Cambridge Studies in Linguistics 23. Cambridge: Cambridge University Press.

Lightfoot, David W. (1979b). Review of *Mechanisms of Syntactic Change*, ed. by C. Li. *Language* 55: 381–395.

Lightfoot, David W. (1981). A reply to some critics. *Lingua* 55: 351–368.

Lightfoot, David W. (1986). Syntactic change. In *Linguistic Theory: Foundations*, ed. by Frederick J. Newmeyer, pp. 303–323. Cambridge: Cambridge University Press.

Lightfoot, David W. (1991). *How to Set Parameters: Arguments from Language Change*. Cambridge: MIT Press.

Longacre, R. E. (1979). The paragraph as a grammatical unit. In *Discourse and Syntax*, ed. by Talmy Givón, pp. 115–134. Syntax and Semantics 12. New York: Academic Press.

Lord, Carol (1973). Serial verbs in transition. Studies in African Linguistics 4: 269–296.

Lord, Carol (1989). Syntactic reanalysis in the historical development of serial verb constructions in the languages of West Africa. Unpublished Ph.D. dissertation, UCLA.

Ludlow, Peter (1992). Formal rigor and linguistic theory. Natural Language and Linguistic Theory 10: 335–344.

Lyons, John (1977). Semantics. Cambridge: Cambridge University Press.

MacNamara, John (1982). Names for things: A study in human learning. Cambridge: MIT Press.

MacWhinney, Brian, and Csaba Pléh (1988). The processing of restrictive relative clauses in Hungarian. Cognition 29: 95–141.

Maling, Joan (1983). Transitive adjectives: a case of categorial reanalysis. In *Linguistic Categories: Auxiliaries and Related Puzzles*, vol. 1, *Categories*, ed. by Frank Heny and Barry Richards, pp. 253–289. Dordrecht: Reidel.

Mallinson, Graham, and Barry J. Blake (1981). *Language Typology: Cross-Linguistic Studies in Syntax*. North-Holland Linguistic Series 46. Amsterdam: North Holland.

Manaster-Ramer, Alexis (1979). The other side of accessibility. *Chicago Linguistic Society* 15: 207–219.

Manning, Alan, and Frank Parker (1989). The SOV > ··· > OSV frequency hierarchy. *Language Sciences* 11: 43–65.

Manzini, M. Rita, and Kenneth Wexler (1987). Parameters, binding, and learning theory. *Linguistic Inquiry* 18: 413–444.

Marchese, Lynell (1986). *Tense/Aspect and the Development of Auxiliaries in Kru Languages*. Arlington, Tex.: Summer Institute of Linguistics.

Marslen-Wilson, William D. (1975). The limited compatibility of linguistic and perceptual explanations. In *Papers from the Parasession on Functionalism*, ed. by Robin E. Grossman, L. James San, and Timothy J. Vance, pp. 409–420. Chicago: Chicago Linguistic Society.

Martinet, André (1962). *A Functional View of Language*. Oxford: Oxford University Press.

Masica, Colin (1976). *Defining a Linguistic Area: South Asia*. Chicago: University of Chicago Press.

Mathesius, Vilém (1929). Zur Satzperspektive im modernen Englisch. *Archiv für das Studium der neureren Sprachen und Literaturen* 155: 202–210.

Matisoff, James A. (1991). Areal and universal dimensions of grammaticalization in Lahu. In *Approaches to Grammaticalization*, vol. 2, *Focus on Types of Grammatical Markers*, ed. by Elizabeth C. Traugott and Bernd Heine, pp. 383–453. Amsterdam: John Benjamins.

Matsumoto, Yo (1988). From bound grammatical markers to free discourse markers: history of some Japanese connectives. *Berkeley Linguistics Society* 14: 340–351.

Matthews, P. H. (1993). *Grammatical Theory in the United States from Bloomfield to Chomsky*. Cambridge: Cambridge University Press.

May, Robert (1991). Syntax, semantics, and logical form. In *The Chomskyan Turn: Generative, Linguistics, Philosophy, Mathematics, and Psychology*, ed. by Asa Kasher, pp. 334–359. Oxford: Blackwell.

McCawley, James D. (1981). *Everything That Linguists Always Wanted to Know about Logic (but Were Ashamed to Ask)*. Chicago: University of Chicago Press.

McCawley, James D. (1982). *Thirty Million Theories of Grammar*. Chicago: University of Chicago Press.

McCloskey, James (1996). Subjecthood and subject positions. In *A Handbook of Theoretical Syntax*, ed. by Liliane Haegeman, pp. 197–236. Dordrecht: Kluwer.

Meillet, Antoine (1912/1926). *Linguistique historique et linguistique générale*. Vol. 1. Paris: Librairie Ancienne Honoré Champion.

Meillet, Antoine (1931). *Linguistique historique et linguistique générale*. Vol. 2. Paris: Librairie C. Klincksieck.

Meinunger, André (1998). Topicality and agreement. In *Functionalism and Formalism in Linguistics*, vol. 2, *Case Studies*, ed. by Michael Darnell, Edith Moravcsik, Frederick J. Newmeyer, Michael Noonan, and Kathleen Wheatley, pp. 203–220. Amsterdam: John Benjamins.

Merton, Robert K. (1949). Manifest and latent functions. In *Social Theory and Social Structure*, ed. by Robert K. Merton, pp. 19–84. Glencoe, Ill.: Free Press.

Mervis, Carolyn B., and Eleanor Rosch (1981). Categorization of natural objects. *Annual Review of Psychology* 32: 89–115.

Michaelis, Laura A., and Knud Lambrecht (1996). Toward a construction-based theory of language function: the case of nominal extraposition. *Language* 72: 215–247.

Milsark, Gary (1977). Toward an explanation of certain peculiarities of the existential construction in English. *Linguistic Analysis* 3: 1–30.

Mithun, Marianne (1984). The evolution of noun incorporation. *Language* 60: 847–893.

Mithun, Marianne (1987). Is basic word order universal? In *Coherence and Grounding in Discourse*, ed. by Russ Tomlin, pp. 281–328. Amsterdam: John Benjamins.

Moore, Terence, and Christine Carling (1982). *Language Understanding: Towards a Post-Chomskyan Linguistics*. New York: St. Martin's Press.

Moravcsik, Edith A. (1978). Language contact. In *Universals of Human Language*, vol. 1, *Method and Theory*, ed. by Joseph H. Greenberg, Charles A. Ferguson, and Edith A. Moravcsik, pp. 93–122. Stanford, Calif.: Stanford University Press.

Moravcsik, Edith A. (1983). On grammatical classes—the case of 'definite' objects in Hungarian. *Working Papers in Linguistics, University of Hawaii* 15: 75–107.

Moravcsik, Edith A. (1991). Review of *The Semantics of Grammar*, by A. Wierzbicka. *Studies in Language* 15: 129–148.

Moravcsik, Edith A., and Jessica R. Wirth, eds. (1980). *Current Approaches to Syntax*. Syntax and Semantics 13. New York: Academic Press.

Moravcsik, Edith A., and Jessica R. Wirth (1986). Markedness—an overview. In *Markedness*, ed. by Fred R. Eckman, Edith A. Moravcsik, and Jessica R. Wirth, pp. 1–11. New York: Plenum.

Mühlhäusler, Peter (1986). *Pidgin and Creole Linguistics*. Language in Society 11. Oxford: Basil Blackwell.

Muysken, Pieter, and Henk van Riemsdijk (1986). Projecting features and featuring projections. In *Features and Projections*, ed. by Pieter Muysken and Henk van Riemsdijk, pp. 1–30. Dordrecht: Foris.

Na, Younghee, and Geoffrey J. Huck (1993). On the status of certain island violations in Korean. *Linguistics and Philosophy* 16: 181–229.

Nettle, Daniel (1995). Segmental inventory size, word length, and communicative efficiency. *Linguistics* 33: 359–367.

Nettle, Daniel (1998). Functionalism and its difficulties in biology and linguistics. In *Functionalism and Formalism in Linguistics*, vol. 1, *General Papers*, ed. by Michael Darnell, Edith Moravcsik, Frederick J. Newmeyer, Michael Noonan, and Kathleen Wheatley, pp. 443–466. Amsterdam: John Benjamins.

Nevis, Joel A. (1986a). Decliticization and deaffixation in Saame: abessive *taga*. *Ohio State University Working Papers in Linguistics* 34: 1–9.

Nevis, Joel A. (1986b). Decliticization in Old Estonian. *Ohio State University Working Papers in Linguistics* 34: 10–27.

Nevis, Joel A. (1986c). Finnish particle clitics and general particle theory. Ph.D. dissertation, Ohio State University. *Ohio State University Working Papers in Linguistics* 33: 1–159.

Newmeyer, Frederick J. (1983). *Grammatical Theory: Its Limits and Its Possibilities*. Chicago: University of Chicago Press.

Newmeyer, Frederick J. (1986a). *Linguistic Theory in America*. Second edition. New York: Academic Press.

Newmeyer, Frederick J. (1986b). *The Politics of Linguistics*. Chicago: University of Chicago Press.

Newmeyer, Frederick J. (1987). The current convergences in linguistic theory: some implications for second language acquisition research. *Second Language Research* 3: 1–19. Reprinted in *Generative Linguistics: A Historical Perspective*, by F. Newmeyer, pp. 155–168. London: Routledge, 1976.

Newmeyer, Frederick J. (1991). Functional explanation in linguistics and the origins of language. *Language and Communication* 11: 3–28.

Newmeyer, Frederick J. (1992). Iconicity and generative grammar. *Language* 68: 756–796.

Newmeyer, Frederick J. (1994a). Competing motivations and synchronic analysis. *Sprachtypologie und Universalienforschung* 47: 67–77.

Newmeyer, Frederick J. (1994b). A note on Chomsky on form and function. *Journal of Linguistics* 30: 245–251.

Newmeyer, Frederick J. (1995). Linguistic diversity and universal grammar: 40 years of dynamic tension within generative grammar. In *History of Linguistics, 1993*, ed. by Kurt R. Jankowsky, pp. 327–348. Amsterdam: John Benjamins.

Newmeyer, Frederick J. (1996). *Generative Linguistics: A Historical Perspective*. London: Routledge.

Newmeyer, Frederick J. (1997). Genetic dysphasia and linguistic theory. *Journal of Neurolinguistics* 10: 47–73.

Newmeyer, Frederick J. (in preparation). Language evolution: a linguistic perspective.

Nichols, Johanna (1984). Functional theories of grammar. *Annual Review of Anthropology* 13: 97–117.

Nichols, Johanna (1986). Head marking and dependent marking grammar. *Language* 62: 56–119.

Nichols, Johanna (1992). *Linguistic Diversity in Space and Time*. Chicago: University of Chicago Press.

Niyogi, Partha, and Robert C. Berwick (1995). The logical problem of language change. AI memo 1516. Cambridge: MIT Artificial Intelligence Laboratory.

Noonan, Michael (1998). Non-structuralist syntax. In *Functionalism and Formalism in Linguistics*, vol. 1, *General Papers*, ed. by Michael Darnell, Edith Moravcsik, Frederick J. Newmeyer, Michael Noonan, and Kathleen Wheatley, pp. 11–30. Amsterdam: John Benjamins.

Norde, Muriel (1997). Grammaticalization versus reanalysis: the case of possessive constructions in Germanic. In *Papers from the 12th International Conference on Historical Linguistics*, ed. by Linda van Bergen and Richard M. Hogg. Amsterdam: John Benjamins.

O'Dowd, Elizabeth (1990). Discourse pressure, genre, and grammatical alignment—after Du Bois. *Studies in Language* 14: 365–403.

Oehrle, Richard (1976). The grammatical status of the English dative alternation. Unpublished Ph.D. dissertation, MIT.

O'Grady, William (1987). *Principles of Grammar and Learning*. Chicago: University of Chicago Press.

Onodera, Noriko O. (1995). Diachronic analysis of Japanese discourse markers. In *Historical Pragmatics: Pragmatic Developments in the History of English*, ed. by Andreas H. Jucker, pp. 393–437. Amsterdam: John Benjamins.

Osgood, Charles (1980). *Lectures on Language Performance*. New York: Springer-Verlag.

Osgood, Charles, and Thomas A. Sebeok, eds. (1954). *Psycholinguistics*. Baltimore: Indiana University Press.

Pagliuca, William (1982). Prolegomena to a theory of articulatory evolution. Unpublished Ph.D. dissertation, SUNY Buffalo.

Pagliuca, William (1994). Introduction. In *Perspectives on Grammaticalization*, ed. by William Pagliuca, pp. ix–xx. Amsterdam: John Benjamins.

Palmer, Frank (1971). *Grammar*. Harmondsworth: Penguin.

Partee, Barbara H. (1975). Comments on C. J. Fillmore's and N. Chomsky's papers. In *The Scope of American Linguistics*, ed. by Robert Austerlitz, pp. 197–209. Lisse: Peter de Ridder Press.

Partee, Barbara H. (1987). Noun phrase interpretation and type-shifting principles. In *Studies in Discourse Representation Theory and the Theory of Generalized Quantifiers*, ed. by Jeroen Groenendijk, D. de Jongh, and Martin Stokhof, pp. 115–144. Dordrecht: Reidel.

Pateman, Trevor (1987). *Language in Mind and Language in Society*. Oxford: Oxford University Press.

Paul, Hermann (1880/1920). *Prinzipien der Sprachgeschichte*. Fifth edition. Halle: Niemeyer.

Payne, Doris L. (1987). Information structuring in Papago narrative discourse. *Language* 63: 783–804.

Payne, Doris L. (1992). Introduction. In *Pragmatics of Word Order Flexibility*, ed. by Doris L. Payne, pp. 1–13. Amsterdam: John Benjamins.

Payne, Doris L. (1998). What counts as explanation? A functionalist approach to word order. In *Functionalism and Formalism in Linguistics*, vol. 1, *General Papers*, ed. by Michael Darnell, Edith Moravcsik, Frederick J. Newmeyer, Michael Noonan, and Kathleen Wheatley, pp. 135–164. Amsterdam: John Benjamins.

Peirce, Charles Sanders (1867/1931). On a new list of categories. *Proceedings of the American Academy of Arts and Sciences* 7: 287–298. Reprinted in *Collected Papers of Charles Sanders Peirce*, ed. by Charles Hartshorne and Paul Weiss, vol. 1, *Principles of Philosophy*, pp. 287–305. Cambridge: Harvard University Press, 1931.

Peirce, Charles Sanders (1885/1933). On the algebra of logic: a contribution to the philosophy of notation. *American Journal of Mathematics* 7: 180–202. Reprinted in *Collected Papers of Charles Sanders Peirce*, ed. by Charles Hartshorne and Paul Weiss, vol. 3, *Exact Logic*, pp. 249 ff. Cambridge: Harvard University Press, 1933.

Peirce, Charles Sanders (c.1902/1932). The icon, index, and symbol. Manuscript. Printed in *Collected Papers of Charles Sanders Peirce*, ed. by Charles Hartshorne and Paul Weiss, vol. 2, *Elements of Logic*, pp. 156–173. Cambridge: Harvard University Press, 1932.

Pembrey, Marcus (1992). Genetics and language disorders. In *Specific Speech and Language Disorders in Children: Correlates, Characteristics, and Outcomes*, ed. by Paul Fletcher and David Hall, pp. 51–62. San Diego: Singular Publishing.

Perkins, Revere D. (1988). The covariation of culture and grammar. In *Studies in Syntactic Typology*, ed. by Michael Hammond, Edith Moravcsik, and Jessica Wirth, pp. 359–378. Amsterdam: John Benjamins.

Perkins, Revere D. (1989). Statistical techniques for determining language sample size. *Studies in Language* 13: 293–315.

Perkins, Revere D. (1992). *Deixis, Grammar, and Culture*. Typological Studies in Language 24. Amsterdam: John Benjamins.

Perlmutter, David M., ed. (1983). *Studies in Relational Grammar*. Vol. 1. Chicago: University of Chicago Press.

Perlmutter, David M., and Carol G. Rosen, eds. (1984). *Studies in Relational Grammar*. Vol. 2. Chicago: University of Chicago Press.

Piattelli-Palmarini, Massimo (1989). Evolution, selection, and cognition: from "learning" to parameter setting in biology and in the study of language. *Cognition* 31: 1–44.

Piattelli-Palmarini, Massimo (1990). An ideological battle over modals and quantifiers. *Behavioral and Brain Sciences* 13: 752–754.

Piggott, Glyne L., and Martine Kessler Robb (1994). Prosodic organization in familial language impairment: evidence from stress. *McGill Working Papers in Linguistics* 10: 16–23.

Pinker, Steven (1984). *Language Learnability and Language Development*. Cambridge: Harvard University Press.

Pinker, Steven (1987). The bootstrapping problem in language acquisition. In *Mechanisms of Language Acquisition*, ed. by Brian MacWhinney, pp. 399–441. Hillsdale, N.J.: Erlbaum.

Pinker, Steven (1989a). Language acquisition. In *Foundations of Cognitive Science*, ed. by M. I. Posner, pp. 359–399. Cambridge: MIT Press.

Pinker, Steven (1989b). *Learnability and Cognition: The Acquisition of Argument Structure*. Cambridge: MIT Press.

Pinker, Steven (1994a). How could a child use verb syntax to learn verb semantics? In *The Acquisition of the Lexicon*, ed. by Lila Gleitman and Barbara Landau,
pp. 377–410. Cambridge: MIT Press.

Pinker, Steven (1994b). *The Language Instinct: How the Mind Creates Language*.
New York: Morrow.

Pinker, Steven, and Paul Bloom (1994). Humans did not evolve from bats.
Behavioral and Brain Sciences 17: 183–185.

Plank, Frans (1984). The modals story retold. *Studies in Language* 8: 305–364.

Pollard, Carl, and Ivan A. Sag (1994). *Head-Driven Phrase Structure Grammar*.
Chicago: University of Chicago Press.

Postal, Paul M., and Brian D. Joseph, eds. (1990). *Studies in Relational Grammar*.
Vol. 3. Chicago: University of Chicago Press.

Postal, Paul M., and Geoffrey K. Pullum (1982). The contraction debate. *Linguistic Inquiry* 13: 122–138.

Potter, Mary C., and Barbara A. Faulconer (1979). Understanding noun phrases.
Journal of Verbal Learning and Verbal Behavior 18: 509–522.

Primus, Beatrice (1991). A performance based account of topic position and focus
positions. In *Performance Principles of Word Order*, ed. by John A. Hawkins and
Anna Siewierska, pp. 1–33. Working paper 2, theme group 2. Strasbourg: European Science Foundation Programme in Language Typology, ESF Office.

Prince, Alan, and Paul Smolensky (1993). Optimality theory: constraint interaction in generative grammar. RuCCS technical report 2. Piscataway, N.J.:
Rutgers University Center for Cognitive Science.

Prince, Ellen F. (1978). A comparison of *wh*-clefts and *it*-clefts in discourse. *Language* 54: 883–906.

Prince, Ellen F. (1981). Toward a taxonomy of given-new information. In *Radical
Pragmatics*, ed. by Peter Cole, pp. 223–256. New York: Academic Press.

Prince, Ellen F. (1985). Fancy syntax and "shared knowledge." *Journal of Pragmatics* 9: 65–82.

Prince, Ellen F. (1988). Discourse analysis: a part of the study of linguistic
competence. *Linguistic Theory: Extensions and Implications*, ed. by Frederick
J. Newmeyer, pp. 164–182. Cambridge: Cambridge University Press.

Prince, Ellen F. (1991). On "Functional explanation in linguistics and the origins
of language." *Language and Communication* 11: 79–82. See Newmeyer 1991.

Prince, Ellen F. (1995). On the limits of syntax, with reference to left-dislocation
and topicalization. Conference on the Limits of Syntax, Ohio State University.

Pullum, Geoffrey K. (1977). Word order relations and grammatical relations. In
Grammatical Relations, ed. by Peter Cole and Jerrold Sadock, pp. 249–277. New
York: Academic Press.

Pullum, Geoffrey K. (1979). *Rule Interaction and the Organization of a Grammar*.
New York: Garland.

Pullum, Geoffrey K. (1989). Formal linguistics meets the Boojum. *Natural Language and Linguistic Theory* 7: 137–143.

Pullum, Geoffrey K. (1996a). Learnability, hyperlearning, and the poverty of the stimulus. *Berkeley Linguistics Society* 22, *Parasession on Learnability*, 498–513.

Pullum, Geoffrey K. (1996b). Review of *The View from Building 20*, ed. by K. Hale and W. O'Neil. *Journal of Linguistics* 32: 117–147.

Pullum, Geoffrey K., and Deirdre Wilson (1977). Autonomous syntax and the analysis of auxiliaries. *Language* 53: 741–788.

Pullum, Geoffrey K., and Arnold M. Zwicky (1991). Condition duplication, paradigm homonymy, and transconstructional constraints. *Berkeley Linguistics Society* 17: 252–266.

Pustejovsky, James (1991). The syntax of event structure. *Cognition* 41: 47–81.

Pustejovsky, James (1995). *The Generative Lexicon*. Cambridge: MIT Press.

Radford, Andrew (1981). *Transformational Syntax*. Cambridge: Cambridge University Press.

Ramat, Paolo (1987). (Rand)bemerkungen über Morphologisierungs- und Entmorphologisierungsprozesse. *Zeitschrift für Phonetik* 40: 455–462.

Ramat, Paolo (1992). Thoughts on degrammaticalization. *Linguistics* 30: 549–560.

Randall, Janet (1984). Grammatical information in word structure. *Quaderni de Semantica* 5: 313–330.

Rappaport, Malka, and Beth Levin (1988). What to do with θ-roles. *Thematic Relations*, ed. by Wendy Wilkins, pp. 7–36. Syntax and Semantics 21. New York: Academic Press.

Ravid, Dorit D. (1995). *Language Change in Child and Adult Hebrew*. New York: Oxford University Press.

Reinhart, Tanya (1976). The syntactic domain of anaphora. Unpublished Ph.D. dissertation, MIT.

Reinhart, Tanya (1981). Definite NP anaphora and c-comand domains. *Linguistic Inquiry* 12: 605–636.

Reinhart, Tanya (1982). Pragmatics and linguistics: an analysis of sentence topics. *Philosophica* 27: 53–94.

Reinhart, Tanya (1983). *Anaphora and Semantic Interpretation*. Chicago: University of Chicago Press.

Reinhart, Tanya (1984). Principles of gestalt perception in the temporal organization of narrative texts. *Linguistics* 22: 779–809.

Reuland, Eric J. (1985). Representation at the level of logical form and the definiteness effect. In *Grammatical Representation*, ed. by Jacqueline Guéron, Hans-Georg Obenauer, and Jean-Yves Pollock, pp. 327–362. Dordrecht: Foris.

Reuland, Eric J. (1986). A feature system for the set of categorial heads. In *Features and Projections*, ed. by Pieter Muysken and Henk van Riemsdijk, pp. 41–88. Dordrecht: Foris.

Riemsdijk, Henk van, and Edwin Williams (1981). NP-structure. *Linguistic Review* 1: 171–218.

Riemsdijk, Henk van, and Edwin Williams (1986). *Introduction to the Theory of Grammar*. Cambridge: MIT Press.

Rijkhoff, Jan (1990). Explaining word order in the noun phrase. *Linguistics* 28: 5–42.

Rijkhoff, Jan, Dik Bakker, Kees Hengeveld, and Peter Kahrel (1993). A method of language sampling. *Studies in Language* 17: 169–203.

Rizzi, Luigi (1982). *Issues in Italian Syntax*. Studies in Generative Grammar 11. Dordrecht: Foris.

Roberts, Ian (1992). *Verbs and Diachronic Syntax*. Dordrecht: Kluwer.

Roberts, Ian (1993). A formal account of grammaticalization in the history of Romance futures. *Folia Linguistica Historica* 13: 219–258.

Roberts, Ian, and Anna Roussou (1997). Interface interpretation. Paper presented at GLOW 20, Rabat, Morocco.

Roberts, Julian M. (1996). On the role of diffusion in creole genesis. Unpublished manuscript, Stanford University.

Rochemont, Michael S. (1986). *Focus in Generative Grammar*. Studies in Generative Linguistic Analysis 4. Amsterdam: John Benjamins.

Rochemont, Michael S., and Peter W. Culicover (1990). *English Focus Constructions and the Theory of Grammar*. Cambridge: Cambridge University Press.

Rohdenburg, Günter (1996). Cognitive complexity and increased grammatical explicitness in English. *Cognitive Linguistics* 7: 149–182.

Rosch, Eleanor (1971/1973). On the internal structure of perceptual and semantic categories. In *Cognitive Development and the Acquisition of Language*, ed. by Timothy E. Moore, pp. 111–144. New York: Academic Press.

Rosch, Eleanor (1973). Natural categories. *Cognitive Psychology* 4: 328–350.

Rosch, Eleanor (1978). Principles of categorization. In *Cognition and Categorization*, ed. by Eleanor Rosch and B. B. Lloyd, pp. 27–48. Hillsdale, N.J.: Erlbaum.

Rosch, Eleanor, and Barbara B. Lloyd, eds. (1978). *Cognition and Categorization*. Hillsdale, N.J.: Erlbaum.

Rosch, Eleanor, Carolyn Mervis, Wayne Gray, David Johnson, and Penny Boyes-Braem (1976). Basic objects in natural categories. *Cognitive Psychology* 8: 382–439.

Rosen, Sarah (1990). *Argument Structure and Complex Predicates*. Hamden, Conn.: Garland.

Ross, John R. (1969). On the cyclic nature of English pronominalization. In *Modern Studies in English*, ed. by David Reibel and Sanford Schane, pp. 187–200. Englewood Cliffs, N.J.: Prentice-Hall, pp. 1669–1682. Originally published in *To Honor Roman Jakobson*. The Hague: Mouton, 1967.

Ross, John R. (1972). The category squish: Endstation Hauptwort. *Chicago Linguistic Society* 8: 316–328.

Ross, John R. (1973a). A fake NP squish. In *New Ways of Analyzing Variation in English*, ed. by C.-J. N. Bailey and R. Shuy, pp. 96–140. Washington: Georgetown University Press.

Ross, John R. (1973b). Nouniness. In *Three Dimensions of Linguistic Theory*, ed. by O. Fujimura, pp. 137–258. Tokyo: TEC Company, Ltd..

Ross, John R. (1975). Clausematiness. In *Formal Semantics of Natural Language*, ed. by E. L. Keenan, pp. 422–475. London: Cambridge University Press.

Ross, John R. (1981). Nominal decay. Unpublished manuscript, MIT.

Ross, John R. (1987). Islands and syntactic prototypes. *Chicago Linguistic Society* 23: 309–320.

Ross, John R. (1995). Defective noun phrases. *Chicago Linguistic Society* 31: 398–440.

Rouveret, Alain, and Jean-Roger Vergnaud (1980). Specifying reference to the subject: French causatives and conditions on representations. *Linguistic Inquiry* 11: 97–202.

Rubino, Carl (1994). Against the notion of unidirectionality in lexeme genesis. *Linguistica Atlantica* 16: 135–147.

Rudzka-Ostyn, Brygida, ed. (1988). Topics in cognitive linguistics. Amsterdam: John Benjamins.

Sadock, Jerrold M. (1980). Noun incorporation in Greenlandic: a case of syntactic word formation. *Language* 56: 300–319.

Sadock, Jerrold M. (1984). Whither radical pragmatics? In *Meaning, Form, and Use in Context: Linguistic Applications*, ed. by Deborah Schiffrin, pp. 139–149. Washington: Georgetown University Press.

Sadock, Jerrold M. (1986). Some notes on noun incorporation. *Language* 62: 19–31.

Safir, Kenneth J. (1985). *Syntactic Chains*. Cambridge: Cambridge University Press.

Salmon, Wesley C. (1984). *Scientific Explanation and the Causal Structure of the World*. Princeton: Princeton University Press.

Salmon, Wesley C. (1989). *Four Decades of Scientific Explanation*. Minneapolis: University of Minnesota Press.

Sankoff, Gillian, and Suzanne Laberge (1973). On the acquisition of native speakers by a language. *Kivung* 6: 32–47.

Sapir, Edward (1921). *Language*. New York: Harcourt, Brace, and World.

Sasse, Hans-Jürgen (1987). The thetic/categorial distinction revisited. *Linguistics* 25: 511–580.

Saussure, Ferdinand de (1916/1966). *Course in General Linguistics*. New York: McGraw-Hill. Translation of *Cours de linguistique générale*. Paris: Payot, 1916.

Schachter, Jacqueline (1989). Testing a proposed universal. In *Linguistic Perspectives on Second Language Acquisition*, ed. by Susan M. Gass and Jacqueline Schachter, pp. 73–88. Cambridge: Cambridge University Press.

Schlegel, August Wilhelm von (1818). *Observations sur la langue et la littérature provençales*. Paris.

Schlegel, Friedrich von (1808/1977). *Über die Sprache und Weisheit der Indier*. Amsterdam: John Benjamins.

Schleicher, August (1848). *Sprachgesichtliche Untersuchungen*. Vol. 1, *Zur vergleichenden Sprachengeschichte*. Bonn: H. B. König.

Schleicher, August (1869). *Die deutsche Sprache*. Second edition. Stuttgart: Cotta.

Schmerling, Susan (1975). Asymmetric conjunction and rules of conversation. In *Speech Acts*, ed. by Peter Cole and Jerry Morgan, pp. 211–231. New York: Academic Press.

Schmidt, Wilhelm (1926). *Die Sprachfamilien und Sprachenkreise der Erde*. Heidelberg.

Schütze, Hinrich (1997). *Ambiguity Resolution in Language Learning: Computational and Cognitive Models*. CSLI Lecture Notes 71. Stanford, Calif.: CSLI Publications.

Searle, John (1972/1974). Chomsky's revolution in linguistics. In *On Noam Chomsky: Critical Essays*, ed. by Gilbert Harman, pp. 2–33. Garden City, N.Y.: Anchor Books. Originally published in *New York Review of Books*, June 29, 1972, pp. 16–24.

Searle, John (1975). Indirect speech acts. In *Speech Acts*, ed. by Peter Cole and Jerry Morgan, pp. 59–82. Semantics and Semantics 3. New York: Academic Press.

Sedlak, Philip A. S. (1975). Direct/indirect object word order: a cross-linguistic analysis. *Working Papers on Language Universals* 18: 117–164.

Sgall, Petr (1995). Prague School typology. In *Approaches to Language Typology*, ed. by Masayoshi Shibatani and Theodora Bynon, pp. 49–84. Oxford: Clarendon Press.

Sheldon, Amy (1974). On the role of parallel function in the acquisition of relative clauses in English. *Journal of Verbal Learning and Verbal Behavior* 13: 272–281.

Shibatani, Masayoshi, ed. (1988). *Passive and Voice*. Typological Studies in Language 16. Amsterdam: John Benjamins.

Shibatani, Masayoshi, and Theodora Bynon, eds. (1995). *Approaches to Language Typology*. Oxford: Clarendon Press.

Siewierska, Anna (1988). *Word Order Rules*. London: Croom Helm.

Silverstein, Michael (1976). Hierarchy of features and ergativity. In *Grammatical Categories in Australian Languages*, ed. by R. M. W. Dixon, pp. 112–171. Canberra: Australian Institute of Aboriginal Studies.

Simon, Walter (1937). Has the Chinese language parts of speech? *Transactions of the Philological Society*, pp. 99–119.

Simone, Raffaele, ed. (1995). *Iconicity in Language*. Current Issues in Linguistic Theory 110. Amsterdam: John Benjamins.

Skalička, Vladimir, and Petr Sgall (1994). Praguian typology of languages. In *The Prague School of Structural and Functional Linguistics*, ed. by Philip Luelsdorff, pp. 333–357. Amsterdam: John Benjamins.

Slobin, Dan I. (1977). Language change in childhood and in history. In *Language Learning and Thought*, ed. by John MacNamara, pp. 185–214. New York: Academic Press.

Smith, Carlota (1991). *The Parameter of Aspect*. Dordrecht: Kluwer.

Smith, Edward E., and Daniel N. Osherson (1988). Conceptual combination with prototype concepts. In *Readings in Cognitive Science: A Perspective from Psychology and Artificial Intelligence*, ed. by Allan Collins and Edward E. Smith, pp. 323–335. San Mateo, Calif.: M. Kaufman.

Sobin, Nicholas (1997). Agreement, default rules, and grammatical viruses. *Linguistic Inquiry* 28: 318–143.

Speas, Margaret (1986). Adjunctions and projections in syntax. Unpublished Ph.D. dissertation, MIT.

Sperber, Dan, and Deirdre Wilson (1986). *Relevance: Communication and Cognition*. Oxford: Blackwell.

Stassen, Leon (1985). *Comparison and Universal Grammar*. Oxford: Blackwell.

Steedman, Mark (1993). Categorial grammar. *Lingua* 90: 221–258.

Steele, Susan (1978). Word order variation: a typological study. In *Universals of Human Language*, vol. 4, *Syntax*, ed. by Joseph H. Greenberg, Charles A. Ferguson, and Edith A. Moravcsik, pp. 585–623. Stanford, Calif.: Stanford University Press.

Steele, Susan (1994). Review of *Auxiliaries: Cognitive Forces and Grammaticalization*, by B. Heine. *Language* 70: 818–821.

Stowell, Timothy A. (1981). Origins of phrase structure. Unpublished Ph.D. dissertation, MIT.

Strozer, Judith R. (1994). *Language Acquisition after Puberty*. Washington: Georgetown University Press.

Swart, Henriëtte de (forthcoming). Aspect shift and coercion. *Natural Language and Linguistic Theory*.

Sweetser, Eve E. (1988). Grammaticalization and semantic bleaching. *Berkeley Linguistics Society* 14: 389–405.

Tabor, Whitney, and Elizabeth C. Traugott (forthcoming). Structural scope expansion and grammaticalization. In *The Limits of Grammaticalization*, ed. by Anna G. Ramat and Paul J. Hopper.

Tai, James (1985). Temporal sequence and Chinese word order. In *Iconicity in Syntax*, ed. by John Haiman, pp. 49–72. Amsterdam: John Benjamins.

Tallal, Paula, Randall Ross, and Susan Curtiss (1989). Familial aggregation in specific language impairment. *Journal of Speech and Hearing Disorders* 54: 167–173.

Talmy, Leonard (1978a). Figure and ground in complex sentences. In *Universals of Human Language*, vol. 4, *Syntax*, ed. by Joseph H. Greenberg, Charles A. Ferguson, and Edith A. Moravcsik, pp. 625–652. Stanford, Calif.: Stanford University Press.

Talmy, Leonard (1978b). The relation of grammar to cognition. In *Theoretical Issues in Natural Language Processing*, vol. 2, ed. by David Waltz, pp. 14–24. Champaign, Ill.: Coordinated Science Laboratory, University of Illinois.

Talmy, Leonard (1985). Force dynamics in language and thought. *Chicago Linguistic Society* 21, *Papers from the Parasession on Causatives and Agentivity*, 293–337.

Talmy, Leonard (1988). The relation of grammar to cognition. In *Topics in Cognitive Linguistics*, ed. by Brygida Rudzka-Ostyn, pp. 165–205. Amsterdam: John Benjamins.

Taraldsen, K. T. (1981). The theoretical interpretation of a class of marked extractions. In *Theory of Markedness in Generative Grammar: Proceedings of the 1979 GLOW Conference*, ed. by A. Belletti, L. Brandi, and L. Rizzi, pp. 475–516. Pisa: Scuola Normale Superiore.

Taylor, John R. (1989). *Linguistic Categorization: Prototypes in Linguistic Theory*. Oxford: Clarendon.

Thompson, Sandra A. (1978). Modern English from a typological point of view: some implications of the function of word order. *Linguistische Berichte* 54: 19–35.

Thompson, Sandra A. (1988). A discourse approach to the cross-linguistic category "adjective." In *Explaining Language Universals*, ed. by John Hawkins, pp. 167–185. Oxford: Basil Blackwell.

Thompson, Sandra A. (1991). On addressing functional explanation in linguistics. *Language and Communication* 11: 93–96.

Thompson, Sandra A., and Yuka Koide (1987). Iconicity and "indirect objects" in English. *Journal of Pragmatics* 11: 399–406.

Tobin, Yishai (1990). *Semiotics and Linguistics*. London: Longman.

Tomblin, J. Bruce, and P. R. Buckwalter (1994). Studies of genetics of specific language impairment. In *Specific Language Impairments in Children*, ed. by R. V. Watkins and Mabel L. Rice, pp. 17–34. Baltimore: Paul H. Brookes.

Tomlin, Russell S. (1986). *Basic Word Order: Functional Principles*. London: Croom Helm.

Tomlin, Russell S. (1990). Functionalism in second language acquisition. *Studies in Second Language Acquisition* 12: 155–177.

Tomlin, Russell S., and Richard Rhodes (1979). An introduction to information distribution in Ojibwa. *Chicago Linguistic Society* 15: 307–320.

Trager, George L., and Henry Lee Smith (1951). *An Outline of English Structure.* Norman, Okla.: Battenburg Press.

Trask, R. L. (1997). *The History of Basque.* London: Routledge.

Traugott, Elizabeth C. (1974). Explorations in linguistic elaboration: language change, language acquisition and the genesis of spatio-temporal terms. In *Historical Linguistics*, vol. 1, ed. by John Anderson and Charles Jones, pp. 263–314. Amsterdam: North Holland.

Traugott, Elizabeth C. (1985). Conditional markers. In *Iconicity in Syntax*, ed. by John Haiman, pp. 289–310. Amsterdam: John Benjamins.

Traugott, Elizabeth C. (1997). The role of the development of discourse markers in a theory of grammaticalization. In *Papers from the 12th International Conference on Historical Linguistics*, ed. by Linda van Bergen and Richard M. Hogg. Amsterdam: John Benjamins.

Traugott, Elizabeth C. (forthcoming). Constructions in grammaticalization. In *A Handbook of Historical Linguistics*, ed. by Richard Janda and Brian D. Joseph. Oxford: Blackwell.

Traugott, Elizabeth C., and Bernd Heine (1991). Introduction. In *Approaches to Grammaticalization*, vol. 1, *Focus on Theoretical and Methodological Issues*, ed. by Elizabeth C. Traugott and Bernd Heine, pp. 1–14. Amsterdam: John Benjamins.

Traugott, Elizabeth C., and Ekkehard König (1991). The semantics-pragmatics of grammaticalization revisited. In *Approaches to Grammaticalization*, vol. 1, *Focus on Theoretical and Methodological Issues*, ed. by Elizabeth C. Traugott and Bernd Heine, pp. 189–218. Amsterdam: John Benjamins.

Travis, Lisa (1989). Parameters of phrase structure. In *Alternative Conceptions of Phrase Structure*, ed. by Mark R. Baltin and Anthony S. Kroch, pp. 263–279. Chicago: University of Chicago Press.

Trubetzkoy, Nicholas (1931). Die phonologischen Systeme. *Travaux du Cercle Linguistique de Prague* 4: 96–116.

Tsimpli, Ianthi-Maria, and Anna Roussou (1991). Parameter setting in L2? *UCL Working Papers in Linguistics* 3: 149–169.

Tsohatzidis, Savas L., ed. (1990). *Meanings and Prototypes: Studies in Linguistic Categorization.* London: Routledge.

Ultan, Russell (1978). The nature of future tenses. *Universals of Human Language*, vol. 3, *Word Structure*, ed. by Joseph H. Greenberg, Charles A. Ferguson, and Edith A. Moravcsik, pp. 83–123. Stanford, Calif.: Stanford University Press.

Vachek, Josef (1966). *The Linguistic School of Prague: An Introduction to Its Theory and Practice.* Bloomington: Indiana University Press.

Vainikka, Anne, and Martha Young-Scholten (1991). Verb-raising in second language acquisition: the early stages. In *Theorie des Lexicons*, vol. 4, *Universal Grammar in Second Language Acquisition*. Düsseldorf: The LEXLERN Project, Universität Düsseldorf.

Vallduví, Enric (1992). *The Informational Component*. New York: Garland.

Van Gelderen, Elly (1996). The reanalysis of grammaticalized prepositions in Middle English. *Studia Linguistica* 50: 106–124.

Van Gelderen, Elly (1997). *Verbal Agreement and the Grammar behind Its "Breakdown": Minimalist Feature Checking*. Tübingen: Niemeyer.

Van Oosten, Jeanne (1986). *The Nature of Subjects, Topics, and Agents: A Cognitive Explanation*. Bloomington, Ind.: Indiana University Linguistics Club.

Van Valin, Robert D. (1981). Toward understanding grammar: form, function, evolution. Review of *On Understanding Grammar*, by T. Givón. *Lingua* 54: 47–85.

Van Valin, Robert D. (1990). Functionalism, anaphora, and syntax. Review of *Functional Syntax*, by S. Kuno. *Studies in Language* 14: 169–219.

Van Valin, Robert D., ed. (1993a). *Advances in Role and Reference Grammar*. Amsterdam: John Benjamins.

Van Valin, Robert D. (1993b). A synopsis of role and reference grammar. In *Advances in Role and Reference Grammar*, ed. by Robert D. Van Valin, pp. 1–164. Amsterdam: John Benjamins.

Van Valin, Robert D. (1994). Extraction restrictions, competing theories, and the argument from the poverty of the stimulus. In *The Reality of Linguistic Rules*, ed. by Susan D. Lima, Roberta L. Corrigan, and Gregory K. Iverson, pp. 243–259. Amsterdam: John Benjamins.

Vargha-Khadem, Faraneh, Kate Watkins, Katie Alcock, Paul Fletcher, and Richard Passingham (1995). Praxic and nonverbal cognitive deficits in a large family with a genetically transmitted speech and language disorder. *Proceedings of the National Academy of Sciences* 92: 930–933.

Vendler, Zeno (1967). *Linguistics in Philosophy*. Ithaca, N.Y.: Cornell University Press.

Vennemann, Theo (1973). Explanation in syntax. *Syntax and Semantics*, vol. 2, ed. by John Kimball, pp. 1–50. New York: Seminar Press.

Vennemann, Theo (1974). Topics, subjects, and word order: from SXV to SVX via TVX. In *Historical Linguistics, I*, ed. by John M. Anderson and Charles Jones, pp. 339–376. Amsterdam: North-Holland.

Vennemann, Theo (1975). An explanation of drift. In *Word Order and Word Order Change*, ed. by Charles N. Li, pp. 269–306. Austin: University of Texas Press.

Verhaar, John W. M. (1985). On iconicity and hierarchy. *Studies in Language* 9: 21–76.

Voegelin, C. F., and F. M. Voegelin (1976). Some recent (and not so recent) attempts to interpret semantics of native languages in North America. In *American Indian Languages and American Linguistics*, ed. by Wallace L. Chafe, pp. 75–98. Lisse: Peter de Ridder Press.

Ward, Gregory, and Betty Birner (1995). Definiteness and the English existential. *Language* 71: 722–742.

Ward, Gregory, Richard Sproat, and Gail McKoon (1991). A pragmatic analysis of so-called anaphoric islands. *Language* 67: 439–474.

Warner, Anthony R. (1993a). *English Auxiliaries: Structure and History*. Cambridge: Cambridge University Press.

Warner, Anthony R. (1993b). The grammar of English auxiliaries: an account in HPSG. York Research Papers in Linguistics, Research Paper YLLS/RP 1993–1994: 1–42.

Watkins, Calvert (1963). Preliminaries to an historical and comparative analysis of the Old Irish verb. *Celtica* 6: 1–49.

Watkins, Calvert (1964). Preliminaries to the reconstruction of Indo-European sentence structure. In *Proceedings of the Ninth International Congress of Linguists*, ed. by Horace G. Lunt, pp. 1035–1045. The Hague: Mouton.

Weil, Henri (1844/1887). *The Order of Words in the Ancient Languages Compared with That of the Modern Languages*. Boston: Ginn. Reprinted in 1978 in the series Amsterdam Classics in Linguistics, 14. Amsterdam: John Benjamins.

Weiner, E. Judith, and William Labov (1983). Constraints on the agentless passive. *Journal of Linguistics* 19: 29–58.

Weinreich, Uriel, William Labov, and Marvin I. Herzog (1968). Empirical foundations for a theory of language change. In *Directions for Historical Linguistics*, ed. by W. Lehmann and Y. Malkiel, pp. 95–188. Austin: University of Texas Press.

Wexler, Kenneth, and Y. C. Chien (1985). The development of lexical anaphors and pronouns. *Papers and Reports on Child Language Development* 24: 138–149.

Wexler, Kenneth, and Peter Culicover (1980). *Formal Principles of Language Acquisition*. Cambridge: MIT Press.

White, Lydia (1990). *Universal Grammar and Second Language Acquisition*. Amsterdam: John Benjamins.

Wierzbicka, Anna (1986a). The semantics of "internal dative" in English. *Quaderni di Semantica* 7: 155–165.

Wierzbicka, Anna (1986b). What's in a noun? (Or: How do nouns differ in meaning from adjectives?). *Studies in Language* 10: 353–389.

Wierzbicka, Anna (1988). *The Semantics of Grammar*. Amsterdam: John Benjamins.

Wierzbicka, Anna (1990). "Prototypes save": on the uses and abuses of the notion of 'prototype' in linguistics and related fields. In *Meanings and Prototypes: Studies in Linguistic Categorization*, ed. by Savas L. Tsohatzidis, pp. 347–367. London: Routledge.

Wilkins, Wendy K. (1988). Thematic structure and reflexivization. In *Thematic Relations*, ed. by Wendy K. Wilkins, pp. 191–214. Syntax and Semantics 21. New York: Academic Press.

Willett, Thomas (1988). A cross-linguistic survey of the grammaticization of evidentiality. *Studies in Language* 12: 51–97.

Wilson, Deirdre (1975). *Presupposition and Non-truth-conditional Semantics*. New York: Academic Press.

Winters, Margaret E. (1990). Toward a theory of syntactic prototypes. In *Meanings and Prototypes: Studies in Linguistic Categorization*, ed. by Savas L. Tsohatzidis, pp. 285–306. London: Routledge.

Woolford, Ellen (1991). VP-internal subjects in VSO and nonconfigurational languages. *Linguistic Inquiry* 22: 503–540.

Wu, Andi (1994). The spell-out parameters: a minimalist appraoch to syntax. Unpublished Ph.D. dissertation, UCLA.

Wundt, Wilhelm M. (1900). *Völkerpsychologie*. Vol. 2. Leipzig: Engelmann.

Zagona, Karen (1988). *Verb Phrase Syntax: A Parametric Study of English and Spanish*. Dordrecht: Kluwer.

Žegarac, Vladimir (1993). Some observations on the pragmatics of the progressive. *Lingua* 90: 201–220.

Zipf, George (1935). *The Psychobiology of Language*. New York: Houghton Mifflin.

Zwicky, Arnold M. (1986). *Wh*-Constructions in English. *Ohio State University Working Papers in Linguistics* 32: 114–124.

Zwicky, Arnold M. (1987). Constructions in monostratal syntax. *Chicago Linguistic Society* 23: 389–401.

Zwicky, Arnold M. (1994). Dealing out meaning: fundamentals of syntactic constructions. *Berkeley Linguistics Society* 20: 611–625.

Name Index

Abney, Steven P., 291, 346
Adger, David, 187 n.
Akmajian, Adrian, 52, 345
Allen, Cynthia, 275
Allen, Shanley E. M., 93
Andersen, Henning, 70–71
Andersen, Paul K., 328, 330 n., 347 n.
Anderson, John R., 78
Anderson, Mona, 193
Anderson, Stephen R., 132, 300 n.
Aoun, Joseph, 53, 99
Ariel, Mira, 66
Armstrong, Sharon Lee, 168
Asher, Nicholas, 120 n.
Aske, Jon, 333

Babby, Leonard H., 205
Bach, Emmon, 105, 186, 332
Bailey, Charles-James N., 284 n.
Baker, Mark C., 291, 306 n.
Bar-Lev, Zev, 120 n.
Barlow, Michael, 14 n., 119
Bartsch, Renate, 35
Bates, Elizabeth, 13–14, 154, 167, 180 n.
Battistella, Edwin, 197 n., 198 n.
Battye, Adrian, 293 n.
Bazell, C. E., 116
Becker, A. L., 61
Beckman, Mary, 178
Behagel, Otto, 116, 122 n.
Bell, Alan, 308–309, 313 n.
Berlin, Brent, 118
Bertoncini, Elena, 257
Berwick, Robert C., 69, 106
Bever, Thomas G., 106
Bichakjian, Bernard H., 324
Bickerton, Derek, 75
Bird, Charles, 133
Birner, Betty, 65
Bishop, Dorothy V. M., 92–94

Blake, Barry J., 122 n., 301, 310, 319, 327–328, 333–334
Bley-Vroman, Robert D., 74–75
Bloom, Paul, 43, 180, 363
Bloomfield, Leonard, 26
Bock, J. Kathryn, 25 n.
Bolinger, Dwight, 34 n., 115, 118, 189, 291
Borer, Hagit, 363
Borsley, Robert D., 51, 183 n.
Bouchard, Denis, 31
Brent, Michael, 88
Bresnan, Joan W., 11, 186
Brody, Jill, 331–332
Brody, Michael, 11 n.
Broselow, Ellen I., 76
Brugman, Claudia M., 15, 46
Buckwalter, P. R., 94
Bybee, Joan L. (Joan Hooper), 8, 116, 118, 151 n., 230, 235–237, 239–240, 248, 268, 280 n., 281–284, 333. See also Hooper, Joan
Bynon, Theodora, 299, 303

Campbell, Lyle, 132, 225 n., 227 n., 237, 241, 243, 248–249, 268 n., 271, 273, 275, 295
Cann, Ronnie, 12, 192 n.
Capell, Arthur, 328
Carling, Christine, 37
Carstairs, Andrew, 268 n.
Carston, Robyn, 12, 120 n.
Chafe, Wallace, 41 n., 122 n., 149
Chao, Yuen Ren, 195
Chien, Y. C., 363
Chierchia, Gennaro, 12, 294 n.
Chomsky, Noam, 6, 8–9, 11, 13, 25, 27, 29–30, 32–33, 36–37, 52 n., 53, 61–62, 72, 79, 81–82, 85–87, 98–100, 104, 137 n., 154–160, 178–179, 203, 221, 225 n., 227 n., 244, 304, 339–340, 350–351, 353–355, 360–361, 363

Subject Index

Accessibility hierarchy (AH), 316-320
Acooli, 184
Adjectives, 41-43, 172-173, 184, 195, 201.
  See also Categories
Agreement, 196
Akkadian, 269
Amharic, 310, 332
Analogy, 232-233, 276
Anaphors, 76, 86-87, 160. *See also* Binding
  Theory
Animacy Hierarchy, 198-199
Animated-First Principle, 146
Antisymmetry theory, 359-360
A-over-A Principle, 156
Arbitrariness in grammar, 28-31, 55, 102,
  139, 155
Argument Fusion, 129, 158
Asymmetry, cognitive, 160-161
Australian languages, 307
Autonomist functionalism, 10
Autonomy of grammar as a cognitive
  system (AUTOGRAM), 19, 24-25, 77-94,
  366
  cognition and, 80-84
  functionalist approaches and, 78-80
  genetic dysphasia and, 90-94
  innateness and, 84-94
Autonomy of knowledge of language with
  respect to use of language (AUTOKNOW),
  19, 24-25, 55-77, 90-91, 289-290, 365-
  366
  creoles and, 72-73
  discourse and, 55-66
  language change and, 67-72
  second-language acquisition and, 74-77
Autonomy of syntax (AUTOSYN), 18, 23-55,
  153-164, 365-367
  competing motivations and, 163-164
  content and, 27-32
  data sources and, 38-39

empirical support for, 46-55
external explanation and, 153-164, 366-
  367
frequency and, 39-44
historical roots of, 26-27
internal explanation and, 100-101
intuitions and, 36-38
meaning and, 44-46
methodological considerations for, 34-44
scope of, 32-34
Auxiliaries, 99-100, 345-346
  inverted, 46-49

Bantu, 264
Barriers, 203
Basque, 269, 333
Binding Theory, 156, 159
Bini, 141
Blackfoot, 250
Bleaching, 229-230, 233, 249
Bounding Theory, 156
Branching-direction theory, 344-346

Canonical Structural Realization (CSR),
  178-180
Case, 52-53
Case Filter, 98-99, 103-105
Categorial Grammar, 11
Categories, 19-20, 117-118, 165-208
  in Emergent Grammar, 59-61
  features and, 178-179
  fuzzy, 167-169, 178, 200-205
  identifying, 338
  notional definitions of, 168-169, 206-208
  prototype, 166-200
  radial, 173-174
Cayuga, 123
C-command, 160
Celtic, 277
Chadic, 278

CPSIA information can be obtained at www.ICGtesting.com
Printed in the USA
BVOW04s1635050514

352607BV00003B/5/P